# EIGHTEEN DAYS in OCTOBER

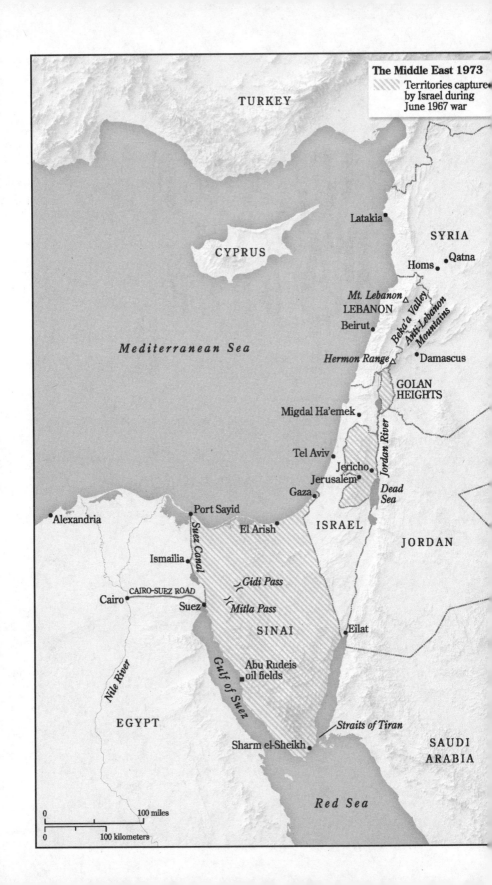

**The Middle East 1973**

Territories captured by Israel during June 1967 war

TURKEY

CYPRUS

Latakia

SYRIA

Homs • Qatna

*Mediterranean Sea*

*Mt. Lebanon* △
LEBANON

Beirut •

*Beka'a Valley*
*Anti-Lebanon Mountains*

*Hermon Range* △
• Damascus

GOLAN HEIGHTS

Migdal Ha'emek •

*Jordan River*

Tel Aviv •

Jericho

Jerusalem •

Gaza •

*Dead Sea*

ISRAEL

JORDAN

Alexandria •

Port Sayid •

El Arish •

Ismailia •

*Suez Canal*

CAIRO-SUEZ ROAD

Cairo •

Suez •

)( *Gidi Pass*

)( *Mitla Pass*

SINAI

Eilat •

Abu Rudeis oil fields •

*Nile River*

*Gulf of Suez*

EGYPT

*Straits of Tiran*

SAUDI ARABIA

Sharm el-Sheikh •

*Red Sea*

0 ___ 100 miles

0 ___ 100 kilometers

# EIGHTEEN DAYS in OCTOBER

## The YOM KIPPUR WAR and
## How It Created the Modern Middle East

# URI KAUFMAN

ST. MARTIN'S PRESS
NEW YORK

First published in the United States by St. Martin's Press, an imprint of
St. Martin's Publishing Group

EIGHTEEN DAYS IN OCTOBER. Copyright © 2023 by Uri Kaufman.
All rights reserved. Printed in the United States of America. For
information, address St. Martin's Publishing Group, 120 Broadway,
New York, NY 10271.

www.stmartins.com

Design by Meryl Sussman Levavi

Maps © Mapping Specialists, Ltd.

The Library of Congress Cataloging-in-Publication Data is available
upon request.

ISBN 978-1-250-28188-3 (hardcover)
ISBN 978-1-250-28189-0 (ebook)

Our books may be purchased in bulk for promotional, educational,
or business use. Please contact your local bookseller or the Macmillan
Corporate and Premium Sales Department at 1-800-221-7945, extension
5442, or by email at MacmillanSpecialMarkets@macmillan.com.

First Edition: 2023

10  9  8  7  6  5  4  3  2  1

*To Esther and the kids, Yosef, Shragie, Bracha,*
*and Naftali, with love.*

# CONTENTS

1. A Parade in Jerusalem     1

2. "That Which Was Taken by Force Will Be Returned by Force"     9

3. The Wars Between the Wars     20

4. Yesmanship: Peace and Its Process     35

5. To Prepare for the War That Must Come     47

6. The Angel and the Noise     61

7. Judgment Day     79

8. "The Third Temple Is at Risk"     97

9. Syrians at the Gate     113

10. *Mikhdal*: The Counterattack     129

11. Valleys of Tears     145

12. Command and Control     162

13. Frenemies     172

14. Never Call Surrender     184

15. Armageddon on a Road Called Talisman          190

16. "We Will Cross with What We Have"              205

17. The War of the Generals                        221

18. The Chinese Farm and the Men Who Conquered It  231

19. The Race to the Bridgehead                     249

20. Bridges                                        264

21. Africa                                         272

22. Embargo                                        281

23. Defcon 3                                       295

24. A Funeral in Jerusalem                         308

Acknowledgments                                    333
Notes                                              335
Index                                              377

# MAPS

The Middle East, 1973                          ii

Maozim and Egyptian Attack                     80

Motzavim and Attack by Syria                   96

Mikhdal                                        128

Valley of Tears and Bulge into Syria          144

Chinese Farm                                   206

Attack into Egypt                             250

# EIGHTEEN DAYS in OCTOBER

# 1

# A PARADE IN JERUSALEM

The U.N. Security Council deeply deplores the holding by Israel of the military parade in Jerusalem on 2 May, 1968 in disregard of the unanimous decision adopted by the Council on
April 27, 1968.

—UN Security Council Resolution 251

In the spring of 1968, the State of Israel announced that it would
mark the twentieth anniversary of its founding by holding a military parade in the recently reunited city of Jerusalem. The governments of the world took great pains to voice their displeasure.
And the government of Israel took equally great pains to hold the
parade as planned.[1]

The route was carefully mapped out. Armored and infantry
columns would mass in a staging area near Shuafat, a newly captured Arab section in the northern part of the city. From there,
the soldiers would march south through the Arab neighborhood
of Wadi el-Joz, past the walls of the Old City, then turn right and
continue through the Jewish sections of Western Jerusalem. It was
a long route—more than five miles—and not just because the Israelis were eager to march in newly acquired warrens of the city.
Organizers planned for half a million spectators—as it turned

out, even *that* estimate was surpassed—and it was important to disperse the crowds over as wide an area as possible.[2]

Counting the Arab residents that completed the shotgun marriage now called Greater Jerusalem, the sleepy hill city numbered only 240,000 souls, and this was to triple in size for one afternoon. In a country with fewer than 54,000 registered vehicles, somehow, impossibly, 45,000 arrived for the festivities.[3] A grandstand was built on a mile-long clearing to accommodate 60,000 people, more than double the seating capacity of the nation's largest stadium.

And, for the first time, Israeli television was there as well. Television came relatively late to the Jewish state, first crackling on the air just two years earlier, in 1966. Executives of state-owned Channel 1—"1" because it was the only station in the country—finally had an excuse to get the Finance Ministry to upgrade their equipment. Show the proceedings live, they argued to jittery officials, and fewer will come to Jerusalem. A used mobile camera was hastily purchased in London and operated under the direction of an Irish technician who did not speak a word of Hebrew. Large crowds indeed gathered in TV-equipped homes, though only in cities far from Jerusalem. One newspaper reported that the streets of Haifa "remained almost deserted, as if an air raid alarm had been sounded." The previous year, Israelis with televisions could watch the armies of their neighbors mobilizing against them. Now Israel returned the favor. The signal from Jerusalem was strong enough to reach homes in Egypt, Syria, Jordan, and Lebanon.[4]

At 9:40 A.M., the ceremonies began. Amid a sea of waving flags, the Presidential Guard and the army band strode before the reviewing stand. The grandstand area was decorated in colors commemorating the previous campaigns of 1948, 1956, and, of course, 1967.

The aerial show came next. Three hundred planes filled the

skies, the largest assemblage of aircraft since the opening hours of the Six-Day War. Five jets led the formations trailing blue and white smoke, the national colors. Then came two additional formations, one forming the number twenty and the other a Star of David.[5]

Saving the best for last, the air force rolled out its finale. A single, needle-nosed MiG-21, painted red, screamed low over the crowd.[6]

Until 1966, few people in the West would have recognized a Soviet-made MiG-21. Only the vaguest details were then available on the fighter jet the Russians called the best in the world. On August 15, 1966, all that changed. Mossad, Israel's fabled intelligence service, scored one of the great intelligence coups of the Cold War by persuading an Iraqi pilot to defect with his aircraft. Had the parade been held in any country besides Israel, no one would have understood the significance of the streaking red plane.

But this was Israel. Where practically every man and woman served in the army. Where ordinary citizens could distinguish calibers of ammunition merely from the sound of gunfire in the distance.

The crowd looked up and erupted in joy.

In the middle of the grandstand sat Prime Minister Levi Eshkol. Ever the kibbutznik, even in the last year of his life, Eshkol wore his dark suit open-shirted without a necktie. Sitting next to him were his cabinet ministers, most without suit jackets. As always, Defense Minister Moshe Dayan stood out, this time by ignoring protocol and wearing his old army uniform with the chief of staff insignia embroidered on the shirt. The then-serving chief of staff, Chaim Bar-Lev, sat in his uniform on the other side.[7]

\* \* \*

The men sitting on the grandstand understood just how far they had come. They remembered what it was like at the military parade the year before when Eshkol's aide slipped him a handwritten note informing him that Nasser had mobilized his army and sent it marching into the Sinai Peninsula.

The nerve-shattering weeks that ensued even had a name, the *Hamtana*, or "Waiting." Weeks of waiting that saw Israel's worst nightmare realized, the IDF's Everything Scenario, in which King Hussein of Jordan placed his troops under Egyptian command and the entire Arab world closed ranks to wipe the Jewish state off the map. When they tuned in to their radios, the Israeli public heard Eshkol botch a speech meant to raise public spirits.[*] At the very moment the nation needed to be rallied for battle, its coalition government collapsed. What the public mercifully did not know, but the men on the grandstand did, was that Chief of Staff Yitzchak Rabin had experienced a mental collapse, the nation's leaders debated resorting to nuclear weapons, and General Ariel Sharon dropped a suggestion to carry out a military coup.[8] [†]

Those who experienced it could never forget the desperation with which they entered the war. With nothing to lose, they wagered everything on a single, spectacular throw of the dice, doing what no nation has done before or since: use *the entire air force on a single tactical mission*, a single mission to destroy Arab air forces on the ground. Doing that meant that once the first bombs landed on Arab airfields, the State of Israel would effectively have no air force for two hours, for that was how long it took the pilots to return to base, land, refuel, rearm, and get back up into the sky. In those two hours, the nation stood naked to a counterattack from

---

[*] Individuals friendly to Eshkol have removed the recording of the "Mumble Speech," as it is known, from Israel's national archive. It is lost to us. In the absence of any known copy, there are several versions of what went wrong. By all accounts, Eshkol stopped in the middle, muttered something, and shuffled through his papers before turning to an aide in front of a live mike and asking, "What does this say?"

[†] The story came to light in 2004 when Sharon was prime minister. He chose not to respond. Instead, his close friend journalist Uri Dan said, probably at Sharon's behest, that any such statement would only have been intended as a joke. Mr. Dan did not indicate whether Rabin laughed when Sharon uncorked that knee-slapper.

Arab fighter jets, or even Jordanian artillery fired from the hills of the West Bank.

And that was if everything went perfectly. Another thing Eshkol learned was that—again, if everything went perfectly—the nation did not have enough planes to get the job done in one wave. After returning to the air, the pilots would have to go back for a second trip and then a third. A computer model gave them no more than a 30 percent chance of success.[9]

And then, as if in a biblical tale, it ended almost as quickly as it began.

At a 1996 symposium, the Israelis revealed that they had hacked into their enemies' radar systems, permitting them to view what Arab radar operators saw in real time. This allowed them to experiment over a period of months, sending jets along different low-altitude routes to determine what the enemy could see and when. On D-Day, the fighter jets slipped through unhindered, the Arabs were as surprised by the second and third attacks as by the first, and four hundred planes were destroyed on the ground. It was over in a few hours. General Ezer Weizman, former commander of the air force, called his wife and exclaimed, "We won the war!" to which she replied, "But Ezer, it's only ten in the morning. How could you have won so quickly?"[10]

From there, everything fell into place as if choreographed by the Almighty himself. Egyptian troops were told to retreat, something Anwar Sadat later called "an order to commit suicide."* King Hussein believed false Egyptian reports of victory, jumped onto the bandwagon, and before anyone knew it, Jews were praying at the Western Wall. During the 1996 symposium, Jordanian officials were seen off to the side screaming at their Egyptian counterparts, "You lied to us!."[11]

By all rights it should have ended there, and the conflict should

---

* Fittingly, when Israeli troops fought their way to the center of Gaza City, the marquee of the local cinema read: "Help!"—not as a cry for assistance but because it was the movie playing.

have been known as the Four-Day War. But then Damascus fool-
ishly turned down a ceasefire offer.[12] The Israelis obliged them
and took the fight to the Golan Heights. Thirty-six hours later,
the Syrian army suffered the same fate as the others, toppling like
the biblical walls of Jericho. The Bible records that the ancient
Hebrews needed seven days to bring down the walls of Jericho. In
1967, Arab armies collapsed in only six.

The State of Israel was now four times larger. An undivided
Jerusalem was under Jewish sovereignty for the first time since
63 BCE. Just a week before, the Israelis were clinging to the shores
of the Mediterranean wondering if they would survive, and now . . .
*it did not seem possible.* Some looked to the Bible and found evidence of divine intervention. The secular year 1948, the year the
State of Israel was founded, corresponds to the Jewish calendar
year 5708. The 5,708th verse of the Bible reads: "And the Lord
shall bring you to the land that your fathers inherited, and you
shall inherit it and the Lord shall bless you to prosper far beyond
your fathers." The verses before that, which correspond loosely to
the Holocaust years, speak of the "fire and brimstone" the Lord
shall rain down upon his people. And what of the 5,727th verse,
corresponding to the Jewish year 5727 and the secular year 1967?
It reads: "And the Lord shall do to them as he did to Sihon and
Og, the kings of the Amorites and to their lands, that he destroyed
them."

The men sitting on the grandstand watching the festivities
that day in 1968 were less interested in the Bible. They realized
what a close shave it had been.

Under conditions of perfect surprise and execution, the Israeli
air force lost 10 percent of its fighter jets on the very first day of
the war. Though in complete control of the skies after that, the
IAF still lost a third of its strength by the time the guns fell silent
just five days later. Three hundred planes flew overhead at the
parade because the Israelis put every contraption they had into

the sky. Those in the know understood that if war broke out tomorrow, the air force had only 130 fighter jets.[13]

Egyptian resistance on the ground likewise crumbled quickly. But still, 50 percent of the officers in Israel's elite 84th Armored Division were either killed or wounded. Worse, if the war had lasted just two more weeks, Israeli tanks would have run out of ammunition. In short, Israel won the war. But only because everything went perfectly.[14]

What might happen if things did not go perfectly was the furthest thing from the minds of the cheering, flag-waving crowds. Instead, in the time since the rapturous summer of 1967, the Israeli public took to the roads and explored the new territories of their accidental empire. Dotting the landscape were numerous signs along the old 1948 line that read: DANGER! BORDER AHEAD. As a joke, someone spray-painted the word No onto one of the signs. And so, until it was pulled down with all the others, it read: DANGER! NO BORDER AHEAD.[15]

The parade ended and soon things returned to normal, or at least what passed for normal in Israel. Eighteen Palestinian guerillas would be killed over the following weekend, along with four Israelis.[16] A submarine was missing. France reneged on the sale of Mirage fighter jets. And in July, Israelis would be introduced to a new tactic: airplane hijackings.

David Ben-Gurion was invited to speak before a special session of the Knesset on June 5, 1968. Twenty years before, the conventional wisdom held that the Jewish state would expire long before Ben-Gurion's first term in office. Now, at an age when most politicians revel in self-congratulation, Ben-Gurion might have struck the high note of winds blowing and pages turning.

That was not the speech he delivered. The situation in 1968, Ben-Gurion declared, was almost as perilous as the one he confronted twenty years before: "Never since the creation of the Jewish State has our international weakness been so much in evidence as in recent years . . . even the finest army—and it is doubtful whether an army in the world surpasses the IDF in quality, capability and devotion—cannot fight empty-handed, and we are still far from producing all the equipment we need for our defense . . .

"We have heard what the Egyptian President, Gamal Abdel Nasser, said on June 9, 1967, after the defeat of the Egyptian Army: No matter what the circumstances, and no matter how long it takes . . . when imperialism has been liquidated in the Arab world and Israel stands alone, the day of revenge will come."[17]

# 2

# "THAT WHICH WAS TAKEN BY FORCE WILL BE RETURNED BY FORCE"

We went looking for donkeys and we found an empire.

—Levi Eshkol, June 11, 1967

When he stood on the dock in 1952, moments before sailing into exile, King Farouk warned Gamal Abdel Nasser and the military leaders who ousted him that they would find out one day just how difficult Egypt was to govern.[1]

In the days after the 1967 war, that prophecy materialized in its darkest incarnation. Egypt was bankrupt, its army defeated. As the nation deteriorated, Nasser's health deteriorated with it. One of his aides wrote that Nasser aged ten years in just six days.[2] Once, Nasser had prevented the Israelis from using the Suez Canal. Now it was the Israelis that prevented him. In 1948, Farouk's army had lasted more than six months against the Israelis. Nasser's was defeated in less than a week.

Egyptian morale rose momentarily on October 21, 1967. Naval command in Alexandria sent a message to its base in Port Sayid not to fire at any target in its jurisdiction. As expected, the false order was intercepted and lured the Israeli ship *Eilat* closer to Egyptian territorial waters (whether it actually entered Egyptian waters is still the subject of controversy). Just before dusk, two Egyptian boats fired four Soviet-made missiles. Three scored direct hits and the *Eilat,* a WWII destroyer the Israeli navy bought on the cheap, went to the bottom, killing 47 of its crew of 199.

Crowds cheered the missile boats as they returned to port. October 21 was established as a national holiday honoring the Egyptian navy.* A Lebanese newspaper declared, "The Israeli legend was shattered in those moments and things have begun to return to their normal place."[3]

The jubilation was short-lived. The Israelis responded by shelling the canal cities of Suez and Port Ibrahim, igniting more than a hundred fuel tanks and flattening refineries, petrochemical plants, and port facilities. Israeli soldiers reported being able to read books at night by the light of the flames. To the loss of revenue from Sinai oil wells and the closure of the Suez Canal could now be added millions Egypt once earned refining and exporting petroleum. Henceforth, Cairo had to find the foreign exchange to buy those products abroad in order to meet domestic needs.[4]

The commander of Egypt's army, Marshal Abdel Hakim Amer, attempted a coup and committed suicide after it failed. Dozens of top military and political leaders, including the defense minister, the intelligence chief, and the commander of the air force, were all jailed.[5] Refugees streamed out of the Canal Zone and flooded Cairo.

The shelling of the canal cities bought Israel a precious year of quiet. Nasser's army was in no condition for another round with the Israelis, and Marshal Matvei Zakharov, chief of the general staff of the Soviet Union, was sent to Cairo to squelch any notion to the contrary. Zakharov approached the situation with the tact and charm of a communist apparatchik, telling his Egyptian counterparts that if every Soviet-made tank had merely fired off ten shots instead of being abandoned, they would have won the war. General P. N. Lashenko, the chief Soviet military officer, said

---

* It was the first time a warship was sunk using surface-to-surface missiles, and it caused a complete rethinking of naval strategy around the world.

of Egyptian Chief of Staff Abdul Munim Riad that "the general impression of him is a good one, although he shows off a bit, like most Arabs."[6]

Of course, in the eyes of the Egyptians the Soviets were no bargain, either. It was true that what the Soviets lacked in diplomatic skills they made up for in iron and steel. Weapons poured into the country, supplied at no cost. But much of that equipment was shoddy, a problem compounded by corruption. In the building of the Aswan Dam, observers quipped that the Russians had to supply three of everything. One item arrived broken, one was stolen, and only the last one made it into the field. Of the Egyptians in 1967, a Russian adviser said, "They were stealing like hell." Worse still, the Soviets estimated that 80 percent of Egyptian soldiers and 60 percent of the officers had no idea how to operate the equipment they were given.[7] *

Israel suffered from the opposite problem. It had soldiers of every rank worthy of the title but lacked weapons. The French imposed an embargo on fifty Mirage fighter jets ordered before the war, and fighter jets were what Israel needed most of all. The only other potential source was the United States.

The campaign to persuade America to sell Israel the F-4 Phantom fighter jet was important enough that Yitzchak Rabin—who was appointed ambassador to Washington in early 1968—dedicated an entire chapter to it in his memoir.† Johnson was advised to hold Israel's feet to the fire and demand, at a minimum, that Jerusalem abandon its nuclear program. He could have demanded far more than that. Any offer was an offer the Jewish state could not refuse.[8]

Johnson ignored the advice. On October 18, 1967, the Israelis were relieved to learn that Washington had lifted its arms em-

---

* Among other things, they also discovered that soldiers were not given food but money to buy food. Since many had large families to support, they gave the money to their loved ones and attempted to perform their duties while suffering from malnutrition.

† It says much about international affairs that Clark Clifford, LBJ's secretary of defense and a central figure in the drama, made no mention of it in his seven-hundred-page memoir. What is an existential issue for one nation is but an afterthought for another.

bargo. Then, in January 1968, Eshkol was invited to a coveted meeting at LBJ's ranch, dubbed the Texas White House. They sat together in LBJ's convertible, a study in contrasts, Johnson at the wheel speeding with Eshkol next to him clutching his homburg. At one point, LBJ nudged a cow off the road, saying it was "as pigheaded as a Texan senator with colic." Eshkol turned to an aide, and above the roar of the engine asked, "*Vus rett der goy?*" (Yiddish: "What's the gentile talking about?").[9]

Once they got down to business, they quickly found common ground. Johnson agreed to sell additional F-4 Phantom fighter jets, demanding only that Israel present a peace plan in return. Eshkol even persuaded Johnson to speed up production so that the IAF could take delivery in 1969 instead of 1970.[10]

With these actions, Lyndon Johnson did more to guarantee the security and survival of the Jewish state than any American president before or since. Israel would receive far less generous treatment from Richard Nixon and his secretary of state, Henry Kissinger. LBJ was an unlikely patron given his record championing America's oil interests, a record that went back to his days as a Texas congressman and senator. Some have attributed his commitment to Israel to a cynical pursuit of Jewish donors. But this seems misplaced given that he did the most when his presidency was winding down and he no longer needed support from anyone.[11] Whatever the motive, it cannot be denied that Lyndon Johnson delivered for Israel in its hour of need.

The Israeli army grew exponentially in the period between 1967 and 1973 adding, among other things, 178 A-4 Skyhawk fighter jets, 110 F-4 Phantom fighter jets, and 1,764 tanks. One would not have known it looking at the meager forces in the field. During the year of quiet that followed the shelling of the canal cities, only 50 Israeli tanks were stationed along the Suez Canal and 50 more to their rear. That, plus a brigade of infantry and three brigades of artillery, was all that was needed. Egypt, a nation of almost thirty-three million, was held off by just five thousand men.[12]

* * *

On June 29, 1967, the barriers dividing Jerusalem were removed, allowing Arabs and Jews to commingle for the first time in nineteen years. In the morning, only a few brave souls ventured into opposing territory. By afternoon, the ice was broken and crowds flowed in both directions. Israelis were surprised to learn that under Jordanian rule, schoolchildren received free public education through high school. Israeli schoolchildren received free public education only through the tenth grade. They were also pleased to find how cheap things were outside of high-tariff Israel. "The bargains flew off the shelves," was how one journalist described it.[13]

That surprise paled in comparison to the shock that awaited the Arabs. For years they had been assaulted with propaganda assuring them that Israel was a failed state on the brink of collapse. What they found instead was a consumer society of overflowing shops and cafés. For some, it was their first glimpse of a modern city. An Israeli policeman remembered seeing Arabs crowded around a traffic light, cheering each time it automatically changed from red to green.[14]

Elsewhere, the occupation worked well because it was guided by Moshe Dayan, who followed the principle "the lighter the grip, the firmer the hold." Less than two weeks after the war ended, he ordered the army to exit Arab cities and position itself in military bases outside. German television crews were stunned to see Arabs listening to Egyptian and Jordanian radio stations. In World War II, listening to enemy radio was a crime punishable by death.[15]

As for the holy sites, Dayan the atheist had it down to a science: separate the two faiths and pray to God they coexist. In Hebron, the Ibrahimi Mosque built atop the Cave of the Patriarchs (*Me'arat HaMakhpela*) was divided in two. In Jerusalem,

Muslims prayed in the Temple Mount above, while Jews prayed at the Western Wall below. King Solomon could not have crafted a more elegant compromise.

The splendid little war that Israel fought in 1967 stood alone upon the bomb-cratered battlefields of the twentieth century as perhaps the only conflict that turned a profit. The direct cost of the war was only about $1 billion and was largely paid for with foreign donations. The opening of the territories to Israel and vice versa created forces of its own, and within a year the two sides realized that they were estranged halves comprising an economic whole. In early 1968, economic growth in Israel reached the unheard of level of 9 percent. From the third quarter of 1967 to the third quarter of 1973, the Israeli economy grew by fully *85 percent*. Palestinians did even better, finding work in Israel—Cairo had never allowed Gazans to work in Egypt—and achieving annual growth rates of close to 20 percent in the years 1969 to 1972. At Israel's economic peak in 1996, 120,000 workers—or fully 40 percent of the entire Palestinian workforce—found employment in Israel.[16]

For publishers, there was a new book genre, the Album of Victory, which amounted to nothing more than a collection of pictures taken during the war, usually by amateur photographers. They were easy to produce and even easier to sell. Approximately four hundred of them flooded the market. Of the more serious books, the most famous was *Exposed in the Turret* by Shabtai Tevet, a hagiographic account of the armored division that fought in the northern Sinai under General Yisroel Tal. The book described young men eager to join the battle ("in the IDF . . . a unit is jealous of others given the privilege to fight") and ended, suitably, with the death of a handsome young officer. In a nation of fewer than two million adults, it sold eighty-five thousand copies.[17]

In this ecosystem, army generals were giants who bestrode the earth. It was enough for a senior officer to dine at a restaurant to turn it into the next hot spot, and owners happily plied them with free food and drink. After feasting on shrimp, caviar, and liquor, a general might hobnob with top businessmen and leave them with a memento from the battlefield, such as a piece of a downed MiG fighter.* Years after General Rehavem Ze'evi's death, several women stepped forward and claimed that he had sexually harassed and even raped them. Ze'evi's daughter scoffed at the charge and said that her father had no need to rape anyone: "Women threw themselves at his feet."[18]

Sadly, unfairly, the one face that never appeared in any of the books, "Collector's Edition" magazines, or on souvenirs or other trinkets was Prime Minister Levi Eshkol. Not even a victory in six days was enough to overcome the damage he inflicted upon himself with his failed speech before the war. Thirty years later his wife, Miriam, said in an interview that the two never discussed the episode. The subject was too painful. She was enraged in 1968 when someone put out a book of jokes poking fun at her husband. Eshkol got a copy and good-naturedly said, "It's not worth getting upset over, I told better jokes about myself."[19]

Atop Olympus stood a national deity, the man who became not only the world's most recognizable Israeli but the very icon of the nation itself.

Moshe Dayan was born in Kibbutz Degania on May 20, 1915, only the second child born in the very first kibbutz. He quickly rose to prominence in the ranks of the Haganah, so much so that when he lost an eye on June 8, 1941, in one of the forgotten battles of World War II, the newspapers did not report that a soldier was wounded, but that Moshe Dayan was wounded. It was a hideous injury. Not only was his eye shot out, the eye socket and surrounding bones were shattered. In later years he was sent to specialists all over the world, and even underwent an attempted bone graft in France. After the procedure nearly killed him, doc-

---

* The Arabs apparently did the same thing. The Jewish star on the fuselage of an IAF plane shot down over Iraq was brought to one of Saddam Hussein's palaces. The American army discovered it in 2003 and returned it to Israel.

tors concluded that with the medicine of the day, the best they could prescribe was an eye patch.[20]

He was considered a mediocre commander in the 1948 war, at least until it ended. It was then that Dayan distinguished himself. At the negotiating table.

Somehow, he persuaded the Jordanians to free 670 Israelis in return for just 12 Jordanian soldiers.* He then talked his counterparts into a land swap that allowed Israel to maintain the train tracks supplying Jerusalem. The train tracks ran through a place called Bet Sefafa; the land swap effectively split the Arab village in two. The Jordanians agreed to the deal anyway. Ben-Gurion could hardly believe his eyes.[21]

A star was born, and born at the right time. Following the impossible victory of 1948, David Ben-Gurion was a government of one, with the power to make or break careers. An ambitious young man in the good graces of the Old Man could be catapulted through the ranks in ways that would be impossible at any other time in history. Shimon Peres was placed in charge of the Israeli navy at the age of twenty-five. Abba Eban was appointed ambassador to the UN at the age of thirty-three. And at the age of thirty-eight, with no formal military education, Moshe Dayan was appointed chief of staff of the Israeli army.[22]

Ben-Gurion sent loyalty down to those that sent it back up, but Dayan tried the Old Man's patience like no other. His womanizing was legendary, so open, so brazen, that it sparked its own collection of jokes ("Does he do it with the patch on, or the patch off?"). He even carried on affairs with the wives of officers who served under him. In one story, possibly apocryphal, an aggrieved officer found Dayan's shirt in his bedroom—only one man's shirt was embroidered with the insignia of the chief of staff—and sent it to Ben-Gurion with the verse from Genesis 37:32, "Look at the cloak and determine if it is your son's." Ben-Gurion, not to

---

* As this account is written, the most recent prisoner swap resulted in Israel trading 1,027 convicted terrorists to obtain the freedom of exactly one soldier, a corporal.

be outdone biblically, responded that King David had slept with Bathsheba, the wife of one of *his* officers, and the Lord had forgiven him.[23]

What no biblical hero could excuse was Dayan's other great vice: illegally digging up archeological artifacts. Dayan was sometimes described as an amateur archeologist. In truth, he was a professional grave robber. Archeologists dig with a spoon and a toothbrush, carefully sifting through soil as they search for clues. Dayan showed up with a shovel and a pickaxe and dug for treasure. He had no other hobbies. Israeli scholar Mordecai Kedar claimed—based on conversations he said he had with two anonymous Dayan aides— that one reason Dayan placed the Temple Mount in the hands of the Arab Waqf was that he had a quiet understanding that he could come at night and dig for antiquities, something he never could have done if it had remained under Israeli jurisdiction.[24]

It was not for nothing that Ben-Gurion tolerated his vices. More than any other single individual, Moshe Dayan is credited with establishing the strategy and ethos of the Israeli army.[25] Upon assuming command in 1953, he inherited a hesitant force commanded by officers whose only priority was avoiding casualties. Upon leaving in 1958, he handed his successor an aggressive fighting machine that vanquished its enemies. The 1956 Suez conflict ended badly for England and France. But it was an elegant victory for Israel that opened the Straits of Tiran to Israeli shipping and bought eleven years of peace on the southern border. Dayan published his *Diary of the Sinai Campaign* and became a global celebrity. The million-dollar eye patch was now as recognizable as Lincoln's beard and top hat. What few knew was that he lived in pain that was so bad he told one of his aides he had thoughts of suicide. Not surprisingly, his personality matched the accounts we have of European royalty that suffered from gout: he was irritable, impatient, and short-tempered. Moshe Dayan was a confirmed misanthrope and he made no effort to conceal it. Indeed, he took a perverse pride in it, often saying that he had only one friend and even he had stopped being a friend. The feeling, of course, was mutual. His own sons could not stand him. A typical account was offered in the memoir of General Rafael Eitan, who wrote, "I hated him with all my heart."[26]

Everyone loved him after the Six-Day War. An American senator suggested in perfect seriousness that Dayan be hired to solve the quagmire in Vietnam. Muckraking journalist and politician Uri Avneiri made a career of enraging the Israeli public, even meeting with Yasir Arafat in Beirut during the siege in 1982 when it was illegal to do so. But he said he never felt so much raw hatred as when he stood in the Knesset and accused Dayan of breaking the law with his amateur archaeology. He would have had an easier time impeaching King David for sleeping with Bathsheba. These were the years of Moshe Dayan.[27]

\* \* \*

Nasser later confided to a friend that the weeks following the 1967 war were "one continuous nightmare." If the Israelis were to cross the canal, he told his friend, there was nothing to stand between them and Cairo.[28]

It was plain to all that Egypt desperately needed peace. The price would be heavy, requiring abandonment of cherished principles that defined the regime. But even Nasser could see his calamities cementing into permanence. Principles were a luxury he could no longer afford. And so, on August 29, Cairo agreed to the unthinkable. There would be a dramatic conference in which Egypt would at last make peace with one of its bitterest enemies: Saudi Arabia.

The Arab League summit was arranged in Khartoum, the capital of Sudan. Nasser's plane was held up so that King Feisal of Saudi Arabia could land first. Had Feisal landed second after Nasser's motorcade drove off, he would have arrived at an empty airport. Keeping the wealthy monarch in good spirits was a key aim of the organizers. Nasser arrived to a hero's welcome. The masses burst through security barriers on the tarmac and formed a human chain around him, shouting, "Long live Nasser!" and demanding revenge against the United States and Israel.[29]

The Syrians boycotted the conference, refusing even now to close ranks with the hated Arab monarchies. But the Khartoum Conference would still be remembered as a success. Nasser patched up his differences with the Arab kings he once condemned as "imperialist stooges," and Saudi Arabia agreed to cover much of Egypt's lost revenue. Peace did not come cheap. Nasser had to agree to withdraw from the long war in Yemen. His ally President Abdullah al-Sallal stormed out of the summit in protest. And then there was the matter of oil sales. Saudi Arabia, Libya, and Kuwait had imposed an embargo on the United States and Britain. But oil was so plentiful they had hurt none but themselves. Nasser agreed they could go back to business as usual. The decision seemed sensible enough. "What is the use of shutting the oil wells," Feisal declared, "and how can the Arabs enable their armies to surmount these setbacks when some of them do not possess enough resources to buy a loaf of bread?"[30]

The foreign press took little interest in any of this. Reporters were there to see if there might be some change in policy toward Israel. On that front, Nasser laid down the "Three No's" that would give the Khartoum Conference its name in the history books: no negotiations with Israel, no recognition of Israel, and no peace with Israel.[31]

Nasser had lost his land and his army, but he still had his supporters. The Prophet Muhammad united the Arabs with the sword; Nasser did it with the radio. His determination was undiminished, as were his powers of communication. And so, as the terrible year of 1967 came to a close, Gamal Abdel Nasser made a declaration to the world that was simple, poetic, and as succinct as a message in a fortune cookie: *That which was taken by force will be returned by force.*

# 3

# THE WARS BETWEEN THE WARS

For all their troubles, Egyptians could take heart from one thing. Their country was an island of stability compared to Syria.

The seven-member Military Committee that governed the country included Abdel Karim al-Jundi, described by East German Stasi agents as a psychopath. Wanting to deter those who might bring down the government in the aftermath of the war, the committee handed political prisoners to Jundi with instructions that liberated the sadistic man's most savage instincts. The mangled corpses he left behind were recorded with horror by the East Germans.[1] Syria turned in on itself, becoming a North Korean–style "hermit kingdom."

Coup and countercoup, victory and betrayal, torture and exile, all worked to whittle the field down to just two camps. One was headed by former chief of staff Salah Jadid and the other by Defense Minister Hafez el-Assad, described by a Russian diplomat as "a strange man that lacked any principles." Both belonged to the Alawite faith, and—in the dismissive tone common in all the Russian memoirs of the period—that same diplomat described it as "that weird religious sect that lived in the mountains."[2]

Attempts within the Alawite community to broker a truce failed. The two factions hoarded weapons for the coming showdown. The wealthy sent assets abroad. Reliable information during this period is difficult to come by, but records of the East German Stasi indicate that the mayhem peaked in the summer of 1968, when hundreds of people disappeared. East German leader Erich Honecker called the situation in Syria "catastrophic."[3]

Syria's chaos kept the country's leadership preoccupied and left the border with Israel quiet. Meanwhile, Nasser saw the clock running out on his political standing—to say nothing of his physical health—and felt he had to act. For all its shortcomings, the Egyptian army still enjoyed two advantages over the Israelis. It had a higher capacity for absorbing casualties. And it had a lot more artillery.

Egyptian Defense Minister Mohamed Fawzi announced in early September that the period of *tzumud*, or "steadfastness," was over and a new period of "active defense" had begun. A round of artillery battles broke out in September and October of 1968, killing twenty-five Israeli soldiers and more than one hundred Egyptians. In a speech in July 1969, Defense Minister Fawzi announced that Egypt had launched the *Harb al-Istanzaf*, literally the "War of Bloodletting." The Israelis called it the War of Attrition.[4]

The war started, as wars often do, with glowing support in the local press. But the Egyptians might as well have trained their guns upon themselves. The war lacked even basic planning and demonstrated that Nasser and his sycophants had learned nothing from their experience in 1967. As in 1967, Nasser had no trouble articulating lofty war goals. This time they included restoring Egyptian honor and forcing Israel to withdraw from the entire Sinai Peninsula. But when Soviet ambassador Vladimir Vinogradov asked Egyptian leaders how they planned to achieve all that, their answers grew vague. In Vinogradov's words, they responded that "one had to start and then see what happens."[5]

Among the things they might have considered was that for all their artillery, the Egyptians' capacity to inflict pain on Israel was but a fraction of the pain the Israelis could inflict upon them in return. Israel had no civilians in the Canal Zone, whereas Egypt had industry, infrastructure, and whole cities to protect. Hundreds of thousands of civilians had already streamed out of places like Suez and Ismailia to pitch tents in the Cairo cemetery. And then there was the problem of the Israeli air force, which from bases in Sinai could hit any target inside Egypt. Gone were the days when Egyptian officials could sit comfortably in Cairo and send Palestinians to attack Israel from Gaza. The tables were now turned: Israel could take the fight into Egypt. Egypt could not take the fight into Israel, at least not with its army or air force.

Nasser could, however, hit Israel's soft underbelly through Palestinians based in Jordan. Over the next three years, the Palestine Liberation Organization would launch almost six thousand attacks across the border. Most were shelling and rocket fire, but there were also land assaults by guerillas that crisscrossed the Jordan Valley, a place with some of the most extreme weather on the planet.[6] No Palestinians ever made it through the Jordan Valley to population centers in Israel along the shores of the Mediterranean. They never sparked a popular uprising among Palestinians in the territories, either. But they scored one minor symbolic victory. They prevented Levi Eshkol from being buried in accordance with his wishes.

Eshkol's cancer returned in 1968. By October, government meetings were being held at his bedside. A terrorist bombing on November 22, 1968, in Jerusalem killed twelve and forced Eshkol to leave his sickbed for a public appearance. He barely had the strength to get out of his car. One of his aides wept as it became clear he could not take a single step. Eshkol died three months later on February 26, 1969, at the age of seventy-three. He could not be buried in his hometown of Kibbutz Degania, as he wanted, because of the risk of shelling from nearby Jordan. Instead, he was buried in Jerusalem on Mount Herzl.[7]

History has few cautionary tales to match that of Levi Yitzchak Eshkol. It can be plausibly argued that he was the greatest prime minister in Israeli history. Yet he was underappreciated by the Israeli public and largely ignored by Israeli historians as well. Only one full-length biography of him has been written so far, and it did not come out until 2003. He had no charisma. Short of stature and wearing his pants above a potbelly with a belt that ran high up his chest, he did not cut a dashing figure. He was cerebral. One aide said that watching him read the newspaper was like watching a rabbi study the Talmud. But these superficialities, and even the infamous Mumble Speech, should not obscure the fact that practically all his major decisions turned out to be correct. And, paradoxically, he stands alone among the principal Israeli leaders of his day—David Ben-Gurion, Moshe Dayan, and Yitzchak Rabin—as the only one who never suffered a collapse in a crisis.[8]* When others wilted under the pressure, Levi Eshkol stood straight as steel.

In his lifetime, no one thought Eshkol an "irreplaceable man." He proved hard to replace all the same. The Labor Party deadlocked between two men, Moshe Dayan, the hero of 1967, and Yigal Allon, the hero of 1948. Eventually a compromise was reached. If the party could not agree on the best man for the job, then that left only one alternative: the job would go to the best woman.

* * *

Golda Mabovitch was born on May 3, 1898, in Kiev, then part of Czarist Russia.[9] Her family immigrated to the United States in 1906, and though she grew up in Milwaukee, she had the scrappy bravado more commonly associated with Brooklyn. Not wanting to be what she called a "parlor Zionist," she moved to Palestine with her husband, Morris Meyerson, in 1921 and settled in a kibbutz.

Behind every great woman is a man, but in Golda's case that

---

* David Ben-Gurion took to his sickbed in the early hours of the 1956 war when it seemed the British had double-crossed him. Rabin collapsed on the eve of the 1967 war. Dayan's breakdown would come in 1973.

man was not Meyerson but David Remez, cofounder of the Labor Party, signatory on Israel's Declaration of Independence and minister in Ben-Gurion's first two governments. He would have been a candidate for prime minister had he not died suddenly of a heart attack in 1951. Remez took an instant liking to Golda and sent her abroad on fundraising missions where the Zionist cause could make use of her charisma and American-accented English. In the words of Teddy Kollek, she had "an unequalled gift for turning emotion into cold cash."[10]

The collateral damage to her career was her marriage to Meyerson, a sensitive young man who loved books and classical music and had no interest in Palestine, let alone manual labor on a kibbutz. The two grew apart, and in the style of the day, Golda had affairs with at least two of the leading Zionist leaders, Remez, and Zalman Shazar, a brilliant author and politician who later rose to become Israel's third president. Of course, her private indiscretions played at best a minor role in her career and might have even hurt it. When she began her romance with Shazar in the 1930s, she cheated not only on her husband but on Remez as well (he took it badly). Golda rose to the highest echelons of the Labor Party because she was spectacularly successful at every job she was given. In 1948, she was sent by Ben-Gurion to the United States on a life-or-death fundraising trip that raised an eye-popping sum estimated between $50 million and $75 million. It was a decisive event in paying for a war that cost $274 million. Ben-Gurion later said, "When the history of the 1948 War is told, it will be said that it was a Jewish woman that got the money that made the country possible."[11]

She served in every government between 1949 and 1966. As labor minister, she is credited with founding the National Insurance, Israel's equivalent of social security. She also passed numerous laws, such as child labor laws, that remain at the foundation of Israel's social contract.[12] But it was as Israel's longest-serving foreign minister—a post she held for almost ten years—that she became known around the world. By then she had long since changed her last name from Meyerson to Meir, but few noticed. To everyone she was simply Golda. A play was written called *Golda's Balcony*, in reference to an observation deck inside Israel's nuclear reactor in Dimona. Mordecai Vanunu, the Israeli traitor who leaked pictures of the reactor to the British *Sunday Times*, said that there really is such an observation deck. It is in the second sublevel of Building 2.[13]

In the vacuum left by Eshkol's death, she was a compromise candidate made in heaven. She was tough, she was experienced, and best of all she was unlikely to hold power for long. It was one of the best kept secrets in Israel that she was diagnosed with lymphoma in 1965. She went through periodic bouts of chemotherapy; the idea of being prime minister was broached to her in a rehabilitation clinic in Switzerland. With her cancer in remission, doctors cleared her to serve. Outwardly, the only sign of infirmity was her preference for orthopedic shoes (to this day, they are known in Israel as "Golda shoes"). But those same doctors always cautioned that people rarely lived long with her illness. She was already seventy, young by the standards of our time, but old by the standards of hers. When friends, family, and physicians pleaded with her to cut back on her chain-smoking, she always replied that it did not matter if she died; she was already an old woman. For a Labor Party split in two, she was the perfect caretaker. Abba Eban wrote that he was assured Golda "would take the office only for the year remaining until an election would be necessary."[14]

For some power corrupts, for others it cures. When asked how it was that she seemed twenty years younger, Golda replied, "The reason is very simple. My disease was that I wanted to be prime minister. Once it was given to me, I was cured."[15]

Golda Meir assumed office on March 17, 1969, the first woman in the history of the world to rise to be head of state without being related by blood or marriage to a king or male politician. Her reputation as a feminist icon was cemented when she engaged in the blood sport of world affairs as naturally as stepping into a warm bath.

Most politicians are given a political honeymoon. Golda did not even get a one-night stand.

On March 8, 1969, Nasser ordered his army to fire up the artillery. Again Israelis were killed, four on this occasion, but again Egypt got the worst of it. The following day, March 9, Egyptian Chief of Staff Abdul Munim Riad and several of his staff officers were killed by Israeli tank and artillery fire as they toured the front. A million Egyptians attended Riad's funeral and turned it into a protest, chanting cries for revenge. Egyptian artillery fire resumed on April 10. This time it would not let up for another sixteen months.[16]

Egyptian shelling turned Israel's side of the canal into a hellish moonscape reminiscent of World War I. But instead of poppies in Flanders Field there were flies, sandstorms, and desert heat. As early as mid-1969, an Israeli general estimated there were thirty-six thousand shell craters just in the area south of the Gidi Pass.[17] Shelling farther north was even worse.[18]

The hardships along the canal rivaled the worst horrors of the trenches in World War I. For Israeli soldiers, the seaside town of el-Arish, near Gaza, was the last outpost of civilization. From there, they would travel through the nine concentric circles of Dante's Inferno, before entering the innermost sanctum of hell along the canal.[19] The shelling rarely let up, making it all but impossible to emerge from the bunkers. Basic hygiene was impossible. The men had to relieve themselves inside their shelters, leading to outbreaks of hepatitis.[20]

Extracting the wounded through the shelling was an elaborate operation requiring columns of armored vehicles.[21] The dead often could not be extracted at all. Their bodies were hung to prevent them from being gnawed at by rats.[22] Garbage was burned in pits outside, which attracted legions of them. When the rats were poisoned, the odor of their rotting corpses would be added to that of human excrement. The men often wore gas masks, not because of chemical warfare, but to ward off the stench and the dust. Decades later, soldiers who survived the ordeal jumped at the sound of a refrigerator door closing. It was identical to the sound of distant artillery launching a salvo.[23]

The Israelis initially responded with commando raids. Seventeen such missions were launched inside Egypt. All achieved their goals, and Israel lost soldiers to hostile fire in only two of them. The missions were often designed with a touch of Israeli chutzpah, the better to undermine Nasser's political standing by humiliating him. In one celebrated operation on December 26, 1969, the Israelis dismantled a five-ton Soviet radar, hitched the pieces to helicopters, and—without taking a single casualty—flew them back to Israel with all the Russian manuals.[24]

General Mordecai Hod might have made his living as a riverboat gambler had he not been commander of the Israeli air force. Delivery of the first F-4 Phantom jets was still two months away, and thus potentially in doubt, but he decided to try the patience of the Americans anyway. Israeli jets were sent to patrol west of the canal, daring the Egyptian air force to challenge them. The Egyptians rose to take the bait and twenty of their planes were shot down in July 1969 alone. In all, during the War of Attrition the Israeli air force downed seventy-three Egyptian planes in air-to-air combat and lost only three, a 24:1 ratio that exceeded that of every previous conflict.[25]

Washington let these incidents pass without protest. Once the Israelis knew there would be no embargo on the shipment of new fighter jets, they went on the attack. The IAF flew no fewer than eight thousand sorties in the Canal Zone, hitting 620 artillery pieces and hundreds of other targets. The Egyptians were forced to shift to mortars and snipers—less lethal but harder to bomb.[26]

The commando operations, the aerial dogfights—all these burnished the reputation of the Israeli army and air force. What they failed to do was end the war.

The natural next question for the Israelis was whether they could push their luck even further and have the air force bomb targets outside the Canal Zone deep inside Egypt. Such a move could potentially finish the war. With the right amount of luck, it might even finish off Nasser. But it carried two distinct risks: the Soviets might get angry and intervene in the conflict. And the Americans might get angry and cut off arms sales.

Despite the risks, the so-called deep-penetration bombings were approved. Starting on January 7, 1970, Israel flew 119 sorties in nineteen missions attacking military bases, military colleges, and ammunition dumps. Many attacks centered on bases near Cairo, forcing ordinary Egyptians to go into nightly blackouts reminiscent of those in London during the Blitz. Nothing in Egypt, it seemed, was beyond the long arm of the IAF. Planes struck as far as the Ras Banas naval base, six hundred miles down the shore of the Red Sea. The Israelis did not lose a single plane.[27]

Egyptian General Sa'ad Shazly later wrote that, with the deep-penetration bombings, "the calamity reached its climax." Those that went to Egypt to see ruins no longer had to travel as far as the ancient city of Luxor. Jihan Sadat remembered that "in the Canal Zone cities, the scene was one of *mahgoura*, no life, no people living there anymore. Not a single building was left standing in Isma'iliya on the western side of the Canal. . . . I could not hold back my tears."[28]

In desperation, Nasser traveled to Moscow on January 22. Without a touch of irony in his voice, he informed his patrons that "perhaps" the Egyptian army was not yet ready to confront the Israelis. Nasser pleaded for surface-to-air missiles, but then, noting that it would take six months to train Egyptian crews, he "dropped a bombshell" in the words of newspaper editor Muhammad Heikal: Soviet troops and technicians would have to come to defend his country. The bombshell was not well received. Brezhnev said that missiles were but one element of a complicated system that also required fighter jets. To that, Nasser replied, "Send the planes too."[29]

The Nasser who pleaded before the Soviets was much diminished. Paradoxically, his weakness was his strength. He had only one card left to play: if the Soviets did not defend his country, he said, he would resign and hand the reins to a "pro-American president." That did the trick. It took eight days of hard bargaining; the question made it all the way to the Politburo. But in the end, Nasser got what he wanted.[30]

On April 18, 1970, two Israeli planes heading back from a reconnaissance mission near Cairo were pursued briefly by MiGs. It was a routine encounter in which no shots were fired, except that Israeli radio operators heard Russian spoken in the cockpits. It was then that the Israelis realized, as the distinguished military commentator Chaim Herzog later put it, that the deep-penetration bombings were a "major error."[31]

Dayan immediately canceled further missions, but it was too late. On April 9, he tried to reach an understanding with the Russians to stop the deep-penetration bombings if Israel was permitted to maintain its air superiority in the Canal Zone. Moscow never even responded. Instead, the Soviets rushed surface-to-air missiles into the Canal Zone. On June 30, the first two Israeli F-4 Phantoms were shot down.[32]

The fighter jets were assets the IAF could ill afford to lose. For at this sensitive juncture, any jet lost was a jet that Israel could no longer replace.

If Hubert Humphrey had won the 1968 election, there seems little doubt that the supply of arms to Israel would have continued unhindered. Instead, the fate of the Jewish state and its arms needs were determined by one Richard Milhous Nixon. At first, Israeli officials saw no trouble on the horizon. It was Nixon himself who established a "doctrine" in Guam on July 25, 1969, committing the United States to "furnish military and economic assistance [to allies] when requested." The hawkish president was so proud of the principle that he worked hard to ensure that journalists change the initial label it had been given—the "Guam Doctrine"—to the "Nixon Doctrine."[33]

The Nixon Doctrine would have been reliable were it not for the fact that it was overseen by Nixon. He delighted in telling associates and visitors that he was impervious to pressure from the "Jewish lobby," often joking that the few Jews who voted for him "had to be so crazy" that they would stick with him even if he turned on Israel.[34] It did not take long for him to do just that.

In February 1970, French president Georges Pompidou went to the United States on a state visit to which Nixon attached great importance. By coincidence, the month before, Pompidou had concluded a deal to sell Libya's Mu'ammar al-Qaddafi the one hundred Mirage fighter jets that were originally earmarked for Israel. The French rubbed salt in the wound by including top-secret improvements that Israeli engineers had developed and shared with their French counterparts. As Libya lacked the pilots to fly advanced aircraft, it was obvious that the planes were destined for Egypt. Pompidou's advance men did a poor job scouting out the American visit, and Israel's supporters greeted him with angry protests wherever he went. It was a rebellious age, and in Chicago pro-Israel protesters hurled what Henry Kissinger later described as "especially offensive" insults at Pompidou's wife.* An enraged Pompidou threatened to cut the visit short and return to Paris. An equally enraged Nixon retaliated against the protesters—by cutting off arms sales to Israel.[35]

For Israel, these were the darkest days of the War of Attrition. The Americans had turned their backs, even as the Israelis were fighting the Soviets. In May 1970, the IDF took seventy killed

---

* Press accounts of the day failed to describe the exact nature of the insults (such were journalistic norms before the advent of social media). But the visit occurred shortly after the Markovic Affair, a sordid tale of sex parties, mobsters, and murder in which French police uncovered sexually explicit photos of Madame Pompidou in the murdered man's car.

along the canal, the highest monthly toll of the war. It was also around this time that Israeli intelligence saw yet another of its core assumptions disintegrate in the face of a "first." The Soviets deployed the SAM-3 antiaircraft missile in Egypt, the first time it was sent outside the Warsaw Pact. Israeli intelligence was dumbfounded; the Soviets would not even share it with the North Vietnamese. The IAF had enjoyed great success against the SAM-2 in late 1969, destroying twelve batteries without losing a plane.[36] Against the more advanced SAM-3—which now gave Egypt an integrated defense system, SAM-2s covering high altitude, SAM-3s low altitude—the IAF had no answer.

Egypt's new missiles were fired with reckless abandon. So reckless, in fact, that they often hit their own aircraft. The first fighter jet downed by a Soviet-made SAM was Egyptian. A civilian Egyptian passenger plane was later hit, though the pilot managed to land safely on just one engine. The skies were so saturated with missiles that Soviet pilots complained they had to "maneuver like snakes" to avoid them.[37]

But the missiles accomplished what Nasser and the Soviets wanted. The Israeli air force was devastated. Of the fifty F-4 sorties flown to attack SAM batteries in the Canal Zone, five of the jets were shot down, and two more were badly damaged. Counting the two damaged jets as the equivalent of one lost—they returned to base "only by a miracle," in the words of one pilot—the IAF lost 12 percent of its F-4 aircraft on each mission. Such losses would be unacceptable in any air force. This was doubly the case in Israel, where the loss of six F-4s amounted to a quarter of all those in the nation's arsenal. At that rate, the air campaign would quickly succumb to the tyranny of arithmetic. A simple calculation showed that after just 350 more sorties, the IAF would run out of its best planes.[38]

To be sure, the Israelis experienced their share of success. The bombing runs prevented the Egyptians from building SAMs in the Canal Zone. Muhammad Heikal wrote that "no fewer than

four thousand" Egyptian workers and engineers were killed attempting to build SAM batteries in the Canal Zone. Israeli photo
reconnaissance revealed eighteen thousand graves dug for Egyptian workers.[39]

Moreover, on July 30, 1970, the Israelis sent four planes into
Egypt on what seemed like a routine reconnaissance mission.
The Soviets took the bait, scrambled jets, and were ambushed
by twelve Israeli fighters. The Israeli jets were flown by a handpicked "dream team" that collectively had fifty-nine recorded kills
between them. As a final touch, the Israelis had radio operators
that spoke perfect Russian send the hapless Soviets confusing orders. Five Soviet jets were shot down against no losses for the
Israelis.[40] *

In the end, the War of Attrition ground to its conclusion not in
the typical fashion, when one of the two sides reached the point
of exhaustion, but when the two patron states reached the point
of exhaustion. The Russians even called it the "War to Exhaust."
Soviet soldiers were dying by the dozens, Soviet taxpayers were
footing the bill, and between the two, the conflict exceeded the
budget of bad news the Kremlin was prepared to swallow.[41]

Like the Soviets, the Americans were never more than a reluc-
tant ally. Kissinger noted wryly that unhappy State Department
officials knew how to exhaust recalcitrant superiors with position
papers and memoranda, but when they agreed with a policy, the
bureaucracy sprang into action. In implementing Nixon's decision
to hold up arms sales to Israel, the State Department was a well-
oiled machine.[42]

The endgame took shape on June 2, 1970, with a meeting
between Secretary of State William P. Rogers and Soviet ambassador Anatoly Dobrynin. A little more than two weeks later, Rogers

---

* The event was hushed up by all sides. The commander of the Soviet air force flew to
Egypt and stated that anyone who breathed a word of the incident would be brought
back from Egypt and "the next plane they flew would be the one taking them to Siberia."
The Egyptians had suffered numerous insults at the hands of the Russians and could not
disguise their glee.

released a plan christened "Stop Shooting and Start Talking." The plan was controversial in Israel because it seemed to tilt toward the Arabs, being definitive in its call for Israeli withdrawal but vague on the peace it would receive in return. Nevertheless, as Rabin later remembered, "it was explained to us politely that re-supply of arms to Israel was dependent upon our accepting the Rogers Plan." Faced with this offer she could not refuse, Golda made the obvious decision.[43]

On July 22, Nasser surprised the Americans by agreeing to the Rogers Plan as well. The ceasefire came into effect at 1:00 A.M. local time on August 8, 1970. When the last shells fell at around midnight, Israeli soldiers emerged from their bunkers. But instead of quiet, they heard the sound of truck engines.[44]

It was Ambrose Bierce who famously said that peace is the period of cheating in between periods of fighting. The Egyptians planned a very short period in between fighting, so they wasted no time in cheating. Working hard through the night, they intro-duced twenty-eight missile batteries into the Canal Zone.[45] For the first time, Egyptian SAMs could hit Israeli planes flying up to six miles east of the canal.

Israeli cries of outrage fell on deaf ears in Washington. The Americans wanted the war to end, violations or not. Ariel Sha-ron, all bluster and heedless energy, proposed crossing the canal, destroying the missiles and even holding on to a "limited bridge-head."[46] The question was, with whose weapons? The Americans still pushed for an end to the war, and without their support, the IDF would grind to a halt. Chief of Staff Chaim Bar-Lev told the government they had no choice but to bend to the will of Wash-ington. Barring resupply, the army would run out of planes in a year and tanks even sooner than that.[47]

Nevertheless, for Egypt the War of Attrition was another costly failure. Nasser had launched his ill-planned adventure seeking two strategic goals: to restore Egyptian honor and restore Egyp-tian land. He achieved neither. To the contrary, on both objectives

Egypt ended the war further from its goals than it had begun. The army was humiliated in every battle. At the height of the war, during the deep-penetration bombings, the Egyptians were forced to move military assets *away* from the fighting, out of range of Israeli fighter jets. The air college and naval college were relocated to Libya. The military college was relocated to Sudan. As for recovering territory, the goal was to inflict so many casualties that the Israelis would withdraw. Nothing of the kind ever happened. From June 11, 1967, until the ceasefire on August 8, 1970, the Egyptians managed to kill only 440 Israelis. That was even fewer than the 459 Israelis who lost their lives to terrorism and fighting on other fronts. The low casualty level failed to create any cracks of support among the Israeli public, which perceived the conflict as a war of survival. As for Egypt, Anwar Sadat called the period from June 1967 through September 1970 "one of intense suffering, unprecedented, I believe, in the entire stretch of Egyptian History."[48] The entire stretch of Egyptian history is a very long time.

By the time the war ended, Nasser was a spent force. He went to bed early on September 28 and died of a heart attack. He was fifty-two. His funeral was attended by millions. Foreign Minister Riad said that Nasser died "after steering the destiny of Egypt during some of its darkest hours."[49] It would have been more accurate had he substituted the word *during* with the word *into*.

One of Nasser's most famous quotes is, "Events are not a matter of chance."[50] Events after his death would prove him wrong. Nasser never voiced any desire to groom a successor. But shortly before he died, completely by chance, he appointed a vice president. His name was Anwar Sadat.

# 4

# YESMANSHIP: PEACE AND ITS PROCESS

One of the arts of diplomacy is to clothe a rejection in the form
of an acceptance in principle.[1]

—Henry Kissinger

To onlookers, the Soviet team sent to Egypt immediately after
the 1967 war reaffirmed Egypt's special place on the global stage.
For heading the delegation was no less a figure than Nikolai Podgorny, chairman of the Presidium of the Supreme Soviet and one
of the troika that led the communist world together with Pre-
mier Alexei Kosygin and General Secretary Leonid Brezhnev. The
Egyptians took heart from the show of importance but still braced
for the worst. They knew from experience that Podgorny was the
man Moscow sent to deliver bad news.[2]

Podgorny performed as expected. He informed the Egyptians
that it contradicted "Marxist and Leninist philosophy" to "wipe
Israel off as a state" and that Moscow could never support this
goal. Podgorny personally urged Nasser to be "more flexible and
realistic." The Egyptians sat silently, seemingly adjusting to the
new reality. But then Podgorny mentioned an unrelated topic,
and Nasser responded that he would take the matter up "after
Israel's withdrawal," as if this were a given. A KGB agent later

remembered that Podgorny "had difficulty absorbing information, either because Soviet-Israeli relations were a new subject for him, or because of the 100-degree heat." Upon listening to Nasser he became irritable, fumbled for cigarettes, and demanded glasses of water.[3]

The meeting adjourned. The Soviets were stunned. So much for flexibility and realism. But as one official later put it, "We had no choice other than to respect the radical attitudes of our Arab friends."[4] With that in mind, attention turned to the next theater of battle, the United Nations.

In that forum, the Jewish state was even more outnumbered than it was on the battlefield. In 1967, the United Nations comprised 122 states, of which all but a small minority were either Arab, Islamic, communist, or members of the Non-Aligned Movement, an organization that counted Nasser as one of its founders. Nevertheless, Israel won two stunning diplomatic victories, beating back resolutions calling for full withdrawal. The first was due to the support of West African nations, where Israel sent a large aid contingent modeled on the Peace Corps.* The second UN resolution, a slightly watered-down version of the first, had the support of even those African countries. But it failed anyway, due to support Israel received from unlikely allies—the Arab nations. In what can only be described as an astonishing act of folly, the Arabs voted *against* a measure calling for full Israeli withdrawal because—though it made no mention of peace or normalization—it called for "coexistence." Israeli diplomats thought it nothing less than a miracle. Abba Eban returned home to a hero's welcome.[5]†

By the time the UN took up the Middle East again in November, the Arabs had declared the "Three No's" in Khartoum,

---

* In 1972, Israel had consulates in thirty-two African countries, whereas the United States had only twenty-eight.

† Eban wrote, "The stunned look on the faces of [Soviet Minister of Foreign Affairs Andrei] Gromyko and the Arab delegates gave me almost sensual satisfaction." As a result of the fiasco, Soviet UN ambassador Nikolai Fedorenko lost his position and vanished from international diplomacy.

the international community had lost patience, and the paradigm had shifted. On November 7, US ambassador Arthur Goldberg proposed a Security Council resolution calling for "withdrawal of armed forces from occupied territories." Previous drafts called for withdrawal from "*all* occupied territories" or even "*the* occupied territories." The absence of those three-letter words, *all* and *the*, was no coincidence. It meant that Israel could satisfy the resolution by withdrawing from less than everything it had conquered. The resolution also dictated the right of every state in the region to "live in peace within secure and recognized boundaries." Egypt's Foreign Minister Riad was enraged, calling it nothing more than "an Israeli draft under a U.S. name." The measure passed unanimously.[6]

It is weirdly fitting that the UN Security Council resolution that guided Middle East diplomacy for a generation carried the palindromic number of 242. It could be read the same way backward as forward. The extent of Israel's withdrawal was subject to interpretation. So was language requiring a "just settlement of the refugee problem," with no indication as to what that settlement might be. And there was the word *peace* but no description of the relations that would exist between the parties. Did "peace" include embassies, trade, and normalization, or merely a state of non-belligerency? The text of the resolution was so vague that, upon hearing it for the first time, Henry Kissinger thought the speaker was joking.[7]

In deference to the Arabs, the resolution did not call for direct talks. Instead, the secretary-general named Gunnar Jarring, the Swedish ambassador to the Soviet Union, to act as a special representative. It was a curious choice. Jarring was admirably discreet, so discreet that reporters nicknamed him "The Clam."[8] But he had limited experience in the region and almost none mediating disputes.

In the Nasser era of the "Three No's," he had little to do. The only thing the two sides agreed upon was their total and absolute commitment to carry out Security Council Resolution 242. In Cairo, that meant no direct negotiations, no normalization, and a complete withdrawal by Israel from all territories conquered in the 1967 war, including the Western Wall. In Jerusalem, it meant the exact opposite. Jarring handed the parties questionnaires in March 1969 asking them to state their respective positions. Upon receiving their responses, he promptly gave up and returned to his post in Moscow.

* * *

It was with special care that fate tapped Anwar Sadat to replace Gamal Abdel Nasser as Egypt's president. Even in the Egypt of the twentieth century, leaders did not typically hail from places as grindingly poor as his hometown of Mit Abu el-Kom. Until it received electricity and running water in 1968, its villagers rose by the light of the sun and went to bed by the light of the moon. Most of the houses were divided into just two rooms. One was used by the family to cook, sleep, and pray. The other was used to house water buffalo, donkeys, and other livestock.

The Israelis had humiliated a nation obsessed with not being humiliated. Anwar Sadat was the living embodiment of that resentment. He was the dark-skinned grandson of a Sudanese slave, maligned in Egypt as "Nasser's black poodle." After divorcing his first wife and marrying Jihan Safwat Raouf, an attractive fifteen-year-old with European features, his relatives asked her, only half-jokingly, "How did our lucky brother get someone as white as you?" It left Sadat something of a psychological rarity: a near six-footer with a Napoleonic complex.[9] *

To the young nationalists determined to remake Egypt, none of these things mattered. What mattered instead was that he was in a position to bring them information on the comings and goings

---

* Muhammad Heikal writes that what attracted the thirty-year-old Sadat to a girl exactly half his age was the fact that she was white. "Color had been, and was always to be, almost an obsession with him."

inside King Farouk's palace. Apart from that, he had little to offer the group that called itself the Free Officers. Sadat missed the 1948 Arab-Israeli War while in prison. He also missed the Free Officers coup on July 23, 1952, because Nasser changed the date at the last minute while Sadat was at the movies.[10]

Among the ten-member Revolutionary Council he was a relatively minor figure, distinguishing himself only in the degree of his fealty to Nasser. That loyalty often came in handy, such as in 1954 after the Muslim Brotherhood attempted to assassinate Nasser. Sadat was personally appointed by Nasser to serve on the three-judge People's Court, even though he had no legal background; he promptly sentenced the six ringleaders to death.[11]

In the eighteen years that he served under Nasser, Sadat opposed him only once. That came after the 1967 debacle when Nasser advocated democratic reforms that included the formation of two political parties. In other words, the only time Anwar Sadat opposed Nasser was when Nasser suggested loosening his own personal grip on power.[12]

By 1969, Nasser was a physical wreck, smoking six packs of cigarettes a day, fingernails bitten to the quick, a survivor of both a stroke and a heart attack, and tortured by a painful skin rash that was treated with what Sadat called "female hormones" that "gave rise to severe fits of nervous tension." At least once, Nasser locked himself in his bedroom and screamed at the top of his lungs. By then, only Sadat and one other figure remained from the original Revolutionary Council that had brought Nasser to power, many of the others having been lost in the failed Amer coup. Sadat's home became a place where Nasser could relax in the company of an old and supportive friend. According to one account, Nasser named Sadat vice president in December 1969 to allow him to earn a higher pension. According to another, he simply believed "it was Anwar's turn to be Vice President." Regardless of whose turn it was, Nasser must have been motivated in part by the fact that he could appoint him without needing to hire a food taster.[13]

No one expected Sadat to become president. When he did, upon Nasser's sudden death, a rumor made the rounds that Minister for Presidential Affairs Sami Sharaf pocketed instructions from Nasser to name someone else, figuring that Sadat would be easier to control. Outside Egypt, disdain for Sadat was universal. On the record, officials spoke of him as a "transitional figure." Under Secretary of State Elliot Richardson represented the United States at the Nasser funeral—the two countries still had no diplomatic relations—and filed a report upon his return giving Sadat no more than six weeks in office. In private conversations, Kissinger is said to have called him a "buffoon."[14]

Of the peace process in the time of Nasser, there is little enough to say. He refused to meet Israelis even quietly, insisting that any negotiation amounted to "capitulation." His concept of "linkage" kept Middle East diplomacy virtually frozen for years. The idea was first articulated by Egyptian Foreign Minister Riad when he interrupted Secretary of State Dean Rusk and declared that any agreement with Israel required withdrawal from *all* territories conquered in 1967, including those previously occupied by Jordan and Syria. "It would be unethical," he explained, "to set Israeli withdrawal from Sinai as the basis for a settlement, leaving out the rest of the occupied Arab territories." Rusk was stunned: "But I got you total Israeli withdrawal from Egyptian territories!"[15]

No one in Jerusalem or elsewhere expected any of this to change under Sadat.[16] Nevertheless, UN representative Gunnar Jarring figured it might be time for another try and presented the parties with what he termed a "package deal." Jarring chose not to engage in any of the hard negotiations required to bridge differences. Instead, he asked a simple, direct question: Would Egypt sign a peace treaty if Israel withdrew to "the former international boundary between Egypt and the British Mandate of Palestine"?[17]

For Israel, the Egyptian response signaled there was trouble ahead. Sadat pointedly made no break with the past. Following the policy of the "Three No's," he refused to accept a document delivered by Jarring until the title, "A Message from the Government of Israel," was erased. Like Nasser, he insisted that he was in talks with Jarring and Jarring alone.[18] Then, in his reply to Jarring, delivered on February 15, 1971, Sadat rehashed Nasser's "linkage" position set forth in 1968. A withdrawal from the entire Sinai Peninsula to the "international boundary" was not enough. Israel had to come to terms *with the entire Arab world*. Thus, it had to withdraw not just from Sinai but from "all the territories occupied since June 5, 1967." Finally, Israel also had to conclude a "just settlement for the refugee problem."

In one respect, though, Sadat's response was groundbreaking and for some even historic. The reply to Jarring is the first document in which a major Arab leader used the "p-word." Sadat stated that if these conditions were met, Egypt was prepared to live with Israel in "peace."[19]

In the wake of this bombshell, Sadat immediately took steps to see to it that his conditions would never be met. On March 8, 1971, less than a month later, he met with Palestinian representatives and urged them not to settle on any terms. King Hussein might sign a peace treaty; they should not. Rather, it was for them to "see that the cause of Palestine was not allowed to die."[20]

To those in the know, it was obvious that Sadat was engaging in what might be termed "yesmanship," the fine art of appearing to say yes. The goal was not to achieve a peace treaty. The goal was to see to it that the Israelis shouldered the blame when it all inevitably failed.

Israel's response to this challenge should have been obvious. Jerusalem could have responded with a hazy "yes, however" of its own, agreeing to withdraw to "secure boundaries" once all issues were resolved. Abba Eban and the Foreign Ministry advocated doing exactly that.[21]

Golda and a majority of her cabinet rejected the advice. Jarring's "package deal" included an Israeli withdrawal only from Sinai to "the former international boundary between Egypt and the

British Mandate of Palestine." Sadat demanded withdrawal from *all* the territories and even a solution to the refugee problem. Golda and her cabinet figured that if Sadat could deviate from the Jarring formula, then they enjoyed the same luxury as well. Accordingly, Jerusalem responded on February 26, 1971, that it, too, was prepared to live in peace; that it was prepared to withdraw to "secure, recognized and agreed boundaries"; and that it was even willing to negotiate compensation for Palestinian refugees. But then the statement added that "Israel will not withdraw to the pre-5 June 1967 lines."[22]

This turned out to be one of the biggest blunders of Golda Meir's premiership. The roof of world opinion collapsed on her. The worst of the criticism was heard inside Israel, coming from the nascent peace movement. Of course, with the exception of perhaps Jarring himself, no one expected either party to make their best offer first. In negotiations of this kind, or any kind, no one ever does. But Sadat was credited with merely stating an opening position that might soften at the negotiation table. Golda was seen as ruling out full withdrawal and thereby sinking the initiative. In truth, it was the other way around. Golda offered to negotiate with Egypt to see if the gap could be bridged. Sadat refused to negotiate at all. This experience should have set off warning bells in Jerusalem. It was, in fact, the first indication that the Israelis were dealing with an adversary who was far shrewder than Gamal Abdel Nasser.

As was his custom, Jarring gave up the moment he saw the parties were at an impasse and returned to his posting in Moscow. His exit left one door closed. But it set the stage for another to open.

The idea was Moshe Dayan's. If it was impossible to sign a *final* peace deal, perhaps it was possible to sign an *interim* one instead. Israel, he said, would withdraw some thirty miles east of the canal to the Mitla and Gidi passes. In return, Egypt would withdraw its forces—and most importantly, its surface-to-air missiles—a comparable distance west of the canal. The Suez Canal would be reopened, the canal cities rebuilt, and a period of non-belligerency would ensue. With the "interim agreement," Israel would not achieve a reversal of any of the "Three No's." But once the surface-to-air missiles were removed, the Israeli air force would reclaim command of the skies in the Canal Zone. Moreover, once Cairo rebuilt the canal cities and reopened the canal, it would have a powerful incentive to stick to the interim agreement so as not to lose them all over again. In short, Egypt would receive the Suez Canal if in return it gave up any realistic military option of invading Sinai.[23]

From Anwar Sadat's memoir, one might conclude that such a limited withdrawal was all that Egypt demanded in return for an interim agreement. Sadat writes that all he requested was a withdrawal "to the Passes." This statement is contradicted by the entire historical record as well as by all other memoirs (including that of his wife). In an interview on February 14, Sadat stated that the "partial withdrawal" had to cover roughly *two-thirds* of the Sinai Peninsula. Sadat followed that up with a speech on May 1 that stated the "partial withdrawal" had to be a "first stage" to an "all-out withdrawal" from "all Arab territories occupied after June 5, 1967." In other words, even an interim agreement had to satisfy the need for linkage, the only difference being that it was "linkage light": Israel did not have to solve the refugee problem. But it had to withdraw from all the other territories, including East Jerusalem.[24]

And then there was the problem of the duration of the interim agreement. Sadat stated that after the partial withdrawal, he was prepared to offer only a six-month extension of the cease-fire. During this period, Egypt would be permitted to send forces, including tanks, across the canal into Sinai. If after the six-month period Israel had not withdrawn from all Arab lands captured in 1967, then "the Egyptian Armed Forces would be entitled to maintain the freedom of action" and use force to bring about "the complete liberation of the entire occupied Arab territory."[25]

Needless to say, Sadat's reply to Dayan's plan received a tepid response in Jerusalem. An interim agreement, as envisioned by Cairo, was not a first step toward peace. It was a first step toward war. And yet Sadat put Golda on the defensive by skillfully dangling the word *peace* to all who would listen.

By contrast, Golda was cast as obstructionist. In truth, many of her wounds were self-inflicted. On February 10, 1970, she gave an interview in which she said that there was no Palestinian nation.[26] To a person of Golda's generation, that statement seemed self-evident. When the United Nations issued its Partition Plan in 1947, it spoke of dividing the land between Arabs and Jews. No one, including the Arabs themselves, thought to refer to the non-Jewish residents as "Palestinians." And if someone had used the term "Palestinian," the obvious next question would have been: "Which Palestinians are you referring to, the Jews or the Arabs?" But Golda had failed to keep up with the times. One could argue that there was no Palestinian nation in 1947. There was plainly one in 1970.

A last attempt at peace was made in early 1973. Sadat sent National Security Adviser Muhammad Hafiz Ismail to Washington for talks with Kissinger. Kissinger found Ismail impressive; he said the latter's appearance and bearing reminded him of the faces etched on the statues of Egypt's ancient temples. The stage also seemed set for a breakthrough. The previous month saw the signing of the Paris Peace Accords that ended the Vietnam War. Optimism was in the air.[27]

The air went out of the room the moment Kissinger heard what Ismail had to say. In effect, nothing had changed. Cairo still clung to linkage, insisting that peace could come only after a comprehensive settlement with all parties, including Syria and the Palestinians. In Kissinger's words, the Egyptian position was "not essentially different from what had produced the deadlock" and "more compatible with a come-on to get us involved than with a serious effort to negotiate."[28] *

Still, Kissinger pressed forward. He asked Ismail if Egypt would agree to "sovereignty for security," allowing Israel to retain military posts for long periods of time, if in return Israel recognized full Egyptian sovereignty over the entire Sinai Peninsula. Ismail promised to explore the idea with Sadat.[29]

The following day, Golda arrived for a meeting with President Nixon to plead for more weapons. Golda was told by Henry Kissinger and everyone else she met to forget about any further delivery of fighter jets. "I have never seen Golda Meir so depressed," Rabin remembered. She murmured from her guest suite in the Blair House that she might cut her trip short.[30]

It was an empty threat. Golda had nowhere else to turn and both sides knew it. She reluctantly gave the green light for Kissinger to explore "sovereignty for security," as long as it was not put forth in her name. With this, Golda retreated from her response to Jarring in 1971 and agreed to withdraw from the entire Sinai Peninsula, albeit with military posts, for a duration to be determined. She was rewarded with an American agreement to sell Israel more fighter jets. The meeting with Nixon was crowned a success.[31]

The next meeting was held with Ismail in Paris on May 20, 1973. By the time it occurred, Kissinger already knew it was a waste of time. In a March 26 speech, Sadat gave his answer. "Israel's security needs require many concessions on our part. We will not accept them . . ."[32]

By now Kissinger had had enough. He had demonstrated a willingness to push the Israelis hard on the issue of withdrawal.

---

* Ismail made only three minor concessions. First, though he demanded a withdrawal by Israel from all the '67 lands, including the Golan Heights and East Jerusalem, he hinted that Egypt might be amenable to minor border adjustments in the West Bank if they were acceptable to King Hussein. Second, after the withdrawal, Israel could use the Suez Canal (Egypt made this commitment after the '56 war and later broke the promise). Finally, Egypt would end the third-party boycott of Israel, though it would not trade with Israel. "It will be some time before Madame Meir can come to Egypt to shop," Ismail remarked.

He was willing to be equally hard with Egypt on the issue of peace. "To ask Israel to withdraw from all occupied territories," he later wrote, "without offering what is normal between most states, namely peace, would have been an absurdity." He believed it equally absurd to pressure an ally on behalf of countries like Egypt and Syria, which "had broken relations with us, pursued policies generally hostile to us, and were clients of Moscow." As Ismail tells it, Kissinger told him that if Sadat were to commence another war, "Israel will win once again and more so than in 1967." The State Department issued a sharp denial that he used those words though acknowledging he "attempted to explain the realities which were needed to frame a settlement." Whatever he said, Kissinger's words stung, as did the news that Washington had approved more fighter jets for Israel. Cairo was enraged.[33]

In March, 1973, *Newsweek* magazine editor Arnaud de Borchgrave traveled to Egypt to interview Sadat. He had to wait three weeks in Cairo, but eventually he got the scoop he was looking for. "The time has come for a shock," Sadat told him. "Everything in this country is now being mobilized in earnest for the resumption of the battle which is inevitable."[34]

The Soviets, perhaps alarmed that this time Sadat meant it, asked to send Podgorny to Cairo for a meeting. Sadat told him not to come.[35]

# 5

## TO PREPARE FOR THE WAR
## THAT MUST COME

Upon visiting the Negev Desert in southern Palestine, Mark Twain remarked that "such roasting heat, such oppressive solitude, and such dismal desolation cannot surely exist elsewhere on earth." Twain would have found just such a place had he continued to the next stop on his journey by land rather than by boat ("It was worth a kingdom to be at sea again").[1] For had he traveled to Egypt by land, he would have traversed the hotter, drier, and more sparsely populated wasteland known as the Sinai Peninsula.

Topographically, the inverted triangle could be divided into two parts. The northern half is a parched world of sand made passable by only a few thin bands of asphalt. A tracked vehicle could sometimes travel off-road, but only if it had a strong engine—an engine driven hard—and a large supply of fuel. The 1956 and 1967 wars reminded military commentators of the North African campaign in World War II, where the taking of a narrow road was recorded on the maps of the world as a huge conquest of land.

The southern half of Sinai is a tight patchwork of stony mountains and sterile gorges that are likewise impassable, except for two routes: the narrow Mitla Pass and the even narrower Gidi Pass. In a few places in northwestern Sinai, and along the approaches to the Suez Canal, there is a break in the topographical monotony.

Here the wasteland presents itself, not in the form of sand and stone, but in the form of swampland.[2] *

When Ferdinand de Lesseps dug the Suez Canal in the 1860s he unwittingly created what Moshe Dayan called "the best anti-tank ditch in the world." The Israelis could hardly have built a better defensive line themselves. The canal was straight as a ruler, offering a good line of sight along a wide horizon.[3] And de Lesseps was kind enough to pile the extracted sand along the banks of the waterway, creating a steep berm roughly forty-five feet high. Crossing any body of water is one of the most difficult feats in the tracts of the military art. The attackers must send a vanguard to establish a bridgehead, those few men must hold out using nothing but the weapons they can carry, and then combat engineers have to lay a bridge under fire to allow vehicles to cross. Soldiers crossing the canal had the additional challenge of having to remove an enormous pile of dirt to plow a passageway through.

Israeli military doctrine changed with the geography. Before 1967 there was no ground to give, so the IDF always took the fight to the enemy. An army that dared attack Jerusalem or Tel Aviv soon had to worry about defending Cairo or Damascus. After 1967 the Israelis no longer had to substitute offense for defense. For the first time there was strategic depth and a high-class problem to go with it: How do you defend defensible boundaries?

It was a difficult problem to tackle because the core arithmetic of the conflict had not changed. On the battlefield, the Arabs outnumbered the Israelis by better than three to one, and it took every ounce of energy the country had to maintain even that lopsided ratio. The Israeli army was often likened to an iceberg. The largest portion of it was unseen because it was comprised of reservists, citizen-soldiers who left their homes and donned uniforms.

---

* In 1970, two armored Israeli jeeps drove across a spit of land in the northwestern swamps of Sinai. When they stopped to eat, a soldier read from a Bible and said that this had to be the spot where Moses parted the Red Sea and the Egyptians chasing them were drowned in their chariots. At that moment, the winds shifted, the pathway flooded, and the jeeps sank underwater. The vehicles could not be extracted until the next day when the waters receded.

The obvious strategy was to stop the Egyptians in the canal where they were most vulnerable. But the army lacked the numbers to man large defensive works on a regular basis. The next best thing was to have tanks and planes near the front to immediately attack an enemy that crossed. The Israelis knew that those tanks and planes had to work quickly. The enemy would be easiest to defeat before armored vehicles crossed, which is to say, before the lead force laid any bridges. The Israelis also understood that they would have to win before the UN Security Council imposed a ceasefire.[4] It was therefore important to quickly identify the location of any attacker.

For this reason, and to create a permanent forward presence, Chief of Staff Chaim Bar-Lev thought it was necessary to build a string of miniature forts called *maozim* along the canal. Each one was heavily fortified, and they had periscopes to allow soldiers to safely view what was happening outside even if they came under fire. The forts were sparsely manned because their mission was not to stop the enemy but rather to locate him. In later years, that real-time intelligence could be gathered by pilotless drone aircraft. In 1973, there was no substitute for having eyes and ears on the front lines. The men would report the position of the enemy from the *maozim* and the tanks would ride to the rescue.[5]

Thus was born a two-phase strategy. The first phase was known as Operation Dovecote. Three hundred tanks manned by soldiers from the regular army would be permanently stationed ten miles behind the front. A line of earthen battle ramps, nicknamed "fins," were built a mile east of the canal to give tank gunners a clear field of fire down to the embankment. The men in the *maozim* would guide the tank drivers into position to act as the first line of defense. The second phase of the plan, code-named Operation Stone, assumed that by this point the reservists would have been mobilized. They would spearhead a counterattack with hundreds of fresh tanks that would expel the remnants of the attacking vanguard and carry the fight across the canal into Egypt.[6]

The plan was controversial. The thirty forts that were ultimately built took up fully 17 percent of the entire defense budget
in 1969. An Israeli general later said that with the funds used to
build the *maozim* he could have purchased another fifteen hundred tanks or one hundred fighter jets. Ariel Sharon was an especially sharp critic of the *maozim*, and as was often the case with
Sharon, the controversy soon leaked to the press. The clash grew
ugly, so ugly that Bar-Lev tried to drum Sharon out of the service
in 1969. What intervened to save his military career was politics.
Elections were scheduled for 1969, Sharon was close to opposition leader Menachem Begin, and it was feared if he left the army
he might run against the ruling Labor Party. Labor Party boss Pinchas Sapir spoke to Bar-Lev, and Sharon was promoted to general
officer commanding the southern theater.[7]

There were other disagreements. General Dan Laner—who in
1972 was the officer in command of the division along the canal—
said that three hundred tanks, or just three per mile, were not
enough to stem an invasion.[8] Strangely, his was the only voice
on the General Staff questioning the viability of Operation Dovecote. Stranger still was the fact that everyone, including Laner, assumed that Israeli intelligence could give enough warning to have
the reservists in place for the Operation Stone counterattack.

To be properly mobilized along the canal, the IDF needed a
week. The defensive line opposite Syria on the Golan Heights
could be manned more quickly but still required twenty-four
to forty-eight hours of preparations. What took so long? Reservists had to be gathered from all over the country in a time when
few owned cars. The countless pieces of equipment all had to be
armed and fueled. The tanks were not designed for long drives on
their tracks and thus had to be loaded onto transporters for the
journey to the canal or the Golan Heights. Even Operation Dovecote could not be properly carried out without a bare minimum
of twenty-four to forty-eight hours of preparation. The army had

no plan for a situation in which it was caught completely by surprise. That scenario was thought to be impossible.[9]

As irresponsible as that might seem, it paled in comparison to the assumptions that guided the army to victory in 1967. That war plan assumed there would be even more advance warning (there was; Nasser mobilized openly); that the air force could neutralize Arab air forces in four successive attacks, maintaining the element of surprise after each one (it did); and most important, that Jordan would stay out of the war. The last assumption turned out to be wrong. But everything worked out all the same. Like Egypt and Syria, the Jordanian army turned out to be hollow.

That last fact, the quality of Arab armies in the previous conflict, weighed heavily on every aspect of planning. In war games in 1971, the Israelis played out a scenario in which the Egyptians managed to get three divisions of infantry and seven hundred tanks across the canal in sixteen hours. General Bar-Lev discounted the whole thing. "I don't think," he said, "that there is even a ten percent chance they could pull off something like that."[10] He was further quoted as saying that "the Arab soldier lacks the qualities necessary for modern warfare. Advanced weaponry and modern military doctrines require a level of intelligence, adaptability, fast-reaction, technological proficiency—and more than anything else, the ability to see a situation and tell the truth, no matter how difficult that might be—that the Arab soldier simply lacks."[11] Ezer Weizman said, "the Arab is a killer, but he isn't a fighter. He wasn't born for this, and I don't think he'll change."[12] Yitzchak Rabin's statements at the time were not as cringeworthy but followed a similar line of thought. "There is no need for a full mobilization [to fend off an Egyptian attack]," he said, "so long as Israel's defense line is along the Suez Canal."[13] Dayan said, "the Arabs know that if they attack us, they will be wiped out."[14]

On one point, however, everyone agreed. If all else failed, there was still an insurance policy that covered all calamities. Even if they

found themselves fighting in the valley of the shadow of death, the Israelis knew they had nothing to fear. For hovering above them in the
heavens was their salvation and their protector: the Israeli air force.

* * *

For the Arabs, the Israeli air force flew above the clouds and
blocked out the sun itself, casting a permanent shadow over every battlefield. On the chessboard of military planning, the plane
with the Star of David on the fuselage was by far the largest piece.
Israel and the fighter jet were made for each other. Only with this
wonder weapon could a nation of 3.3 million—less than half the
population of New York City—hold off combined populations of
over 80 million.

In the competition for funding, members of Israel's other service branches often felt as if they lived inside an old Broadway
show with the pilots singing the tune "Anything You Can Do, I
Can Do Better." Israel made a minimal investment in its navy;
fighter jets could guard the coastline more efficiently. Israel invested little in artillery. "Flying artillery" was more accurate. The
breakdown of the budget said it all: the air force received 48 percent of the defense budget, all branches of the army received 44
percent, and the navy received 6 percent (the final 2 percent went
to other purposes). In the years 1969–1972, the State of Israel
spent *10 percent of its entire GDP* on its air force.[15]

With the arrival of Soviet surface-to-air missiles, the Arabs
found a partial solution. In Vietnam, American pilots had a saying: "The SAMs come up, and the boys go down." Once the radar
locked onto a target, the missiles would launch at Mach 3, which
was about three times the speed of a fighter jet. This strength was
also the missile's greatest weakness. At that speed it could not
overcome its own momentum to make sharp turns. Pilots who
saw the infamous "flying telephone pole" knew to "dive for the
deck" and take the plane into a sharp tailspin to a lower altitude.
But other perils awaited them if they got there. There was flak

from more traditional antiaircraft guns or other low-flying missiles fired in dense salvos.[16]

The only thing more frightening than facing a surface-to-air missile battery was serving inside one. The shifts ran twelve hours in stifling desert heat ("Everyone was sitting in their underpants wearing gas masks, laughing nervously looking at one another"). As one Russian soldier remembered, "The radar screen would fill with dots, and each one of them carried death. They all seemed to be flying right at you." The war of nerves took place in total silence, the only sound in the command cabin being flies buzzing overhead and fans that circulated the dry desert air. The silence only added to the tension. One minute you were sitting inside the stifling cabin, the next minute you were gone. Sometimes soldiers threw off their helmets and ran away.[17]

For the Israelis, the biggest challenge was finding the missiles. The SAM-2 and SAM-3 launch sites were easy to spot, so they were concealed by placing them among dozens of dummy sites. Harder to find were the mobile SAM-6s. It took a minimum of four hours to send reconnaissance planes over the battlefield, snap photos, and then develop the pictures. Sometimes, the pictures that reached the hands of the pilots were taken the day before. By the time the fighter jets were up in the air, the SAM-6s often had been moved to other locations.[18]

Hardest to find were the small flak guns that peppered the skies with hot metal as the fighter jets streaked through at low altitude. In Vietnam, the United States lost a devastating 3,374 fixed-wing aircraft to the Soviet air defense system. Sixty percent were shot down by flak guns, 31 percent by missiles, and only 9 percent by MiG fighters in aerial dogfights.[19] Obviously, the Israelis could not afford to lose even a tiny fraction of that figure.

\* \* \*

Before settling on a military plan of his own, Sadat had to first attend to the basic business of survival. In the minds of all, he compared poorly with his predecessor. The Arab gift for rhyme and sloganeering manifested itself among crowds in the streets that chanted "*Rah al-wahsh, gaa al-gahsh*" ("Gone is the giant, the donkey has taken his place"). A coup attempt by senior officials was thwarted in May 1971. The coup plotters were described as "Nasserists": they were so devoted to their spiritual leader they attempted to communicate with him through séances. Sadat traveled to Moscow to plead for more weapons and returned after two long sessions that he described as "nine hours of insults." With respect to Israel, he declared 1971 the "Year of Decision" and exposed himself to further ridicule when nothing happened.[20]

The Egyptian army became the butt of merciless jokes. Some were recycled one-liners from World War II about the Italian army, such as the one about the Egyptian army selling used weapons that were "only dropped once." Others were more original, like the one that said the Egyptians were preparing for the aftermath of the next war: "The Cairo Hilton is taking reservations for Bar Mitzvahs."[21]

Sadat made changes in the army, removing all those who believed that Egypt could paddle across the canal and conquer Sinai. For chief of staff, he chose Sa'ad Shazly, a highly regarded career soldier, elevating him over thirty more senior officers.[22] In the 1967 war, he had commanded the elite 4th Division. And of all the retreats of the Egyptian army, his was the only one that could be considered orderly.

Shazly was appointed on May 16, 1971, and quickly discovered that Egypt "had no real plan" for retaking the Sinai Peninsula.[23] The Egyptian army had always been led to disaster, and it was slogans and high emotion that had guided them to that destination ("That which was taken by force will be returned by force!"). Shazly was determined that this time was going to be different. There was only one thing that could protect the army from the Israeli air force, and that was the surface-to-air missiles. Thus, Shazly argued that the depth of the Egyptian army's advance could not exceed the range of the SAMs, which was only six miles east of the canal.

Such a limited campaign, if successful, would still leave the Israelis holding over 95 percent of Sinai. Nevertheless, it could achieve two important war goals. The first was restoring Egypt's national honor. In a climate of low expectations and a controlled media, crossing the canal and holding two slivers of land in Sinai would suffice.[24] * The second was inflicting as many casualties as possible on the Israelis.

Up to that point, all Egypt's war plans resembled the Normandy landing in World War II. Shazly's resembled the Tet Offensive in Vietnam. Another example Shazly could have drawn upon was the Battle of Verdun in World War I. The German Supreme Army Command realized that it was impossible to conquer France. Accordingly, they planned to seize a historic town they knew the French would attempt to retake. They then planned to break the will of the French public by inflicting catastrophic casualties. The strategy very nearly worked.[25]

Egypt had two crucial advantages that neither the Viet Cong nor the Germans enjoyed. First, the weight of international power politics was tilted heavily in its favor. With nothing tangible to offer, Israel had only one ally—the United States—which had to weigh its support against its interests in the Arab world. If the diplomatic stalemate could be broken and the international community made uncomfortable, perhaps the superpowers would impose a settlement on Jerusalem. On this point, Shazly had a willing listener in Anwar Sadat. "I used to tell Nasser," Sadat later wrote, "that if we could recapture even four inches of Sinai territory (by which I meant a foothold, pure and simple), and establish ourselves there so firmly that no power on earth could dislodge us, then the whole situation would change."[26]

Second, unlike the French and the Americans, the Israelis

---

* The Suez Canal comprises two man-made channels, separated by the Great Bitter Lake in the middle. No crossing was planned at the Great Bitter Lake because of its width.

could not remain on a war footing for any length of time. The bulk of the army was reservists. Once these citizen-soldiers were called up, the country came to a standstill. A nation can hold out only so long with darkened factories and shuttered stores. If the war dragged on long enough, Cairo could dictate terms. All the Egyptian army had to do was cross the canal and survive.

But could it survive? Military offensives are typically planned around reaching a natural barrier. In Verdun, the German objective was to seize an easy-to-defend ridgeline known as the Meuse Heights and a string of easier-to-defend forts. In Sinai, the Egyptian objective was to advance six miles and then stop in the middle of the desert. The land was flat and perfectly suited for a counterattack.[27] The SAMs might protect them from the Israeli air force. But what of Israeli tanks?

Recent history was less than encouraging, to put it mildly.* In the Six-Day War—which actually lasted only four days in Sinai—Israeli tanks destroyed two Egyptian divisions in the first ten hours of the war, inflicting some five thousand killed. They accomplished this without the aid of the IAF, which was still busy neutralizing Arab air forces.[28] In that fight, the Egyptians had hundreds of tanks of their own. The force crossing the canal would be nothing but foot soldiers.

This was the great weakness of the Shazly plan.[29] For this reason, he and Egypt's minister of war, Mohammad Ahmed Sadek, came to a compromise. Sadek relented in his ambition to conquer the entire Sinai Peninsula. But he still insisted upon a military operation up to the easily defensible Mitla and Gidi passes, approximately thirty miles east of the canal. This plan, known as Operation 41, was adopted by the Armed Forces Supreme Council and shared with Egypt's allies and senior officers.

However, Sadek agreed that Shazly could work quietly on a secret alternative. This plan, shared with only a few handpicked

---

* On a trip to the US, reporters asked Golda if Israel would resort to nuclear weapons. To gales of laughter, she said, "We haven't done so badly with conventional weapons."

officers, was known as Operation High Minarets. It shared much in common with Operation 41, at least when it came to crossing the canal. But its stated objective was for the army to advance just six miles—the extent of the protection offered by the SAMs— and then stop cold in the middle of the desert. As far as Shazly was concerned, this was Egypt's only realistic option.[30]

The secrecy surrounding the limited operation was not just to fool the Israelis. By now the president of Syria was the wily Hafez el-Assad, who successfully vanquished his opponents in 1970. Sadat knew that Assad would not go to war unless he, Assad, thought that Egypt would keep up the pressure against Israel and draw forces from the Golan Heights. Sadat therefore lied to Assad, presenting an ambitious plan to first attack the passes, and then conquer the entire Sinai Peninsula. Shazly later wrote that neither he nor any of his subordinates thought they would attack beyond the six-mile protective range of the SAMs. Of the lies told to the Syrians about a grand invasion, Shazly said, "I was sickened by the duplicity."[31]

\* \* \*

In 1939, a fifteen-year-old boy from Zagreb named Chaim Brotzlewsky boarded a train bearing a precious immigration certificate that entitled him entry into Palestine. As a going-away present, the members of his Youth Aliyah group, Hashomer Hatzair, handed him an album with the pictures of all forty of its members. Only Brotzlewsky and three other children pictured in the album would survive the Holocaust. One of them was his best friend. His name was David Elazar.[32]

Brotzlewsky had family in Palestine. Elazar, who was born in Sarajevo in 1925, arrived in Palestine alone in the world. His father stayed behind in Zagreb. His mother died when he was young; until the day he died he carried a picture of himself as a small boy standing alongside her grave. As the war clouds gathered in Palestine and Israel's untaught army quickly cobbled together, the two young friends joined an elite strike force known as the Palmach. Both were natural leaders and both rose quickly through the ranks. Brotzlewsky was known for his unflappable calm. A story made the rounds about a recruit who accidentally stabbed him in the leg with a bayonet, and how Brotzlewsky quietly told him to please remove it. Elazar, known universally by his nickname Dado, possessed a volcanic temper.[33]

It can be said that Dado Elazar and the Israeli army grew up together. Both had little or no schooling, both were educated in the field, and both shared a crucial formative experience. That experience took place on May 1, 1948, in a battle over a south Jerusalem hilltop on whose summit stood the Monastery of San-Simon.

Of the two hundred men under the command of twenty-two-year-old Major Elazar, only fifteen would emerge unharmed. Sixteen hours into the battle, eighty-five were dead, a hundred were wounded, and all seemed lost. Elazar witnessed the carnage from the monastery's rooftop and began to give orders to retreat. But then he was reminded of words uttered by Yitzchak Sadeh, the legendary founder of the Palmach: *When it is raining on you and you are tired and soaked to the bone, always remember that the enemy is also getting wet.*

Elazar waited. Then, at the very breaking point, with men and ammunition all but exhausted, the watchman looked below and gave the word: the Arabs were withdrawing.[34] The battle was won.

This episode passed into legend, and Elazar's tenacity became a core tenet of the Israeli army. At the decisive moment of battle, the side that held out just one minute longer was the side that won the day.

A little over twenty-three years later, on January 1, 1972, Chaim Brotzlewsky, now Chaim Bar-Lev, completed his four-year term as chief of staff of the Israeli army. His replacement was Lieutenant-General David Elazar.

\* \* \*

The Soviets were told that Egypt had abandoned the plan to conquer all of Sinai and would focus instead on Operation 41, the limited campaign to the Mitla and Gidi passes. This "limited" campaign required a seemingly unlimited supply of weapons. The Soviets eventually supplied them free of charge. But the new Soviet MiG-23 and MiG-25 fighters had come into service only a year before in 1970, and Moscow made it clear that it would be years before it had any available for Egypt.

The Soviets reserved a special contempt for Sadat, accusing him, among other things, of "smoking drugs." But the sharpest derision was voiced by the Israelis, who concluded in a top-secret intelligence study in 1970 that Sadat's "intellectual level was low," that he was "narrow-minded, lacking in any principles, a hypocritical demagogue, utterly without talent and unable to contribute anything to the management of his country." The study was updated in late 1972 to add that he was also "weak, impulsive, acting under the pressure of the moment and incapable of taking the initiative to break the Middle East deadlock."[35]

For Sadat, time was running out. The year 1972 marked the fifth anniversary of the 1967 humiliation, and the high emotion carried people to open acts of defiance rarely seen in the Arab world. There was an open letter of protest from Egypt's most prominent writers. There were student protests. Most ominously, an army officer led his men into the Hussein Mosque in central Cairo demanding "immediate war" with Israel.[36]

On October 26, 1972, Sadat relieved General Sadek as minister of war and replaced him with General Ahmed Ismail Ali. The move was greeted with shock. As one of the three key men that helped Sadat turn back the coup attempt, General Sadek was thought to be untouchable. But Sadek never abandoned his dream to fight to the passes and insisted Egypt wait several years until the Soviets delivered MiG-23 and MiG-25 fighter jets that could challenge the Israeli air force. His replacement, General Ismail, was a curious choice. He had a reputation for being something of a lightweight. He also had a strained relationship with Shazly that went back to their service together in the Congo in 1960, when Shazly punched him in the face.[37] But he had two things that Sadat was seeking. He posed no threat because he was battling cancer, a battle he was destined to lose two years later. And he understood that Egypt had to go to war immediately and had to do it with the army that it had.[38]

Shazly and Ismail finalized Operation High Minarets. Both realized that the operation was risky. It started with a sober assessment of the strengths and weaknesses of the two sides and then attempted play to Egypt's strengths. But it was built on a number of questionable assumptions.

The biggest question related to how much could be expected of Egypt's soldiers. These men were called upon to cross the canal in rubber dinghies and then use high-powered water cannons to blast away the mound of sand on the other side. After taking fire while sinking in bottomless mud, these men were then called upon to make a stand in the desert against Israeli armor, using nothing but shoulder-fired weapons. This would continue until bridges could be laid and Egyptian tanks could cross.

Machine guns against water cannons, tanks against foot soldiers—the Israelis would have every advantage in the crucial opening stages of this war. Raw courage was not going to be enough to overcome them. There was only one thing that might carry the Egyptians through the first twenty-four hours. Achieving it required almost as much planning as the rest of the operation.

It was the element of surprise.

# 6

## THE ANGEL AND THE NOISE

Once you have accepted a theory and used it as a tool in your thinking, it is extraordinarily difficult to notice its flaws. If you come upon an observation that does not seem to fit the model, you assume there must be a perfectly good explanation.[1]

—Daniel Kahneman, Nobel Prize–winning psychologist

On October 1, 1972, the highly regarded Major-General Aharon Yariv concluded eight years as the head of AMAN, Israel's military intelligence arm. The Arabs were happy to see him go. Muhammad Heikal—editor of the Egyptian newspaper *al-Ahram* and close friend of both Nasser and Sadat—described him as "an exceptionally astute officer." There is a saying in the Talmud, "It is the wise man that says, 'I do not know.'" Aharon Yariv was just such a wise man. He questioned every assumption, allowed every opinion to be heard, and always highlighted what he knew he did not know.[2]

Chief among the things he knew he did not know was the decision-making of Israel's enemies. AMAN could alert Israel's leaders that an Arab army had mobilized along the border. It could not predict whether an Arab leader would order it to attack.

Put another way, a good intelligence agency could measure an enemy's *capabilities*; it could never predict its *intentions*. This being the case, whenever an Arab army mobilized, AMAN sounded the alert and insisted that Israel do the same. It happened in 1955. It happened again in 1960.[3]

Mobilizing every able-bodied man was an expensive undertaking that brought the nation's economy to a standstill. In an oft-repeated joke, all Israelis were said to be on eleven months' leave from the army. During the run-up to the Six-Day War, even the number of pages in newspapers fell dramatically.[4] It sparked anger if the Arabs stood down and it turned out the mobilization was carried out "for nothing." Yariv and those who preceded him argued that, in the tough neighborhood that Israel called home, mobilizations of this type were a cost of doing business.

Eli Zeira replaced Yariv as commander of AMAN. His arrival resulted in a sea change in the culture of the agency. Part of this was driven by necessity. Tracking capabilities was much easier before 1967. All one had to do was keep an eye on the empty Sinai Peninsula and see if forces entered. But Zeira testified after the war that "given the permanent forces the Egyptians stationed along the Canal, they had the capability to attack at all times, so we were left with no choice but to focus on intentions."[5]

Much of that sea change was tied to Zeira himself, who unlike the cautious Yariv, believed that Israel no longer had to mobilize at the first sign of trouble. For one thing, the Jewish state now had defensible borders, borders that were far from population centers. For another, the Israeli army had shown that it could win victories over the Arabs with relative ease. And then there was Zeira himself, who believed he could accurately predict Arab intentions and who told a Knesset committee, "I can definitely give notice before any crossing of the Canal."[6]

The reason for this newfound confidence was not just Zeira's arrogance (though no one ever accused him of suffering from low self-esteem). It had as much to do with an intelligence source.

A source in Cairo that was seemingly manufactured as a dream come true and was destined to become the central character of the greatest story in the history of Israeli espionage.

\* \* \*

Sometime in 1969, a tall, handsome, impeccably dressed man walked into the Israeli embassy in London and asked to speak to a Mossad agent. "I want to work for you," the man said. "I will give you information that you could only hope to obtain in your wildest dreams. I want money, a lot of money. And believe me, you will be happy to pay."[7]

The Israeli intelligence community was indeed happy to pay. When word made it back to Tel Aviv, the heads of Mossad and AMAN practically fell out of their chairs. Through the 1970s, they would pay the staggering sum of $3 million—equivalent to over $20 million today—and those in the know considered it a bargain.[8] * For the individual who offered his services was no less than the right-hand man of Anwar Sadat.

Ashraf Marwan was born on February 2, 1944, to a well-respected Cairo family. His father was a senior military officer and his grandfather rose to become head of Egypt's Islamic courts. Ambitious and hardworking, his big break came in 1965 when he won the heart of Gamal Abdel Nasser's daughter Mona. The president ordered a background check that came back less than flattering. The flashy young man lived beyond his means and was seen as less than sincere in his affection for Mona. But Mona was smitten with the dashing officer and Nasser finally agreed to the marriage in 1966.[9]

Marwan became an important figure in Nasser's inner circle; when Sadat assumed power, he kept him as one of his most visible

---

* To put that in perspective, only four Americans arrested for spying in the late twentieth century are thought to have been paid more than $1 million. One of the most damaging spies in American history, former CIA officer Aldrich Ames, received only about $4 million (in 2018 dollars).

aides.* He naturally wanted to show continuity in the regime, but Sadat's regard for Marwan seems to have been heartfelt. Sadat referred to Mona, Marwan's wife, as *ya binti*, "my daughter," and she referred to him as *ya ami*, "my uncle." Marwan backed Sadat in the failed coup of 1971 and was rewarded by being named presidential secretary.[10] In that position, he saw everything that crossed Sadat's desk.

It is said that espionage is the world's second oldest profession and a lot less moral than the first. But Marwan's betrayal of Egypt stands out even in that Judas-infested netherworld, leading to the obvious question: Why did he do it? The head of the Mossad at the time, Zvi Zamir, said he had no good answer for that question. Zamir never asked him, wanting to avoid the uncomfortable topic, and Marwan never volunteered a reason. Plainly, Marwan was no Zionist. Zamir writes that he never inquired about Israel and never shared any opinions on history or philosophy because he had none.[11]

What Marwan had was a taste for high living. Zamir thought him a mediocrity who served his own interests and cared about nothing else. But if he married Mona Nasser with the idea of making money, he was soon disappointed. Becoming part of Nasser's family made him poorer, not richer. Russian accounts of the time include admiration for the spartan lifestyle Nasser both lived and imposed upon his family. Nasser once told Khrushchev that in the little spare time he had he liked to make amateur movies, but he could afford only black-and-white film. Nasser died with only six hundred Egyptian pounds in his bank account.[12]

Others in Israel were not convinced. They were certain that Marwan was a double agent, someone sent by Egyptian intelligence to deceive them.

---

* It was important to Sadat to have some visible ties with the Nasser family because of his troubled relationship with Nasser's son Khalid Abdel Nasser. *Time* magazine reported that Khalid refused to let Sadat acquire the elder Nasser's bulletproof limousine and, after a heated argument with Sadat, destroyed the vehicle by setting it on fire.

"How can this be?" Golda would often ask. Israeli master spy Tzvi Malkin was similarly unconvinced. Marwan drove around London without fear of detection, sometimes arriving to meet his handlers in cars that carried Egyptian diplomatic plates. Moreover, in the Egypt of Anwar Sadat, Marwan had many opportunities to enrich himself. Malkin often said in anger that the millions Mossad paid were probably split between Marwan and Sadat.* To that, Marwan's supporters replied that the only thing more unlikely than Nasser's son-in-law spying for Israel was Egyptian intelligence using him as a double agent. It was dangerous work, and it was dangerous work that could be performed by any senior military officer. Of course, if Sadat and Marwan really were splitting the loot, then he, Marwan, might have been only too happy to volunteer for the mission, and Sadat might have been only too happy to send him.[13]

In the end, supporters of Marwan won the debate inside Israel because it was hard to argue with success. Marwan was given the code name "the Angel," and the information he supplied was described as heaven-sent, "once-in-a-history" material. Not one, but two intelligence committees were formed to cross-check it against other Israeli sources. The conclusion was always the same. The Angel's information was spot-on accurate.[14]

Marwan's material filled several binders. But there was one piece of information he supplied that was so important, it took on a life of its own and a new Hebrew term was coined to describe it. Israeli military planners called it the *Conceptzia*, or simply "the Concept."

In its simplest form, the Concept said the following: (1) Syria would not go to war without Egypt; and (2) Egypt would not go to war until it could neutralize the Israeli air force.[15]

The first portion of the Concept regarding Syria proved true

---

* The Russian accounts that speak glowingly of Nasser are filled with contempt for the high lifestyle that Sadat adopted. A KGB agent joked that they should build a "vodka pipeline" to his residence in Giza.

and would guide Israeli intelligence into the 1990s. The primary focus thus turned to Egypt.[16]

This is where things grew complicated. Marwan told Israeli intelligence of Egypt's plan to fight to the Mitla and Gidi passes.[17] But before they could launch it, he said, the Egyptians knew they had to satisfy two conditions. First, they had to find a way to protect their ground forces from the Israeli air force once they pushed more than six miles east of the canal, outside the protection of their surface-to-air missiles. Second, they had to find a way to prevent the Israelis from engaging in the deep-penetration bombings that had devastated Egypt in the War of Attrition.

Protecting the Egyptian heartland was by far the easier of the two conditions to satisfy, because it involved deterring the Israeli air force rather than confronting it. Sadat knew the Israelis would never dare bomb his cities if he had a rocket that could bomb their cities in response. He therefore pleaded with the Soviets to send him Scud missiles, the medium-range missiles that achieved fame eighteen years later when Saddam Hussein used them in the Gulf War. The Israelis understood the logic all too well and kept a close eye on whether the Soviets supplied them.[18]

The first condition was more difficult. There was only one way to protect Egyptian ground forces fighting outside the protective umbrella of the SAMs, and that was with long-range fighter jet aircraft that could challenge Israel's F-4 Phantoms and A-4 Skyhawks. Since the Soviets were not scheduled to supply such aircraft until 1974—MiG 23s and MiG-25s were in short supply—and since it took approximately two years to train pilots to fly them, the Israelis figured they had some breathing room. It would not be possible for the Egyptians to launch an attack up to the passes, at least until late 1975.[19]

Zeira said he knew the Concept could be wrong. But he figured that the exceptional quality of his sources would act as what he called an "insurance policy." "I said to myself," he told the postwar Agranat Commission, "suppose the Concept is wrong? Well, then I have my sources. And what if my sources are wrong too? For that I need *decisive facts* to prove that they are wrong."[20]

If he had thought about it a bit more, he would have realized that that was far too high a bar to call his assumptions into question. Recent experience should have informed him that, for all of its modeling and all of its sources, AMAN was incapable of guessing what foreign leaders would do. AMAN's "Concept" before 1967 was that Egypt would never go to war so long as it was bogged down in the Yemen Civil War. Nasser himself said it in countless speeches—and Nasser himself changed his mind in May 1967 and mobilized his army anyway.

Starting in late 1968, Egypt held war exercises once or twice a year, practicing every aspect of an invasion of Sinai. The constant maneuvers were carried out not just to maintain readiness, but to conceal intentions. This was a tactic learned from the Soviets, who fooled Western intelligence agencies by constantly training along the borders of their satellites. Most of the time they demobilized and went home, but occasionally the drills suddenly turned into surprise attacks, as in Czechoslovakia in 1968. Likewise, once Egypt mobilized along the canal, it was impossible for Israel to determine if the troops were there to train or to cross the canal. In 1973, Egyptian mobilizations grew larger and more frequent. Between January 1 and October 1, Egypt's reservists were called up and sent home no fewer than twenty-two times.[21]

The constant exercises along the border did not just make it impossible for the Israelis to predict if a war was planned. It made it impossible for Egyptian and Syrian soldiers as well. And that was exactly what Arab military planners wanted.

In addition to Marwan, the Israelis had a second super-source inside Egypt, this one an officer in the Egyptian army. The existence of this second agent was not publicly revealed until 2020. The Egyptian officer warned of a surprise attack no fewer than six times in 1969, six times in 1971, and five more times after that in 1972. The constant cries of "wolf" caused Israeli intelligence officers to discount him. But a December 1972 warning set Jerusalem on edge, because for the first time Marwan added his voice to that of the Egyptian officer. Zeira said not to worry; an attack would never happen so long as Egypt had no Scud missiles or MiG-23s and Syria had no surface-to-air missiles. His reputation soared when he was proved right.[22]

The next warning from Marwan and the Egyptian officer came in April 1973. It said the attack would come in May. By now Egypt was mobilizing troops along the border on a constant basis. Seemingly, this was the time to sound the warning. The *capability* to attack was there, showing itself in dozens of data points that the Israelis referred to as "signs of war." And though the conditions of the Concept had not been satisfied—Egypt still did not have the Scuds or the advanced fighter jets, and Syria did not have the SAMs—Marwan told the Israelis that the *intention* to attack was there, anyway.[23]

Why, then, did Zeira tell Golda, Dayan, and Elazar *not* to mobilize the army, and why did they listen?

In the aftermath of the war, the Israelis empaneled the Agranat Commission to explore just this question as part of an investigation of the war. Panel member and former Chief of Staff Yigal Yadin asked a minister why the army and Golda's cabinet were so certain that AMAN could give forty-eight hours warning of any attack. The minister, Yisroel Galili, answered, "Because of major advances in our electronic capability."[24] These advances were obliquely referred to as the "Extraordinary Measures."

The details of the Extraordinary Measures were so sacrosanct that their exact nature bypassed Israel's porous tradition and never leaked out. Decades later, the commander directly involved described them as "battery-powered listening devices attached to telephone and telegram branches . . . which allowed eavesdropping on conversations in places in Cairo." Zeira testified before the Agranat Commission that he knew the Concept might be wrong. But to prove it wrong, he needed "decisive indications." And where would those "decisive indications" come from? Zeira said, "I viewed the [Extraordinary Measures] as my insurance to tell me there is a mistake in the Concept."[25]

Employing the Extraordinary Measures was no simple decision. Activating them placed them at risk of detection and drained their batteries, which could only be replaced manually on a dangerous mission deep behind enemy lines. For all these reasons, the Extraordinary Measures were viewed as AMAN's last resort, to be utilized only under circumstances that matched the title "Extraordinary."[26]

April 1973 was one of those times. The Extraordinary Measures were utilized, and though we do not know the details of what they revealed, it was enough for Zeira to declare that the Egyptians were merely engaging in military exercises. When he was proved correct again, his reputation reached new heights. From then on, the government believed in Zeira, and Zeira believed in the Concept. Internally, AMAN officers referred to the Extraordinary Measures as their "insurance policy."[27]

A few skeptics of the Measures, and Zeira, remained. The commander overseeing the Extraordinary Measures, Colonel Yossi Langotsky, ran into his old friend Ehud Barak, who led the unit that installed the Extraordinary Measures. Red with anger, he told him, "These people are crazy! I don't understand where they have the balls to say, 'there will be war, there won't be war.' We all know how little information we have, and they piece it together into these elaborate theories."[28]

\* \* \*

On August 24, 1973, AMAN learned that the Scud missiles had finally arrived in Egypt.[29]

This alarming news was dismissed by Zeira and AMAN's research team. IAF intelligence officers estimated that it would take the Egyptians at least six months to train their personnel. Of course, the Soviet trainers had the know-how to fire the missiles. But this threat was discounted. During the War of Attrition, the Soviets never allowed their fighter jets to fly east of the canal. The last thing they wanted was a potential entanglement with the United States. It was thought highly unlikely they would ever fire missiles at an Israeli city.[30]

Here was the great flaw in AMAN's analysis. The question was never what the Russians would do. The question was what the Israelis would do. When war broke out, the Israeli air force advised the government not to engage in deep-penetration bombings of Egypt, for fear of reprisal. The Soviets *probably* would not fire the Scuds, but then again maybe they would. This was exactly what Sadat gambled would happen. The Scuds would deter Israel and protect the Egyptian heartland. The SAMs would cover the skies over the battlefield and protect a limited incursion that would stop six miles east of the canal. The Israelis did not grasp it. But by August 1973, the conditions laid out in the Concept had both been satisfied.

Syria was then spending fully 70 percent of its entire government budget on the military. Its war planners likewise understood that it would all go to waste if they could not protect themselves from the Israeli air force. As with Egypt, August 1973 was the month when everything changed. It was then that the Syrians took delivery of more than thirty SAM batteries, of which at least fifteen were the new SAM-6, the most advanced in the Soviet arsenal. The area south of Damascus now *had the thickest air defense on earth*. There were more missiles per square mile defending the approaches to the Syrian capital than there were defending Moscow or Hanoi.[31]

Even more disturbing from the IDF's standpoint was the

placement of the missiles right up on the line. From that location, the entire Golan Heights and even a portion of northern Israel were within range of the SAMs. The positioning also spoke to intentions. Syria's missiles, upon which its entire defense depended, were now just a short drive away from IDF tanks and well within range of Israeli artillery. Israeli intelligence analysts saw reconnaissance photos and said there could be but one reason for Syrian generals to place their SAMs in such peril, and that was to support a ground attack on the Golan Heights. Zeira had by now imprisoned himself inside the intellectual trap of the Concept, skillfully repairing it each time some new piece of evidence offered him a chance to escape. He ignored the obvious and insisted the missiles were there to defend Damascus.[32]

Then, on September 13, 1973, Israel sent a group of fighter jets on a reconnaissance mission over northern Syria. The Syrians sent up MiGs to challenge the Israelis and it resulted, predictably, in five Syrian jets being shot down. It would have ended there, but one of the Israeli pilots got drunk on his own adrenaline, ignored instructions, and lit up his afterburners in pursuit of two MiGs. The Israeli pilot was himself shot down and rescued. But in the ensuing melee, another seven Syrian jets were shot down as well, bringing their total losses to an even dozen.[33]

This was a major provocation, the largest aerial dogfight in the history of the Arab-Israeli conflict fought outside one of the wars. Some sort of Syrian response was to be expected. Israeli intelligence analysts were therefore not surprised when, instead of thinning out their forces, as they did every year when winter approached, the Syrians sent in reinforcements.[34]

What the Israelis did not know was that on August 21, 1973, six of Syria's most senior military officers—including Defense Minister Mustafa Tlass and Chief of Staff Yussef Shakur—had donned casual wear as if on holiday, boarded a Soviet passenger liner, and traveled to Alexandria to meet with their Egyptian counterparts. The officers barely recognized each other when they met on the dock: it was the first time they had seen each other in civilian clothes.[35]

In Alexandria the two sides finalized plans to go to war. The only thing left to decide upon was a date; that decision was above even their pay grade. Sadat subsequently traveled to Damascus and met personally with President Assad in his palatial office. A Lebanese warlord with experience in that office said that upon entering, Assad sat so far away he looked like a pea propped up on a cushion. On August 29, 1973, Sadat and Assad came to an agreement. The war would commence on October 6—Yom Kippur, Israel's most solemn holiday.[36]

On September 30, 1973, Sadat convened his National Security Council for one last meeting. Many of those present were hesitant. They had many reasons to be hesitant. The catastrophic War of Attrition left Egypt arguably even more demoralized than the defeat in 1967. Ordinary Egyptians had felt the war for the first time. Israeli planes and commandos bombed their cities with impunity. Of more immediate concern was Egypt's war plan, which to many looked like something assembled at gunpoint. The Scuds would have to deter the Israelis from laying waste to Egypt's cities. The SAMs would have to protect Egyptian soldiers in the Canal Zone. The Soviets had done little for Egypt in the 1967 war. There was no way to know if this time would be different.[37]

But there was one inescapable fact that prodded them forward. Egypt was in free fall. Every moment of Sadat's day was hostage to its collapse. At the end of the meeting he said, "Our economy has fallen below zero. We have commitments to the banks which we cannot meet. In three months' time we shan't have enough bread in the pantry. I cannot ask the Arabs for a single dollar more; they say they have been paying us although we didn't, or wouldn't, fight."[38] The die was cast.

On October 4, Sadat asked that his War Room be prepared. Inside it hung a large map titled "Operation 41," with arrows pointing all the way to the passes. The map was taken down. In its place was hung a new map. It showed arrows advancing into Sinai with a hard stop six miles east of the canal.

Above the map was a new title: "Operation Badr."[39] [*]

\* \* \*

On September 25, 1973, King Hussein of Jordan flew to a secret Mossad location in Tel Aviv. Coordinating with the Israelis was now routine. This was his fourth meeting with Golda since November 1972.[40] [†] A description of the Black September conflict— the culmination of a bitter struggle between King Hussein and radical Palestinians—is beyond the scope of this account. Suffice it to say that Egypt and Syria had long aided those trying to topple him. The Israelis played a key role in helping him remain in power. At the September meeting he returned the favor, informing the Israelis that Egypt and Syria were planning to go to war against them.

How seriously Israel should have taken the warning remains hotly debated. A transcript of the meeting has never been released, but an Israeli journalist with access to it says the vague warning does not first appear until page nine. Much of the ambiguity surrounds a single word. Speaking in English, the king said that Egypt and Syria "would" go to war. It was unclear if that meant *will* go to war. What can be said with certainty is that he did not give a time and date for the attack, because he did not know it. What can also be said is that a nervous Golda Meir immediately phoned Dayan, who told her not to worry.[‡] The king had issued three false alarms

---

[*] The October war was fought in the Islamic holy month of Ramadan. During the month of Ramadan, in the year 624 A.D., forces of the Prophet Muhammad won their first victory in the Battle of Badr.

[†] The story of King Hussein's meetings with Israeli leaders leaked to the press in 1988. Israel's enraged intelligence community commenced an investigation, but the offender was never apprehended.

[‡] A young intelligence officer named Zusia "Zizi" Kaniezer took the king's warning seriously. Though he was ignored by his superiors, it earned his character the starring role of the Israeli movie about the lead-up to the Yom Kippur War. The Moshe Dayan character was

since May. One even identified July 26 as a possible day for the attack.[41] Most important, Ashraf Marwan, AMAN's super-source, had not given any indication of an impending threat.

While AMAN was attempting to gauge the intentions of Cairo and Damascus, two enormous armies mobilized along Israel's borders. The Syrian army had 185,000 men and boasted 326 fighter jets and 1,170 tanks. The Egyptian army numbered 1.2 million men.* The Egyptians could attack with 420 fighter jets, 1,880 tanks, and 2,400 artillery pieces. To defend against the Israeli air force, the Egyptians had 50 surface-to-air missile batteries. The 50 batteries were concealed among more than 100 bases that contained dummy missiles that, from the air, looked identical to the real thing. Against this, prior to mobilization, the Israelis had only 75 tanks to confront the Syrians (not counting 100 more sent to the Golan just before the attack) and 300 tanks to confront Egypt, assuming they got up to the line in time.[42]

AMAN had long identified forty-five potential "signs of war." By the end of September, thirty of them were spotted in the field. In fairness, the signs of war had been seen many times before, and they were buried in a mountain of other data. The challenge of modern intelligence gathering is not a lack of information but an overabundance. In 1973, AMAN was absorbing tens of thousands of pieces of raw intelligence every month, all without the aid of a computer.[43]

Zeira and those around him thought they could ignore signs in the field and look instead for the magic piece of information that would allow them to separate the signal from the noise. As Zeira's assistant Aryeh Shalev remembered, "The extraordinary quality of the sources at the highest levels of the Egyptian leadership led us to

---

uncannily realistic because the producers threw an eye patch on his actor-son Assi Dayan and cast him in the role of his father.

* In his memoir, General Shazly lamented that the army could have been even bigger, but he was not permitted to enlist women, even as volunteers.

favor those sources over everything else." Lieutenant Colonel Yonah Bendman, chief of AMAN's Egypt desk, told the Agranat Commission that "we made our assessment based on what was happening in Cairo, not the Firdan Bridge [along the Suez Canal]."[44]

A jolt to AMAN's complacency came on September 30, 1973. The Egyptian officer said that Egypt would attack the next day, October 1, and that the Syrians would take part as well.[45]

Say this for Eli Zeira: the man had the courage of his convictions. He kept the warning of the Egyptian officer from Golda and mentioned it to Elazar in a dismissive way ("I saved you a night of sleep") only because he ran into him in the hall.[46] The attack did not come on October 1. Eli Zeira's confidence in his assumptions, to say nothing of himself, was further cemented.

But then, on October 2, the Egyptian officer reached out again and sharpened his message. An attack, he said, was imminent. It would come under the guise of maneuvers that at the last moment would turn real. Zeira decided to keep this, and other information, from Elazar and Golda. There had been maneuvers before, the Egyptian officer had issued false warnings before—the Concept had always proved right in the end.[47]

On that same day, October 2, more disturbing intelligence came in from the field. These were no ordinary signs of war—they were unmistakable. Among other things, the Egyptians removed mines from the canal, drove three hundred trucks filled with ammunition to the front lines, and plowed away dirt to open paths to the canal. These were not things the Egyptians would do for a war exercise; they could have but one purpose. AMAN also overheard a Syrian housewife being told that her husband, an officer in the elite 47th Armored Brigade, had been transferred to the Golan Heights. The Israelis knew from captured prisoners that the 47th was tasked with protecting the Assad regime itself. It would be transferred south only if war was imminent.[48]

This was seemingly an extraordinary moment, tailor-made for the Extraordinary Measures. And to be sure, the team manning the apparatus pleaded for authority to turn it on. In the words of one officer, Zeira "didn't want to listen, didn't want to believe and didn't want to do anything."[49]

Why the stubbornness? It was because a similar listening device was discovered in Egypt in June 1973. Zeira was loath to lose another high-value intelligence resource. Zeira was so sure of himself that he even deceived those above him. On October 2, Elazar asked Zeira if he had employed the Extraordinary Measures. *Zeira told him that he had, even though he hadn't.*[50]

The Arabs were not the only ones the Israelis were watching. AMAN also had a group of two hundred native-speaking Russians who eavesdropped on Soviet communications. The unit in which they served was code-named Knitting Needle. But given the corporate culture and the liberties they were permitted to take, a better name might have been the Vodka Battalion. On the evening of October 4, 1973, the hard-drinking unit intercepted hysterical messages from Syria. The families of Russian advisers were evacuating.[51] *

This was the smoking gun in a smoke-filled room. It jolted even Zeira, who told Elazar and Zamir it was a development for which he had no explanation. At 10:00 P.M. on October 4, Zeira finally relented and allowed the Extraordinary Measures to be deployed. However, he gave strict instructions that this was only a test to see if they worked properly. He ordered that they be turned back off at 6:00 A.M. the following morning. In that brief period, the Extraordinary Measures revealed nothing. Of course, in the middle of the night between the hours of 10:00 P.M. and 6:00 A.M., traffic was presumably at its lowest.[52]

On that morning, October 5, an emergency meeting was held. Dayan opened the discussion with the results of reconnaissance photos taken the day before and said, referring to Arab forces,

---

* The Russians realized that the sudden evacuation might tip off the Israelis as to the attack, but when asked, Foreign Minister Gromyko responded bluntly, "The lives of Soviet people are dearer to us."

"The numbers alone are enough to give you a stroke." Dayan asked Zeira if the Extraordinary Measures had been deployed and Zeira replied that they had, leaving the impression that they were then operating and had been for some time. The news that the Extraordinary Measures were in operation and yielding no indication of war defused any sense of alarm.[53]

There was still concern that the Syrians might retaliate for the shooting down of the twelve planes in September. So the elite 7th Armored Brigade was mobilized and sent to the Golan Heights, bringing the total number of Israeli tanks there to 177. The air force was brought to heightened alert as well. However, Elazar said at 11 A.M. on October 5 that he would mobilize the reservists only when he received "an additional indication."[54]

This complacency cannot be tied completely to the Extraordinary Measures. The IDF leadership also possessed an outsized estimation of the army's capabilities against thousands of Arab tanks. Elazar conferred with his old friend Chaim Bar-Lev—the two were often seen speaking to each other in their native Serbian— and told him there was nothing to worry about. There were three hundred tanks in position along the canal and nearly two hundred in the Golan Heights. With that, Bar-Lev went home thinking that everything was under control. Mossad Chief Zvi Zamir said later, "The Concept wasn't with our intelligence, it was with ourselves. There was a willingness to take enormous chances because of our contempt for the enemy."[55]

Worrisome signs of war continued to stream in. AMAN learned on October 5 that Egyptian soldiers were told to break their Ramadan fast. And at five o'clock that afternoon, AMAN intercepted a message from Iraq's ambassador in Moscow. The message said that Egypt and Syria had informed the Soviets they were about to attack. Zeira kept the last piece of information from Elazar. The Iraqi diplomat was well known to Israeli intelligence and considered a figure of ridicule.[56]

The most worrisome sign of all had come in late on the night of October 4. Marwan finally reached out to his handlers. He asked for an urgent meeting in London.[57] The mere request should have set off warning bells. Instead, Dayan, Elazar, and Zeira chose to wait to hear what he had to say.

It was the day before Yom Kippur, so there were no commercial flights out of Israel, not even for the head of Mossad. Zamir therefore arranged a private plane and arrived on the evening of October 5. There, just past midnight London time on October 6, 1973, he met personally with Marwan, who arrived uncharacteristically late.[58]

Several hours later, Zamir sent an urgent message back to Israel. Egypt and Syria would attack before dark.[59]

# 7

## JUDGMENT DAY

On Yom Kippur our fate is sealed by the Lord . . . who shall
live and who shall die, who in a timely manner and who in an
untimely manner, who by fire, who by water [and] who by the
sword.

> —The Yom Kippur prayer, uttered in the Budapest *maoz* along the
> Suez Canal moments before the war began.[1]

On October 5, General Elazar placed the regular army on a low
state of readiness and went to bed wondering if he had over-
reacted.[2] At 4:30 A.M. on October 6, he was awakened by the red
phone on his night table.

The meeting with Marwan ended at 1:00 A.M. London time,
which was 3:00 A.M. Israel time. The embassy cipher was nowhere
to be found. Not wanting to wait, Zamir picked up an ordinary
phone and dialed. There were no direct phone calls between England and Israel in 1973, so Zamir got the operator on the line and
gave her a number in Tel Aviv. She informed him that "no one is
picking up. I think it is a holiday in Israel."

Zamir lost his temper. "You're telling *me* it's a holiday in Israel?! Keep trying!!"[3]

Eventually, the phone was answered and Zamir read his message:

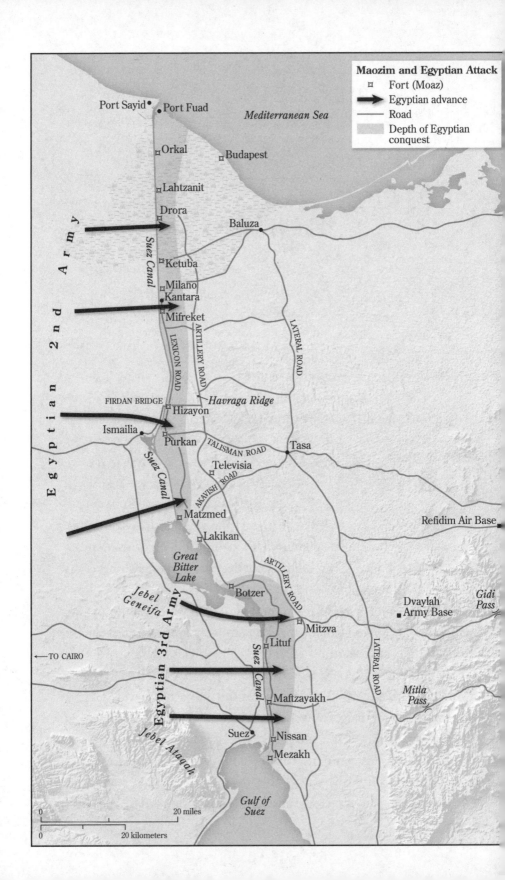

**Maozim and Egyptian Attack**

⌂ Fort (Moaz)
➤ Egyptian advance
— Road
    Depth of Egyptian conquest

*Mediterranean Sea*

Port Sayid •  • Port Fuad

⌂ Orkal
⌂ Budapest

⌂ Lahtzanit

⌂ Drora

• Baluza

Egyptian 2nd Army

*Suez Canal*

⌂ Ketuba

⌂ Milano
⌂ Kantara

⌂ Mifreket

LEXICON ROAD
ARTILLERY ROAD
LATERAL ROAD

FIRDAN BRIDGE

*Havraga Ridge*

⌂ Hizayon

Ismailia •

⌂ Purkan

TALISMAN ROAD

• Tasa

⌂ Televisia

*Suez Canal*

AKAVISH ROAD

⌂ Matzmed

Refidim Air Base ■

⌂ Lakikan

*Great Bitter Lake*

*Jebel Geneifa*

Egyptian 3rd Army

ARTILLERY ROAD

⌂ Botzer

*Dvaylah* Army Base •

*Gidi Pass*

⌂ Mitzva

⌂ Lituf

*Suez Canal*

← TO CAIRO

LATERAL ROAD

*Mitla Pass*

⌂ Maftzayakh

*Jebel Atagah*

Suez •  ⌂ Nissan

⌂ Mezakh

*Gulf of Suez*

0     20 miles

0     20 kilometers

the "deal" would land "before dark." He added that "the Angel believes the chances they will sign the contract are 99.9 percent, but with this fellow [a reference to Sadat] you never know."[4] Decades later, Zamir said he tightened up just thinking back to the tension he felt as he sent word to Tel Aviv.

Though there are many potential times of day that are "before dark"—and in Sinai the sun actually set that day at around 5:30 P.M.—the message over the red phone to Elazar was that war would break out at 6:00 P.M. This time of day fit perfectly in the wheelhouse of a "miniature Concept" embraced by Israeli military planners. Israel's pilots needed daylight to locate targets on the ground, while Egypt's surface-to-air missiles worked by radar and could operate effectively in the dark. Thus, they believed, any attack would come just after twilight.[5]

A second red phone rang alongside Moshe Dayan's bed at the same hour. He quickly dressed and had one of his aides organize a meeting in his office with Elazar, Zeira, and other senior officers.[6]

The men arrived at 5:50 A.M. and quickly got down to business. Zeira was still skeptical, as was Dayan. There had been warnings of imminent attack in all the other months, and now it seemed it was October's turn. "We've heard these warnings before," Dayan said. "Then when the Arabs don't attack, we get the explanation that 'at the last minute' Sadat changed his mind." Dayan also believed that the Extraordinary Measures had been in operation since at least the day before with no indication of war. In truth, Zeira had ordered his men to turn them on again at only five that morning, after the warning came through from Marwan.[7]

Still, the armies were massed, the Russians were evacuating, and it was impossible to deny signs of impending battle. Dayan therefore agreed to a partial mobilization of fifty to sixty thousand men, enough to defend the borders. Elazar wanted to mobilize more than double that figure so that Israel would be prepared not just for defense, but for the counterattack that had been planned in the event of invasion. Dayan scoffed at this. There was no certainty the Arabs would attack, and Elazar was already planning a counterattack.[8]

The debate seems strange given how things turned out. But the 1967 crisis had begun with a Soviet claim that Israel had mobilized to attack its Arab neighbors. The claim was demonstrably false, and yet it sent both sides hurtling down a track that ended in a war no one wanted. In Dayan's mind, preparation for a counterattack was far less important than ensuring Israel not be blamed for fanning the flames of another crisis, or indeed causing one. Elazar pointed out that they would be condemned just as roundly for sending fifty thousand men as two hundred thousand. "I'd rather they say we started it, and then win the war."[9]

Though Elazar and Dayan usually worked well together, they had a difficult past stemming from an incident in the 1967 war in which Elazar lied to Dayan to get him to authorize the attack on the Golan Heights. The 1973 debate over mobilization grew heated and, rather than taking the partial mobilization that Dayan offered and arguing over the rest later, Elazar stalked off saying that Golda would have to decide. Two precious hours were lost.[10]

The tense meeting in Golda's office at 9:00 A.M. commenced under a heavy cloud of cigarette smoke. One general said that the stern portrait of Theodore Herzl hanging on the wall looked even more dour than usual.[11]

To the astonishment of all observers, Golda and Dayan had set aside years of mutual hostility and worked in relative harmony. This was partly because their respective aides worked well together—the two military men were close friends—and partly because Golda deferred to Dayan on all military matters. "Dayan was the dominant minister in the government," Zamir later remembered.[12]

Golda listened to both sides, lighting cigarette after cigarette. When both men were through, she did what she would do in practically every dispute that would arise over the next eighteen days: she sided with Elazar over Dayan. "If there is a war," she said echoing Elazar's words earlier that morning, "better that the world be angry at us, but that our situation be better. [Besides], no one will be able to measure how many men we mobilize."[13]

The decision landed like a clap of thunder. *Moshe Dayan had been overruled in a matter of national security.* It was a difficult decision that would earn Golda high praise from the Agranat Commission. She drew upon nothing other than her own common sense. She is the only prime minister in Israeli history with no military experience either in government or in uniform. Later, she told one of her aides, "They were the experts and I the civilian. What do I know about these things?"[14]

Dayan accepted Golda's decision with admirable deference and at 9:20 A.M. he gave Elazar authority to implement it. The meeting with Marwan had begun at around midnight, Israel time, on the evening of October 5. Though the meeting lasted an hour, the warning of war came right at the beginning. The decision to mobilize did not come until almost ten hours later.[15]

* * *

Having gone over Dayan's head on the issue of mobilization, Elazar turned to the next difficult decision. Should Israel strike first?

Preemption had won the Six-Day War. If the Arabs had struck first, the IDF would have spent the first days of the war defending Jerusalem, rather than destroying Arab air forces. At 4:30 A.M. on October 6, the moment Elazar hung up his red phone, he called Air Force Commander Benny Peled. The air force was ordered to make plans for a first strike on Arab surface-to-air missiles.[16]

In his memoir, Peled said that although Dayan often talked tough, he knew the government would never approve a first strike.[17] The history spoke for itself. In 1967, it took three nerve-shattering weeks, including two diplomatic missions to Washington, the creation of Israel's first national unity government, *and* the Arabs trumpeting plans of annihilation for Eshkol to authorize a preemptive strike.

Weighing on everyone in Golda's office that October morning was the crisis in December 1972. It had been a perfect dress rehearsal. Marwan warned of an attack, the government met in emergency session, and the army argued for a first strike. But all of that was placed on hold when Kissinger told Rabin, "It is critical that Israel not break the ceasefire, even if it has information of an Egyptian intention to restart the war."[18]

Kissinger was no less emphatic on this occasion. While Golda's government was deliberating in Jerusalem, he told Israel's acting ambassador that "there must be no preemptive strike." Of course, it is possible Golda would not have struck first with the IDF unready, even if Kissinger had given the green light. But Kissinger's warning plainly left her no choice. Elazar argued for a first strike; this would be the only time in the war that she rejected his advice. "This isn't 1967," she said. "The world will never believe us."[19]

It was one of the most important decisions of the war. As to whether it was correct, opinion is split right down the middle. Given the difficulties the Israelis experienced later in obtaining American resupply—even after it was obvious that they had *not* fired first—it seems clear that Golda's decision was a reasonable, if painful one. The Agranat Commission does not take a position one way or the other.

\* \* \*

The State of Israel mobilized for war. Among the men who received a call-up notice that morning were those serving in AMAN's signal intelligence corps. Days before, Zeira had refused to call up his own reservists. Later on that October 6, a general passed a pale Zeira in the corridor as the two men ran to the command center in Tel Aviv. "This," the general remembered, "was no longer the Eli Zeira that was so confident in himself."[20]

In the streets of Israel, confusion reigned. One officer pointed to the radio in his car broadcasting the BBC—Israeli radio and television stations were all dark for the Yom Kippur holiday—and said that this was his only intelligence officer. In the synagogue of Kibbutz Sha'alvim, a man approached the rabbi and whispered into his ear. The rabbi turned pale. Someone banged on the table where the Torah scroll lay open and announced there was an emergency call-up. Buses were waiting outside to take the men away in their prayer garments.[21]

Once they got to their bases, they found perfect pandemonium. The Agranat Commission later lamented that "when discipline is allowed to decline in times of peace, you will always find failures in the ultimate test, which is times of war." A senior officer testified before the Commission that day-to-day discipline was widely viewed in the army as "bullshit." When the supply depots were opened, it was every man for himself. Soldiers from one brigade often discovered that their equipment had been "borrowed" by men from another. In one base in the south, soldiers arrived by bus to find that the doors to the warehouses were locked. Ariel Sharon appeared and screamed, "What are you waiting for, break it open!" The warehouses were pried open; the soldiers looted them like peasants in a palace. Equipment was thrown to the ground, and in the words of one, "Whoever managed, took what he could." Sharon himself later made it to the front traveling in a small truck that belonged to a water heater repairman.[22]

Just a few months earlier, Sharon's term as commander of the southern theater had come to an end. Throughout his career, Sharon had stalked through the IDF, spoiling for a fight with anyone that stood in his way. Prime Minister Levi Eshkol called him a *vilda haya*, literally "wild animal," but it is the same term Yiddish speakers use to describe an unruly child. Ben-Gurion said that Sharon could be a great military officer if only he could overcome his habit of lying.[23] In the summer of 1973, at age forty-six, and seemingly at the end of a storied career, he used his going-away party to attack the chief of staff, the defense minister, and the senior leadership of the IDF. His words found their way into the press, as somehow they always did.

The last formality of Sharon's departure was a gathering with the General Staff, which Dayan attended, perhaps to make sure that things did not get out of hand. Dayan offered warm words, and when it ended, Sharon took him aside and made a request. Could he command one of the reserve armored divisions? Surprisingly, Dayan said yes. The remainder of this account would have been very different if he hadn't.[24]

\* \* \*

There was much to admire in General Shmuel Gonen, the man who replaced Sharon as commander of the southern theater. Born Shmuel Gorodish, he studied in an ultra-Orthodox yeshiva in Jerusalem wearing side curls, a shaved head, and a yarmulke. At the age of sixteen he abandoned the yeshiva and joined the Haganah. In the 1948 war he was wounded and returned to the battlefield no fewer than five times. His survival represented a statistical near-impossibility, because he was a *lehavyoran*, or flamethrower, and responsible for performing perhaps the most dangerous job of the war. It is said that Gonen tempted fate even further by crawling up to enemy positions, quietly spraying them with fuel to create a bigger fireball and then letting loose with his weapon. Some thought he was the bravest man in the Israeli army. Some thought he was just crazy.[25]

In the custom of the day, he changed his last name to the more Hebrew sounding Gonen, but his nickname remained his given name of Gorodish. In the 1956 war he was wounded again, but still led the tanks that were first to reach the Anglo-French "ultimatum line" ten miles east of the canal.[26] In the 1967 war he led the elite 7th Armored Brigade, plowing a path across northern Sinai. A photo of a grizzled Gonen—holding binoculars, sternfaced, covered in sand—landed him on the cover of *Life* magazine's special Six-Day War edition.

At the same time, there was much about Shmuel Gonen that was repugnant.

He was the most reviled man in the Israeli army. Men transferred into his command invariably pleaded to be transferred out. Gonen's day was one long tantrum, those under him trembling in fear as he screamed at the top of his lungs. The reason for a tirade and even a stint in jail could be something as petty as a poorly executed salute, a haircut that did not match regulation, or the way a cook made an omelet. Attractive young women had more to fear than just verbal abuse. Though married, Gonen often asked that the prettiest girl on the base be brought to him. At least one nineteen-year-old burst out of his office in tears. Dayan and Elazar were aware of his shortcomings, but they figured war was at least a few years off and hoped he would grow into the job. As commander of the southern theater, he assumed responsibility for defense of the entire line along the Suez Canal. He was forty-three years old.[27]

At noon on Yom Kippur, Golda convened her government in Tel Aviv. As she sat chain-smoking, her stunned ministers heard from Dayan that war would break out later that day, "a little before or after sunset."[28] When the shock wore off, most of the discussion related to the question of a first strike. At 2:00 P.M., Golda wrapped things up and suggested they convene later that day— and was cut off in midsentence by the wailing of sirens. She tried to continue, but then turned to the stenographer.

"What's that?" she asked.

"It would appear the war has begun," the woman replied.

"*Nar das felt min oys,*" Golda muttered (English: "This is just what my life was missing").[29]

* * *

In 1973, a *maoz* along the Suez Canal was considered an easy place for reservists to spend their annual stint on active duty. "I thought I had arrived at a country club," said a soldier who served in the Mifreket *maoz*. The sky was blue, the waters were turquoise, and there had not been an incident with the Egyptians in more than three years. Reduced tension translated into reduced discipline. Motti Ashkenazi, the commander of the Budapest *maoz* in the northern Sinai, arrived in late September to find communication trenches filled with sand, fencing that had rusted away, and stray dogs wandering aimlessly across obsolete minefields. The *maoz* was in such poor condition he decided to abandon a portion of it and station his men in what he termed a miniature *maoz*.[30]

Starting in October, Ashkenazi's men reported a series of disturbing signs. The movement of armor was loud enough for them to hear clear across the canal. It was obvious the Egyptians were not mobilizing for defense, because they plowed openings in their own sand embankments. Ashkenazi reported this up the chain and was told to forget about it.[31]

Then, on October 5, everything went completely quiet. The silence was so deafening that an intelligence officer behind the lines brought in an electrician to see if his listening equipment had suffered a power outage. That quiet carried over to the Budapest *maoz*, where on the morning of October 6, Ashkenazi was reminded of the biblical story of Lot's wife. Perhaps the Egyptians had been transformed into "pillars of salt."[32]

At 1:30 P.M., he received a call from headquarters. "Total war" would break out at 6:00 P.M.

There was no time for preparation. Twenty minutes later, four Egyptian fighter jets bore down on them dropping bombs and firing rockets. Ashkenazi screamed at his men, "Everyone go down into the bunkers!" He did not have to tell them twice. As they squeezed inside, they heard the earth convulse above them. The largest artillery barrage in the history of the Arab-Israeli conflict rained down. Ashkenazi himself counted thirty shells a minute. "I could not hear my own thoughts," he later remembered.[33]

The shelling was as intense everywhere else, and so was the surprise. An enraged Israeli colonel ran outside at the outbreak of war demanding to know who commenced fire without his authorization. (The Egyptians, was the reply.) In the Mifreket *maoz*, the dust cloud created by the bombardment was so thick, the men reported—falsely as it turned out—that they were under a gas attack. The soft sand of Sinai absorbed much of the explosions and shrapnel, creating a strange ripple effect across the landscape. One witness said the ground itself got up and danced.[34]

At the same moment, the Syrians let loose a similar barrage on the Golan Heights, firing an estimated twenty-five thousand shells in the first five minutes of the war. The ground was firmer in the Golan, pushing the force of every blast higher into the air. The clouds of black smoke they created hung over the battlefield for three days.[35]

Intelligence officers listening to Egyptian radios barely heard the blasts in the background. They were drowned out by thousands of men descending to the canal, shouting, "*Allahu Akbar!!*"[36]

At approximately 2:05 P.M. on the afternoon of October 6, 1973, eight thousand Egyptian commandos carried rubber dinghies down to the waters of the Suez Canal and paddled across. On August 22, 1973, barely six weeks earlier, only eight Egyptian officers knew that war was coming. Division commanders entered October thinking they were preparing for just another round of war exercises. The highest-ranking Egyptian officer that Israel captured, a colonel, said that he found out only a half hour before the attack, when he saw the commander of the Egyptian Third Army on the floor, facing Mecca in prayer.[37]

Despite the lack of advance notice, the Egyptian army performed brilliantly. The men had rehearsed the crossing twenty-three times before. They carried it out on October 6 as if they were drilling it for the twenty-fourth. When the order came down the line, they knew they had their work cut out for them. The plan called for the opening of seventy passages through the sand barrier on the east bank of the canal within seven hours. Thirty-five ferries would then begin moving equipment across. Two hours after that, engineers would lay twenty-five bridges of varying sizes.[38]

The Egyptian army had created a new junior rank called "war officer," trained to carry out a single task. The most dangerous of these tasks belonged to combat engineers who were given high-pressure fire hoses to blast through the sand barrier with water pumped from the canal. It took a team manning five cannons a minimum of two hours to create a breach. The teams stood exposed, armed with nothing but fire hoses, soaked to the bone and sinking in mud.[39]

The operation came off without a hitch. Egyptian commandos paddled across, climbed over the steep sand barriers, and laid rope ladders to aid those behind them before dashing across to the other side. Once through, they seized the "fins," the battle ramps the Israelis had built for their own tanks to mount in the event of an invasion. The first Egyptian tank crossed ahead of schedule, just six hours after the war began. In Shazly's telling, by the next day the Egyptians had 1,020 tanks on the east bank of the canal.[40]

The Egyptians poured through the gaps between the *maozim*. These gaps were considerable. In 1972, with Chaim Bar-Lev no longer serving as chief of staff, Ariel Sharon saw his opportunity and reduced the number of *maozim* from thirty to just sixteen. He accomplished this, characteristically, by moving men around in a constant shell game, and then begging for forgiveness instead of permission when some of the *maozim* ended up uninhabited. Among other things, the thinning out created a blind spot of approximately twelve miles smack in the middle of the line between a *maoz* called Purkan and another called Matzmed. The Egyptians seized all the ground between them. One of the places they took was called the Chinese Farm.[41]

Egypt's General Gamasy later said that he considered the possibility of losing as many as 85,000 men in the initial assault. The sun rose the next morning and he found he had lost only 280. The performance had exceeded every expectation and came as a shock, not just to the Israelis but also to Anwar Sadat himself. In the words of Muhammad Heikal, the *al-Ahram* editor, "Nobody expected the Egyptian Army to behave as it did."[42]

Much of the surprise occurred because no one expected the Israeli army to perform as it did.

If it had gone according to plan, the Israelis would have activated Operation Dovecote, and the Egyptians would have been confronted by a force spearheaded by three hundred tanks. As it turned out, only eighty-nine tanks were activated, and all but a handful of them were positioned away from the canal. In ordinary times, there were thirty tanks patrolling along the canal. On October 6, there were only three.[43]

For many, like General Ezer Weizman, this, and not the failure to mobilize the reservists, was the great failure of the Yom Kippur War. "If the regular army had been in position [along the canal], the war would have looked completely different and we would have completed the holding action in 48 hours," he later wrote. The reservists would have arrived, he continued, and these fresh troops would have launched the counterattack against an exhausted Egyptian army.[44]

This was to become one of the enduring controversies of the war. Why wasn't Operation Dovecote implemented?

All agreed that General Elazar ordered Gonen to send two of his brigades up to the line and hold the third one in reserve, as called for in Operation Dovecote. But Gonen claimed that after meeting with Elazar on the morning of October 6, he received a message over his teletype to send only *one* brigade up to the line and keep *two* in reserve. Gonen further claimed that Elazar told him not to send the tanks into the field until 4:00 P.M. The idea was to have them in place at 5:00 P.M. to meet the Egyptian attack expected at 6:00 P.M. Why wait till the last minute? Gonen said that if the Egyptians saw where his forces were spread out, they could change their plans and focus their attack in the gaps between them. Once they were within an hour of the planned invasion, it would be too late for the Egyptians to change anything. As it turned out, the Egyptians had plans of their own.[45]

The confusion was just as great everywhere else. In the Bunker, the army's command center in Tel Aviv, there was not enough time to prepare the war room, so generals crouched over maps on the floor in the corridor.[46] When the day began, IAF commander Benny Peled ordered preparations to attack Syrian surface-to-air missiles. A few hours later, what Peled called "my great fear" was realized: the Golan was covered in low-level clouds. He thus ordered that the mission be changed to attacking Syrian airfields.

At 1:00 P.M., when it became clear that no preemptive strike would be approved, Peled ordered *all* his planes to swap armaments. If Arab air forces had to be destroyed in the air instead of on the ground, then Benny Peled was going to have every available plane in the sky. This took most of his jets out of the fight for four hours because that is how long it took to replace bombs with Sidewinder missiles and other ammunition needed for dogfighting.[47]

There is an admirable ethos in the Israeli air force of speaking truth to power, and one of Peled's aides, Colonel Giora Forman, told him he was making a serious mistake. Long before the war, the IAF had gamed out this very situation. Its planners concluded that it needed only seventy jets to defend the nation's skies.[48]

The IAF had a ready-to-go contingency plan to confront an Arab invasion. It even used the same munitions used to destroy the SAMs or airfields, the only difference being in the fuel tank needed.[49] If a first strike was off the table, Colonel Forman argued, the next best thing was to unleash the IAF's fighter jets minutes after the Arabs opened fire. Stripping the planes of their munitions did not just take them out of the fight, it also left them in a vulnerable position on the ground. The munitions all carried high explosives, the fuel was combustible, everything had to be carefully moved around from place to place.

Peled rejected Forman's advice. The war was not to begin until 6:00 P.M. By that time, it would be dark and the pilots would not be able to locate targets on the ground. Better to use every plane to intercept and destroy as many enemy planes as possible in the air. In the words of a senior IAF officer, "There was no man and no power at headquarters to tell the IAF commander, 'You are making a catastrophic mistake, drop it!'"[50]

An hour after Peled gave his order, a young soldier was manning a radar screen on Mount Meron, near the ancient city of Safed. "Hey Cafri," she said to her superior, "I might be having a technical problem, but it looks like dozens of Syrian planes are heading toward the Golan Heights."[51]

Major Yair Cafri initially went into denial, not unlike a patient given a terminal diagnosis. It was probably just a technical glitch, he told her. But then he overheard one of his assistants breathlessly telling an air base to scramble fighters. Now shocked into reality—and with radar screens filling tighter with flashing lights—he quickly wired the air defense duty officer and told him to fire his Hawk surface-to-air missiles at every bogey in the sky. Like the Arab SAMs, the American-made Hawk missiles could not distinguish between friend and foe. "Are you sure you want me to do that???" the missile officer asked incredulously. Cafri repeated the order: shoot at every plane on the screen.[52]

Major Cafri, the radar's commander, was perhaps the first to realize what would soon horrify those above him. War had broken out, *and the Israeli air force had hardly a single jet in the sky.*[53]

The military academies of the world all study the cautionary tale of the Japanese catastrophe in the Battle of Midway, which occurred because Japanese aircraft were sitting on carrier decks, fully fueled and armed, at the exact moment that American planes came dive-bombing out of the clouds. The Japanese carrier *Akagi* was destroyed by just a single bomb dropped from a lone scout plane. That was enough to ignite a fireball, engulf the floating city in flames, and take her to the bottom.

The Israelis were operating on dry land, and largely underneath concrete canopies, but their bomb-laden planes were sitting helplessly on the ground all the same. With catastrophe just over the horizon, sirens went off, pilots scrambled, and the jets took off, munitions and all. The Phantoms and Mirages were directed out over the Mediterranean, where they were ordered to dump their ordnance in the sea. The less agile A-4 Skyhawks were by design bombers that could be freed of their munitions quickly. They were ordered to detach their bombs on the ground and get up into the sky to defend the air bases. This order caused much bewilderment. A-4 Skyhawks were of limited value as interceptors and had never been used for that purpose before.[54]

The pilots began to wonder what demons had possessed their commanders. In the space of eight hours a mission to attack Syrian SAMs was ordered and canceled, a mission to attack Syrian airfields was ordered and canceled, and then planes were sent up helter-skelter to drop munitions into the sea. Men had been scurrying on the ground since six in the morning. Yet it was Egyptian and Syrian planes that took control of the skies.[55]

It could have been worse. The Arabs would have scored a devastating psychological blow had they done to the Israeli air force in 1973 what was done to them in 1967. Somehow, despite attacking with 450 planes and a similar measure of surprise, the Arabs achieved surprisingly little. Four Syrian MiG-17s swooped down on the control center in Mount Meron. They dropped their bombs and missed. The other Syrian planes strangely avoided Israel's air bases. Instead, they bombed ground positions in the Golan, including the main military base called Nafekh, where power was temporarily cut. Egyptian marksmanship was not much better, and the results were equally dismal. IAF fighter jets even managed to turn back from the Mediterranean and shoot down eighteen Egyptian planes.[56]

This was cold comfort back in the Bunker. The unthinkable had happened. War had come with hardly a tank along the canal and barely a plane in the sky. No one had ever gamed out this situation because no one thought it was possible.[57] Everything from here had to be improvised.

As the sun set that day, it was Major Cafri, once again, who was first to realize the severity of the situation. Still in the command center on Mount Meron, he received a message from a pilot over the emergency rescue frequency. The pilot reported that he had ejected from his plane after it was hit by a Syrian SAM. But he hastened to add that everything was all right. He had parachuted down safely and landed next to the Israeli settlement of Ramat Magshimim in the Golan Heights.

A minute later he wired an urgent message. The Syrians were at the gates of Ramat Magshimim, and he was about to be captured.[58]

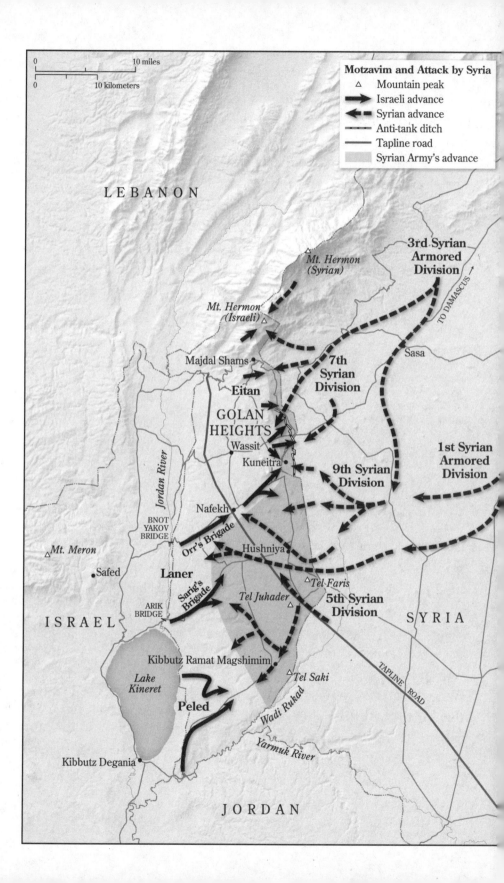

**Motzavim and Attack by Syria**
△ Mountain peak
➡ Israeli advance
⬅ Syrian advance
Anti-tank ditch
Tapline road
Syrian Army's advance

0 ——— 10 miles
0 ——— 10 kilometers

LEBANON

*Mt. Hermon (Syrian)* △

3rd Syrian Armored Division

*Mt. Hermon (Israeli)* △

TO DAMASCUS

Majdal Shams ●

7th Syrian Division

Sasa

**Eitan**

GOLAN HEIGHTS

Wassit ●

Kuneitra ●

9th Syrian Division

1st Syrian Armored Division

Nafekh ●

BNOT YAKOV BRIDGE

Orr's Brigade

△ *Mt. Meron*

● Safed

**Laner**

Sarig's Brigade

Hushniya ●

△ *Tel Faris*

ARIK BRIDGE

*Tel Juhader* ● △

5th Syrian Division

ISRAEL

SYRIA

Kibbutz Ramat Magshimim ●

*Lake Kineret*

△ *Tel Saki*

**Peled**

TAPLINE ROAD

Kibbutz Degania ●

*Wadi Rukad*

*Yarmuk River*

JORDAN

# 8

## "THE THIRD TEMPLE IS AT RISK"

No war plan survives contact with the enemy.
—Field Marshal Helmuth von Moltke

Everyone has a plan until they get punched in the mouth.
—Mike Tyson

No one thought much about Mount Hermon before the 1967 war. The Syrians left the mountain range unmanned, even though the tallest of its peaks was the second highest point between Turkey and Yemen. The Israelis snatched one of the lower ridges on June 12, 1967, two days *after* the ceasefire was declared, by landing a helicopter and planting a flag just hours before UN inspectors arrived. This Israeli Hermon was 6,890 feet above sea level, or 922 feet below the Syrian Hermon located just north of it. Accounts are split as to why the Israelis did not seize the Syrian Hermon. Some say their helicopters could not fly through the thin air to the higher altitude. Others say they simply missed it because it was covered in fog.[1]

From the Israeli Hermon it was possible to see sixty miles in any direction. Advances in technology turned the base into a beehive of artillery spotters, intelligence officers, and air force engineers trained in jamming enemy radar. Strangely, given its value, it never occurred to anyone in Israel that the Syrians might try to retake it. The position was never fortified and did not figure in the plan to defend the Golan Heights. After the war, a brigadier general in Northern Command called the situation a "scandal."[2]

The scandal of planning before the war paled in comparison to what occurred upon its outbreak. Fifty Syrian helicopters were seen on October 5 moving into place near the Hermon. AMAN chose to ignore it. Then on the following day, astonishingly, no one remembered to tell the men in the outpost that war was about to break out. The irony crystalized into a perfect metaphor for AMAN's humiliation: the officers who served in the most important intelligence post in the land were the last ones to find out the war had started.[3]

On October 6 at 1:35 P.M., three Syrian helicopters took off and skillfully flew behind a mountain ridge where Israeli radar could not see them. Under cover of artillery fire, the three helicopters deposited Syrian commandos at strategic points along the mountain. Helicopters were fragile craft in 1973, and the mission suffered an early mishap when one of the three was blown over by a gust of wind and exploded. But more than thirty men took up positions blocking reinforcements, paving the way for other commandos to advance by foot down from the Syrian Hermon.[4]

The battle ended quickly. The Israelis had only ten combat soldiers, and they were caught completely by surprise. A second lieutenant on lookout later said that until the Syrian helicopter exploded, he thought the choppers were carrying senior Israeli officers for a surprise inspection. The confusion was so great that Israeli investigators never pieced together exactly how the base fell. What is known is that the battle ended before anyone received an order to destroy documents or equipment. Soviet experts arrived on October 8 and shouted with joy when they saw the haul. The material was loaded onto mules and carted away.[5]

Of far greater value were the men that were captured. There

were thirty-one of them, not counting "two or three" that the Syrians executed. They were filmed by journalists on October 15 sitting in filthy uniforms, unshaven, hands behind their heads in defeat. It is one of the iconic pictures of the war.[6]

Not far from the Israeli Hermon, the Syrians gouged a large section out of a different mountain and filled it with a two-story command bunker. Inside, intelligence officers and their Soviet advisers peered through the most advanced East-bloc optical equipment and saw the Israeli line spread out before them.[7]

* * *

The Israeli defense in the north bore the stamp of Chaim Bar-Lev and resembled the line in the south along the canal. Of course, there was no waterway separating the two sides in the Golan Heights. Instead, the Israelis dug an antitank ditch that was five yards wide and three yards deep. The ditch extended the entire forty-four-mile length of the front, except along the southern Golan, where nature supplied a steep, impassable dry riverbed named Wadi Rukad. Overlooking the ditch were battle ramps from which Israeli tanks had a clear line of fire to stop any attacker. As in the south along the canal, intelligence was fed in real time by men inside fortified bunkers.[8]

The Syrians had a healthy respect for Israeli gunnery born of painful experience. The plan therefore depended upon surprise. After much study, Assad and his generals concluded that Israeli reservists needed at least twenty-four hours to mobilize. The Syrians hoped to make it to the Jordan River before the reservists made it to the front.[9] This was ambitious but realistic. The Golan is only twenty-seven miles at its widest.

The first step was to drop commandos behind Israeli lines to block roads and destroy bridges over the Jordan River. Had this been carried out, the reservists would not have made it in time, and the fate of the Israelis would have been sealed. But someone in the Syrian High Command apparently did not have the heart to send so many young men to a certain death. The mission was canceled at the last minute with the helicopters already in the air. It was a questionable decision. In Sinai, practically all nine hundred Egyptian commandos on a similar mission were killed or captured, and they delayed Israeli reservists for only a few hours along just one road. But for the Syrians, a delay of a few hours along one road might have made all the difference. Three days later after their offensive stalled, the Syrians would in desperation send commandos in helicopters on a suicide mission. But the better time for suicide missions was at the start of the campaign when it would have mattered most.[10]

After the war, practically the only senior Israeli military officer to avoid reprimand was the commander of Northern Command, General Yitzchak "Haka" Hofi. The Agranat Commission found that "although there were flaws" in his performance, he was the one figure that reviewed the intelligence, arrived at his own conclusions, and "caused the General Staff to strengthen the defense of the Golan Heights just in the nick of time."[11]

The words *just in the nick of time* are if anything an understatement. The "strengthening" of the line was mostly accomplished by redeploying the elite 7th Armored Brigade from its usual posting along the canal. It made it to the Golan only the night before the Syrian attack. On the afternoon of October 5, the IDF had just 75 tanks defending the Golan. On the afternoon of October 6, it had 177.[12]

The Syrians began with a huge artillery barrage from nine hundred guns targeted at the antitank ditch. The idea was to chase the Israelis away so that combat engineers could lay bridging equipment. The shelling did not achieve the desired result. Foot soldiers took refuge inside their bunkers, and tanks ducked behind hills and battle ramps.[13] The shelling stopped, the Syrian attack began, and the Israelis popped out to man the ramparts.

In its initial phase, the Syrians attacked with 500 tanks against Israel's 177, for an advantage of less than three to one. That is

a reasonable ratio for defenders, at least if they deploy their resources wisely. General Hofi might have deployed his men in this
fashion, but he never got the chance. In another of those last-
minute decisions that came in for criticism after the war, General
Elazar met with Generals Gonen and Hofi early on the morning
of October 6, but then called them back to the Bunker in Tel Aviv
for a second meeting instead of letting them hurry back to their
respective commands. The idea that the Arabs might strike before
6:00 P.M. never seems to have crossed anyone's mind. When war
broke out, the shelling made it impossible for Hofi's helicopter to
land anywhere in the Golan Heights.[14]

It left one of the most important decisions of the war in the
hands of a colonel named Uri Simhoni. Compounding the problem was the fact that although AMAN had managed to obtain
Syria's war plans, it never shared them with officers of Simhoni's
rank for security reasons. After the war, the Agranat Commission
asked in exasperation, "What is the point of the enormous effort
of obtaining enemy war plans if in the end they remain in filing
cabinets?"[15]

In Simhoni's words, "I looked left and right and realized that
I was the one that had to make the decision." The reports at that
moment were that the Syrians were attempting to bridge the antitank ditch in the north, but that everything was fine in the south.
Simhoni took stock of the situation, reasoned that the most likely
place for the Syrian main effort would be through the village of
Kuneitra, and sent three of his five battalions to the north.[16]

He guessed wrong.

* * *

As commander of Southern Command, General Gonen had access to all the intelligence in AMAN's filing cabinets. One of the
most prized items was a forty-six-page description of Egypt's war
plan, which AMAN had painstakingly pieced together. The report
was mistaken in several respects. The Israelis apparently received

a copy of Operation 41 and thought that Egypt's war goal was to fight to the passes after an operational pause (though Marwan told Zeira in the dramatic meeting in London that he thought the Egyptian goal was to advance only six miles). But on the main points, AMAN's forty-six-page description was accurate. The Egyptians crossed with infantry only. They spread out over a broad area rather than concentrate a main effort in any one place. And in the initial phase, they advanced only about a kilometer.[17]

When the invasion began, Gonen knew none of this. Though AMAN had captured the enemy's war plan—a singular achievement, the dream of every intelligence agency—Gonen later told a dumbfounded Agranat Commission that he never saw it. When asked how that could be, he responded, "No one directed my attention to it." A Commission member said, "I am stunned." The result was that on the 6th, Gonen wasted a precious hour and a half trying to locate Egypt's main effort, even though AMAN's description made it clear that there would be no main effort.[18]

It was a strange paradox: The Israelis had the Egyptian war plan. What they lacked was a plan of their own. Simply put, the IDF never thought through what to do in the event of an attack that caught them completely by surprise.[19]

The first thing Elazar had to decide was how to use the Israeli air force. Every war plan assumed that the air force would be like a compressed spring, ready to jump into action the moment war began. It was likewise assumed that the air force would destroy the enemy SAMs in short order, perhaps as quickly as five to six hours. The plan thus called for the air force to join in the defense of the Bar-Lev Line only *after* it finished its mission destroying the SAMs. It was the same strategy as in 1967. First, Arab air forces were destroyed on the ground, and only then did the IAF turn its attention to ground support. "Everyone figured," Assistant Chief of Staff General Yisroel Tal said after the war, "that 180 tanks in the Golan and 300 more along the Canal could hold out for just 5–6 hours [until the air force was available]."[20]

As it turned out, when Egypt attacked, the air force was not ready *and* there were no tanks along canal. What to do in *that* situation?

The choices for Elazar were stark. He could stick with the original plan, abandon the men on the ground to their fate, and focus first on destroying the enemy's planes and air defenses. Alternatively, he could order his fighter jets into the fray, knowing that dozens (and possibly more) would be lost to the SAMs. Elazar accepted Peled's recommendation and chose the former.

There is much evidence supporting the wisdom of the decision. Throughout the war, the Arabs fired their surface-to-air missiles as if they were bullets, steeled with the knowledge that there would be ample resupply from their Soviet allies. The same would prove true of antitank missiles, artillery shells, and all the other expensive ordnance in their arsenal. If the IAF had sent wave upon wave of planes through a hail of missiles, it might well have lost them before the war even began. One *maoz* commander saw "four or five planes" shot out of the sky before his eyes. He radioed a message to call off anything further.[21]

Other Israeli officers disagreed. A retired general named Emmanuel Sakal—who, not coincidentally, was a young lieutenant colonel stationed along the canal when the war broke out—later wrote a doctoral thesis arguing that the Israeli air force should have been used to attack Egyptians and Syrians on the ground. Sakal's study includes an unfortunate quote from a senior pilot who said that the plan was never presented to Elazar because "it is not the job of the Air Force to present plans that are bad for the Air Force." If it had been presented, Elazar would have been told that each F-4 could carry eleven cluster bombs, which they could fire from a relatively safe distance using a method called the "slingshot." Fighter jets would go into a steep climb and release their munitions while gaining altitude so that the bombs would continue upward and then travel in a wide arc before descending on the target. The accuracy of this method was poor but effective enough for cluster bombs. Eleven cluster bombs contained 7,150 bomblets that obliterated everything in an area of a quarter mile by two-thirds of a mile. Given that the Egyptians advanced only about a half mile in the initial stage and were packed tightly with their backs to the canal, just sixty F-4 sorties could have wiped out the vanguard before any armor would have crossed. Could Israel have won the war in the opening hours with its air force? This is another of those what-ifs that is impossible to answer.[22]

The next question before Elazar was the *maozim*, or, more specifically, whether to evacuate the men that served inside them. There were 451 such soldiers when the war began. Only 331 of them were combat troops, and most were from the Jerusalem Brigade, a unit of immigrants and middle-aged men with limited training.[23]

How much these men could contribute was anyone's guess. Operation Dovecote called for the *maozim* to be manned by elite units. Ariel Sharon always argued for withdrawing even those soldiers the moment hostilities began. His assistant, General Jackie Even, later said that the *maozim* became worthless a minute after the war began. Others were not so sure. Withdrawal would deprive the army of its eyes and ears along the canal when it needed them most. It would also hand the Egyptians an enormous psychological victory.[24]

In the heat of the moment, facing a situation he thought impossible only the day before, Elazar could not make up his mind. He therefore delegated the decision to Gonen, a man never blessed with a moment of self-doubt. He decided on the spot. There would be no withdrawal. The men of the *maozim* would stand and fight.[25]

In the absence of any plan, the army drew upon its experiences in the War of Attrition. One of the most heavily drilled exercises was rescuing a *maoz*. A tank commander who received a cry for help was expected to drop everything, race to where they could engage the enemy, and send a single tank in to evacuate the wounded. On the evening of October 6, Israeli commanders in the field thought that Egypt had merely restarted the War of Attrition. Because of that, and because all the *maozim* cried for help at once, they split up their tanks and sent them piecemeal into battle. There were twenty such *maozim* along the line. Israeli tanks would reach only five of them.[26]

Earlier that day, the men inside the *maozim* peered through their periscopes and reported that the Egyptians had crossed the canal carrying strange equipment. Some had tubes dangling off their shoulders that from a distance could be mistaken for a woodwind musical instrument. Others carried what looked like suitcases.[27]

The wood-wrapped steel tubes were a Soviet-made bazooka called an RPG-7, perhaps the most widely used shoulder-fired weapon ever produced. The rugged, easy-to-handle RPG-7 fired a projectile that could destroy a small building or pierce the armor of a tank. Accuracy was dodgy beyond two hundred yards, but the weapon was lethal when placed in capable hands. It was the RPG-7 that shot down two American Black Hawk helicopters in Somalia in 1993.[28]

The suitcases Egyptian soldiers carried held a more sophisticated device, part of a class of weapons known as antitank guided missiles, or ATGMs. The Soviets introduced the weapon the year before in Vietnam; it was known in the West as a Sagger. One Israeli soldier described it as a flying tennis ball made of fire that pursued you like a wild animal seeking its prey.[29] What made the Sagger so deadly was that the missile was connected to a thin wire that, when unspooled, extended over a mile long. The wire was itself attached to a joystick that an operator used to guide the projectile onto the target.

It is Confederate general Nathan Bedford Forrest who is credited with saying that military victory was about getting there "firstest with the mostest." The adage was as true in 1973 as it was during the American Civil War. On the evening of October 6,

Egyptian troops reached Israel's battle ramps first. From there, they fired "the mostest," thousands of RPG rockets and missiles. Against that, the Israelis violated the two cardinal rules of tank warfare: never stand still in an enemy killing zone, and never attack one at a time. Israeli tanks split up and rolled into battle in tiny groups, coming to a stop near the *maozim*. One battalion commander received a desperate report from the field, "They're shooting at us with missiles that have wires. The missiles are chasing us and hitting us." And then the radio went dead.[30]

It was only the following morning, October 7, that the Israelis understood the mistake of making the *maozim* their focus instead of stemming the Egyptian invasion. The casualty reports spoke for themselves. One of the three brigades permanently stationed along the canal, the 401st, entered the battle with ninety-eight tanks. By the following morning it was down to just twenty-five. Another brigade, the 14th, started the war with a hundred tanks. The next day it was down to fourteen. Less than twenty-four hours had passed since hostilities began, and the Israelis had already lost 173 tanks, or almost 10 percent of their entire arsenal.[31]

At 9:37 A.M. on the morning of October 7, General Gonen belatedly gave the order to evacuate the *maozim*. By then it was too late for most of the men there, who were now trapped behind enemy lines.[32] Despite all this, Gonen was still living in 1967. He radioed Elazar and suggested launching a counterattack by attacking the center of the Egyptian line and crossing the canal.

In the midst of the calamity unfolding before him, Elazar could not believe his ears. He lost his temper and began to scream. Those who witnessed the outburst were stunned.[33]

* * *

In the Golan Heights, the shelling made it impossible for General Hofi to reach his headquarters until 4:30 on the afternoon of October 6. But when he got there, he was told that the situation was under control.[34] The Syrians had made no attempt to cross the steep dry riverbed of Wadi Rukad. Instead, they divided the remaining thirty-mile front into three parts and sent a division to attack each ten-mile section.

The most difficult task was given to the Syrian 7th Division in the north. The hilly terrain near Mount Hermon was perfect for defense. And though the Syrians were bolstered by an expeditionary force from Morocco, they enjoyed a numerical advantage over the Israelis of only 1.5 to 1. The Syrians experienced some limited success. On the evening of October 6, Druze residents from the nearby village of Majdal Shams, who were branded pro-Israel collaborators by their neighbors, knocked on the door of an IDF outpost and pleaded for protection from Syrian secret police roaming the streets. But overall, the attack lost momentum and failed to gain ground. The northern Golan then remained relatively quiet through the night.[35]

Farther south in the central Golan, the Syrians fought better but with the same outcome. The Syrian 9th Division attacked the city of Kuneitra, hoping to raise their flag above the main government building. The attack failed, so they settled for raising it above a mosque on the outskirts of town. As night fell, at 5:44 P.M., General Hofi reported to Elazar that the line had held everywhere. Estimates later put Syrian losses at no less than 200 of the 276 tanks that attacked in the first wave.[36]

The trouble for the Israelis began almost immediately after that.

A radio message reached General Hofi at 5:53 P.M., less than ten minutes after he hung up on Elazar. The Syrian 5th Division and parts of the 9th Division had achieved a breakthrough in the southern Golan near the town of Hushniya. The Syrians later threw their elite 1st Division into the gap opened up by the 5th Division. It is still unclear whether this was the original plan, but if the attack farther north was a feint, it succeeded completely. In the southern Golan the Syrians enjoyed a numerical advantage of better than five to one. Near Israel's southernmost outpost, numbered 116, only three Israeli tanks confronted forty-one Syrian tanks and over fifteen hundred foot soldiers. Eventually the three tanks ran out of ammunition, but they bought some time by firing their flares as if they were ordinary shells. The flares bounced off the Syrian tanks but created enormous flashes that in some cases caused the alarmed crews to flee their armored vehicles. Once they emerged from the hatches, the Israelis mowed them down with their machine guns.[37] *

Once through, the Syrian force fanned out in three directions. One headed south toward Moshe Dayan's boyhood home of Kibbutz Degania at the southern tip of Lake Kineret. Another headed west toward the crucial Arik Bridge at the northern tip of Lake Kineret. The largest effort turned right and headed northwest. Its objective was a place called Nafekh.

Since at least the time of the German theorist Carl von Clausewitz, military strategists have understood that every belligerent has a "center of power on which everything depends" and that it is against this center that "the concentrated blow of all forces should be directed."[38] For Israel in the Golan Heights, that center of power was the military base in Nafekh, located strategically at an important crossroads. In 1950, the American Bechtel Corporation opened the Trans-Arabian Pipeline, or Tapline, to carry oil from Saudi Arabia to the Lebanese port of Sidon. A section of the Tapline bisected the Golan diagonally, as did an adjacent service road that passed through Nafekh along the way. It was up the Tapline Road that more than a hundred Syrian tanks sped in the early hours of October 7, with little in their path and Nafekh less than fifteen miles away.

All through the night, the Israelis scrambled to throw forces into battle, ready or not, with whatever material was on hand. One soldier complained that his tank was sent in without any

---

* Israeli foot soldiers armed with bazookas managed to destroy two Syrian tanks inside Outpost 116. The picture of one of the disabled Syrian tanks resting atop the outpost is one of the best-known photos of the war.

light ammunition. He was told not to worry. Maybe he knew he could not fire his machine gun, but the Syrians did not. Others extracted unused tank shells from destroyed vehicles, wiped off the blood, and loaded them elsewhere. And then there were reservists struggling to get damaged tanks back into action. One such soldier wandering in the dark through a forward base was a twenty-one-year-old second lieutenant named Tzvika Greengold.[39]

Greengold found a tank that was covered in blood but operable. He climbed inside with three others under his command.* The loader told him that for some reason he could not get the cannon door closed no matter how hard he slammed it. He looked inside and discovered a severed hand. One of the others saw blood and body parts, jumped from the tank, ran over to a tree, and vomited. The soldier returned after emptying the contents of his stomach, the severed hand was tossed out through an open hatch, and the tank rolled off into the night.[40]

Greengold wired his brigade commander seeking orders, but in one of those random acts of luck that often decide the fate of a battle, the radioman forgot to pass the request along to his superior. Had he done so, Greengold would have been ordered up to one of the outposts along the line and the remainder of this chapter would be dedicated to describing the fall of Nafekh. Instead, Greengold headed down the Tapline Road. In the darkness, he came upon what looked like a hundred cats moving toward him. He immediately identified the green "cat's eyes" as infrared night-fighting equipment.[41]

It was the ultimate statement of how the two sides had swapped roles of David and Goliath. Before 1967, the Israelis attempted to blunt their numerical inferiority by fighting at night. After 1967, Israeli military planners figured their days of fighting at night were over. They came in for heavy criticism later for refusing to spend money on night-fighting equipment, even though

---

* Tanks were operated by a four-man crew: the commander, the driver, the loader, and the shooter.

they could have supplied an entire brigade with it for less than the cost of a single tank. The Syrians, by contrast, understood the new battlefield calculus after 1967 and invested heavily in night fighting.[42]

A tank commander with binoculars could see the distinct "cat's eyes" from a distance. A tank gunner peering through a periscope saw nothing but the black of night. Unless someone fired a flare, the only hope was hitting an enemy tank, igniting it, and seeing the others in the light of the fireball. Fortunately (or more accurately unfortunately), there were so many enemy tanks that Greengold's shooter could hit one of them with his eyes closed. Itzik Arnon, the shooter, said in an interview over thirty years later, "You have to remember, the Tapline road is very narrow. It only fits one tank opposite another. The one that shoots first is the one that stays alive." He added that "from that range it was impossible to miss." [43]

Greengold's tank opened fire and pulled back after each shot, taking up a position elsewhere to give the impression of a larger force. Greengold called his commanding officer, Colonel Yitzchak Ben-Shoham, over the wireless. Ben-Shoham asked how large his force was, but knowing that the Syrians were listening, Greengold did not answer. In the blackness of night, Greengold himself did not know how many enemy tanks his shooter hit. He later estimated it at "six or seven definite kills and three or four probable kills." The more important fact was that by the time he fired off his last shell at around midnight, he and the men in his tank had held off the Syrians for two crucial hours.[44]

It was at that very moment that the first reservists arrived. A convoy of seven tanks—it started out as ten, but three broke down along the way—was sent down the Tapline Road with orders to join "Force Tzvika." They discovered that Force Tzvika was a lone tank that was out of ammunition. Greengold said that he had to go back to camp to reload, but the unit commander, Captain Amnon Sharon, ordered him stay. "Don't worry," he said,

"I don't have any ammunition either. It'll be alright." That was only a slight exaggeration. Each of Sharon's tanks had only twelve shells.[45]

Not long after that, the unit was practically wiped out. Greengold's tank was hit with the others, possibly by friendly fire, and it ignited. Greengold made it out with moderate burns. His tank driver was killed. The two remaining crewmen were badly burned and set out on foot seeking medical treatment. They headed northwest up the Tapline Road, hoping to make it to Nafekh.[46]

As in the south along the canal, commanders in the north thought that what they were facing was merely a "battle day," one of the fiery skirmishes that had characterized the War of Attrition. Just after midnight, in the early hours of October 7, General Hofi realized he was facing a full-blown invasion. He called Elazar, advised him that Syrian tanks were less than three miles from Nafekh, and asked for air support. Fighter jets were of extremely limited value at night when the pilots could not make visual contact with targets on the ground, and anyway the area was covered by Syrian surface-to-air missiles. Hofi was told that he would have to hold out until the morning.[47]

Hofi ordered Colonel Avigdor "Yanush" Ben-Gal to send some of his tanks south to plug the breach. Though Ben-Gal's men would later engage in some of the fiercest fighting of the war, in the early stages their sector remained quiet. In one of the more controversial episodes of the war, Ben-Gal refused to send them, insisting he needed those forces in his sector farther north. Ben-Gal escaped punishment because the Agranat Commission concluded that Hofi did not impart just how desperate the situation was farther south. Moreover, Ben-Gal turned out to be correct. Later he needed every tank to hold off the Syrians.[48]

Hofi next turned his attention to the Golan's sixteen Jewish settlements. He was told that women and children had all left, but some of the men had stayed behind. He ordered them to evacuate at once. In one settlement, the last eight men took the

Torah scroll, piled into a single car, and made it out just ahead of the Syrians.[49]

Hofi realized that he could not continue in Nafekh. It was a small base designed for battle days, not invasions. Earlier in the day, a senior officer tried to enter the command bunker and could not get in. There simply was not enough room. Hofi might have also figured that he could do a better job managing his theater of command if he remained alive. Accordingly, at 2:30 in the morning, he and his staff fled west for the main base on Mount Canaan in the town of Safed.[50]

After catching two hours of sleep, Moshe Dayan was awakened at around four in the morning. He was told he had to come at once. The war was going badly. He arrived at the Bunker in Tel Aviv, and under a cloud of cigarette smoke he was apprised of the catastrophe taking shape in the Golan and along the canal.[51]

Dayan, like many others, saw the modern state of Israel as the "Third Temple." The first Jewish Temple had been built by King Solomon and destroyed by the Babylonians; after a seventy-year exile, the Jews built a second, later destroyed by the Romans. As the high command took stock on October 7, what the Jews had built with so much effort was once again trembling on the brink of destruction. In Dayan's memoir, he wrote, "I do not remember ever being filled with such fear and dread." Later that day, he blurted to an aide, "The Third Temple is at risk."[52]

# 9

## SYRIANS AT THE GATE

A small nation is one whose very existence may be put into question; a small nation can disappear and it knows it.[1]

—Milan Kundera

The pecking order within the Israeli army began at the bottom with lowly desk clerks, known in Hebrew slang as *jobniks*. Above them stood those in the artillery corps, and higher still were those serving in tanks, paratroopers, and commandos. Standing on the highest rung atop practically every able-bodied man in the country were the pilots. At the top of this top rung was one man: the air force commander, General Binyamin "Benny" Peled.

Peled had several firsts attached to his name. He was the first Israeli pilot to break the sound barrier, the first to be ejected from a fighter jet, and the first to be rescued after being shot down. He was also a brilliant engineer, who by sheer power of intellect had acquired the final say on all equipment purchases. But he rose through the ranks on the strength of technological savvy, organization, and planning, with only limited experience commanding operations. In an air force piling up combat records, younger pilots wondered why they were led by a man who did not have a single confirmed kill.[2]

On the morning of October 7, Peled sent his planes to carry out Operation Tagar, the mission to destroy Egypt's surface-to-air missiles. It was a complicated opera carried out by a thousand-piece orchestra in multiple acts. In the first, planes were sent up to draw fire, causing Egyptian SAM batteries to give away their positions and empty their launchers.

Then, American-made M-107 artillery barraged the SAM sites with 175-mm long-range shells. The M-107 was supplied to Israel by Washington to compensate it for Egypt's violation of the War of Attrition ceasefire.[3] It was not very accurate when it reached its maximum range of eighteen miles. But the Israelis hoped the shelling would disrupt SAM operators and maybe even cause them to run for cover.

The next target was Egyptian radar. Israel's planes and artillery scattered small pieces of metal in the sky to confuse it, helicopters carried electronic warfare devices to jam it, and missiles were fired to destroy it. After that came an attack on conventional antiaircraft guns, as well as attacks on Egyptian airfields to keep enemy fighter jets grounded.

When all the above was completed, the Israelis rolled out their finale: wave after wave of planes sent to destroy the SAM batteries themselves. This was the most complicated phase of the operation. The pilots were instructed to fly through imaginary pipelines in the sky, spaced tightly together, but attacking from different directions. The "time over the target" for each plane was choreographed not to the minute, but to the second ("That's not a typo!" one pilot wrote in his memoir. "The planning and precision was measured in seconds"). One squadron commander said the mission required more aerobatics than one sees at a demonstration of the American Blue Angels.[4]

The air force needed a minimum of twenty-four hours preparation to attack the SAMs. But the teams worked through the night and the operation got under way at 6:30 A.M. In less than an hour the initial phases were all completed. Dan Halutz, who later rose to command the Israeli air force, said the results destroying conventional antiaircraft guns were only so-so. But Air Force Command was pleased overall. The losses to that point were acceptable—only two A-4 Skyhawks—and everything was teed up for the destruction of the missiles. Peled put the failures of the day before behind him. Egypt's SAMs would soon be destroyed. The IAF would soon control the skies. And then Egypt's force east of the canal would be wiped out as planned.[5]

\* \* \*

It was a shaken Moshe Dayan who arrived at Northern Command at six in the morning on October 7. There General Hofi gave him a report that was far more pessimistic than what Elazar had told Dayan only an hour before. The southern Golan had been breached; Syrian tanks were pouring through. Hofi said he had only thirty-two tanks left in the entire southern Golan, and at least three of them were out of ammunition. Orders had already been given to destroy documents in Nafekh and set up a defensive line along the Jordan River. The bulk of the reservists were not expected to arrive until that afternoon, and without them, there was little preventing the Syrians from driving straight down the Heights through Degania into northern Israel.[6]

The Syrians would already have been in northern Israel if they had not stopped inexplicably the night before, just as victory was within their grasp. The Syrian brigade that turned north was stopped just a few miles south of Nafekh. But in the decades since, historians have struggled to understand why the Syrian forces that turned west and south paused to regroup on the night of October 6–7 when they could have continued unmolested to the Jordan River. It is possible they were afraid the clever Israelis were setting an ambush. It is possible they did not want to expose their right flank while the northern Golan was still in Israeli hands. Yet another explanation was supplied by a former Syrian officer interviewed for this account. He speculated that the men stopped because the war plan called for them to stop, and in the Syrian army, no good deed went unpunished. An officer who took the initiative against the Israelis might just take the initiative back home and topple the regime.[7]

* * *

Dayan and the generals in Northern Command knew it would not be long before Assad gave the green light and the Syrians continued west. They ordered preparations to blow up the Jordan River bridges. General Dan Laner, one of the most respected divisional commanders in the army, told Dayan that the battle for the Golan was lost. Another old warhorse, Colonel Yisachar "Yishka" Shadmi, agreed and said that unlike in 1948, this time there were no Molotov cocktails in Degania to hold off the Syrians. The only thing the kibbutzniks could throw at them were bottles of wine.[8]

An air force officer present said that Dayan looked like a broken man crying for help. Another said that Dayan was so upset it was difficult to understand him. By contrast, Elazar kept his cool. A witness said that he saw him in the darkest hours of the war and "learned a lesson in what leadership is about." Elazar calmly called Peled and told him that the air force was the only thing that could hold off the Syrians, and planes had to be sent north immediately.[9]

After hanging up with Elazar, Peled huddled with his senior officers. What was said in the meeting remained secret for thirty years. It was a lieutenant colonel named Amos Amir that finally broke the silence.[10] Peled told his staff that he planned to call off the operation in Egypt, send all the planes to defend the Golan, and destroy Syria's SAMs.

Peled's officers were dumbfounded. Defending the Golan was an obvious necessity. But the plan to destroy the SAMs, codenamed Operation Dougman 5, made no sense. These were not operations that could be turned on and off like a water tap. Carrying out Dougman 5 at that moment, without preparation, would mean the pilots would have no artillery support, no jamming of enemy radar, and worst of all, no idea where Syria's missile batteries were located. The most up-to-date reconnaissance photos were two days old. Syria's air defense was based largely on the SAM-6, the newest missile battery in the Soviet arsenal, against which the Israelis and even the Americans had no experience. But it was known that unlike the SAM-2 and SAM-3, the SAM-6 was mobile and could be easily moved from place to place.[11]

Lieutenant Colonel Amir called the decision to stop Operation Tagar and initiate Dougman 5 Israel's biggest tactical blunder of the war, worse even than the decision not to mobilize the reservists. "There was no person, no force, that could tell Peled 'you are making a catastrophic blunder. Don't do it.'" Two of Peled's most senior officers pleaded with him to allow the air force to complete Operation Tagar rather than start over with Dougman 5. His chief of operations, Giora Forman, told him that the air force had a plan for just this scenario and had enough planes to complete the job in Egypt and still defend the Golan. The destruction of the Syrian SAMs could wait. By then Forman's relationship with Peled was strained. The two had gotten into a screaming match during the opening hours of the war over Peled's decision to strip the ammunition off the fighter jets and use every one for defense.[12]

Peled was just as unmoved this time. No plane would return to Egypt. Instead, every fighter jet would be sent to hold the line in the Golan and destroy Syria's surface-to-air missiles.

Lieutenant Colonel Yiftach Spector, one of the IAF's squadron commanders, writes that when he landed his F-4 and was told he would be attacking SAM batteries in Syria instead of Egypt, "I began to question the sanity of the world around me." The operation went forward anyway, even though it never had a chance. The pilots who made it into Syria looked down and saw missile sites, but no missiles. Syrian defense minister Mustapha Tlass wrote in his memoir that most of the SAM-6s had been moved that morning to protect the 1st Division in its drive to conquer Nafekh. Out of twenty-five Syrian SAMs, only one was destroyed and one damaged. Against that, Israel lost six planes and saw ten others damaged. Fully 10 percent of the planes that took part in the mission were downed or damaged, a loss rate that is unacceptable in any air force, but doubly so in an air force as small as Israel's. The one silver lining was that Dougman 5 was carried out in such a hurry that only three quarters of the planes planned for the mission actually took off. Had more planes participated, more would have been shot down.[13]

Operation Dougman 5 would be remembered as the biggest disaster in the history of the Israeli air force. Peled later defended himself, saying that he was ordered by Dayan and Elazar to carry it out because the Golan Heights had to be rescued. Decades later, two distinguished Israeli historians working separately were given access to the tape recordings of what was said that morning. Both concluded that Peled's version was untrue. Dayan and Elazar ordered him to rescue the Golan. But they never told him how to deploy his jets, never mentioned stopping Operation Tagar, and never ordered him to carry out Dougman 5.[14]

\* \* \*

Elazar next had to decide where to send the reserve 146th Division, commanded by General Moshe "Mussa" Peled (no relation to Benny Peled, the air force commander). There were three choices.

The fiasco along the canal left practically no Israeli tanks between the Egyptian army and the Israeli border. But would Egypt press farther east through the Mitla and Gidi passes toward Israel? Elazar sent a pilot on a hair-raising reconnaissance mission to find out. To the surprise of AMAN, the pilot reported that the bulk of Egypt's tanks were still west of the canal. There was only one conclusion: there was still time before the Egyptian army might go back on the attack.[15] He decided not to send the 146th there.

Elazar next summoned one of Israel's most highly regarded intelligence officers, a passionate, German-born analyst named Colonel Zev Bar-Lavi. Bar-Lavi taught himself Arabic, dedicated his life to studying King Hussein, and became "top-secret famous" by correctly predicting that Jordan would enter the '67 war.* This time, Bar-Lavi told Elazar he did not have to worry about the Jordanian border. Jordan had no surface-to-air missiles to counter the Israeli air force and no hope of resupply from the Soviet Union. There was no chance that the king would enter the war. Despite the failures of the previous forty-eight hours, Elazar gambled he could still depend on AMAN in a pinch and made one of the gutsiest decisions of the war. Against the advice of Assistant Chief of Staff Yisroel Tal, he left the border with Jordan undefended. Mussa Peled and the 146th Division were sent to the Golan.[16]

Peled's division had already been hard at work through the night preparing tanks for battle. The IDF never thought it would be caught by surprise, so it never trained for preparing tanks under emergency conditions. Luckily, someone remembered that the military base was located near a kibbutz that manufactured forklifts. It had never been tried before, but during the night two forklifts were hurriedly trucked in on a flatbed and used to move shells from warehouses to the bellies of the tanks. Soldiers estimated that this daring (and arguably reckless) move saved six crucial hours.[17]

Peled drove to the command center on Mount Canaan in Safed from where he could look down on the Golan Heights. Dayan's "Third Temple at risk" statement spread through the ranks like a brush fire and scorched Peled's ears as well. But after looking through his binoculars, Peled concluded that the Golan was far from lost, to say nothing of the Third Temple. He could see that

---

* A young officer once reported for duty at AMAN's Jordan desk and asked why the unit was having a party. Bar-Lavi looked at him askance and asked, "Don't you know that today is King Hussein's birthday???"

the Syrians had hundreds of tanks. He could see that they were not far from the Jordan River. But he also saw something else.

Israeli reservists were driving up the rise heading into battle.[18]

* * *

Unlike the canal, where prewar plans were ignored and surprise was total, in the Golan Heights the Israelis were on the line in a state of partial readiness. After the war the Israelis lamented that had they mobilized just one additional brigade—just a hundred more tanks—the Syrians would have been doomed from the outset. The Syrians lamented the same in reverse: had Israel *not* mobilized the 7th Brigade and *not* had an extra hundred tanks on the line, their surprise attack would have succeeded. As for Israel's reservists, the Syrians gambled they would not arrive for twenty-four hours. As it turned out, they made it up to the Heights in only twelve.[19] *

In short, the Israelis had fared badly defending the Golan, but the Syrians had fared only marginally better attacking it. At four in the morning in the early hours of October 7, the Syrian 7th Division made another attempt to conquer the northern Golan. From positions behind their antitank ditch, the Israelis discovered ninety Syrian tanks heading their way and opened fire. There was no need to call in flares for illumination. The fireball of each incinerated tank lit the way for the destruction of the next until the entire Syrian force was wiped out. The Israeli commander, Lieutenant Colonel Avigdor Kahalani, later said that he was startled to see the Syrians fighting to the last tank ("There was not one coward among them").[20]

Farther south, barely five miles east of Nafekh near Outpost 110, another Syrian tank force surged forward in what turned into a modern version of the Charge of the Light Brigade. The Syrian battalion drove west all guns ablaze, fighting practically to the

---

* Hofi and his staff came in for praise from the Agranat Commission for taking steps in 1972 to move supply depots closer to the front and thereby shorten mobilization time.

last man until it was annihilated. The battle ended when the lead
Syrian tank was hit, killing or wounding all inside except the battalion commander. He leaped out of the burning vehicle, charged
on foot toward the Israelis firing his rifle, screaming, "*Allahu Akbar!*" and was gunned down in a hail of bullets. For his valor, he
was posthumously awarded Hero of the Republic, Syria's highest
military honor.[21]

Balanced against its failures in the north and central Golan was
Syria's successful breakthrough in the south. A bird flying over
the Golan on the morning of October 7 would have looked down
and seen Israeli olive-drab uniforms in the north and west, and
Syrian leopard-camouflage uniforms in the south and east. At that
moment there was far less olive-drab balanced against leopard-
camouflage, but the seesaw could still tip in either direction.

In the south, the Syrians charged once more into the breach,
this time with their elite 1st Division and its 326 tanks. The Israelis responded in the only way they could, by throwing in the air
force to slow them down. Before the war, Israel's leading theorist
on armored warfare, General Yisroel Tal, wrote that it was impossible for planes to stop tanks by themselves. Dayan later remarked dryly that "fortunately, the Arabs never read the book." In
truth, the air force flew only ninety-seven sorties before stopping
abruptly at ten A.M. to prepare for Operation Dougman 5. According to one study, they did not hit a single tank (plainly there
was something to what General Tal was saying). But the value of
what the air force accomplished was not measured in tanks, but
in time. The Syrians were slowed just long enough to allow the reservists to win the race. An Israeli reserve brigade commanded by
Colonel Ran Sarig arrived half an hour before the Syrians would
have reached the Jordan River.[22]

The fiercest battles were fought around Israel's command and
control center in Nafekh. Colonel Simhoni told a historian that
if Nafekh had fallen, the Israeli counterattack would have been
impossible and General Peled's 146th Division would have been

ordered to take up positions defending northern Israel. The Syrians understood the calculus all too well and further reasoned that if they could bypass Nafekh and continue north, they could cut off Israel's 7th Armored Brigade from behind and roll up Israel's line like a Persian rug.[23]

When General Hofi fled Nafekh the night before, he left command in the hands of Rafael Eitan, a forty-four-year-old brigadier general reputed to have the hardest head in the Israeli army. The surgeons that extracted a bullet from his skull in 1967 found shell fragments left over from a head wound he received in 1948. His dirt-poor parents told him that they would have terminated him if only they could have scraped together the two Palestinian pounds to pay for the abortion. Fortunately for Eitan and the future Jewish state's army, the doctor did not work on credit.[24]

At 7:30 on the morning of October 7, the order was handed down in Nafekh: the Syrians were at the gates, and everyone had to evacuate. Eitan describes a surreal scene in which he emerged from his bunker and was taunted by a foreign television crew that, "seeing us retreat, could not conceal its schadenfreude." There were still a few broken-down tanks under repair on a nearby helicopter pad. Their damaged tracks rendered them immobile, but the cannons worked, so the crews and repairmen piled inside and blasted away.[25]

At that very moment, the first elements of Israel's 679th Armored Brigade arrived. The 679th was something of a novelty in the army because a quarter of its men were the first to enlist under *hesder*, a program that allowed boys to fulfill part of their military service through religious study in yeshivas. No one yet knew if the army could make soldiers out of Talmudic scholars.[26]

The main Syrian effort came from the south up the Tapline Road. It was a hundred of Syria's best tanks commanded by Walid Khamdun, one of the ablest officers in the Syrian army. But fourteen Israeli tanks blocked their path, and by nine o'clock the pressure on Nafekh eased. One of the fourteen was commanded by none other than Tzvika Greengold, who by now had been forced to abandon two tanks and was fighting inside his third. Another second lieutenant named Nati Levy was forced to abandon no fewer than six different tanks over the course of the previous twenty-four hours. After the last one was hit, he scrambled out and took refuge in a hilltop bunker called Tel Saki.[27]

General Eitan returned to Nafekh with his staff at 10:15 A.M. and attempted to reestablish communications with all the units under his command. For the first time since the Syrian break-through, it looked as if the line was finally holding. Things were stable enough that at 10:00 A.M. General Elazar ordered every fighter jet not engaged in Dougman 5 to fly back to the canal. At 12:50 in the afternoon AMAN gave an "extremely optimistic assessment," in the words of the Agranat Commission.[28] The optimism lasted exactly ten minutes.[29]

Colonel Ori Orr, commander of the 679th Armored Brigade, was positioned opposite Kuneitra, and from his vantage point all was quiet on the eastern front. But from his rear, five miles off to the west, he could hear the distinct sound of tank fire. He tried to raise someone, anyone, on the wireless, but all he heard was silence. It gave him an unsettled feeling, even though he knew the radio silence was to be expected given the damage to antennas in and around Nafekh.

Finally, at around 1:00 P.M. he received word from General Hofi, calling him directly from Northern Command atop Mount Canaan. What was he doing in Kuneitra? Hadn't he received orders from General Eitan? Orr replied that he had not heard anything from anyone. With that, General Hofi told him to drop everything and return to Nafekh.[30]

\* \* \*

Just moments before, the chief intelligence officer in Nafekh was choking on the dense cigarette smoke in the crowded command bunker and went outside to get some air. The officer was tasked with knowing where the Syrians were, and upon emerging he found them. A hundred tanks were speeding directly toward him, the elite Syrian 91st Armored Brigade attacking with everything it had. Syrian defense minister Mustapha Tlass later wrote that all the pent-up anger of the Syrian nation was channeled into those hundred tanks.[31]

What ensued was one of the epic battles of the Yom Kippur War. The Israeli intelligence officer ran back inside the command bunker to report that he had indeed found the enemy. General Eitan absorbed the news calmly. "With ice in his veins," in the words of one historian, he abandoned his command bunker for the second time in six hours. His staff was not quite as coolheaded and bolted without taking coded maps and other sensitive documents. The last man out remembered all the Arab battle flags his father captured and proudly displayed after the '67 war. Wanting to avoid a similar humiliation—and with bullets and shrapnel whizzing in every direction—he ran back, ignored the sensitive material, and retrieved all Israeli army flags.[32]

Orr's tanks were the first to make it to Nafekh. When they arrived the base appeared empty, except for a dog that was tied to the gate "barking like crazy." His brigade was armed with old World War II–era tanks. And though they were confronting T-62s, the finest in the Soviet arsenal, they fought the Syrians to a standstill (it turned out Talmudic scholars made superb soldiers). One Israeli officer's tank was hit, killing his driver. He jumped out with his uniform on fire and ran until he bumped into none other than General Eitan directing the battle from a nearby hill. Not realizing the officer's ordeal, Eitan screamed, "Soldier! Where's your tank?" The officer replied with perfect Israeli chutzpah, "And you! Where's your division?"[33]

At that moment the division was rushing back to Nafekh. Among them was Colonel Yitzchak Ben-Shoham, commander of the 188th Armored Brigade. The 188th was the hard-luck unit that had the misfortune of manning the southern Golan when the war broke out. Ben-Shoham and his assistant were killed on the drive back to Nafekh. When that occurred, at approximately two in the afternoon, the entire 188th—which started the war with approximately two thousand men—was left without a single combat officer. This is the moment when armies often collapse into unorganized retreat. The men of the 188th fought on.[34]

The battle seesawed all afternoon. At one point, the Israelis intercepted a wireless message from a Syrian brigade commander reporting that he had conquered Nafekh. He was mistaken. Among the Israeli soldiers that raced into battle was the ubiquitous Tzvika Greengold, his blond hair now singed black from earlier hits his tanks had sustained. His lone tank drove onto the base and opened fire on seven Syrian tanks that were pressing forward along the fences. There were still other Syrian tanks streaming down a hill toward them. But a second tank joined Greengold's and together they turned back the Syrian assault. At four in the afternoon, the Syrians broke off the attack. Many abandoned their vehicles and headed back to Syria on foot. It was only then that hundreds of Israeli soldiers, hiding in every nook and cranny of the base, emerged. "They didn't look like an army," Greengold later wrote. "They looked like a bunch of people whose lives were saved by a miracle."[35]

That evening, the results of the day's fighting were presented to President Assad and his command. Israeli reservists were pouring in. The Israeli army was estimated to have lost a hundred tanks, but the Syrian army was estimated to have lost six hundred, more than two thirds of the number that crossed the border.[36] An Israeli counterattack was expected. Morale was low.

Assad grew angry and slammed his fist on the table.[37]

\* \* \*

Many Israelis later spoke of the bizarre transition they experienced that Yom Kippur. One minute they were sitting in their homes with family or in their synagogues praying. Just a few hours later, they were sitting in tanks or armored personnel carriers fighting for their lives.[38] Though far from the battlefield, the transition was felt just as acutely in Golda Meir's government. Most of her ministers were kept in the dark as to the brewing crisis in the days leading up to the war. At a meeting on the morning of October 7, most were boiling with anger.

Briefing them, General Elazar put the best face possible on the crisis, taking care to keep the worst of the war news from them. The battle on the Golan was still raging, its outcome very much in doubt. Dayan was still thinking about the Third Temple. Later that day he told his generals that even if the line held in the north, the bigger problem was that Israel had already lost more than two hundred tanks and thirty-two planes. The Arabs to that point had lost only forty aircraft, leaving a near one-to-one loss ratio that was as unthinkable as it was unsustainable. At the current rate, the army would run out of weapons in barely a week. There was only one source of resupply, and it was hardly reliable. Dayan did not know it yet, but later that day, Kissinger would tell Ambassador Simcha Dinitz that there was fierce opposition inside the Pentagon to selling Israel any additional F-4 fighter jets.[39]

Dayan bided his time. Notably, he waited for Elazar to leave and fly off in a waiting helicopter. The meeting ended shortly after that and the ministers filed out, their gray mood mirrored by the gray cigarette smoke that wafted out the door with them. When the government stenographer was no longer present to record what was said, Dayan gestured everyone to come back inside, as if he reminded himself of a minor detail he forgot to raise earlier. Then he closed the door.[40] *

---

* What happened behind that door was revealed by Arnon Azaryahu, an aide to Minister Yisroel Galili, in a six-hour interview that he gave in 2008 just ten months before his death at age ninety-two. The person who interviewed him was Israeli-born historian Dr. Avner Cohen, who after releasing his first book on Israel's nuclear program in 1999 was told that he would be prosecuted if he entered the country. Against the advice of friends and lawyers, Cohen traveled to Israel in 2001 and dared the police to arrest him. He was briefly detained, but after three years of investigations, the state prosecutor had chosen not to bring charges.

Dayan's words jolted everyone in the room: he wanted authorization to "begin preparations for a display of nuclear power." This way, he explained, if the government later gave the go-ahead, it could set off the weapons immediately and save the half day needed to prepare. Dayan brought along Shalhevet Freier, director general of the Israel Atomic Agency Commission, who sat silently outside the meeting room, waiting to receive orders.[41]

Voices rose in tandem with the tension in the room. Deputy Prime Minister Yigal Allon and a highly regarded minister named Yisroel Galili did not just declare their opposition, they shouted it. Dayan, his hand still on the door, pleaded his case with Golda. In an interview not released until more than twenty-five years after his death, Deputy Prime Minister Yigal Allon said that "Dayan seized upon nuclear weapons as a weapon of salvation, out of despair."[42]

Golda Meir's command of the Hebrew language was never perfect. It had a way of becoming even less perfect in moments of stress. She lapsed into Yiddish or English, her two mother tongues, when things were at their worst.

She looked at Dayan dismissively and said in English, "Forget about it."

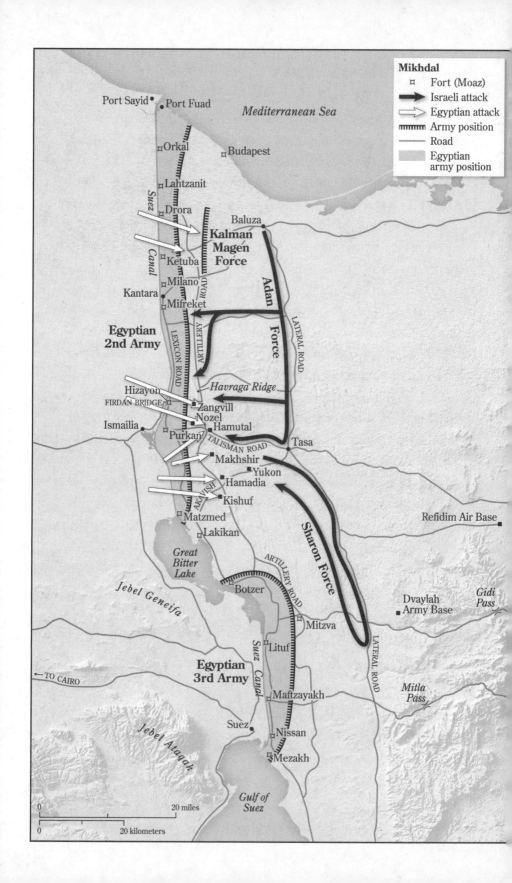

# 10

# *MIKHDAL*: THE COUNTERATTACK

The job of an administrator is only half completed upon the issuance of an order; it is discharged when he determines the order has been executed.

—Report of the Joint Committee on the Investigation of the
Pearl Harbor Attack, US Congress (1946)[1]

It was at the Dvaylah army command center near the canal, at noon on October 7, that Dayan made his "Third Temple at risk" pronouncement. According to Gonen, Dayan was "very upset, nervously rubbing his hands together." Earlier that day Dayan had heard that the battle was lost in the Golan. He arrived at the same conclusion with respect to the battle along the canal. Dayan proclaimed—once again, as a "ministerial suggestion"—that the army should withdraw east to the passes.[2]

Had his advice been taken, Israel would have lost the use of the Dvaylah army base as well as the massive Refidim air base. The Egyptians might not have advanced all the way to the passes, beyond the range of their surface-to-air missiles. But they would have certainly advanced far enough to make any later Israeli crossing of the canal impossible. Dayan's advice was all the more questionable because it was hardly the time to panic. At that moment, the farthest point of Egypt's offensive extended less than two miles from the canal. Later, Dayan's harshest critics accused him of having undergone nothing less than a nervous breakdown. Some pointed to the high incidence of mental illness in the Dayan family, which included his son, numerous nieces and nephews, and a sister who committed suicide. Others who witnessed Dayan throughout the war said that the assertion was untrue. He was more pessimistic than he should have been, but perfectly grounded and far from a state of collapse. And then there was his aide General Ze'evi, who told members of the General Staff that given the risk of running out of weapons and the fear that Jordan might enter the war, Dayan was not overly pessimistic. It was rather that they were overly optimistic.[3]

As was often the case, what changed everything was Ariel Sharon. He arrived at the canal in the early afternoon of October 7, drove right up to the front, and immediately concluded that the situation was not nearly as bad as everyone thought. His optimism seems to have had an immediate effect on Gonen, who then ordered the army to dig in along the Artillery Road, just six miles east of the canal. It was a courageous decision for which Gonen never received proper credit.[4]

Gonen was not the only general who pushed back against Dayan's pessimism. General Peled overheard the General Staff making plans to withdraw to the passes. He stormed out of the Bunker and slammed the door behind him, crying aloud, "If you keep planning a retreat, I'll come back in here personally with an Uzi and mow you all down!" With that, he ran down the corridor to the air force command center and ordered his planes to bomb Egypt's bridges over the canal.[5]

This was another of Peled's impulsive decisions that made sense only in the heat of the moment. The pilots were then returning from Dougman 5. They had only to look down from their cockpits to see Syrian tanks rampaging across the southern Golan. All expected to be sent back north to help hold the line. When they landed, they were told that no, they were not going back to Syria. They were going back to the canal.

"Will we be going back to complete Operation Tagar?" one pilot asked.

"No," came the reply, "you will be bombing bridges over the canal."

Bridges?

Destroying bridges was not in any of the IAF's war plans. Lieutenant Colonel Yiftach Spector said that the only thing he knew about bombing bridges was that there was one in Hanoi that the American air force kept hitting, but which somehow always remained in service. At least the Americans knew where the Hanoi bridge was located. The Israelis could only guess where, along the hundred-mile canal, the Egyptians had laid theirs. Pilots would have just a split second to spot them. From the sky, a bridge appeared as a thread strung across blue velvet. And, of course, the pilots had to find them in an area saturated with surface-to-air missiles. This was why the air force never planned to bomb bridges in the first place.[6]

The initial reports from Syria earlier that morning were jubilant. Dayan told the government that the IAF destroyed fully 70 percent of the Syrian SAMs. Early reports from the air raid along the canal were just as optimistic. The IAF paid a terrible price: ten planes were downed and six more damaged. But Peled told Elazar that his pilots had destroyed seven out of fourteen Egyptian bridges and that he would have the remainder knocked out by nightfall.[7]

At last, there was some good news from the canal front. Elazar told Peled to come immediately to his office so he could give him a kiss.[8]

* * *

AMAN's intelligence coup, obtaining Egypt's war plans, allowed the IDF to predict Egypt's crossing of the canal with remarkable accuracy. The Egyptian Second Army had conquered a tiny sliver of land abutting the northern portion of the Suez Canal. The Egyptian Third Army had conquered a tiny sliver of land abutting the southern portion of the Suez Canal. An Egyptian "First Army," though not referred to as such, was left west of the canal in reserve. There was a large gap between the Second Army and the Third Army, comprising the territory along the eastern shores of the Great Bitter Lake. As expected, the Egyptians left this ground in Israeli hands because it was outside the range of Egypt's SAMs.[9]

AMAN had every reason to believe that the remainder of the captured Egyptian war plan would be followed as well. But then, on the afternoon of October 7, a strange thing happened. The Egyptians did not send more tanks over the canal, nor did they continue their drive farther east to the passes. For some reason, they seemed frozen in place. On that October 7 afternoon— notwithstanding Shazly's assertion in his memoir that the Egyptians had more than a thousand tanks east of the canal—AMAN concluded based on photo reconnaissance that the Egyptians had no more than four hundred tanks on the two slivers of land, divided evenly between the Egyptian Second and Third Armies.[10]

The two Egyptian armies were too far apart to help each other, leaving them dangerously spread out with only about four tanks per mile. General Peled drew what seemed to be the obvious conclusion, one he was not shy about sharing with others: the Egyptian offensive had stalled because his planes had knocked out the bridges.[11]

The Israelis had another reason for cautious optimism, though it was of the good news / bad news variety. The good news was that on the morning of October 8, they had five hundred tanks along the canal, far more than any prewar planner thought possible.[*] The bad news was that two hundred more had broken down on

---

[*] One officer pulled up to a local civilian gas station at the head of a column of tanks. The tanks filled up, the officer handed the bemused station owner an IOU, and the column continued on its journey to the front.

the way to the front. They sat smoking at the side of the road because tanks, especially World War II–era tanks, were supposed to be transported on special flatbed trailers rather than driven hundreds of miles.* Those that made it clogged the narrow roads, making it impossible for artillery to get through.[12]

By this point, over 150 Israeli tanks had been damaged or destroyed by Egypt's RPG-7s and Saggers. Yet no one took the time to study the problem and formulate countermeasures. Likewise, AMAN never seems to have seriously considered the possibility that Egypt *chose* not to continue its drive to the passes, and *wanted* an Israeli counterattack in order to inflict casualties. Mossad Chief Zvi Zamir warned of this possibility but he was ignored. Later, commentators spoke of the Egyptians having entered an "operative pause." But that term was coined only after the war.[13]

In short, IDF commanders should have been concerned with Egyptian infantry armed with RPG-7s and Saggers. Instead, guided by thinking from the last war, they focused more on the number of Egyptian tanks that had crossed. Since the Israelis had a slight advantage in tanks east of the canal, and since it appeared the Egyptian army's offensive had stalled, Gonen and Ariel Sharon advised Elazar to launch a full-scale counterattack. The goal was nothing less than destroying the Egyptian Second Army and crossing the canal.[14]

Golda's government had the final say. It met late on the afternoon of October 7 to decide what to do. Dayan spoke with admirable candor. "I did not properly assess the strength of the enemy," he said, "plus I exaggerated our ability to withstand them." He then opined that there was no chance of retaking the Bar-Lev Line. He repeated his fear that the nation would run out of weapons and recommended withdrawing to the passes. Golda listened to him "in horror."[15]

---

* The IDF had 284 trailers in total, of which only 131 were "fast" trailers. The remainder were either "slow" trailers or civilian trailers that had to be mobilized. These had to transport approximately 1,300 tanks (477 tanks were already on the line when the war began).

Elazar kept his cool. There was no reason for panic, and certainly no reason to retreat to the passes. But neither was it time for any risky counterattacks across the canal, as Gonen and Sharon wanted. The wisest course, Elazar counseled, was to solidify the line and set the stage for a counterattack later. It was a good presentation of a sensible position, and it won the support of Golda and her government. None of the ministers had been in the field to see the situation for themselves, and only two of them had the military background to judge it even if they had. What won the day was Elazar's cool demeanor and ability to instill optimism. "He acted the way I would expect a chief of staff to act," one general who witnessed the scene remembered. "I imagine he was more pessimistic inside than he let on. But he never lost his head once."[16]

This latest rejection of Dayan's advice—an indignity unthinkable before the war—brought him to the breaking point. He took Golda aside and offered to resign. "Unless I have your confidence," he said, "I can't go on." This was only a few hours after the morning meeting in which Dayan recommended preparing nuclear weapons. Golda was resolute. She had not lost confidence in him, she said, and what's more, he *had* to stay on. She later said she never regretted the decision.[17]

* * *

With the government's approval in hand, Elazar rushed to the Dvaylah army base near the canal to put his plan into action. Elazar wanted to firm up the line opposite the Egyptians before they could send reinforcements and before they could push farther east to the passes. "Our estimation was that Egypt wanted to conquer the Passes," Gonen said after the war. "This is what guided all the things we did."[18]

By now Elazar knew that it was Egypt's Saggers and RPGs that were causing the casualties, not its tanks. He also knew that most of the Egyptian Saggers were positioned atop battle ramps near the canal, both on the west bank where the Egyptians had built them and the east bank where they seized them from the Israelis in the early hours of the war. Success depended on staying out of range of those missiles.[19]

Elazar therefore ordered a north–south attack that at all times would remain two to three kilometers east of the canal, out of range of the Saggers. The goal was to box the Egyptians into a tight area no more than three kilometers wide along the east bank of the canal, without going near the canal itself. Driving the Egyptians out, crossing the canal—these would have to wait for later. The IDF could not risk losing any more tanks at this delicate moment. Elazar was also clear that of the three divisions then along the canal, no more than one could be on the attack at any given time. When one of the three divisions went on the attack, the other two had to remain in reserve in case something went wrong.[20]

The plan was improvised and presented in the same tiny room where Gonen slept. Elazar gave all his orders verbally, and this after not having slept for almost forty-eight hours. The assembled commanders had also gone without sleep for a day and were hearing everything for the first time. Ariel Sharon did not hear anything directly from Elazar, because his helicopter was late bringing him to the meeting.[21] *

A conference held after the war revealed that there were no fewer than three different understandings of what Elazar had said. In one version Sharon's division was to attack north to south. In another it was to attack south to north. No one could say for sure which version was correct even after the war, because even after the meeting no written orders were ever issued. Southern Command sent Elazar a written version of what it understood the plan

---

* Sharon got into a heated argument with Gonen earlier that day. Sharon wanted to attempt a rescue of the men trapped in the *maozim*, something Gonen refused. Sharon would go on to charge that Gonen orchestrated the helicopter's delay to prevent him from raising the issue at the meeting. Gonen's evasive answer to the Agranat Commission on this issue lends some credence to the claim. But no hard evidence of a plot ever came to light.

to be. But it did not reach him until the morning of October 8, by which time the battle had already begun. Elazar approved it even though he could not remember later if he ever read it. To the Agranat Commission, he said, "I cannot read every piece of paper put before me in the middle of a battle."[22]

Reading the document probably would not have made any difference. Gonen had plans of his own.

* * *

Strangely, given the importance of the counterattack, Elazar chose not to be present in Dvaylah to personally command the operation but rather went to Tel Aviv for a meeting with the government. Thus, at approximately 8:00 A.M. on the morning of October 8, it was Gonen that gave the order to General Avraham "Bren" Adan to commence the attack. In accordance with Elazar's instructions, the other two divisions under Gonen's command— the 143rd under Sharon and the 252nd under General Avraham "Albert" Mandler—were to remain in reserve until Adan's 162nd carried out its leg of the mission.[23]

Elazar later said that if even one commander had said they were not ready, he would have postponed the operation. No one said anything because, as one general put it, "it was an extraordinarily simple operation; all you had to do was figure out which way was north and which way south." It should not have been difficult to peel off the lead Egyptian forces and firm up a line. In only two places had the Egyptians advanced more than three kilometers.[24]

Adan's division made good progress, albeit for a bad reason. Ariel Sharon stood on the Havraga Ridge, along the front, looked westward through binoculars, and heard tanks out of the north coming up behind him. He immediately recognized them as Adan's tanks heading south. The trouble was, they were traveling some seven to eight miles east of where they were supposed to be. A colonel in Adan's force later testified that on that journey south, he never saw a single Egyptian soldier. The improvised operation had never been practiced, and in an era before GPS, there were few visual landmarks in the monotonous Sinai desert to offer navigational guidance. At 9:05 A.M., Gonen realized that the division was too far east of the canal and sensibly ordered Adan to head west to "look for the enemy."[25]

Then, barely fifteen minutes later, he called Adan back. This time he ordered him to continue west *all the way to the canal.*

Gonen still wanted him to attack from north to south. But now he wanted the attack to proceed along the banks of the canal, not three kilometers to the east as Elazar ordered. Doing this required destroying the entire Egyptian Second Army across a thirty-five-mile front, from Kantara all the way to the Matzmed *maoz.* Adan had only 170 tanks under his command. He could not have carried out this new operation with a force five times that size. A lieutenant colonel approached the canal near the Firdan Bridge, looked down at the enormous army before him, and was reminded of a verse in the Bible: "all the chariots of Egypt."[26]

Not satisfied with that, Gonen also ordered Adan to capture two bridges and use them to cross into Egypt. He might just as well have ordered him to conquer Cairo. It was far from clear if Egypt's bridges could carry Israel's tanks. Egypt's Soviet-made tanks all weighed less than forty tons. Apart from the practically obsolete World War II–era Sherman tanks, Israel's American- and British-made tanks all weighed more than fifty. Captured documents later demonstrated that the Egyptians were aware of the risk of Israel capturing a bridge and took no chances. The bridges that could handle tank traffic were dismantled after October 7 and reassembled only briefly on October 13 and 14. The others could handle only light vehicles like supply trucks and were wired with explosives in case they were captured.[27]

Gonen then radioed Sharon. He ordered him to abandon his position, head south all the way to the Mezakh *maoz* over forty miles away, seize an Egyptian bridge, and cross the canal near the city of Suez. Sharon pointed out to him that Adan's attack was bogged down near the canal and nowhere near complete. Elazar's orders were clear that only one division could attack at a time. Worse, if Sharon abandoned his position atop the Havraga Ridge, it would potentially open a hole in the Israeli line and expose Adan's flank. Gonen told him to ignore this. The mission farther south was "more important."[28]

Gonen's later attempt to explain this brazen act of foolishness made for some of the most dramatic testimony before the Agranat Commission. Gonen explained that, in his mind, Elazar had not put forth a plan, but rather just an "idea." It was Gonen's job, he believed, to translate this idea into an operation. The italicized words in the transcript of the proceeding gives voice to the Commission's anger: "Do you mean to tell me that the chief of staff—*whose plan represented a decisive mission that the entire government and the minister of defense waited upon with bated breath*—that he merely came [to Dvaylah], offered an *idea* and then flew home?"[29]

The only thing one can say in Gonen's defense is that there was plenty of blame to go around. Elazar should have been in Dvaylah commanding the operation personally. Adan passed along rosy intelligence reports from the field without attempting to check their accuracy. These false reports of victory reached the General Staff in Tel Aviv and sparked jubilation. *Israeli forces had crossed the canal!* It was on the basis of this false information that Elazar was fooled into changing his own plan, taking advantage of the "success," and ordering a counterattack across the canal. He thus authorized Gonen to send Sharon's division south.[30]

And then there is the role played by Ariel Sharon. In his telling, he protested Gonen's order in "the strongest terms" but Gonen threatened to sack him if he refused, and so "I had no choice except to obey." This assertion is questionable. If ever there was a general who believed he had a "choice" to disobey orders, it was Ariel Sharon. Moreover, the Agranat Commission's final report makes no reference to any such protest. To the contrary, the report concluded that "there was no sign of hesitation" in Sharon's command once he got the order to head south. One of Sharon's greatest admirers, his assistant, General Jackie Even, writes that "there is no explanation, not even a forced one, for why he carried out Gonen's disastrous order."[31]

If anything, Sharon's actions demonstrated reckless enthusiasm. Upon receiving Gonen's order at about 10:30 A.M., he jumped into his jeep and took to the road to gather his forces and rush south. He was in such a hurry, he left without a radioman by his side and was unreachable for almost two hours. He used the fastest way south, the Lateral Road, which was more than ten miles east of the battlefield.[32]

In his haste, Sharon did not even take steps to ensure that the hills he abandoned were properly handed off to Adan's division. The force guarding the Nozel position atop the Zangvil Ridge was pulled off the line with no force sent in to replace it. It was described by an Israeli commander as "the key to the entire sector." The Egyptians quickly seized it.[33]

Elsewhere, Sharon's horrified staff stepped into the void as best they could. Sharon later claimed that he left his reconnaissance battalion to defend two crucial ridges called Hamadia and Kishuf. This, too, is contradicted by the record. Sharon's assistant, General Jackie Even, actually saved the day, defying orders and ordering the reconnaissance battalion to remain on Hamadia and Kishuf.[34]

The reconnaissance battalion numbered only twenty tanks, far too few to defend two ridges. But the battalion was commanded by Lieutenant Colonel Ben-Zion "Bentzi" Carmeli, an exceptionally able officer who managed to beat back a much larger Egyptian force. Sharon correctly referred to Hamadia and Kishuf as "two absolutely critical ridges." Had the two fallen, the Egyptians could have continued up the Akavish Road, conquered the IDF's canal-bridging equipment at a staging area called Yukon, and threatened the large military base at Tasa. If even *one* of the two ridges had fallen, the Akavish Road would have been blocked by Egypt. Its closure would have rendered any crossing of the canal impossible. In short, if either of the two ridges had fallen to Egypt, Israel would have almost certainly lost the Yom Kippur War.[35]

Carmeli, wounded twice before in other conflicts, had physical limitations that rendered him unfit for combat duty. Fortunately for the State of Israel, he refused to take no for an answer and won a combat commission by sheer determination. He was killed on that October 8 afternoon, leading his men, and thus earned the tragic distinction of being perhaps the greatest hero in the history of the Israeli army that no one has ever heard of. For reasons known only to them, the IDF committee in charge of military awards posthumously awarded him only the Chief of Staff Citation. It is Israel's fourth highest honor.[36]

* * *

Adan was puzzled by the order to push all the way to the canal. He did not find out that Gonen had changed Elazar's plan until after the war. But an order is an order, so he directed tanks from two of his battalions to push west to the canal. The entire force numbered only fifty-five tanks.[37]

One of Adan's battalion commanders, Lieutenant Colonel Asaf Yaguri, made a dash for the canal. A battalion commander in a sister unit said the sight reminded him of Soviet propaganda movies from World War II, in which men fought on through walls of fire until they fell dead. Yaguri's tanks initially shocked and awed the Egyptian defenders—until those defenders realized that there were no other tanks backing them up. That was when the Saggers came raining down in waves. Before the war, Israeli planners did not think much of the Saggers. Yaguri said that he went into battle having never heard of them. He learned the hard way. Yaguri's unit was practically wiped out. He himself was wounded and captured, thus becoming the highest-ranking Israeli ground officer of the war to fall into enemy hands. His commander, Colonel Natan "Natke" Nir, was asked by headquarters how the operation was going. Nir replied that in another minute there would be no one left to ask.[38]

Meanwhile, officers in Sharon's division were struggling to figure out why on earth they were suddenly ordered to head south. There seemed to be only one emergency that could justify pulling up stakes, leaving critical hills exposed, and rushing down the Lateral Road far from the battle. *The Egyptians must have achieved a breakthrough toward the Mitla and Gidi passes.* The source of the dark rumor might have been a colonel on Sharon's staff, referred to behind his back as the division's "Chief Panic Officer." Whatever the source, it created a strange paradox: as rumors of victory circulated upward among senior officers in Tel Aviv, rumors of catastrophe descended downward among junior officers in the field.[39]

At about 2:30 P.M. a helicopter landed near Sharon some forty miles away and ordered him to turn around and head back north. The order came down not a moment too soon. The Egyptians had begun a massive ground assault of their own, which threatened to turn Adan's flank and destroy his division. Adan remembered this as the worst moment of his military career, a career he began as junior officer in the 1948 war.[40]

October 8 would be remembered as the darkest day in the history of the Israeli army. In all, Israel lost sixty tanks, more than two battalions. Not only did the IDF fail to advance, it lost ground, including critical high ground taken by the Egyptian Second Army. Besides Zangvil, two other ridges, code-named Hamutal and Makhshir, were left poorly defended when Sharon's division headed south. Both fell to the Egyptians. Their loss made it impossible for the Israelis to reach the canal via the Talisman Road, which had been paved before the war to create one of the jump-off points across the canal. Over the next week, the Israelis would make no fewer than nine attempts to retake these ridges. All nine failed.[41]

The failures crisscrossed the battlefield. One of Adan's brigade commanders reported that the Hamutal Ridge had been retaken, even though the counterattack had not even begun. Tanks from Sharon's division mistakenly fired upon tanks from Adan's division, and possibly destroyed four of them. The Hamutal Ridge was lost when a platoon of tanks simply turned around and drove off in the heat of battle. The battalion commander ordered the platoon leader to get his men back up on the line. He replied that his men had retreated against orders, and he was not willing to stay there by himself.[42]

And then there was the distrust among senior commanders that undermined the faith of all beneath them. Gonen sent the helicopter to track down Sharon because he could not get him on the radio. Colonel Aharon Tal received the radio call from Gonen and told him innocently that Sharon was not there. Tal was dumbfounded to hear Gonen respond that he did not believe him. "It was only then that I realized how serious our problem was," Tal remembered.[43]

It did not go unnoticed that the only place where the IDF experienced success was where its senior commanders were not involved. A brigadier general named Kalman Magen held the northernmost portion of the line with ninety tanks. When Egyptian tanks attacked, his men destroyed thirty-five of them and suffered almost no losses of their own. The result suggested that if the IDF had simply held the line instead of all the driving around, it could have wiped out the Egyptian assault and possibly gained ground in a classic counterattack.[44]

At General Staff headquarters, the bad news came cascading in all at once. They learned that Dougman 5 had not destroyed 70 percent of Syria's SAMs as initially reported but was instead a costly failure. The bombing of the bridges over the canal had failed as well. Fresh Egyptian tanks were pouring into Sinai. The counterattack was a complete fiasco. Upon hearing the news, a senior general wept.[45]

Fighter jets sent to Egypt, then Syria, then back to Egypt. Tanks driving pointlessly all over the desert. False reports from the battlefield. It was apparent that the Israelis were experiencing the very confusion they were once so good at sowing among the Arabs. Someone—it is not clear who—put it more succinctly: "We taught them how to fight, and they taught us how to lie."

Prior to the war, the dictionaries of the world defined the Hebrew word *mikhdal* as a "failure to carry out something important." After the war, the word took on a new meaning, one that survives to this day: "a fiasco as monumental as the IDF's failures in the opening days of the Yom Kippur War."

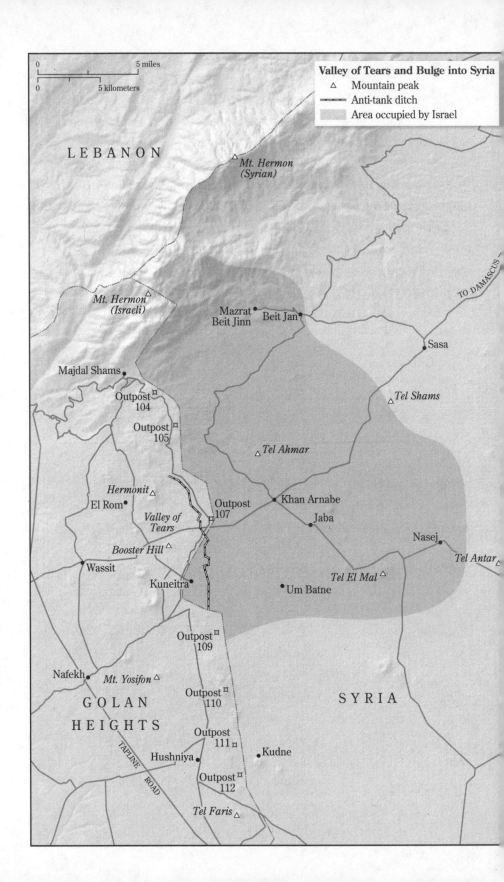

**Valley of Tears and Bulge into Syria**
△    Mountain peak
━━━━━   Anti-tank ditch
     Area occupied by Israel

0             5 miles
0             5 kilometers

LEBANON

△ *Mt. Hermon*
*(Syrian)*

TO DAMASCUS

△ *Mt. Hermon*
*(Israeli)*

Mazrat
Beit Jinn    Beit Jan

Sasa

Majdal Shams

△ *Tel Shams*

Outpost
104

Outpost
105

△ *Tel Ahmar*

*Hermonit* △
El Rom

Outpost
107

Khan Arnabe
Jaba

*Valley of
Tears*

Nasej

*Booster Hill* △

*Tel Antar* △

Wassit

Kuneitra

*Tel El Mal* △

Um Batne

Outpost
109

Nafekh

*Mt. Yosifon* △

GOLAN

Outpost
110

SYRIA

HEIGHTS

Outpost
111

Outpost
109

Kudne

TAPLINE ROAD

Hushniya

Outpost
112

*Tel Faris* △

# 11

## VALLEYS OF TEARS

For Israel, these were the times that tried men's souls.

The government met on the morning of October 9. Veteran politician Victor Shem-Tov remembered it as the gloomiest meeting he ever saw. Dayan now spoke only half-jokingly of bringing in Jewish volunteers from abroad, "cutting their hair and sending them into battle." Whether such long-haired volunteers existed was beside the point. The real problem was that the country was running out of tanks and planes. Everything was mobilized. There were no further reserves of arms to draw upon. The way things were going, there would soon be no more ammunition as well.[1]

There was but one thing that gave Dayan reason for optimism. "I cannot imagine a more listening ear, open mind or courageous heart than that of Golda in that meeting," he remembered. What Dayan and the others did not know was that at that moment Golda was badly shaken and contemplating suicide. Her chain-smoking rose from six packs a day to an impossible eight or nine. Fortunately for those present, her suicidal thoughts were not revealed by those closest to her until after she died five years later. In the moment of crisis, when it mattered, she was a pillar of strength. Minister Uzi Baram said that in raw courage she stood first among equals.[2]

The larger drama occurred earlier that day at 4:00 A.M., when Elazar met with his generals. The false reports of victory during the failed counterattack were as much on men's lips as the defeat itself. That fact, no less than the loss of tanks and men, reinforced the idea that what had occurred was not just a setback, but a cataclysm. For the first time, it really seemed as if Arabs and Jews had traded places on the battlefield. The wisecrack "We taught the Egyptians how to fight, and they taught us how to lie" struck such a deep nerve that the military censor prevented its publication.[3]

After the war, Elazar met with American General Orwin C. Talbott and told him "out of the blue," in Talbott's words, that the Israelis had been "approaching the point where they were ready to use them [nuclear weapons]." Talbott's assistant, Colonel Bruce Williams, forgot the exact wording but similarly remembered a clear message that "Israel was prepared to use nuclear weapons against the Syrians if they'd broken through." The issue was debated seriously enough in the Israeli General Staff on the morning of October 9 that a brigadier general who overheard the discussion burst into the office of Assistant Chief of Staff Yisroel Tal and told him in a voice choked with tears, "You have to save the nation from those lunatics." The transcript of the October 9 government meeting is unusual in that, to this day, it contains several lines that remain blacked out by military censors. Whatever was said about nuclear weapons is probably in that text. Given the sober decisions Golda's government arrived upon, it can be surmised that cooler heads prevailed.[4]

Nevertheless, all agreed that some aggressive demonstration of military force was needed. Without it, other Arab countries, and particularly Jordan, might enter the war to deliver the knockout blow. Egypt had Scud missiles that could be fired at Israeli cities; Syria did not. Dayan thus proposed bombing civilian infrastructure and bombing the Syrian Defense Ministry right in downtown Damascus. Golda had her doubts. This was a major escalation that might jeopardize resupply from America. But the Israelis believed they had a legitimate reply for Kissinger should the issue come up. The Syrians had fired over thirty Frog-7 missiles into northern Israel. The missiles seemed to have been aimed at air bases. But several strayed and hit nearby civilian targets, including the town of Migdal Ha'emek.[5]

It was the Frog missiles that tipped the scales. Golda and her government approved Dayan's proposal and did so unanimously. It resulted in one of the most famous operations in the history of the Israeli air force.[6]

* * *

When those around him grew discouraged, Elazar lifted their spirits by repeating what he had heard from his commanding officer, Benny Marshak, in the 1948 war: when it rains on you, the enemy gets just as wet.[7]

Hafez el-Assad would no doubt have agreed. Before the war, he told Soviet ambassador Nuritdin Mukhitdinov that Syrian forces were not capable of a protracted campaign. The plan was thus for a massive surprise attack that would conquer the Golan Heights in two days, followed by a quickly imposed ceasefire. The role of the Soviets, he explained, was to deliver the ceasefire in the UN before Israel could mobilize and launch a counterattack.[8]

For Assad, the first two days of the war had been a disappointment. The losses had been devastating, yet the Syrians had little to show for it—only a toehold on Mount Hermon and a small chunk of the southeast Golan. Nevertheless, Assad stuck to the plan and told the Soviets to arrange a ceasefire. Israeli reservists were pouring into the Golan far more quickly than expected. Desertion in the Syrian army was becoming a problem; there were even rumors of a mutiny in the elite 1st Division. One Soviet officer said of his Syrian counterparts, "I came and saw all those gloomy faces, as if everyone had a turd inside their cheek." In the words of a senior Soviet diplomat, "My impression was that Assad was beginning to panic."[9]

The Soviets were only too happy to oblige Assad. Brezhnev deemed the decision by Egypt and Syria to go to war "a gross miscalculation," predicting "certain and speedy defeat of the Arabs." Though pleasantly surprised by the early success of the attack, Moscow pushed its allies to accept a ceasefire as early as the evening of October 6.[10]

The problem was Sadat. He was drunk on victory and unwilling to stop until his objective was achieved, which he described as "shattering the Israeli theory of security." The Soviets pleaded with him every day to quit while he was ahead, even mobilizing Marshal Tito of Yugoslavia, a close friend, to see if he could talk sense into him. It was all to no avail. "He can't see farther than his nose," Gromyko grumbled.[11] *

Assad, by contrast, could see his situation perfectly and now did his best to pick up the pieces. First, he reached out to King Hussein, asking him to open a third front by invading across the Jordan River.[12] Not surprisingly, the king declined. Syria was, after all, the country that invaded his kingdom just three years before in support of Palestinians seeking to topple him. Hussein promised only to think about it and get back to him.†

The truest measure of Assad's desperation was his next request: asking Saddam Hussein to send forces from Iraq. Everyone in the region, including Assad, knew that getting Iraqi soldiers to enter your country was easy. Getting them to leave was another story. In Jordan, they remained after the 1967 war and brazenly helped radical Palestinian groups undermine King Hussein until

---

* When confronted by Sadat, Assad denied that he ever sought a ceasefire. Not unlike the Claude Rains character in the movie *Casablanca*—who expresses "shock" to learn that gambling is taking place—Assad feigned surprise at having been misunderstood by the Soviet ambassador. "Unfortunately," a senior Soviet official later observed, "in the history of diplomacy such conversions are not unusual."

† There was no love lost between King Hussein and Sadat, either. Jordanian prime minister Wasfi Tal was assassinated on November 28, 1971, in Cairo, while attending an Arab League summit. It became one of the most notorious acts of terrorism by the Palestinian group Black September, because one of the gunmen got down on his knees and licked Tal's blood off the marble floor. Sadat sided with Black September, allowing the men to go free on minimal bail and then leave the country.

Israeli infantry moving to Golan Heights under air cover. *Government Press Office.*

Long-range 175 mm artillery in action on the Syrian Front. *Azouri Menashe / Government Press Office.*

Soviet-made Katyusha missiles captured by Israel in 1967 and fired upon their former owners. *Ron Ilan / Government Press Office.*

David Elazar. To his right, partially obscured, is Avraham Adan. *Sa'ar Ya'acov / Government Press Office.*

Moshe Dayan briefing the press. *Herman Chanania / Government Press Office.*

Golda Meir visits the front, being led by Shmuel Gonen, in sunglasses, to the left. *Segev Yitzhak / Government Press Office.*

Syrian oil tanks set afire by the Israeli navy in Latakia.
*Reininger Alon / Government Press Office.*

Israeli tank on the right and Egyptian on the left, destroyed near
the Chinese farm. *Tomarkin Yigal / Government Press Office.*

Ariel Sharon in bandage, conferring with Chaim Bar-Lev. *Greenberg Yossi / Government Press Office.*

Crocodile mobile raft, with pontoon bridge in background. *Ron Ilan / Government Press Office.*

Pontoon bridge over the Suez Canal. *Ron Ilan / Government Press Office.*

Israeli armor crossing into Egypt over the rolling bridge.
*Ron Ilan / Government Press Office.*

SAM-2 missile, captured in Egypt. *Government Press Office.*

Mobilized Israeli civilian buses carrying troops across the Suez Canal.
*Kogel Avraham / Government Press Office.*

Israeli soldiers near an irrigation canal west of the Suez Canal.
*Kogel Avraham / Government Press Office.*

Egyptian soldiers supplying surrounded Egyptian Third Army through a breach in the sand barrier along the canal. *Government Press Office.*

Agranat Commission. From left to right: Yigal Yadin, Moshe Landau, Shimon Agranat, Yitzchak Nebentzal, and Chaim Laskov.
*Sa'ar Ya'acov / Government Press Office.*

losing the Black September struggle. Predictably, Saddam Hussein agreed to send an *enormous* force onto Syrian soil. "If tanks had wings," he said ominously, "they would be there today."[13]

Assad's next decision had to have been the most difficult of the war. More than half his army was gone. Much of what remained were his Defense Companies (*Siraya ad-Difaa*), whose job it was to protect the regime and whose men were commanded by his brother Rifaat.[14] The history of modern Syria to that point was a chronicle of chaos. In its first twenty-four years, the nation experienced twenty-three changes of government, of which fifteen were military coups. To risk the Defense Companies was to risk his regime, his rule, and his life. Most leaders would have scraped together what was left and gone on the defensive. Few would have let Saddam Hussein into the country through the back door.

Hafez el-Assad gambled everything on victory.

\* \* \*

American Lieutenant General Daniel P. Bolger once likened service in an armored personnel carrier to living inside a garbage dumpster. Service inside a tank in 1973 was, if anything, even worse. To the tank designers of the world, the comfort of the men inside was not even an afterthought. They were expected to function in sweltering heat, wearing heavy asbestos suits and helmets; eating, drinking, and sleeping in tiny steel spaces. Unless they were servicing their tank—or fleeing a fireball after taking a hit—soldiers were not permitted to leave their vehicles for any reason. Going to the bathroom was a particular hardship. Men defecated into bags they carefully affixed inside their unworn helmets, which served as chamber pots. If someone had diarrhea—and given the conditions, someone always did—the stench filled the entire compartment. On the Golan Heights, tank treads crushed the basalt rock into dust, which somehow found its way inside and clung so firmly to sweat-covered skin it was hard to get off weeks later, even after a long shower. The size of the driver's compartment, particularly in Soviet-made tanks, put a premium on soldiers who were five foot three or shorter. A historian who served said the Israeli armored corps sought out men who were "short, muscular savages."[15]

Only after a hard day of fighting could soldiers open their hatches and emerge, but there was no time to take in the fresh air. Each day, a tank needed a minimum of five hours for refueling, reloading, and mechanical servicing. In the Golan, the Israelis broke safety rules and bounced trailers off-road to bring fuel and ammunition right up to where it was needed. Nevertheless, the cycle of fighting and servicing filled practically all twenty-four hours. On a good night, a filthy, sweat-covered soldier might be left with two hours of sleep.[16]

By October 9, the men had been at this for more than three days and were completely exhausted. Colonel Yossi Peled, commander of the 205th Armored Brigade, went to sleep on the hood of his jeep and woke up later to find that he was by himself in no-man's-land. He drove "like a missile," in his words, to catch up with his unit almost a mile away and angrily demanded to know why they had withdrawn. He was told that they were compelled to pull back when they came under heavy fire. No one thought to wake him up because no one thought they had to. The colonel had slept through an artillery barrage.[17]

The 205th Armored Brigade, which Colonel Peled commanded, was the backbone of the 146th Division, the unit that Elazar sent to the Golan Heights rather than hold in reserve in case Jordan invaded. They first crossed the Jordan River on the morning of October 8 after a long drive, and were jolted by a sight no soldier had seen since 1948: Israeli civilian refugees. The people who fled settlements in the Golan Heights were huddled not far from antitank guns set up near Lake Kineret. Colonel Peled and his assistant looked at each other. *Had the Syrians penetrated this far?*[18]

Once the brigade was in the Heights, Peled's orders were simple: spread out and attack north. Peled likened his multipronged drive to a giant comb. The two most important objectives were the volcanic hills of Tel Juhader and Tel Faris, but Peled's men were first ordered to relieve Tel Saki, a tiny outpost crammed with nineteen wounded men who had miraculously held out for over two days.[19]

The story of Tel Saki became one of the most famous of the war. On the first night, it was the rallying point for the ragtag forces that held off the Syrian army. For a time, those forces were the only thing standing between the Syrian army and the Israeli kibbutzim and villages at the foot of Lake Kineret. When they ran out of water and ammunition, their commander, an Orthodox Jew named Menachem Ansbacher, ordered them to destroy their maps and codes and retreat into a tiny bunker. Ansbacher—a giant slab of a man who looked like a piece of the Wailing Wall that broke off and walked away—then gathered whoever was still alive and did the only thing he felt he could. He led them in prayer. One of the men volunteered to go outside and surrender to the Syrians; somehow, he convinced them that no one else was left alive in the bunker. The Syrians still rolled grenades inside, but the bodies of two dead men positioned near the door absorbed the shrapnel. Later, two Syrian soldiers took cover from Israeli artillery fire inside the bunker's entrance and were just inches from Ansbacher. Ansbacher held a grenade in his hand with the pin removed. The men sat motionless without uttering a sound. The two Syrians never saw them and left when the shelling stopped. Ansbacher then discovered to his horror that he could not find the grenade pin in the dark. So he neutralized the live grenade with a bobby pin taken from his yarmulke. Thirty hours after entering the bunker, Ansbacher and his men were rescued.[20]

Peled's unit made steady progress. A key victory occurred in the early hours of October 9 when two volunteers crawled to the top of Tel Faris—the highest such "tel," or volcanic hill, in the Heights—and eliminated what was left of the Syrian defenders using nothing but guns and grenades. The seizure of Tel Faris made all the difference. After the war, the Israelis acknowledged that Syrian artillery was far more effective than their own. It became far less effective once their spotters lost Tel Faris.[21]

In the end, the Syrian 76th Brigade was completely wiped out, but Peled's 205th did not fare much better. The 205th arrived on the morning of October 8 with a hundred tanks. By the evening of October 9, it was down to fewer than twenty. The Israelis had a well-earned reputation for their ability to buy surplus equipment on the cheap and upgrade it for modern use. The World War II–era Sherman tanks of Peled's unit were an example: they had been outfitted with modern 105-millimeter cannons, a process known as "up-gunning." But there was only so much Israeli engineers could do with a lightly armored tank that had been inferior to the German tanks they had faced thirty years earlier. In General Peled's estimation, the Sherman was "a terrible tank" whose armor "concealed the tank crew but did not protect them." All it took was a single shot from a Soviet-made T-55 and the Sherman went up in flames. "The heroism of the men that served in those tanks," General Peled remembered, "was beyond anything I could describe."[22]

\* \* \*

On the morning of October 9, Hafez el-Assad went for broke. The Syrian army advanced in a classic pincer movement. The elite 1st Division was to attack from south to north in a final attempt to conquer Nafekh. After that, it was to continue up the Tapline Road and hook up with a second drive by the elite Defense Companies, attacking north of Kuneitra from east to west.

By now the Syrian 1st Division was down to half its original strength. But the Defense Companies commanded by Assad's brother were fresh troops and the best equipped in the Syrian army. Against them were weary Israeli forces of which contemporary descriptions repeatedly come back to the four words "what was left of." Facing Syria's Defense Companies north of Kuneitra was what was left of the 7th Brigade, about fifty-three battered tanks. Facing the 1st Division opposite Nafekh was what was left of the 679th Brigade, perhaps sixty tanks in similar condition. Farther south near the town of Hushniya were fragments of four other brigades, all low on ammunition and all exhausted after forty-eight to seventy-two hours of uninterrupted combat.[23]

The Syrians first sent eight helicopters filled with commandos to fly behind enemy lines in broad daylight. They never had much of a chance. One group of four helicopters landed near the Wassit road junction and took heavy casualties, but it carried out an ambush that drew Israeli forces from the battle farther south. The second group of four flew right next to the Israeli base at Nafekh. The force was commanded by a captain named Hassan Tarif, who ordered his pilot to land knowing he was on a suicide mission. The Israelis initially mistook the helicopters for their own, not expecting the enemy to brazenly land right in their midst in broad daylight. The surprise gave the pilots enough time to deposit the commandos, though three of the four helicopters were shot down on the return trip. The commandos were mostly Palestinians, and they fought to the last man. Fifty were killed and nine captured, though according to Syrian records, a handful managed to make it back across Syrian lines. For his heroism, Captain Tarif was posthumously awarded Syria's highest military honor.[24]

South of Nafekh, Colonel Ori Orr snatched two hours of sleep and awoke to find the Yeshiva *hesder* soldiers wearing phylacteries (*tefillin*), swaying in prayer. He was pleased to discover yet again that they really did make good soldiers. The time they carved out for prayer did not come at the expense of their tanks, which were fueled, oiled, and loaded. Many of the tanks were covered in twisted metal, pockmarked with bullet holes and shrapnel. But those that could still move took to the hills a mile south of Nafekh and waited.[25]

The attack began, as it always did, with an enormous artillery barrage. The Syrians headed north between six and seven in the morning, hoping the dawn sun would blind the Israeli defenders.

Years before, General Yisroel Tal conducted a study and concluded that what decided tank battles, to the exclusion of practically everything else, was marksmanship. The side that hit the target more quickly and more frequently was the side that won. Israeli training invested heavily in gunnery and it showed. In Colonel Orr's estimation, the Israelis fired just a little faster and a little straighter. One by one the Syrian tanks lit up the battlefield. Unbowed, they kept surging forward, even as the sun rose high in the sky and they became easy targets in the valley below. The Syrians also kept up the artillery fire, saturating the Israelis with fire and shrapnel.[26]

The battle stalemated. The Syrians could not advance north to Nafekh, but neither could the Israelis push east to reach the lines the two sides held on October 6. In the "Hushniya Wedge"—the triangle of land that jutted into Syria just south of the town of the same name—Colonel Peled's 205th stalled under a curtain of artillery fire. He asked for an air strike to help break the logjam. He was told there were no planes available.[27]

\* \* \*

There were two ways for Israeli fighter jets to get to Damascus: the hard way and the harder way. For some, the obvious flight path was to come in low behind Mount Hermon where radar could not see them, go into a steep climb, and then head north at maximum speed. It took only two minutes to get from Mount Hermon to Damascus once pilots lit their afterburners. But in those two minutes they had to fly over the thickest air defenses in the world. The preferred path was therefore flying north over the Mediterranean, cutting across Lebanon, and surprising the Syrians from the rear. Of course, there was no guarantee they would make it to Damascus or achieve surprise if they did. They had to destroy a Lebanese radar station, clear two mountain ranges, and hope that thousands of Syrian soldiers deployed west of Damascus did not recognize the jets flying overhead as F-4 Phantoms.[28]

Twenty-four planes took off in complete radio silence and

split up into three groups of eight. They flew low over the Mediterranean to avoid enemy radar, so low that the pilots created a wake across the sea. Just north of Beirut they turned right and made a break for it across the width of Lebanon. They cleared Mount Lebanon and flew over the Bekaa Valley, which looked like a green checkerboard crisscrossed with orchards. But just when it seemed the gamble had paid off, only five minutes from Damascus, they looked up and realized their luck had run out.[29]

The Anti-Lebanon Mountains were covered with clouds.

The cumulus white blanket merged perfectly with the mountains to form a huge, solid mass. There was not a crack in the curtain. They could not fly into the clouds where they might collide with the side of the mountain. But neither could they fly above them at the altitude where SAMs were most effective. With seconds to decide, Major Arnon Levoshin, the lead pilot, remembered being told years before by a meteorologist that clouds often terminated at the spot where the Anti-Lebanon range ended and the Hermon range began. He led the team south, and sure enough, there was a tiny crack where the meteorologist said. Once through, the skies cleared and there was perfect visibility all the way to Damascus.[30]

In 1973, pilots still relied more on what they saw outside their cockpit windows than on their instrument panels. Using a soccer field and a city square as a point of reference, the planes raced to downtown Damascus. The pilots had only a few seconds to identify the target, line it up in their sights, and drop their ordnance. In an era before smart munitions, they still managed to hit the headquarters of the Syrian High Command.[31]

The Syrians were caught completely by surprise. No sirens went off before the first bombs landed. But they recovered quickly, and—forgetting that what goes up must come down—they saturated the skies with missiles. A report from Damascus by CBS's Dean Frelus said that "many Syrian residential areas were hit by Israeli bombs," but this was probably Syrian ordnance that plummeted back to earth. The Syrians also fired streams of .50-caliber munitions from their flak guns. An Israeli pilot likened it to fleeing a swarm of angry bees. One plane was shot down. Another was badly damaged but made it back to base with one engine out and the other on fire.[32] *

Photo reconnaissance revealed that most of the Israeli bombs missed. Nevertheless, the mission passed on into legend, not unlike the raid carried out by America's Jimmy Doolittle over Tokyo in World War II. It supplied the country with a morale boost and forced the enemy to divert SAM batteries to better protect the capital.[33] It might have also played a role in King Hussein's decision in the end to refrain from opening a third front as Sadat and Assad wanted, and merely send a brigade into Syria.

And then there was the psychological effect it had on Syrian counterintelligence. Unknown to the pilots, several Israeli POWs were being held in the Syrian General Staff headquarters. By coincidence, the bombs landed on the other side of the building. The Syrians lined up the bewildered POWs and demanded an answer: *How did Israeli pilots know which side of the building to bomb?*[34]

* * *

Farther west, the second group of eight fighter jets could not find the opening in the clouds. The squadron commander, Lieutenant Colonel Yiftach Spector, said he had to make a split-second decision or the mountain would make it for him. They were turning back. There was not enough room to make a turn. Instead, they lit their afterburners, rocketed straight up through the clouds—Spector said they were so thick they felt like damp wool—and headed south back toward Israel.[35]

Upon crossing the border, Spector radioed in. His squadron did not make it to Damascus and he wanted another mission. The

---

* The pilot won a medal for steering his plane into a net while going 240 mph, despite a tire blowing out on the runway and the loss of his hydraulic system.

eight planes collectively carried sixteen tons of bombs under their wings. Perhaps they could be put to use somewhere else.*

The operations officer remembered that there was a colonel on the Golan Heights who had called in an air strike. With the fuel indicators in Spector's planes near empty, he knew there was no time to plot proper coordinates. So he breathlessly radioed Spector and gave the kind of directions one might give a lost driver ("Head down the Jordan River till you hit the Kineret, then hang a left and go up the highway until you see two hills . . .").[36]

Using nothing but a compass and a timer, the squadron headed up to the Heights and came in for the kill. Israeli tank commanders stood back and watched in awe as the fighter jets obliterated the Syrians with cluster bombs. Colonel Peled likened the bomblets to hailstones made of fire. The IAF flew 136 sorties in the Golan Heights that day. By all accounts it was the bombing by Spector's planes that broke the back of the Syrian 1st Division's south-to-north pincer movement. Paradoxically, the only time in the war that the IAF gave effective air support to ground forces was in an improvised mission with no planning and no proper coordinates. Put another way, the only time the IAF played the role that everyone expected was when it did so by accident.[37]

\* \* \*

There might be nicer country farther north in Lebanon. But when the sunlight lies upon it, and the winds off the snowcapped Hermon Range push the shadows of white clouds across the grassy hills, the valley between the Hermonit and Booster Hill just north of Kuneitra is about as beautiful as anything the Golan has to offer.† It was good terrain for hiking and kite flying. Less so for tank warfare.

---

\* The last group of eight planes came in for criticism for dropping their bombs over the Mediterranean and flying back to base.

† Hermonit—literally "Little Hermon"—is the southernmost mountain in the Hermon Range. Booster Hill was so named because it contained a booster pump, used by farmers to move water and then spray it across their fields.

In the cheap light of hindsight, it was probably not the best place for the Syrians to mount their main pincer movement, attacking east–west. The better strategy might have been to stick with one point of attack and add resources to the drive heading from south to north. There were only a few places north of Kuneitra flat enough for tanks, and everyone knew where they were. There would thus be no element of surprise on the morning of October 9. The plan relied instead on the more fundamental element of brute force. The Syrians had tried to cross the valleys north of Kuneitra for three straight days and failed to advance an inch. But they left Israel's 7th Armored Brigade with only fifty-three working tanks, a third of which were practically out of ammunition. All were manned by exhausted soldiers who had barely slept in three days.[38]

Against this, the Syrians had 150 fresh tanks that had not yet been committed to battle. Practically all were Soviet-made T-62s, which had a 115-millimeter cannon that was widely viewed as the finest on the battlefields of the 1970s, superior to anything in Western arsenals. Sixty-two of the 150 tanks belonged to the Defense Companies commanded by Rifaat Assad, Hafez's brother.[39]

The Israeli 7th Armored Brigade was commanded by Avigdor "Yanush" Ben-Gal, a thirty-seven-year-old Holocaust survivor born to a wealthy Polish businessman. The family summer home, a mansion located west of Lodz, was seized by the Germans in September 1939 and turned into the local headquarters of the Gestapo. Ben-Gal was tall and thin with a moon-shaped face that jutted out under a large shock of hair. Whenever superiors asked why his hair was not cut to regulation, he pulled it back to show that it covered an ear mangled years before by a land mine.[40]

Any attack following Soviet military doctrine begins with an artillery barrage. But the one that ushered in the Syrian attack in the northern Golan on the morning of October 9 was exceptional even by that standard. Three hundred eighty cannons fired off at once. Amid the "rolling curtain of fire," as one officer called it, it is likely the assaulting tanks could not see their enemies even though they were charging across open ground. They knew only to continue west over the antitank trench, the fire and smoke closing around them as they advanced. It was not much different for the Israelis. For a period of a half hour, Ben-Gal said that he and his officers lost control, it being impossible for tanks to be seen or orders to be heard. Each tank fought its own private battle.[41]

The main effort came exactly where the Israelis expected it, in the valley between the Hermonit and Booster Hill. Nevertheless, Ben-Gal was spread thin and had only twenty tanks to deploy in the valley, eight more on the Hermonit and a meager four on Booster Hill. By happenstance, this tiny force was backed up by a relatively large number of artillery pieces. When the reservists had hauled them up to the Heights, the Syrians controlled the southern Golan, so by default they brought them to the north instead. There, a lieutenant colonel named Aryeh Mizrahi skillfully clustered them into a "fist" to achieve a multiplier effect. Among the weapons in the artillery convoy were twelve trucks laden with Soviet-made BM-24 rockets, 240-millimeter monsters captured in Sinai in the '67 war. They were practically the only ones the Israelis possessed. And they were saving them for a special occasion.[42]

Each of the twelve trucks carried twelve launchers. At the decisive moment, all 144 rockets were fired off at once, together with all the artillery in the fist. The ordnance landed in a single thunderous crash, creating an effect that one Israeli officer likened to an atomic bomb. Still the Syrians surged forward blindly, managing somehow to bridge the antitank trench. The confusion and poor visibility were such that both sides shelled the Hermonit at the same time, because each thought the other held it.[43]

Once Ben-Gal called in his reserve, there would be not a single tank between the valley and northern Israel. He called it in anyway. He wired Lieutenant Colonel Meshulam Retes and ordered him to reinforce the Hermonit with whatever he had,

which turned out to be just eight tanks, the remainder of a battalion that started the war with thirty-six. Retes was one of the
IDF's old warhorses, who had befriended Ben-Gal when the latter served under him earlier in their careers. Retes met Ben-Gal
in the field and told him, "This is a suicide mission and we both
know it. If anyone else gave me this order I'd refuse it. But you're
asking, so I'll do it for you." With those words he closed the hatch
on his tank and rolled off into battle. He took a direct hit an hour
later and was killed instantly.[44]

At around noon, after five hours of combat, Lieutenant Colonel Avigdor Kahalani, commander of the force on the Hermonit,
ran out of ammunition. Kahalani moved off his position to look for
a second line where they might retreat. Realizing that there was no
such place, he told his driver to return and position the tank in a
prominent place. Perhaps seeing a tank would scare the Syrians off.
A sister battalion likewise ran out of ammunition. Its commander,
Captain Meir Zamir, filled his pockets with grenades and prepared
for a last stand.[45]

Ben-Gal radioed General Eitan. His men were out of ammunition. They had no choice but to withdraw. Eitan pleaded with
him to hang on for just five more minutes, certain that the Syrians
would break first. He also promised reinforcements, though Ben-
Gal was convinced these were reinforcements he did not have.[46]

Moments later those reinforcements appeared under Yossi Ben-
Hanan, a lieutenant colonel who had rushed back to Israel from
his honeymoon and was now in the Heights with twenty tanks.
Ben-Gal told him to head to a position marked on Israeli maps as
Outpost 107 to outflank the Syrians from the south.[47]

Shortly after that, a soldier from the crack Golani Brigade radioed in from Outpost 107, which was well behind enemy lines.
The Syrians were retreating.[48]

Avigdor Kahalani emerged from his tank. He looked down at
the hundreds of burned bodies and vehicles strewn before him
in the valley, smoke rising, air filled with the stench of cordite

and burning flesh. He said, "It looks like a valley of tears." The statement reached a reporter for the IDF newspaper *Bamahane*. Israelis have known it by that name ever since. The Syrians know it as the "Wadi of Death."[49] The battle passed on into Israeli lore, joining the 1948 Battle of San-Simon and others in which the IDF won, by virtue of holding on just a few minutes longer than the enemy.

It might have ended differently.

Rifaat Assad brought the finest unit of the Syrian army with him into battle. Unfortunately for the Syrians, he also brought himself. The Defense Companies existed outside the regular army's chain of command and took orders straight from President Assad himself.[50] This disturbed hierarchy might have played a decisive role in the outcome.

Most Syrian tanks were nominally attached to the 7th Division, commanded by General Omar Abrash, an able professional soldier educated in America's staff college in Fort Leavenworth. Abrash died during the battle. At various times, the Syrians have claimed he committed suicide, or was killed by an artillery shell or by a direct hit to his tank. During the war, rumors surfaced that he was executed. The details emerged only years later when a retired Syrian officer revealed that the bulk of the 7th Division was sent into the valley unbeknownst to General Abrash, earlier than he wanted, on direct orders from Damascus. The casualty reports came in and an enraged Abrash called President Assad directly to complain. In reference to Assad's background as a pilot, Abrash screamed, "You are nothing but a chauffeur for MiG-17s!"[51]

Assad hung up and sent a senior officer from his Alawite clan to "discuss the matter" with General Abrash. The officer shot him dead.[52]

# 12

## COMMAND AND CONTROL

Our strategy was always to force the enemy to fight on our terms, but we never expected him to collaborate.

—General Sa'ad Shazly[1]

When Egypt attacked on October 6, most of Israel's *maozim* along the canal were manned by just twenty men or fewer, and all from the Jerusalem Brigade, a collection of immigrant soldiers with limited training. All held out for at least twenty-four hours, which was a good deal more than anyone had a right to expect. But fighting for God and country was but a partial motivator. The Yom Kippur War offers a case study in how tenaciously men will fight once they learn, as the Jerusalem Brigade did, that surrender is not available to them.[2]

In the Hizayon *maoz*, the Egyptians tried Israeli prisoners in a kangaroo court in the field for the crime of having participated in the 1967 war, convicted eleven, and executed them on the spot. The first six Israelis bearing white flags who emerged from the Maftzayakh *maoz* were gunned down as well. In a particularly tragic story, a sergeant named Shlomo Arman led the last five survivors from the Orkal *maoz* across the swamplands of northern

Sinai in a lone tank, destroying five Egyptian tanks along the way. Miraculously, after a forty-eight-hour ordeal of firefights and narrow escapes, he reached Israeli lines—only to be gunned down by friendly fire. He was posthumously awarded Israel's highest military honor.[3]

Late on the night of October 8, the men of the Purkan *maoz* radioed Ariel Sharon and informed him that they, too, were going to make a break for it. Sharon told them what they already knew—namely, that their chances were not good. But if they could slip across six miles of enemy territory into no-man's-land, he would see to it that there were tanks in place to pick them up.[4] He told them the rendezvous point with the rescue party would be near Hamutal.

The hill that Sharon had lost during the counterattack the previous day.[5]

* * *

The failed counterattack had not changed Ariel Sharon's thinking in the least. Writing years later, he said, "This was not the time to sit back and allow the Egyptians to build up their bridgeheads and their defenses . . . we should be pushing them, probing for their weak points, looking for openings to exploit." He added, "It is no exaggeration to say that by this time my confidence in . . . Southern Command or General Headquarters . . . was down to zero." His assistant, General Jackie Even, said that because of this loss of confidence, Sharon concluded that he was no longer bound to "automatically accept" the judgment of Elazar or Gonen. General Even goes on to say in his memoir that after the October 8 fiasco, Sharon believed he could defy his orders, "so long as he covered his tracks."[6]

North of the Great Bitter Lake, the Egyptian Second Army held a narrow strip of land that, apart from the Lexicon Road hugging the east bank of the canal, left all north–south roads in Israeli hands.[7] The only place where the Egyptians held a bulge that included other north–south roads was in Sharon's sector near the Hamutal and Makhshir hills. Sharon had lost those hills on October 8. He had every intention of taking them back.

Elazar's orders were crystal clear: as long as the army's main effort was focused on Syria in the north, there were to be no adventures near the canal in the south. Launching any sort of offensive action was, according to General Even, "a complete violation of the Chief of Staff's orders."[8]

To this problem, Sharon had a creative solution. Because he had authorization to rescue the men who fled the Purkan *maoz*, Sharon declared this the primary objective of the mission. He went out of his way to say that this was a purely "defensive mission." But, he added, proper defense would be impossible without first straightening the line *by seizing the hills that were lost the day before.*[9]

Those who received Sharon's orders knew exactly what he was up to. One of his brigade commanders, Colonel Chaim Erez, said that the rescue was merely a by-product. The main goal of the mission was to "return to the line atop the hills [of Hamutal and Makhshir]." At dawn on October 9, a major jotted down, "The order was issued to conquer Makhshir and Hamutal."[10]

When the tanks rolled off into battle at about seven in the morning, one could plausibly argue that Colonel Erez's 421st Armored Brigade was sent to the Hamutal hill to rescue the men of Purkan. But at the very same moment, Sharon also sent the 600th Armored Brigade to retake the Makhshir hill just south of Hamutal. The men of Purkan were nowhere near Makhshir. There was not even a pretense that the 600th was sent for any reason other than retaking the hill.[11]

The Agranat Commission initially limited the scope of its inquiry to events occurring on or before October 8. But once it heard testimony, it could not resist the urge to wade into the events of October 9. It concluded that "it would appear that Sharon intended to return to his first plan from Monday [October 8], meaning to attack with two brigades."[12]

Of course, while it was happening, these facts had to be hidden from Elazar and the General Staff. Sharon and his divisional officers therefore could not command and control the operation. Sharon knew that his superiors would be listening in on his division's wireless. The General Staff in Tel Aviv had already realized it could not trust the information it was getting, so it formed the "Library," a group of senior officers pulled from retirement to listen in on radio traffic and try to form a picture of what was really happening. Accordingly, Sharon gave orders to brigade commanders in person and met each one separately. Once in the field, the brigade commanders were left to work things out among themselves, though this covered only basic things like avoiding friendly fire. There could be nothing over the radio from divisional headquarters suggesting a coordinated assault. To the extent that anyone spoke, it was General Even, not Sharon, and always in vague generalities, such as "stabilizing the line" and "establishing order." In 2015, General Even acknowledged that Sharon sat next to him and quietly signaled what to say and do.[13]

In short, when the tanks rolled west toward the hills of Hamutal and Makhshir early on the morning of October 9, they did so not as an armored division carrying out a well-planned offensive. Rather, they went on a rogue operation as separate brigades attacking one at a time.[14]

The thirty-three men of Purkan crawled through a crack in the bunker at three in the morning and headed out on foot under the light of a nearly full moon. They first moved south to avoid the Egyptians camped outside. Then they turned east, hiking across a surrealistic hell of smoking tanks and burning bodies. Walking along the path of earlier battles, they took cover in bomb craters to hide from passing Egyptian soldiers.[15]

To have any hope of rescue they knew they had to make it to

no-man's-land before first light. By equal parts perseverance and luck, they hiked eleven miles in under four hours over soft sand to arrive within sight of Israeli lines, just as the sun was appearing on the horizon. Hours passed. They missed the rendezvous point by a mile and a half. But luckily, a battalion commander named Lieutenant Colonel Shaul Shalev discovered them and sprinted across no-man's-land to pick them up. Everyone piled aboard his tank; thirty-three men grabbed on to whatever they could, and the driver sped back toward Israeli lines. From a distance, the vehicle no longer looked like a tank, but like a strange multi-limbed monster crawling over the dunes with arms and legs dangling over the side.[16]

It was a dramatic rescue, albeit at high cost. Five men were killed elsewhere trying to reach them. And when it was over, at around nine o'clock in the morning, Ariel Sharon's mission had ostensibly ended. But no one returned to their previous position. Instead, there was a long day of fighting ahead. After dropping off the thirty-three men of Purkan, Lieutenant Colonel Shalev turned around, went back into battle, and was killed soon thereafter.[17]

A battalion in Colonel Erez's brigade took heavy casualties in its attack on the Hamutal hill. Nineteen of its twenty-two tanks were hit, the Egyptians screaming *"Allahu Akbar!"* with each strike. An Egyptian corporal named Sid el-Shakhat crawled underneath an Israeli tank clutching a land mine and set it off. Nevertheless, at 8:30 A.M., the battalion reported that it had taken the position. Hamutal was back in Israeli hands.[18]

This was music to Sharon's ears. The mission was going well. At that moment the rescue of the men from Purkan was still ongoing, so Sharon could plausibly claim he was following Elazar's orders. He felt secure enough to call Gonen and ask for air support. Gonen understood what Sharon was up to. But far from enforcing Elazar's orders, he told him to take another hill just north of Hamutal to straighten the line.[19]

Trouble was not far behind. The 600th could not take the sister hill of Makhshir just south of Hamutal. Though it had the best equipment in the army, and its commander Colonel Tuvia Raviv was given first dibs on the best officers, its tanks were rushed into battle without machine guns. It was Egyptian infantry firing Sagger missiles that Israeli tanks most feared, and the main weapon Israeli tanks used to neutralize infantry was machine guns. One tank officer said that fighting infantry without machine guns was like boxing with both hands tied behind your back. Another said it was suicide.[20]

The best the hapless Israelis could do was fire their personal weapons and throw grenades. But their personal weapons were Uzi submachine guns, and those had an effective firing range of only about a hundred yards. One tank crew beat Egyptian infantry off their hatches with their fists. Not surprisingly, the attack quickly came unstitched. The 409th Battalion of the 600th Armored Brigade spearheaded the drive west. It was decimated under a hail of missiles. The battalion commander, a lieutenant colonel named Uzi Ben-Yitzchak, was wounded when his tank was hit by a Sagger and he was catapulted out of the turret.[21] *

For Israel, the hero of the day was Ben-Yitzchak's assistant, Major Amos Unger. He assumed command and from atop his tank among the dunes made a critical decision: the 409th had to cut its losses and call off the attack. The responsibility Unger assumed cannot be overstated. His order essentially rendered the day's effort a failure. Colonel Erez, commander of the 421st, soon realized that he could not hang on to the Hamutal hilltop if the twin hilltop of Makhshir was in Egyptian hands threatening his flank. After Major Unger pulled back from Makhshir, Erez ordered his tanks to withdraw from Hamutal. The head count taken at the end of the day spoke for itself: twenty more tanks were lost, fifty more were damaged—and Israel was back to square one.

---

* The driver of the destroyed tank was a twenty-two-year-old law student named Amnon Abramovitch. Abramovitch survived near-fatal burns, endured two years of skin grafts, and went on to become one of Israel's leading columnists. Though his face bore severe scars from the ordeal, he is as of this writing one of the nation's best-known television commentators.

The Agranat Commission was scathing in its criticism, finding, among other things, that the attack was "planned hurriedly, without proper preparation . . . and without learning any of the lessons of earlier battles."[22]

Nevertheless, it was Unger's decision, taken in the field from the ranks of middle management, that prevented the adventure from becoming a disaster. The 409th exited the battlefield and hustled back to defend the Hamadia hill. As noted earlier, the loss of this crucial position would have closed off the Akavish Road to the Israelis and rendered any future crossing of the canal impossible. To lose the Hamadia hill was to lose the war. Unger's tanks made it back just in time to defend it against a massive Egyptian assault. This "snap ambush," in the words of General Even, won the day and beat the Egyptians back. The scale of Egyptian losses speaks to how well they understood the battlefield calculus and how badly they wanted the hill. Eighty Egyptian tanks were destroyed. Brigadier General Shafik Matri Sadrakh, commander of Egypt's elite 3rd Brigade, was killed.[23]

The defense of Hamadia was by far Israel's most important success of the day. It was successful enough for Sharon to see an opportunity for fresh scheming. The Egyptians were on the run. This was the time to "exploit the success." He radioed Gonen and sought authority to chase the Egyptians to the canal. Gonen told him, "Do not attack. Keep your distance and don't lose any tanks."[24]

At two o'clock in the afternoon, Sharon reported to Gonen that "in accordance with your instructions, we are advancing slowly [west] toward the Missouri hill." Of course, those were not his instructions. Gonen traveled personally to Sharon's headquarters and ordered him to break off the attack. Sharon agreed to stop the effort. But when Gonen got back to his headquarters, he listened to the radio and discovered that the attack was ongoing.[25]

Just after dark, Sharon radioed Gonen. His men were along the banks of the canal. He wanted authorization to cross.[26]

From atop the hills of Hamadia and Kishuf, the Israelis could see that the Egyptians left a thirteen-mile gap between the Second and Third Armies. This "seam," as it became known, began and ended along the widest portion of the Great Bitter Lake. That section was so wide that the east bank in Sinai was out of range of SAMs on the west bank in Egypt. Any force outside the protective umbrella of the SAMs was doomed. Earlier in the day, fifty Egyptian tanks from the Third Army had ventured outside that umbrella in an attempt to conquer the Abu Rudeis oil fields, attacked south, and were mauled by Israeli fighter jets.[27]

But the Egyptians made a crucial mistake. An Israeli reconnaissance battalion drove into the seam, turned north, and discovered that the Egyptians had left the Lexicon Road undefended all the way up to the Matzmed *maoz*. This area was inside the protective umbrella of the SAMs, where their ground forces would have been safe. Nevertheless, they left this back door wide open. What they did not know was that it was the very spot that Ariel Sharon had long planned to use as the jump-off point to cross the canal.[28]

Sharon's request to cross the canal reached Elazar at 6:00 P.M. on October 9. The events in Sinai and the Golan Heights are described separately in this account, but they happened at the same time. It had been a roller-coaster day in which Damascus was bombed, the Golan Heights almost fell, the use of nuclear weapons was debated, and the Americans were still refusing desperately needed resupply. Only then, at 6:00 P.M., did Elazar learn that his orders had been ignored in Sinai and more tanks had been lost. His biographer writes that it was at this moment that his "Montenegrin blood boiled over."

Elazar exploded. "Get him out of there! Get him out!"

Gonen attempted to get a word in. Elazar exploded again. "I am telling you do not cross! Do not cross! Do not cross!"[29]

* * *

The busy day in Sinai seemingly ended in a draw. Both sides took heavy losses. Both sides gained no ground. To Sharon's supporters, the Israelis still came out ahead. They now knew of the open back door to the canal. To Sharon's detractors, this was cold comfort given the losses. They argue that the seam between the Egyptian Second and Third Armies was well known before the attack. The back door would have been discovered once the Israelis attempted to cross.

Both Israel and Egypt paused to regroup. The Sinai front would thus remain relatively quiet for the next four days, until October 14.[30] The Egyptians used the time to bring more tanks across the canal. The Israelis brought in more tanks as well, repairing those that could be fixed or that broke down on the drive to the front. They also brought in machine guns for the tanks already on the line. Finally, they took the time to study the previous four days of fighting to learn lessons and devise new tactics.

There was one other important outcome of the Sinai battles. David Elazar had finally had enough of Shmuel Gonen.

He called Dayan. The two agreed to appoint Chaim Bar-Lev, the former chief of staff, to take over Southern Command. The matter had to be handled delicately. If Gonen resigned or, worse, if he committed suicide—and there was a real fear that he might— the Israeli public would assume the southern front had collapsed. They therefore decided that Bar-Lev would serve "above" Gonen but not "in place" of him. Gonen screamed and shouted upon receiving the news. But he did not resign. He did not commit suicide, either.[31]

That left the question of what to do about Sharon. Elazar told Bar-Lev that if it turned out that he'd attacked against orders, he should relieve him of command and appoint Gonen in his place. Dayan told Elazar ruefully that there was nothing new about Sharon lying. But years before, when asked why he put up with it, Dayan famously remarked, "Better to struggle with stallions you can't control, than donkeys you can't get to move." Still, Dayan said that what Sharon had done enraged him more than anything else he had seen so far. If Bar-Lev wanted to get rid of him, he was fine with it.[32]

That was probably what he expected. Southern Command was manned by generals as divided as the builders of Babel. But there was no relationship in the army as fraught as the one between Sharon and Bar-Lev. Sharon said having Bar-Lev on top of him was "the last thing I needed to hear."[33] But at last there was someone to control the wild stallion called Ariel Sharon. On at least two occasions between October 10 and 13, Sharon proposed attacking the Egyptians.

Bar-Lev told him no.[34]

# 13

## FRENEMIES

*If I learned one thing from this war, it's that in radical times
the bitterest enmities are born as are the strongest friendships.*[1]
—One Israeli officer to another, October 9, 1973

After the failed offensive on October 9, Hafez el-Assad could still
win the war or lose it. What he could no longer do was control
it.[2] He could not even control the messaging. The bombing of
the television station in Damascus by the IAF on October 9 was
such a surprise, the Syrians did not have a chance to stop a live
radio broadcast. The sound of the bombs falling and the terrified
cries of the presenter were heard throughout the land. For Assad,
this raised concerns that transcended the implications of victory
or defeat. For as he surely knew, of all the leaders involved in the
conflict, he was the one that had the best chance of ending up
dead in a ditch.

Only a fifth of the Syrian forces that rolled off into battle
on October 9 made it back. Israeli photo reconnaissance revealed
that Syria was left with at most 450 tanks. Of that, 150 belonged
to Rifaat Assad's Defense Companies and had to be stationed in
Damascus to protect the regime. Morale was low. A Syrian interpreter probably spoke for many when he told a Russian coun-

terpart that he lived in grinding poverty and had no intention of dying for some lofty ideal.[3]

Meanwhile, Assad and his generals waited desperately by the teletype for word that Egypt was launching its offensive to the passes. Each time they expected the next telegram, or the one after, to bring news of the assault. Each time they were disappointed.[4]

Equally unnerving for Assad was the fact that Egypt had reneged on its prewar promise to fire Scud missiles into Israel if the IAF bombed targets deep inside Syria. In addition to bombing central Damascus, the Israelis had also struck a nearby power plant and a refinery in Homs. Egypt did nothing. Syria had no Scud missiles of its own. It was obvious that the IAF would be back again. There was nothing Assad could do to prevent it. Outwardly, Assad remained calm, even as his entreaties to Cairo were ignored and it became clear that he had been double-crossed. Assad's biographer notes with evident understatement that "communications between the two high commands lost the brotherly warmth of the prewar period."[5]

Any relief would have to come from Iraq, Assad's nemesis to the east. Saddam Hussein held a brief ceremony north of Baghdad before sending an enormous army off to Syria. The expeditionary force numbered sixty thousand men and included seven hundred tanks, dozens of artillery pieces, and hundreds of vehicles. An Israeli intelligence analyst estimated that the Iraqis sent fully half their army and two-thirds of their armor into Syria. Such a generous show of force left many suspecting that Saddam had designs on Syria that went well beyond fighting the Israelis. What they did not know was that Saddam had similar worries of his own. None of the Iraqi vehicles were permitted to load ammunition until they were well west of Baghdad for fear some enterprising general might spring a surprise coup while in the nation's capital.[6] *

---

* The Moroccans had a small land force in Syria from the start of the war. They originally planned to send badly needed fighter pilots as well, but they were sitting in jail as a result of a failed coup against Moroccan king Hassan II.

That left only one other country that could make a sizable contribution.* Pressure built on King Hussein to open a third front, or at least send an expeditionary force to Syria. More than half the kingdom's population had its origins west of the Jordan River, fleeing east in 1948 or thereafter. These ethnic Palestinians expected him to do *something*. Nevertheless, during the Black September crisis of 1970, it was to Israel that the king turned for help. Alliances come and go quickly in the Middle East. But the last thing he needed was Israeli fighter jets laying waste to his country. The king therefore reached out quietly to the Israelis through British prime minister Edward Heath to see what might be acceptable to them. The answer was, not very much. Henry Kissinger remarked that it was only in the Middle East that belligerents asked for an adversary's permission before waging war against them.[7]

In the end, the king sent a sizable force—160 tanks, 40 artillery pieces, and highly trained soldiers to man them—but held them back until October 13. It was a generous gesture, especially when you consider that these were the very brigades that fended off a Syrian invasion of Jordan during the Black September crisis only three years earlier. And it displayed yet again the king's gift for survival, maneuvering a middle path that placated Palestinians in his kingdom but did not burn bridges with Jerusalem. The one person that was not placated was Hafez el-Assad. In his authorized biography, Jordan's contribution earns mention in just half a sentence.[8]

There was one ally, however, to whom Assad knew he could turn in times of trouble and receive unquestioning support. One ally that gave its word to Syria and remained true throughout the war. That ally was the Soviet Union. A Soviet resupply effort of both Egypt and Syria began on October 9.[9]

By contrast, Israel's standing in Washington was precarious.

---

* Saudi Arabia sent a small contingent to Syria on October 12. After the war, Kuwait sent a contingent of twenty to forty-five tanks. Cuba might have sent six hundred soldiers as well.

On October 6, Henry Kissinger convened a committee called the Washington Special Action Group, or WSAG, to best manage the crisis among the different arms of America's sprawling national security establishment. The surprise attack on October 6 caught Kissinger in New York, so WSAG's first meeting was chaired by Secretary of Defense James Schlesinger. Schlesinger said the only question the group should consider was whether to label the Israelis "aggressors." Schlesinger found a ready ally in the Chairman of the Joint Chiefs of Staff, Admiral Thomas Moorer. Moorer harbored deep hostility toward Israel, possibly as a result of Israel's accidental attack on the USS *Liberty* in the 1967 war. After he retired from the service, he was quoted as saying, "I've never seen a President . . . stand up to them [Zionists]. If the American people understood what a grip those people have got on our government, they would rise up in arms." At the October 6 WSAG meeting, he said, "If we give [the Israelis] a single item of equipment, we will have taken sides."[10]

Mostly, the WSAG feared what support for Israel might mean for oil supplies. In the hectic moments just before the war began, a young NSC staffer named William Quandt drafted a memo for the White House. The truncated grammar speaks to how quickly he typed it. It states, among other things, that "if hostilities are imminent," the United States had to "convene oil task force to prepare on a contingency basis for cutoff of Arab oil." A second memo drafted immediately after hostilities began laid out a seven-item agenda for the first WSAG meeting. Item one on the agenda was evacuating Americans from the region. Item two on the agenda was "Oil."[11]

Standing athwart these currents was Henry Kissinger. No one quite knew what to make of him. To some, it was plain that the first Jewish secretary of state was going to be an advocate for the Jews. Others were not so sure. On October 6, Kissinger told China's ambassador that "our strategic objective is to prevent the Soviet Union from getting a dominant position in the Middle East." He added that he "took very seriously . . . the importance of maintaining good relations with the Arab countries." As for the Israelis, he said, they were "a secondary emotional problem having to do with domestic politics."[12]

In the statement that perhaps best revealed his thinking, he also told the Chinese that "within 72 to 96 hours the Arabs will be completely defeated."[13] Even a person wholeheartedly in favor of Israel would not resupply it within those first seventy-two to ninety-six hours and risk an oil embargo if he thought the IDF was going to win anyway. There would be plenty of time for resupply later, after the crisis passed, after Israel's inevitable victory.

At 8:20 on the morning of October 9, Israeli ambassador to the United States Simcha Dinitz arrived at the Map Room of the White House for a meeting with Kissinger. He came right to the point. In the first seventy-two hours of the war, the Israelis had lost forty-nine planes and *five hundred tanks*. Kissinger was so stunned his response in the official transcript includes a rare exclamation point: "500 tanks! How many do you have?"

Dinitz softened the news a bit by pointing out that an unspecified number—as it turned out, a little less than half—had not been lost in battle but merely broke down on the long drive to the front. But then he dropped another bombshell: the loss ratio with Egypt was "about one-to-one." The Israelis, Kissinger knew, were accustomed to loss ratios of twenty-to-one or better. "So that's why the Egyptians are so cocky," he sighed.[14]

The Israelis had fared better against the Syrians, Dinitz reported. But Iraq was sending an enormous force that would be there in two to three days. Israel needed resupply, and it needed it badly.[15]

Kissinger was staggered by the news. He told Dinitz, "You can't get tanks from here."

General Mordecai Gur, Israel's military attaché replied, "We could get them from Europe and take them by ship. . . . It's important; it's urgent. Your Air Force used to deliver it [planes and tanks] in civilian planes."

"But not in the middle of a war," Kissinger replied. "You have to realize that to take planes from combat units will be in every newspaper in the world." Kissinger then complained, "I don't understand how it could happen. Our strategy was to give you until Wednesday evening, by which time I thought the whole Egyptian army would be wrecked."

The official government transcript ends with the following: "Kissinger and Dinitz confer alone from 8:43 to 8:48 a.m."

It was, no doubt, a very interesting five minutes. Unfortunately, at the time of this writing, there is no publicly available transcript of what was said. Many have speculated that Dinitz threatened to use nuclear weapons if Israel's requests for conventional arms were not met. In his memoir, Kissinger says that Dinitz used the time to request that Golda be permitted to come to Washington secretly to plead for military aid, a request that Kissinger dismissed out of hand. This assertion is echoed in Dinitz's unpublished memoir. Putting aside the difficulty of proving a negative, if Dinitz had engaged in "nuclear blackmail," Kissinger would have almost certainly told someone, and that someone would have almost certainly written it down somewhere. A former senior American diplomat interviewed for this account said that he reviewed all the documents of the era, including those that remain classified. There is no reference to any such threat.[16]

\* \* \*

The very busy day of October 9 came to an end, and with it the first phase of the war. Syria ceased its offensive and braced for an Israeli response. Egypt ceased its offensive and the lines firmed up east of the canal. Winston Churchill would have said that it was not the beginning of the end, but it was the end of the beginning.

Overall, the Egyptians were satisfied, though they held a bit less than they had planned. The objective was to reach all the north–south roads six miles east of the canal.[17] They made it that far only along the Hamutal and Makhshir hills that Ariel Sharon's division negligently abandoned on October 8. The Syrians were pushed back to the original line, except for their toehold atop Mount Hermon.

Israel's leadership sat down on October 10 to take stock of the situation. Before the war, the army had defined its goals as "preventing the enemy any military gains and dealing him a serious defeat in order to give Israel a military advantage for the next few years."[18] These were the modest goals of a small war. In the much larger war that Israel found itself fighting, it was self-evident that "preventing the enemy any military gains" was not going to be possible along the canal. The IDF pushed the Syrians back to the original ceasefire line. It lacked the strength to do the same to the Egyptians.

The next best thing was acquiring bargaining chips for the coming negotiations. But bargaining chips where?

The obvious place was in Syria. The Syrian army was reeling. A thrust toward Damascus might just knock Syria out of the war, freeing resources to fight Egypt. At a minimum it would give Israel something to trade. This, at least, was the view of Elazar. He even allowed himself to fantasize that there could be a package deal: Israel withdraws from Syria if Egypt withdraws from Sinai.[19]

Others, led by Dayan, disagreed. Few seriously thought that Sadat would ever give up an inch of Egyptian soil for Syria. Moreover, if Assad did not agree to a ceasefire, then Israel would find itself overextended, trapped in a grinding war of attrition inside Syria. The original October 6 line was much easier to defend. Once Mount Hermon was retaken, Israel would have realized its war goals in the north, denying the Syrians any gain. Best to hold firm in the north, move forces south, and take Port Sayid on the west bank of the canal. It was against Egypt that Israel needed something to trade, not Syria. Admittedly, Port Sayid was not much of a bargaining chip. But it was lightly defended and was unprotected by surface-to-air missiles.[20]

Those present remembered it as one of the most difficult decisions of the war. And, not surprisingly, opinion was split right down the middle. What tipped the balance was a telegram from Washington. The Soviets were proposing a ceasefire. To all the shortages weighing upon Jerusalem was now added a shortage of time. Moving forces from the Golan to the canal would take close to a week; Golda needed bargaining chips before a ceasefire was declared. She sided with Elazar. The invasion of Syria was to commence the next day.[21]

Meanwhile, as the government debated where to attack, the Israeli air force calmly went about its business laying waste to Syria. The attacks on Syrian infrastructure the day before had been psychological victories, but caused little physical damage on the ground. Now, with some experience under their belts, Israeli pilots returned to finish the job. The bombing of a fuel depot in the port of Latakia ignited a spectacular fireball, as did the destruction of a refinery in Homs. Perhaps the most significant attack took place on a power plant in Qatna, not far from the Homs refinery. Its destruction is thought by Israeli intelligence to have caused power shortages inside Syria into the 1980s. This might be true. But a Syrian professor interviewed for this account said that there was so much corruption and so little electricity to begin with, it was hard to know for sure what caused rolling blackouts.[22]

These successes masked what critics of the IAF remembered as two of the worst failures of the war.

The first related to the enormous Iraqi army that AMAN warned was rolling into Syria. There were only two roads from Iraq into Syria. Iraqi forces traveled bumper to bumper across just one of them, trailing blizzards of dust behind them. Practically all six hundred miles they covered was in the desert, where there was no place to hide and no SAMs to protect them. In the 1967 war, the IAF obliterated the Egyptian army fleeing over identical terrain in

Sinai. There is no good explanation for why it did not do the same to the Iraqis in 1973. Only one halfhearted attempt was made at locating the Iraqis, on the evening of October 9.[23]

The second failure was arguably even greater. Though the Syrians received high marks for aptitude from their Soviet advisers, they had only three months to train in operating the SAMs. In the first days of the war, the inexperienced crews saturated the skies with a reckless abandon that outpaced resupply. Some time on October 9, the Syrians ran out of missiles. The now quiet airspace handed the IAF its best opportunity to win the war. For twenty-four crucial hours, the SAM batteries stood helplessly on the ground, naked to attack. The Israelis bombed Syrian runways to prevent resupply. But for reasons that are not clear, they never attempted to destroy the SAMs themselves.[24]

* * *

The entire Israeli army in the north was down to just 378 tanks, which was a little less than what the Syrians had. But the Syrians had to leave over 100 in Damascus to protect the regime. Ordinarily, a ratio of one-to-one greatly favored the defender. The Syrians knew better. In the words of his biographer, "Assad's mind was wholly taken up with the defense of Damascus." The wives and children of prominent Syrians were moved farther north to the Alawite mountains. Defense Minister Mustafa Tlass writes that the government handed out a half million rifles for guerilla warfare. If true, it was a bold gamble on national unity, and one that proved correct. After the war, ordinary Syrians did not turn those weapons on the regime, or upon one another.[25]

Spearheading Israel's attack was the brigade commanded by Colonel Yanush Ben-Gal, now a man with a valley to cross and a score to settle. In a speech to those he commanded—those that had survived the Valley of Tears—he minced no words: "We are going now to avenge the blood of our comrades that fell in battle. . . . The Syrian army and the Syrian nation are cruel by their nature. You must kill them, or they will kill you without mercy."[26]

Ben-Gal was too smart to cross into Syria along the main road from Kuneitra to Damascus. Instead, he made his main effort farther north in the hilly terrain between Outposts 104 and 105. It was a classic Israeli operation, driving toward the enemy's capital over the route that was least expected. Moshe Dayan boasted to reporters that the Syrians were about to find out that the road that led from Damascus to Israel also led from Israel to Damascus. It was a pithy quote that rolled nicely off the tongue, but it angered Kissinger, who was already upset over the bombing of Damascus. "What in the hell am I now going to tell the Russians?" he screamed at an Israeli diplomat.[27]

When officers cautioned Ben-Gal about the rugged terrain in the northern Golan, he told them that he saw it as an advantage. The hills offered good visibility for one tank battalion to lay covering fire to aid the advance of another. The results in the field proved him correct. The tanks forced their way through over the few narrow roads, plowing forward behind a rolling box of smoke and fire. Syrian resistance became uneven, fierce in some places, but light in others. The Israelis moved nine miles in two days, taking several important ridgelines and the hilltop village of Mazrat Beit Jinn.[28]

For all its failures leading up the war, AMAN performed well after fighting broke out, accurately predicting that King Hussein would not open a third front and supplying timely warnings of major Arab attacks. The one exception was the arrival of Iraqi forces on the Syrian battlefield. AMAN estimated that they could not get there before October 13. They arrived on October 12. The bigger failure belonged not to AMAN but to the staff officers working inside Northern Command. As early as October 9, AMAN had warned them of an Iraqi force heading for Syria.

Somehow, though intelligence was constantly delivered as if through a fire hose, this warning never trickled down to the commanders in the field. They had no idea that *any* Iraqi force was headed their way. When tanks painted in an unfamiliar color were first seen approaching their southern flank, the spotters assumed they were Syrians covered in some strange dust.[29]

If Iraqi tanks had arrived at night, they might have scored the dream of every strategist, landing a surprise attack on the enemy's flank. The Israelis avoided disaster only because someone happened to see them through their binoculars and because tanks of Israel's 679th Armored Brigade happened to be on a nearby hilltop rearming and refueling.[30] With only minutes to spare, the 679th's commander, Colonel Ori Orr, positioned his tanks along the ridgetop as calmly as if he were directing maneuvers back in training camp.

The line of Iraqi vehicles was so long that Orr could not see the end of it. Fortunately for Orr, the Iraqis were just as oblivious as the Israelis, and they drove straight into an ambush. The Israelis were positioned in the shape of the letter "U" turned upside-down; the Iraqis drove north through the opening on the bottom. Surrounded on three sides, they never had much of a chance. Dozens of Iraqi vehicles were destroyed. The Israelis did not lose a tank. The Iraqis launched a halfhearted attack the next day, October 13, but they accomplished little. With that, the lines of what became known as the "bulge" firmed up.[31]

The Israelis were now twenty-seven miles from Damascus. That was just beyond the range of artillery. But it was close enough to shell the Kisweh military base south of the city. And that was close enough for Assad to hear in his presidential palace. The Israelis had their bargaining chips. One could bomb Damascus from the air as readily as with artillery. But, as Dayan liked to point out, the Syrians knew that one does not conquer cities with planes.[32]

Unfortunately, bargaining chips alone were not going to solve Israel's military predicament. To defeat Egypt was to defeat Syria, but the same was not true in reverse. The Israelis now had to dig in for a grinding war of attrition with Syria. And they had no plan for victory against Egypt.

Egypt's General Sa'ad Shazly understood this. He had his army dig in as well. He planned for a war of attrition at this stage of the operation because it was a war he knew that Egypt was well suited to fight. Egypt had the manpower and the resources to outlast the Israelis. It had the unflinching support of a superpower.

Unfortunately, it also had one other thing. A president to snatch defeat from the jaws of victory.

# 14

## NEVER CALL SURRENDER

As the first week of the war ended, one could question the wisdom of the *maozim* that made up the Bar-Lev Line. No one could question the courage of the men that served inside them. Two of the forts were still holding out almost a week into the war.

One was the northernmost *maoz* called Budapest. It was easier to defend because it was located at the edge of an impassable swamp near the shores of the Mediterranean. A road led to it, one laid at great difficulty. Tanks that ventured off it sometimes sank all the way up to their turrets. Budapest also had sixty-three men, more than triple the number in most of the others. For these reasons, it was one of the few *maozim* that had a happy ending. A rescue party reached it late on the night of October 11 and relieved its beleaguered defenders.[1]

The second stubborn holdout was the southernmost *maoz*, perched where the canal met the Gulf of Suez. It was called Mezakh.

The men of Mezakh covered themselves in glory. Like the soldiers of all the *maozim*, they were third-line troops never meant for combat. Yet they held out against intense shelling and waves of attacking Egyptian soldiers. "They were crazy," one Israeli remembered, "in a kind of ecstasy where they shouted and screamed."

The commander of the *maoz* was a twenty-year-old religious student named Captain Shlomo Ardenest. By October 11, five of his men were dead, twenty-seven lay on the floor groaning from war wounds, and only twelve were still healthy.[2]

Sea commandos in six Zodiac rubber boats were sent up the Gulf of Suez on October 11, led by a legendary Israeli officer named Dov Bar. Bar had successfully carried out numerous missions deemed impossible. This one was beyond even him. When the men in Mezakh saw the Zodiacs turn back to the mother ship, they knew there would be no rescue.[3] It left them with only two options: fight to the death, or something unthinkable.

On December 8, 1954, an Israeli commando force was captured inside Syria while on a mission to replace the battery in a listening device. One of the captured soldiers committed suicide in Damascus's notorious el-Mazah prison. The name of the soldier, Uri Ilan, passed on into legend when on his body a note was found in which he had written, "I didn't betray." The remaining soldiers broke under torture and told all they knew. When they returned home in a prisoner swap, they were court-martialed for "surrendering." In the words of one journalist, the army chief of staff "pressed for a conviction at any cost" in order to "make an example out of them." The army chief of staff was Moshe Dayan.[4] *

Captain Ardenest radioed headquarters and sought permission to surrender. Dayan initially gave the authorization. But then a half hour later he canceled the first order and sent new instructions: Captain Ardenest would have to decide what to do on his own.[5]

Ardenest grew up in the era of Israel's military adolescence, hearing war stories about Uri Ilan and others. But he found the courage to put his men first, and on the morning of October 13, he negotiated a surrender through the Red Cross. The Egyptians

---

* Fifty years later, the commander told a reporter, "The Army and the establishment would have preferred to receive us in coffins rather than on our own two feet because then they could have created a legend of Israeli soldiers fighting, dying and not surrendering. . . . In those days the ethos was all communist, the individual was secondary, and the collective was what was important."

made sure to have a television crew on hand to create a "victory photo." The crew unwittingly filmed what would become one of the iconic photos of the war for Israel: a bearded, nineteen-year-old rabbinical student named Hillel Unsdorfer emerging with a Torah scroll. The scroll's cover indicated that it originated in one of the communities in Europe lost in the Holocaust.[6] *

The men emerged, saluted their Egyptian captors, and were taken west over the canal. From there they were driven to Cairo.

* * *

Of the three bad outcomes for a soldier in war—killed, wounded, or captured—it was the third that scared Israeli soldiers the most.

To be sure, the Israelis' own record regarding prisoners was hardly perfect. In the early days of the war, a Bedouin helping Egyptian commandos in the Sinai was captured and acknowledged killing an unarmed Israeli journalist. The Bedouin was promptly executed. But the enraged Israelis were not mollified and received orders from their field officer not to take prisoners. As one Israeli put it, "When we got that order we were not happy, we were doubly happy." The next day they executed twenty more captured Egyptians.[7]

The soldiers involved in the incident waited decades to reveal the story, after they could no longer be prosecuted. It was the threat of criminal prosecution that undoubtedly had a restraining effect on Israeli soldiers at the time. One Syrian POW complained to an Israeli doctor about cigarette burns on his abdomen. The Israeli doctor saw the scars, shouted at the policeman who brought him, and treatment of the prisoner improved. Research for this account failed to uncover any other executions, but there were credible stories of beatings. Some occurred in the field, like the Sinai killings, after Israeli soldiers discovered that their comrades

---

* Unsdorfer made it back to Israel in the prisoner swap, though he died tragically in a car accident some years later. The Torah scroll was returned to Israel by Egypt in the 1990s.

had been executed. But others occurred while prisoners were in transit or while under interrogation.[8]

Israeli prisoners in Arab hands had no one to complain to and abuse was predictably far more widespread. Amnesty International concluded, in dry understatement, that "abuses . . . perpetrated against the former Israeli prisoners of war held in Syria appear generally to have been of a more severe nature."[9] *

There are dozens of memoirs of the Yom Kippur War. None are as harrowing as Amnon Sharon's *Sane in Damascus*, a chronicle of his time in Syrian captivity. He describes being beaten regularly (once losing a tooth), being burned with cigarettes, and having his toenails ripped out. He walked in pain for the rest of his life. Other Israeli soldiers came back to tell similar stories of fingernails ripped out, feet beaten while being hung upside down, burns, and electric shock torture. An Israeli pilot named Avi Lanier had information so sensitive it remains classified to this day. He refused to disclose it; the Syrians beat him to death. An Israeli who fell into Egyptian captivity, David Senesh, was the nephew of Hannah Senesh, an iconic Holocaust hero who was captured and executed by the Nazis. He said what he endured "was not cold, ideological torture like the Nazis administered. It was driven by pure hatred."[10]

A young intelligence officer named Amos Levinberg made his own pact with the devil. When senior Israeli intelligence officers saw his name among those captured on Mount Hermon, they knew they were in trouble. Levinberg possessed the nightmare trifecta: an insatiable curiosity about Israeli intelligence, a spectacular memory, and an ego that drove him to show everyone just how much he knew. He once boasted that he could match every officer on the base to their car with nothing but the license

---

* The Yom Kippur War marked the first time that nations at war cooperated with Amnesty International in a postwar investigation of abuses, giving access to former prisoners. Only Israel and Syria participated. Egypt had good reason to decline. An investigation in Israel concluded, to the surprise of all, that prisoner abuse was worse in Egypt than in Syria.

plate number, and then he did it on a dare. Levinberg told the
Syrians everything, not just informing them but training them
on every aspect of Israel's signal intelligence, where they put listening devices, how they put them there, et cetera. The Syrians
were stunned by the quality of the information and flew in Russians to interview him as well. Immediately after the war ended,
Israeli intelligence overheard a Syrian officer tell his men, "The
Jewish professor says that the Jews hear everything and listen to
everything. You must be very careful as to what you say." Sometime during his ordeal, Levinberg was brought back to the cell
he shared with other Israeli prisoners. He murmured that he had
been beaten, but Amnon Sharon—the tank officer who authored
*Sane in Damascus*—tore his shirt off and saw that there was not
a mark on him. Sharon screamed, "Liar!!!," pounced on him, and
beat him, releasing all his pent-up rage. In Sharon's words, if a
one-legged fellow prisoner had not pulled him off, "I would have
torn him to pieces."[11]

Both sides showed moments of humanity, some of which bordered on the surreal. At the end of the war, the Egyptian general
Ismail Ali assembled Israeli POWs and informed them that they
would soon be going home. With what one called "typical Israeli
chutzpah," someone asked if they could see the pyramids, seeing
as they were in Egypt anyway. The general good-naturedly agreed
that they could. Buses were brought in and drove them past the
pyramids of Giza, located just a few miles from their prison cells
in Cairo.[12]

The ordeal of the 314 Israelis who fell into captivity during
the 1973 war—248 in Egypt, 66 in Syria—did not end when they
returned home. All were sent to a facility—not to be treated for
post-traumatic stress, which was then only thinly understood—
but to find out what they had told their captors. The facility was
located in the Israeli town of Zichron Yakov; the men sent there
nicknamed it "Stalag Zichron." It was a nice play on words because
it literally translated to "Stalag Memory." Interrogators plumbed

the depths of their memories, even giving some "truth serum," ostensibly to treat shell shock. In interviews of these soldiers years later, the word that comes up again and again is *humiliation*. Elazar himself asked the men, "Why didn't you do what Uri Ilan did? Why didn't you commit suicide?" On a radio program interviewing the survivors of Mezakh, former chief of staff Chaim Laskov said that "falling into captivity, surrendering, these are evasive things. An order to surrender is illegal. The only proper order is 'every man for himself.'"[13]

Still, the Yom Kippur War was the moment in which Israeli society finally began to take a more realistic approach to prisoners of war. Perhaps they were affected by the way the United States treated returning POWs from Vietnam as heroes, even though the war itself was controversial. Perhaps they came to their senses and realized that it was absurd to expect men to commit suicide in captivity.

The decision was made at the highest levels not to prosecute Captain Levinberg for handing over information to the Syrians and Russians. Golda Meir, ever the Jewish mother, even agreed to meet with him. More than forty years later, Levinberg remembered her fondly for the compassion she showed him.[14]

While he was imprisoned in Egypt being tortured, Ardenest wondered if it paid to survive, given that he would be court-martialed once he got home. But then, as he waited to return to Israel, a pilot who had fallen into captivity later in the war hugged him and said, "You're the commander of Mezakh? You guys are all heroes."[15] Those words flooded him with relief. As it turned out, he was not court-martialed. But his actions holding off the Egyptian Army for an entire week did not earn him any medals, either.

Years later, Ardenest saw Moshe Dayan and approached him. Couldn't Dayan have given the order to surrender? Couldn't Dayan have saved Ardenest from having to make that decision himself?

Dayan refused to respond.[16]

# 15

## ARMAGEDDON ON A ROAD
## CALLED TALISMAN

All of military history indicates that battles in the desert are
short and decisive, more like naval battles than land battles.[1]

—Henry Kissinger

In the first twenty-five years of its life, the State of Israel labored
to equip a modern army at a time when horses and carts were still
a common sight. In between periodic wars, it also absorbed Jewish
refugees whose numbers surpassed that of the original population.
Something in all this was bound to get the short end of the stick
and that something was the Israeli navy. It was the only branch of
the service that did not share in the glory of 1967, because it failed
in every mission it was given. The biggest failure of all had tragic
consequences. The navy accidentally attacked the USS *Liberty*, an
American spy ship operating legally in international waters.[2]

The men who commanded the navy were determined to do
better the next time. The sinking of the *Eilat* in 1968 convinced
the Israelis that destroyers and frigates were as relevant to modern
warfare as dreadnoughts and cannons. They were all removed from
service and replaced with small, fast-moving missile boats. The
boats were armed with the Gabriel missile, a homegrown weapon
that was the pride of Israel's armament industry. The Gabriel had

a range of twelve and a half miles. The Soviet-made Styx missiles they faced had a range of over thirty miles. To overcome the disparity, the Israelis employed electronic jamming and fired metal chaff to confuse enemy radar.[3]

On the first night of the war, five Israeli missile boats attacked the Syrians right in their main base in Latakia. It was the first naval engagement in history fought exclusively with missiles.[4] In theory, the Syrians should have been able to sink the Israeli boats with their Soviet-made missiles before the Israelis got into range to fire theirs. But this was also the first time that the arms makers of the world learned there was a new player on the global stage. Israeli countermeasures worked perfectly. Fifty-four Soviet missiles went flying off to hit imaginary targets, while every Syrian boat went to the bottom. Four Egyptian missile boats challenged the Israelis two nights later. Three of them went to the bottom as well. The Israelis did not take a single casualty in either encounter.

After that, nothing on Egypt's or Syria's shoreline was safe. The Israelis went on a rampage. They felt confident enough that, after their missiles hit fuel tanks near the Syrian port of Latakia on the evening of October 10, the commander of one missile boat allowed men to come up from the engineering room to enjoy the spectacle illuminating the night sky. The Syrians and Egyptians never left port.[5] To this day, the Israeli navy has an upside-down heritage. In the navy, the '67 war is remembered as the bad war. The Yom Kippur War is remembered as the good one.

Meanwhile, other fertile minds inside Israel took a hard look at the events of the previous week and began to craft solutions. What made the Sagger missiles so lethal was the mile-long wire connected to a joystick that allowed operators to direct them onto the target. One had only to look at the multitude of wires lying in the sand, crisscrossing the dunes as if hung on a weaver's loom, to realize that the Egyptians had to fire a lot of Saggers to destroy a single Israeli tank. Put another way, the raw courage of Egyptian soldiers was not enough to score a hit. Sagger operators also had to sit undisturbed while they guided their missiles from distances that were usually over half a mile away. The obvious solution was to subject them to artillery fire. The exploding shells did not have to kill or wound the operators. It was enough to kick up dust, force operators to take cover, or simply disturb their concentration.[6]

A similar process took place in the air force. Once the shock of the first few days wore off and things entered a more predictable rhythm, Peled and others could take the time to do what they did best: analyze a sticky problem and come up with a solution.[7]

A study early in the war revealed that the SAMs were first and foremost an intelligence challenge. Wherever pilots knew the location of the SAMs, they were destroyed, with the same holding true in reverse. Photo reconnaissance did not offer a solution. The dummy sites could not be distinguished from the real ones, and the SAM-6s could be moved in the time it took to develop the photos and analyze them. Thus was born a new tactic: sending up a plane to draw fire so the enemy would give away its position. The Israelis nicknamed the decoy planes with a slang Hebrew term that loosely translates to mean "a sexually attractive woman used to dupe unsuspecting men."[8]

But sending up flying femme fatales offered no solution, at least within the plans that had been painstakingly drawn up before the war. The thinking then was that you could not defeat the SAMs unless you overwhelmed them. This opera in the sky sent planes on numerous preplanned flight routes that could not be changed at the last minute. Here Peled and his subordinates showed their genius for adaptation under pressure. The hardest thing for anyone to do is acknowledge a mistake and cut their losses. The IAF did it with aplomb, throwing years of hard work, and all the assumptions that went with it, right into the trash bin. The SAMs would no longer be overwhelmed with squadrons of fighter jets. Instead, smaller, flexible "hunter" groups would wait for the "femme fatale planes" to be fired upon. Once they saw the source of the fire, they would quickly close in to destroy the SAMs.[9]

This was hardly a perfect solution. Israeli planes were still lost in the process. But at least multiple SAMs were destroyed as well. There was another advantage. After the failure to destroy the SAMs in the early days of the war, the IAF never launched another large-scale attack on Arab air defenses.[10] This was not just because of a loss of confidence. Many still believed in Tagar and Dougman 5. Indeed, for the rest of their lives, Peled and his predecessor, Moti Hod, insisted that the SAMs would have been destroyed had the air force not stopped in the middle. But therein lay the problem: it was not possible to take such a large portion of the air force out of the battle to carry out Tagar and Dougman 5. It was also too dangerous to risk so many planes on one throw of the dice. The new approach allowed smaller fighter wings to do the job piecemeal while the rest of the air force remained in the fight.

These lessons were acquired at great cost, more than the Israelis could afford to pay. The army, the air force, the Israeli economy itself—these could remain on a war footing only with resupply from outside. That could come from only one place.

* * *

Late on October 9, Henry Kissinger met with Israeli ambassador Simcha Dinitz to deliver good news. The president formally agreed to replace all of Israel's tank and fighter jet losses, and to supply all "consumables"—ammunition—that it requested, apart from laser-guided bombs. The message must have relieved Dinitz because he felt comfortable enough to report to Kissinger that Israel's situation no longer looked as dire as it did when they met in the morning. Except on Mount Hermon, the Syrians had been pushed back to the original line, and there had been progress in Sinai as well. Kissinger relaxed and even cracked a joke at the expense of his aide Brent Scowcroft. But before the two men parted, he choked up. "As long as I am here," he said, "I won't abandon Israel."[11]

It was comforting in Jerusalem to hear that there would be resupply. But resupply when?

A memo drafted by the NSC on October 9 noted that "Kuwait is calling for the use of oil as part of the battle." The memo went on to note that if an oil embargo took place—even just a limited one affecting Western Europe only—then "we should be prepared to issue a statement on rationing if necessary." Finally, "most of our Ambassadors in the Arab world seem to feel the best outcome we can hope for now is an immediate ceasefire."[12]

The next day, October 10, the CEOs of Exxon and Gulf Oil met with State Department officials. They warned that there was a real risk that their oil-producing assets would be nationalized. One added that "we survived the 1967 crisis but now the Arabs have the oil companies at their mercies." Gulf Oil chairman Bob R. Dorsey expressed alarm because if Kuwait followed through on its threat and nationalized Gulf's interests, his company stood to lose 1.5 million barrels per day out of total production of 2.5 million barrels per day.

Moreover, the world needed the oil and there was nowhere else to get it. The United States had spare capacity of only 1 percent. Already, in talks in Vienna, the Saudis were demanding that the fee charged to oil companies by OPEC countries—the so-called posted price—be raised from $3 per barrel to $6 per barrel. This 100 percent increase meant that Arab governments would now receive 85 percent of oil profits.

Worse still, Saudi Arabia's representative, Sheikh Zaki Yamani—a name soon to become a household word—threatened to cut production by 5 percent per month until Israel withdrew to the 1967 boundary. The deputy secretary of state who chaired the meeting, Kenneth Rush, pointed out that Israel had forgone a first strike but agreed that "prolongation of the fighting is undesirable."[13]

In the face of these countercurrents, Kissinger attempted to chart a middle course. He could not please everyone. So he played for time.

On October 10, he received a message from the Soviet embassy stating that Moscow was interested in an immediate ceasefire. Sensing how precarious Sadat's position was, the Soviets sought no preconditions, only "coordinated actions of the U.S.S.R. and the U.S. [to] facilitate the ceasefire in the Middle East." Kissinger wanted to buy time for Israel to launch its counterattack into Syria and acquire some bargaining chips. Fate handed him a perfect excuse. Coincidentally, October 10 was the day that Spiro Agnew resigned as vice president over corruption charges. Kissinger called Dobrynin and told him that Washington was in crisis and so "the President cannot possibly address this question [the ceasefire]." Kissinger was coy as to the nature of the crisis, but two days later he joked that he would make Dobrynin vice president, if Dobrynin made him a member of the Politburo.[14]

Meanwhile, Kissinger learned of what he termed "the ominous news of a Soviet airlift to Syria." Despite this, and despite promises made to Israel in Nixon's name on October 9, no weapons were sent by Washington. Kissinger handed Dinitz off to Defense Secretary Schlesinger, knowing that Schlesinger was hostile to Israel and any notion of sending assistance.* Kissinger would later claim that Scowcroft and top aide Joseph J. Sisco worked tirelessly to arrange a resupply effort but were "given the runaround."[15]

Any assertion that Kissinger could not overcome bureaucratic stonewalling—and this at the very height of his influence, while Nixon was preoccupied with Watergate—would have to clear a very high bar of skepticism. The Israelis never believed a word of it. Military attaché General Motta Gur and air force attaché General Shyka Barkat understood Washington as well as anyone. Both concluded that if there was any "runaround," the perpetrators did so only after receiving a wink, a nod, and the tacit approval of Dr. Henry Alfred Kissinger. There would be no resupply. And soon there would be no time, either. Kissinger sidestepped the Soviet ceasefire proposal, hoping the Israelis would win bargaining chips

---

* Schlesinger brushed off Dinitz's request, saying, "Everybody hates you, no one will give you the right to fly over their territory."

on the battlefield. He received a call from Scowcroft late on the night of October 11. The Israelis had indeed broken through and seized sizable chunks of Syria that could be traded at the negotiating table.[16]

Early the next morning, Kissinger called Nixon. By now they had stalled the Soviet ceasefire proposal for forty-eight hours. The delay had paid off. There had been no supply of Israel, so the Arabs remained mollified. King Feisal sent a message on October 11 that the State Department judged "relatively moderate." Now, in Kissinger's words, "there's a sort of balance in the sense that the Israelis gained in Syria and lost in Egypt." With all the pieces in place, Kissinger said that it was time for a ceasefire. In a few hours, he told Nixon, he would meet with the British and ask them to introduce the resolution in the UN Security Council. The Soviets had presumably lined up the support of Egypt for a ceasefire. Now Washington would line up the support of the Israelis.[17]

It seemed the perfect outcome. American honor had been preserved. The Israelis had fought the Arabs to a draw, so Washington had avoided the specter of Soviet weapons defeating American weapons. The Arab world had been mollified, so there was no disruption in oil supplies. And the crisis would soon be over.

* * *

Late on the night of October 11, Elazar almost fainted from exhaustion. He was revived with caffeine administered by that most American of delivery systems, copious glasses of Coca-Cola. With that he went right back to work.[18]

Less than an hour later, ten minutes into October 12, he was given some of the worst news of the war. General Peled informed him that the Americans were refusing to supply Israel with more fighter jets and the IAF was rapidly reaching its "red line." The IAF began the war with 301 combat-ready planes. It was now down to 220. Once it dipped below what Peled called the "critical level of 210–220," it could no longer provide air support for ground operations. At that level, the most the IAF could do was defend Israeli skies, and even that would have to be limited to major cities only. Peled said that it would be best to enter a ceasefire in the next thirty-six hours, on the morning of October 13.[19]

Some have claimed that Peled exaggerated the IAF's predicament. The figure of 301 combat-ready did not count another 82 that were in hangars for repairs and maintenance when the war started. Moreover, of the 80 planes hit by enemy fire, only about 50 were completely lost, and a portion of the remainder were in the process of being repaired and returned into service. Of course, no one then knew it, but now armed with experience and better tactics, the IAF would go on to lose only another 36 planes over the remainder of the war. Nevertheless, Peled's words had a devastating effect on the General Staff. What he said was echoed by Chaim Bar-Lev, who reported that—although mechanics were working feverishly to restore equipment to service—the three divisions along the canal were down to just 672 working tanks. It was also echoed by Golda's military secretary, General Yisroel Lior, who reported that the army had an immediate need for forty-five thousand tank shells.[20]

On the morning of October 12, Washington time, Dinitz contacted Kissinger. The Israelis were willing to enter a ceasefire. The plan was for the British to introduce the resolution before the UN Security Council the following day.[21] The war would end on October 13, with the Israeli army holding difficult-to-defend lines in both the north and the south. The Israeli economy would grind to a halt, because it would be impossible to demobilize the reservists. Israeli Foreign Minister Abba Eban said of the ceasefire, it "would have meant that the Egyptians and Syrians had won the first round of the war. From these new positions they would have pressed for Israel's return to the pre-1967 lines [without giving a peace treaty in return]."[22]

Those involved in the negotiations questioned whether Syria would agree to a "ceasefire in place" with Israeli troops practically within artillery range of Damascus. But everyone thought that Sadat understood the situation and would readily sign on. What Kissinger did not know was that, in the words of Dobrynin, there was a "general lack of stability in the behavior of the Egyptian leader," and therefore, when speaking of the ceasefire, Brezhnev avoided the question of its terms. The moment of truth came on the evening of October 12. The British ambassador to Egypt handed Sadat a message in the name of Prime Minister Heath, asking him to agree to a ceasefire in place. The ambassador, Sir Phillip Adams, pointed out that "this was a concession the Israelis had already been compelled to agree to."[23]

To the astonishment of all, Sadat turned down the proposal.

On the morning of the following day, October 13, Egypt responded with a list of demands. Israel had to withdraw within a predetermined time to "behind the pre-5th June 1967 lines." Gazan Palestinians would be given statehood, despite refusing to recognize Israel's right to exist. And Israel would have to rely upon UN observers to guarantee freedom of shipping through the Straits of Tiran—guarantees that had previously proved worthless—and this for only "a specified period." In return for all this, Israel would receive no recognition and no peace. All Sadat was prepared to give was a vague statement of non-belligerency.[24] In substance, the Egyptian demands sought not just to roll back Israel's victory in 1967, but its victory in 1956 as well.

This was an overreach, to put it mildly. Upon hearing of it, Senator J. William Fulbright—perhaps the best friend the Arabs had in the United States Senate—growled that Anwar Sadat was "not a very bright man." Diplomats around the world spent October 13 scrambling to find a formula that might work. There was even talk of introducing the ceasefire resolution anyway, in the hope that Sadat would yield to the consensus of the UN Security Council. Sadat replied that if such a resolution was brought, he would ask the Chinese to veto it.[25]

Kissinger now knew what he had to do.* He called Scowcroft and told him to get ready "to pour stuff in there." Magically, the "bureaucratic delays" disappeared. The largest airlift in history was about to commence.[26]

Giving Sadat every benefit of the doubt, one could argue that he did not know his rejection of the ceasefire would cause Kissinger to green-light the airlift to Israel. Accordingly, given that the goal was to engage Israel in a war of attrition, it arguably made sense to reject the ceasefire to keep up the pressure and not give the IDF a chance to regroup. From declassified documents, we now know that the Israelis were very much afraid of this scenario.[27] But then Sadat followed up his strategic blunder with a tactical one of equal proportion.

Egypt went to war of two minds. Shazly was convinced that the plan was to advance just six miles and remain within the protective umbrella of the SAMs. Gamasy, and probably General Ismail Ali, were just as convinced that this was merely an operative pause, and the plan was to push on to the passes. Early in the war, Sadat made remarks suggesting that he agreed with Shazly that "territory isn't important; what is important is to exhaust the enemy . . . make the enemy bleed."[28]

Starting on October 11, General Ismail Ali broached the idea of "building on the success" of the first five days and continuing the offensive farther east to the passes. Shazly was horrified, arguing against it, in his words, "passionately, continuously, and in front of many people."[29] It is difficult to see how anyone in Cairo could have opposed him. *The Shazly plan had worked.* The weakness in the plan was that it forced Egyptian ground soldiers to hold out in the desert, without fighting behind a natural barrier.

---

* William B. Quandt, who served on the NSC in 1973, ultimately as its director for Middle Eastern Affairs, wrote, "The resupply of arms to Israel had been deliberately delayed as a form of pressure on Israel and in order not to reduce the chances of Sadat's acceptance of the cease-fire proposal." Schlesinger made similar comments at a press conference on October 26, 1973.

The events of the previous week proved that the gamble had paid off. Egyptian troops had beaten back every Israeli counterattack. There was nothing to be gained tactically by reaching the passes. The line could be defended one way or the other.

There was nothing to be gained at the negotiating table, either. The Egyptians had the same leverage whether they penetrated six miles or twenty. The key was surviving and forcing the Israelis to fight a war of attrition they could not win. The events of the previous week likewise proved the wisdom of remaining inside the protective range of the surface-to-air missiles. The one Egyptian foray outside that protection—the October 9 attempt to conquer the Abu Rudeis oil fields—ended with the IAF wiping out the attacking force.[30]

Despite all the above, which was as visible in real time as it was in hindsight, Sadat ordered the offensive to the passes anyway. After the war, the Egyptians argued that they had to carry out the attack to relieve pressure on their Syrian allies. This assertion was repeated so many times in so many different forums that it acquired a measure of acceptance.[31] Upon closer examination, it appears unconvincing.

Sadat demonstrated callous disregard for Syria's needs throughout the war. In the words of Patrick Seale, Assad's biographer and confidant, "by October 13 . . . relations between Syria and Egypt were barely civil." The October 14 offensive offered a chance for Egyptians to salvage their honor and argue that they had in fact assisted their beleaguered ally. Some went so far as to spin the events of October 14 in courageous terms, casting it as a victory of sorts (the outcome notwithstanding) because it relieved pressure on Damascus. The trouble with this argument is that by the time Sadat ordered the attack, word had reached Cairo that Iraqi and Jordanian forces were in Syria and that the Israelis had been stopped. The time to rescue Syria was on October 11, not October 14.[32]

The Egyptians tried to use the Syrians as the excuse for their other great blunder. After the war, Kissinger asked Egyptian Foreign Minister Ismail Fahmi why Egypt did not accept the October 13 ceasefire proposal. Before abruptly changing the subject, Fahmi replied that "Sadat could not accept the ceasefire while the Syrians were refusing."[33] This answer is absurd. On October 20, just a week later, the Egyptians did exactly that—accept a ceasefire that the Syrians angrily refused.

Then why did Sadat cast aside the Shazly plan just as it was working?

The evidence points in but one direction. It is the phenomenon that appears throughout military history—the age-old sin of hubris. After the initial surprise of October 6, the Egyptians experienced little success *attacking*, only *defending*. In fact, every attack had failed at great cost. The only exception was the taking of the two hills on October 8, because Ariel Sharon's division drove off and left them unprotected.

And yet, in the face of this, Sadat was drunk enough on victory to conclude that this was the time for an all-out offensive. An American intelligence source inside Egypt issued the following report: "The Egyptian goal now has been broadened because of what is described as President Sadat's view that his armies are capable of taking all the Sinai."[34]

* * *

Meanwhile, on the afternoon of October 12, Elazar convened the senior leadership of the government and the army—eighteen people in all—for what he called "a very, very fateful decision." Elazar reviewed the dire situation of planes and tanks before concluding that Israel needed a ceasefire and needed it badly. But what if Sadat refused? Should they attempt to cross the canal? Practically the only criteria for the decision, he said, was whether a crossing made a ceasefire more or less likely. Elazar said that he had not yet made up his mind himself.[35]

The opportunities west of the canal were obvious. A tank

force, once set loose, could destroy the SAMs or at least cause them to retreat, thereby opening the skies to the air force. Seemingly, this was the only way to defeat the Egyptian army and avoid a war of attrition. The trouble was that Egypt had 550 tanks west of the canal, and the most the Israelis could send was 400. This was hardly a favorable ratio for an attacker. Worst of all, Israel had only one heavy bridge—the so-called rolling bridge—and two vulnerable pontoon bridges. If they were destroyed, the force west of the canal would be cut off. "Let me ask an idiotic question," Golda said. "Where could we get a bridge if we needed one?" Elazar explained that the only source was the Americans, but they would never supply one because it was deemed an "offensive weapon." Dayan added that if the attack failed, and a large force was lost west of the canal, they might find themselves fighting outside Tel Aviv. General Tal added that in all their war games, the IDF assumed it was controlling the east bank of the canal. No Israeli soldiers had drilled battling to the canal and then crossing under fire. Something this complicated was not the sort of thing you could improvise in the field.[36]

As he spoke, someone knocked on the door and asked Mossad chief Zvi Zamir to step outside. The others in the room, nervously chain-smoking, could barely hide their annoyance. What could he possibly have that was more urgent than the matter at hand?[37]

He soon returned with news that more than justified his brief absence. The Egyptian officer who had been passing secrets to Mossad had made contact. Egypt was about to helicopter three brigades of commandos to the passes. Zamir immediately understood what that meant: an offensive was coming.[38]

Zamir had his aide rush to the Mossad office nearby and bring the file containing Egypt's war plan. The plan, which Mossad had carefully stitched together from multiple sources, called for Egyptian commandos to block the passes while nine hundred tanks attacked east to hook up with them. To carry this out, the Egyptians would have to move between two hundred and three hundred tanks from the west bank of the canal to the east. Once that happened, the ground west of the canal would be undefended, vulnerable, and ripe for an Israeli attack. As for the ground east of the canal, the Egyptians would be sending nine hundred tanks against Israel's seven hundred. "With a ratio like that," General Tal declared, "we will light up the battlefield."[39]

All the fear drained out of the room. Golda spoke for everyone. "It would appear that Zvika [Zamir] just settled the debate."[40]

* * *

On the morning of October 14, the Egyptians launched what would be recorded as one of the largest tank battles in world history. The Egyptian main effort was the conquest of the Israeli military base at Tasa, north of the passes. At first light they fired five thousand shells and then sent hundreds of tanks straight down the Talisman Road. Waiting for them on the other side were hundreds of Israeli tanks that were locked, loaded, and under the command of Ariel Sharon.[41]

When it came to defense, the American-made and British-made tanks in Israeli hands had a major design advantage insofar as they were tall enough to point their cannons downward. This allowed them to be positioned at a 45-degree angle toward the top of a dune and aim the cannon down the other side of the slope so that the body of the tank was still protected behind the dune. Soviet tanks were designed shorter and lacked this feature. A Soviet adviser who fought in Syria said that from a distance, an Israeli tank looked like a man sitting on a stick.[42] *

The rising sun was at the backs of the Israelis. Visibility was good atop the dunes and the Egyptians approached with their hatches closed. From inside closed tanks, it is unlikely the Egyptians

---

* In tank warfare, using sloping ground to hide all but a tank's cannon has a name. It is called *defilade*.

saw what was in front of them. The Israelis waited patiently until they were just five hundred yards away, point-blank range for a 1970s tank. Then they commenced a turkey shoot.[43] Fire off the dunes tore through Egyptian columns, leaving scorched wreckage wherever it landed.

In the afternoon the Egyptians made another attempt, hoping the setting sun would blind the Israelis. The results were the same. The only place where the Egyptians had a chance was farther south, in a place called Wadi Mabouk, where they attacked with 140 tanks against Israel's 29. The Israelis did not panic. They did what they were trained to do whenever they got into a fix. They called in the Israeli air force. The Egyptians were beyond the range of their SAMs, so Israeli pilots did what *they* were trained to do and "hit the entire convoy in order."[44]

The tally taken at the end of the day's carnage was the most lopsided of any battle of the war. The Egyptians lost 250 tanks. The Israelis lost 6.[45]

Far to the rear, Israel found further salvation on the hard road traveled. C-5 Galaxies, leviathans with wings, landed in Lod airport laden with American weapons. The US resupply arrived like a transfusion of blood into a sick patient bled white. The effect was as much psychological as physical. For the first time since the war began, Golda allowed herself to cry.[46]

And for the first time, Elazar and the General Staff were of one mind. That is not to say there was harmony. Gonen chafed under Bar-Lev, Elazar clashed with Dayan, and everyone hated Sharon. Still, on one point, there was finally agreement. The following day, the Israeli army would cross the canal.

# 16

## "WE WILL CROSS WITH WHAT WE HAVE"

He knows all eyes are upon him. He lives for this.[1]
—Moshe Dayan, speaking about Ariel Sharon, October 15, 1973

On October 14, at 3:30 in the afternoon, just moments after the guns fell silent—and while the desert blue skies over Sinai were darkened by pillars of black smoke—Israel's 14th Armored Brigade was pulled off the line atop the Hamadia Hill. Its commander, Colonel Amnon Reshef, was handed orders. He opened them and his mood instantly shifted from the euphoria of victory. For his orders contained something that all soldiers dread: the objective that had to be taken at all costs.[2]

The details were sketchy. But the upshot was that he and the men of the 14th had to plow a path to the canal so that others could cross into Africa, the territory west of the Suez Canal. Back in Tel Aviv, the old strategy of taking the fight to the enemy was back, and a little of the old swagger as well. "The Egyptians have returned to themselves, and we have returned to ourselves," declared General Chaim Bar-Lev. One of Golda's ministers supported the mission to cross into Africa only after Dayan assured him that there were no plans to build settlements there.[3]

Settlements were the last thing on Dayan's mind. There were

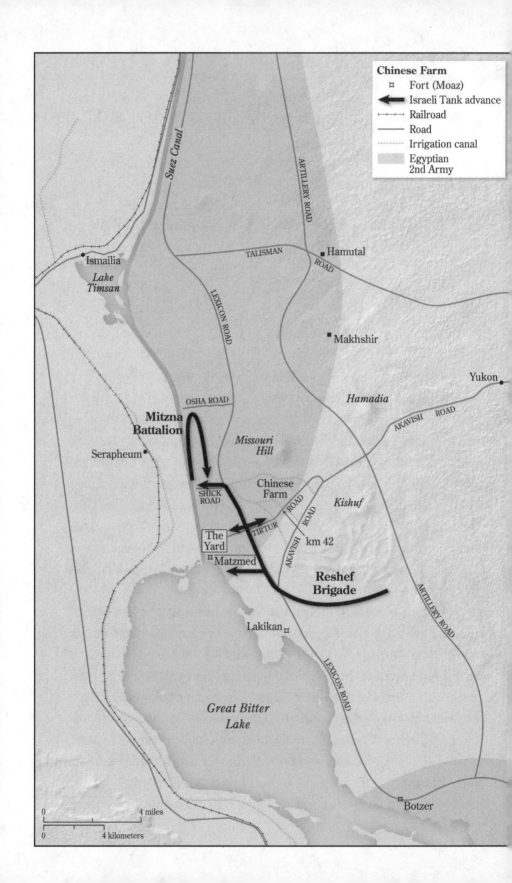

many brutal dilemmas weighing on him. And he could not address any of them until he settled the first one: What to do about Ariel Sharon?

On October 12, Bar-Lev recommended sacking Sharon, a recommendation he repeated on a later occasion, as well. Dayan rejected the advice each time. Some said that Likudnik Sharon held on to his appointment because Laborite Dayan feared that relieving him could, in the words of one commentator, "create political problems."[4]

Dayan had another reason to keep him. "As a general, he was head and shoulders above everyone else," said Reshef. Another officer—who spearheaded antiestablishment protests after the war—said Sharon "was the best divisional commander the IDF had." His failures to that point notwithstanding, Sharon still inspired an almost mystical confidence in those he commanded. The spell he cast on the battlefield crossed enemy lines. The wireless radio was an endless cacophony of voices, all competing to be heard above the whooshing static caused by Egyptian jamming. Everyone recognized Sharon's confident voice. When it came on the air, everything fell silent. Even the Egyptians operating jamming devices paused to allow a clear connection. When Ariel Sharon spoke, everyone listened.[5]

The affection of those Sharon commanded was matched in equal measure by the contempt of his superiors. "If you give Sharon a mission that he agrees with," Gonen said, "you can sleep soundly. You know he's going to do it. And if you give him a mission he does not agree with, you can also sleep soundly. You know that he won't do it." When Ezer Weizman was defense minister, he met an old woman who told him she knew Sharon when he was just a baby. Weizman replied, "You knew Sharon when he was peeing in his diapers, I knew him when he was pissing on everyone else."[6]

But somehow, when war came, it was always Sharon that was given the most difficult task, as in 1956 when he was sent to the Mitla Pass or in 1967 when he was sent to conquer Egypt's largest military base. Sharon's assistant Jackie Even said that the actions of the General Staff spoke for themselves. They knew that to cross the canal the IDF needed a miracle. And though none of them would admit it, they also knew that Sharon was the only general that might just pull it off.[7]

Every previous attack in the war on Egyptian-held territory had failed. This would be by far the most ambitious. It required tanks to drive all the way to the canal. It required paratroopers to paddle across in rubber dinghies and set up a bridgehead on the other side. And it required the 421st Armored Brigade to deliver bridges to the jump-off point and install them over the canal, possibly while under fire, so that tanks and other vehicles could cross.[8]

But the linchpin upon which everything else would depend was handed to Reshef and the men of the 14th Armored Brigade.[9] * The endless sea of vehicles and bridging equipment could reach the canal only one way, and that was over two roads, one code-named Tirtur and the other Akavish. The dunes surrounding the roads were so soft they might as well have been quicksand. Wheeled vehicles that wandered off-road immediately sank to the chassis. Tracked vehicles often filled with sand and broke down as well.

The worst-case scenario was not even failing to open the roads or, for that matter, failing to set up the bridges. Rather, the worst-case scenario was opening the roads, getting hundreds of vehicles across into Africa, and *then* having the line of communication severed. The margin between victory and disaster would be as narrow as the corridor Reshef and his men opened. In short, the Tirtur and Akavish roads had to be taken at all costs, and then they had to be held at all costs.

A three-ring circus of this scale and complexity should have received an enormous amount of thought and preparation. The most obvious thing to do would have been to review photo recon-

---

* Prior to going into battle, Reshef gave his men a pep talk in which he said, "The entire Nation of Israel is behind you." A reservist rose and asked, "Is there a way we can put the entire nation in front of us?"

naissance of the battlefield to see what forces the Egyptians had and where they were positioned. The perception, at least before the battle, was that the paratroopers had drawn the short straw and that the worst of the fighting would take place west of the canal. Reshef was told that his assignment would be relatively easy since the Egyptians were positioned well north of the two roads.[10]

A cursory review of the reconnaissance photos in AMAN's possession would have shown that the opposite was true. The Egyptians were well dug in along the Tirtur Road. Any intelligence officer who saw this would have recommended softening up the area before going on the attack. IAF fighter jets could have saturated it with napalm and cluster bombs, fired from a safe distance using the "slingshot" method. Not only was this not done, Reshef was never even told of the dangers he would encounter. As he put it, sending his men into battle without intelligence that was readily available amounted to "criminal negligence."[11]

Why were the Israelis in such a hurry to get the offensive started? No one was then pushing for a ceasefire, there was no longer any pressure from Washington, and they had just fought one of the largest tank battles in world history. Why not wait another day and plan things properly?

Sharon told his men there was no time to waste. He was not afraid of what the Arabs might do, he was afraid of what the Jews might do. Put bluntly, he feared that those above him might change their minds. As Sharon later said, "Right now we had approval to cross. Tomorrow might be a different story." In a conversation with one of his colonels, Sharon used a contemptuous slang word that loosely translates to mean "chicken out" (in Hebrew slang, rabbits—not chickens—are the cowards, so the word literally means "become like frightened rabbits").[12]

But sending tanks blindfolded into battle was hardly Sharon's mistake alone. In the end, it was Gonen, Bar-Lev, and Elazar—the men Sharon most feared would change their minds—who gave the green light. Why were *they* in such a hurry?

There is no good answer to this question. The best theory is that the operation depended on the element of surprise, and with Israeli forces gathering in the area, it was feared the Egyptians might figure out what was coming. It was well known that Egypt had Bedouins in Sinai reporting on the movements of Israel forces. Sadat called them his "human radar." Nevertheless, this was a somewhat exaggerated fear. The Egyptians were still licking their wounds from the October 14 battle and Israeli jets controlled the skies above the area, making aerial reconnaissance impossible. Despite this, Elazar thought the cost-benefit analysis pointed to moving immediately and scoring even a limited gain on the west bank, rather than waiting and perhaps obtaining nothing. "I said to myself," Elazar later told a group of officers, "that if we have just one bridge in the water by October 16 it will be enough."[13]

But that, more than anything, spoke to the reason for waiting. Plainly, when the entire goal of a mission is to lay a bridge, you need to know that the bridge will be there when you reach the shoreline. Sharon's bridges were miles from the front. The colonel in charge of delivering them told Sharon that there was no way that any of them would be there within his timeframe. Upon hearing this, Sharon relieved the colonel of command and appointed someone else.[14]

Promised armored personnel carriers, the next requirement for this assault, were nowhere to be found, either. Gonen told Sharon that he had complete confidence in his ability to steal vehicles from someone else's division. Sharon laughed and told him he had already sent a major to the rear to find transport by any means fair or foul. The major managed to "borrow" thirty APCs. But that was only about half of what was needed.[15]

The commander of the paratroopers, Colonel Danny Mat, asked his battalion commander, Lieutenant Colonel Dan Ziv, if he was comfortable crossing with only half the planned force. In Ziv's telling, "Mat's body language said that he expected me to tell him, 'Under these circumstances I'm not willing to risk my men and cross.'" But Ziv was among Sharon's most fervent followers, having fought under him as far back as the 1950s. He responded that his single battalion would do the work of two.[16]

Reshef's men were not as confident. On this, their tenth day of fighting, the men of his 14th Armored Brigade were stripped of any illusions as to what was being asked of them. This was the unit that had borne the brunt of the Egyptian onslaught on October 6 and had to be rebuilt almost from scratch. An officer who commanded a company in the brigade just a month before returned and discovered to his horror that he hardly recognized a soul. An elaborate walkie-talkie was erected to allow soldiers to call home. The officers claimed it was done because soon they would all be in Africa where communications were spotty, but it was widely interpreted as a chance to say goodbye.[17]

\* \* \*

Reshef's tanks set off at dusk, at 6:05 P.M. on October 15. The armored line traveled over sand dunes just south of the Akavish Road heading west toward the canal. The paratroopers tasked with setting up the bridgehead on the west bank of the canal set out a half hour later. It was deemed a minor miracle that they made it into battle at all. To the lack of APCs was added the lack of rubber dinghies, which were nowhere to be found. Sharon told the paratroopers that if they did not find them, they would swim across. The dinghies materialized at the last minute, but there were so few of them that there was no room for combat rations. The only food the paratroopers brought was what they could stuff in their knapsacks. There were so few APCs that the paratroopers loaded twenty to twenty-five men into each vehicle instead of the usual ten, and carried the rubber dinghies bobbing across the top. Some of the soldiers rode part of the way on mobilized civilian transit buses as if they were commuters heading to work.[18]

It is said that Napoleon's first question about any officer was, "Is he lucky?" In asking the question, it was soldiers like Colonel

Danny Mat, commander of the paratroopers, that he had in mind. To save time, Mat decided to drive straight down the Akavish Road under the light of a full moon. The column drew small-arms fire and even a few stray missiles but made it through, miraculously, without delay or casualties. Ariel Sharon had driven ahead in his command APC and personally directed the paratroopers into the Yard, a staging area prepared before the war for crossing the canal.[19]

The men expected a fearsome battle to retake the Matzmed *maoz*—one of the forts along the canal that fell in the war's opening assault. But Mat, still hot with the dice, continued his extraordinary run of luck. Somehow, Matzmed sat quietly in the night, unoccupied and open for the taking. The Israelis entered it like homeowners returning after a brief vacation. That it was left completely unguarded fueled conspiracy theories in Egypt after the war (and even a few in Israel).[20]

By the time Mat's paratroopers put the first rubber boats in the water, they could already hear the tank guns booming in the distance. But the men quietly paddled across the canal and remained there undetected through the night. This, too, was deemed something of a miracle, for even a small Egyptian armored force would have cut them to pieces. A high-risk element of a high-risk operation had come off without a hitch, and it offered badly needed encouragement to those higher up the chain. After radioing the code word "Acapulco," the paratroopers received a warm reply from a familiar voice listening in. It was General Elazar himself.[21] *

Reshef's 14th Armored Brigade found slower going over the dunes. He had only ninety-three tanks. It would have been a difficult trip even in broad daylight when the drivers could see where they were going. In the dead of night, five tanks crashed into each

---

* A startled woman living near Tel Aviv was awakened in the middle of the night when her telephone rang and a strange, excited man exclaimed, "We crossed, we're in Africa!" It was Ariel Sharon, who thought he was speaking to his wife. His radioman had dialed the wrong number.

other, two broke down, and three more flipped over or sank in the sand. The remaining eighty-three tanks emerged along the Lexicon Road at 8:00 P.M. and turned north. The lead force came to the intersection of the Tirtur and Lexicon roads, and, with luck and surprise still with them, drove quietly past. Egyptian soldiers, thinking the tanks were their own, waved to the Israelis. The Israelis did not wave back. But they did not open fire, either. There was no reason to. The spotty intelligence seemed accurate. Apart from these unsuspecting Egyptian foot soldiers, the area appeared to be undefended.[22]

Two battalions, numbering forty-five tanks, drove through. The lead battalion split up, turned left along three smaller roads, and took up positions along the canal, encountering only light opposition along the way. The second battalion, commanded by Lieutenant Colonel Amram Mitzna, continued farther north. His orders were to create a two-and-a-half-mile-wide corridor. But he encountered no resistance, and so, following classic Israeli military doctrine, he kept going, traveling with his force for what turned out to be over five miles. At 9:12 P.M. Mitzna arrived at a small east–west road called Osha and stopped to have a look.[23]

There, through the darkness, he saw what looked like the entire Egyptian army.

It was the command and supply center of the Egyptian 16th and 21st Divisions. The Egyptians expected any attack to come from the east and figured themselves safest to the west, along the canal. They never expected the Israelis to appear from the south. Mitzna's men let loose and ignited thousands of explosions. Fuel, ammunition, SAM missile batteries, supply trucks—everything went up in a spectacular fireball. Ariel Sharon radioed Reshef and told him the inferno was visible from his position over five miles away.[24]

What Sharon saw through his binoculars the Egyptians saw through theirs, as well. At that very moment, an Israeli soldier at the head of another tank battalion passed by the Tirtur-Lexicon intersection. He saw the previous two battalions drive through without taking fire and had just enough time to relax and think, "It's the Six-Day War II." Instantly, missiles lit up the tanks beside him and shook the ground underneath. In the words of one commander, "The gates of hell opened up."[25]

Sagger missiles rained down, seemingly from every direction. Twenty tanks of the 184th Armored Battalion entered the intersection. Only eleven made it out. One man who fought through the night said he fully expected to die and soldiered on, praying like Samson in the Book of Judges, "Let me die with the Philistines." Meanwhile, Mitzna's armored battalion, the 79th, fought for its life farther north until it pulled back two and a half miles to the Shick Road. The 79th entered the inferno with twenty-one tanks and returned with only six. However, its losses were not in vain. According to Egyptian records, it struck a huge blow in Egypt's divisional headquarters and nearly decapitated the entire senior military leadership.[26]

By now Reshef realized that the Egyptians were not "north of the Tirtur Road" as he had been told. They were dug in along the Tirtur-Lexicon intersection spewing fire in every direction. Reshef positioned himself on a hill overlooking the junction, thinking it was far enough in the rear for him to properly manage the battle. Instead, as he stood inside his tank he heard bullets crashing against the turret "like hail on a tin roof."[27]

Tank crews are trained to fight across distant battle lines. Along the canal that night there were no battle lines. An Israeli tank traveling south down the Lexicon Road almost collided with an Egyptian tank heading north. Meanwhile, a few hundred yards away, an Egyptian tank fell in line between two Israeli tanks. The Egyptian commander realized his mistake and turned his turret to the left, but was killed first by the Israeli tank to his right. Reshef reported to Sharon that "we are barrel to barrel."[28]

In the dead of night, the only way to know the enemy's location was to look for the source of fire, which was not much of a guide because fire was coming from every direction. The Israelis hit the Tirtur-Lexicon intersection with a barrage of artillery that descended in a screaming whistle and raised a great conical cloud of dust, debris, and human remains.[29] It silenced the area, allowing Reshef to drive through undisturbed and assist in stabilizing the northern line along the Shick Road. As late as 11:30 P.M., one of Reshef's officers reported that he had driven through the intersection five times without incident.

But then, at around 2:30 A.M. in the early hours of October 16, Reshef received word that the Egyptians had returned. When the tanks that had escorted the paratroopers to the jump-off point on the shores of the canal headed back east, they were mauled when they reached Tirtur-Lexicon. The intersection was closed once again.[30]

Of all the hard luck units of the Yom Kippur War, there was none to match the record of the 87th Armored Reconnaissance Battalion. It entered the war with approximately twenty tanks. Only one would emerge at war's end with its original tank crew intact. Its first commander, Bentzi Carmeli, was killed in the defense of the Hamadia and Kishuf hills on October 8. At 2:30 A.M., Reshef ordered his replacement, Lieutenant Colonel Yoav Brome, to retake the Tirtur-Lexicon intersection.[31]

Brome made it to the intersection and headed east down the Tirtur Road, supported by tank and artillery fire that blazed a path before them. Resistance was light. But then, fifty or so yards in, the Egyptians sprung their ambush. Brome placed himself in the lead tank from where he could best see the battlefield and report directly to Reshef. He stood in the turret, radio in hand—and was killed in midsentence.[32]

Reshef was unbowed. This time he planned to hit the Tirtur Road from the west and the east. He ordered his assistant to gather up whatever was left of the 87th plus a group of paratroopers, go back to the Tirtur-Lexicon intersection, and attack from west to east. For the attack in the other direction, from east to west, he borrowed two battalions from a sister unit, the 600th Armored Brigade.[33]

By then there was not much of the 87th left to gather up, so the paratroopers arrived at the jump-off point first, with only two tanks ahead of them leading the way. It started well enough. At 5:03 A.M., when they were about halfway through at kilometer marker 42, the paratroopers reported that they were "moving east quickly," taking nothing but small-arms fire. But when they reached a small bridge that spanned a dry irrigation canal, they came under a shower of Sagger missiles. A paratrooper described them as fast-moving fireballs "like spinning tops made of flames." One of the two tanks in the lead stood its ground and fought through the night, spewing fire and hot lead in every direction. Its commander, Captain Gideon Giladi, was killed and posthumously awarded Israel's highest military honor.[34]

The paratroopers piled out of their World War II–era half-tracks and took cover in the canal under the bridge at kilometer marker 42. They had gone into battle being told they had only to "mop up some tank hunters." When they looked up, they saw an entire Egyptian division, legions of commandos backed by tanks and artillery. Omer Ron, the assistant commander, made it out of the inferno and ran in every direction seeking help. Ron, who was later elected to the Knesset, eventually tracked down an assistant brigade commander and asked why he had not sent in a rescue party. The officer told him, coldly, that he was not willing to sacrifice another unit on a suicide mission. Realizing that there was no hope of rescue or reinforcement, the paratroopers' commander, Lieutenant Colonel Natan Shuneri, gave the only order he could: "Every man for himself."[35]

* * *

Israeli military planners had prepared three ways to get men and material over the canal.

The centerpiece was the "rolling bridge," a steel monster on

wheels that was practically impervious to enemy fire.[36] General
Jackie Even wrote in his memoir that the long-shot mission to cross
the canal was approved only because senior commanders placed
great faith in the rolling bridge. So firm was that faith, the bridge's
creators were awarded the coveted Israel Defense Prize before it
was tested in battle. The bridge won accolades, General Even wrote,
because no one understood just how flawed it really was.

Before the war, the logic behind the rolling bridge seemed
sound enough. Every military bridge going back to Napoleon was
premised on the idea of bringing numerous pieces to shore and
then assembling them in the water under fire. It was dangerous
work for the combat engineers and resulted in a vulnerable bridge.
To solve this problem, a legendary Israeli engineer named Colonel
David Laskov designed something revolutionary: a single-piece,
already-assembled bridge that was rolled into action and then
floated directly onto the water.[37]

Of course, there are no free lunches in engineering. What was
gained in durability was lost in mobility. It took up to seventeen
tanks to move the 450-ton monstrosity, with a bulldozer in front
clearing every obstacle great and small. The tank crews that had
been trained to move the bridge were all fighting on the Golan
Heights, so new tank crews had to be trained on the fly. Worst
of all, *the bridge had no turning capability whatsoever*. The steel
behemoth—which was almost two hundred yards long—had to
move in a straight line from its staging area twelve miles east
of the canal all the way to the shores of Africa. That is why the
cash-starved IDF had laid the straight-shot Tirtur Road in the first
place. The bridge could not be moved via the Akavish Road, or
any other road, because it could not make the hard right turn at
the Lexicon Road intersection. The only way to get the rolling
bridge into place was to open the Tirtur Road.[38]

A second crossing method was pontoon bridges. These could
be disassembled into parts, driven down the Akavish Road, then
maneuvered onto the Lexicon Road and ultimately the canal. It

sounded easy enough, at least on paper. In reality, each pontoon was over fifty-five feet long and thirty-six feet wide. Loads this size took up the entire width of every road and created a logistical nightmare. Hundreds of vehicles clogging the narrow arterials had to be pushed aside to make way for the special wagons that carried the pontoons. Like the wagons, the vehicles all sank in the soft sand the moment they moved off the asphalt. Once in the Yard—the staging area along the canal—it took hours to assemble the pontoons, even if the combat engineers were not taking fire. A "fast assembly" mechanism was under development, but the war broke out before it could be perfected.[39]

As an afterthought, and because they could be acquired secondhand on the cheap, the Israelis also purchased amphibious boats that were nicknamed the "crocodiles." The crocodiles could drive short distances over land, reach the jump-off point in the Yard, and then ferry tanks across the canal. The problem was that they cost only $5,000 apiece, and the Israelis got what they paid for. The crocodiles were extremely vulnerable to enemy fire and constantly broke down. Perhaps worst of all, there were not many of them. The army initially planned to buy sixty old crocodiles and cannibalize the parts to make thirty-two. Budget cuts left them with only nineteen. One fell off its wagon on the trip down to the canal. Two were broken before the war. There were only sixteen available for duty.[40]

* * *

The Tirtur Road was still blocked, and with it any hope of getting the rolling bridge to the canal. The Akavish Road was still passable, but the pontoons were trapped miles away behind a wall of gridlocked vehicles.

That left nothing but the crocodiles. Somehow, late in the hectic chaos of the war's first week, someone had the good sense to free up enough trailers to send the crocodiles from northern Israel up to the head of the Akavish Road (to this day, no one knows for sure who it was). The strange, enormous vehicles looked like net-covered houseboats on trailers. When they passed through Israeli cities, onlookers did not know what to make of them. They sparked rumors of some secret wonder weapon.[41]

As they came closer to the canal, they passed the smoldering wreckage of battle on both sides of the road and got stuck in the same traffic jam that stalled the entire army. But here again, someone—the record is not clear who—had the good sense to put a bulldozer in the lead to shove everything out of the way. Most vehicles that landed on the sand sank below the wheel hub and required a winch, a tracked tow truck, or even a bulldozer to be extracted. But the crocodile convoy continued, sometimes moving just a hundred yards at a time, its drivers inching behind the bulldozer absorbing curses and verbal abuse as they went.[42]

The crocodiles were little more than large trucks with inflatable flotation devices attached to each side. To get tanks across water with them, you had to lash several of them together.[43] As ferrying craft, the crocodiles were slow, had practically no armor, and were extremely vulnerable to enemy fire. In short, they were the least reliable means of crossing the canal. But there they were in the Yard, engines idling under the moonlight.

Combat engineers went nervously into battle with tiny bulldozers they knew were too small to remove the enormous mound of dirt separating the Yard from the canal. But in what one called a minor miracle, on the way to the canal they found a full-size bulldozer that got lost on its way to a military base. Sharon was in the Yard to show the combat engineers the spot he had marked out before the war to indicate where the dirt was thinned out and could be removed quickly. The path was hastily cleared and the far bank of the canal came into view, its palm trees illuminated by the moonlight reflecting on the water.[44]

Fresh tanks from the 421st Armored Brigade began arriving. They were available to either cross the canal or turn back and (hopefully) open the Tirtur Road so that (hopefully) the rolling bridge could be laid. Sharon knew that Elazar, Bar-Lev, and Gonen wanted him to first open the roads before crossing with any armor. He knew that they wanted him to first establish a safe corridor so the bridges could be laid.[45]

And so, with the battle raging behind him, and his face illuminated by the red flicker of fires in the distance, Ariel Sharon gave the order: *"We will cross with what we have."*[46]

# 17

## THE WAR OF THE GENERALS

On the morning of October 16, it was clear to the Israeli General Staff that the course of the fighting had followed their pre-battle assessment—only in reverse. The dividing line separating what was expected and what was not was the waters of the Suez Canal.

The west bank of the canal, where the worst of the fighting had been expected, was a paradise. It even looked like paradise, covered in palm trees and greenery that was nourished by irrigation channels. A few of the paratroopers apparently forgot there was a war in progress and were seen shirtless, sunbathing on the banks of the canal. Colonel Chaim Erez, commander of the 421st Armored Brigade, said that he heard birds tweeting in the background as he crossed on a crocodile. One of the soldiers asked Ariel Sharon if he wanted the honor of crossing in the first tank. Sharon politely declined; he had too much to do in the Yard.[1]

The crocodiles worked through the night and ferried twenty-eight tanks and seven armored personnel carriers. One combat engineer said that his orders were the simplest he had ever received, some variant of "just get across the damn Canal." In addition to carrying a full belly of fuel and shells, the tanks were each loaded with boxes of bullets, food, water, cigarettes, and anything else that could be tied down to the sides. They also got a final pep talk from their commander, Giora Lev. "Who is the best unit in the Army?" he asked, to which the men shouted, "We are! We are!" The paratroopers cheered as they came off the crocodiles on the other side.[2]

Twenty-one of the tanks broke out of the bridgehead and drove, in the words of one soldier, "as if there were no wars in the world." The tanks headed west and destroyed five surface-to-air missile batteries, tearing a hole in Egypt's air defenses. It later emerged that the Egyptian brigade commander in charge of the sector was killed as well. Lieutenant Colonel Lev reported destroying ten Egyptian tanks, twenty APCs, and various other vehicles without taking a single casualty along the way. He later said that had he not been ordered back to the beachhead to refuel, he could have driven all the way to Cairo. Lev's immediate superior, Colonel Chaim Erez, radioed Sharon and told him in perfect seriousness that he could drive his tanks to the Nile.[3]

By contrast, the east bank of the canal, where resistance was expected to be light, was hell on earth.

The flat moonscape of Sinai seemed to be torn open to reveal the earth's inner organs. Fire and smoke erupted from the desolation, sending black pillars into the skies. Ariel Sharon, now in his fifth war, declared it "the most terrible sight I had ever seen." Moshe Dayan said the same thing. The smell of cordite, scorched flesh, and burning metal hung over hundreds of blackened vehicles of every size. The twisted, smoldering wrecks left little doubt as to what happened to the men inside at the moment of calamity. At least 108 Egyptian tanks were destroyed against about 50 Israeli tanks; many had their barrels interlocked in the armored equivalent of hand-to-hand combat. An Israeli who survived by pretending to be dead had a gold chain pulled off his neck and witnessed Egyptians going from tank to tank shooting survivors.[4]

Seeing the difference between what happened to soldiers on the east bank of the canal from those on the west, a medic was reminded of the selections the Nazis did at the entrance to concentration camps. Those sent to one side lived, and those sent to the other died.[5] The bodies were so severely burned that it was often impossible to tell who was Israeli and who was Egyptian. A medic worked across the battlefield, asking, "Are you a Jew? Are you a Jew?" A sound came up from a blackened, ash-covered man with a mangled right hand missing fingers. He turned out to be Yitzchak Rabin's nephew.

"I am a Jew," he said. And then he sighed. "It's hard to be a Jew."[6]

* * *

At 6:00 P.M. the night before, just as the mission got under way—and before anyone knew if the Tirtur or Akavish roads were open—the final preparations were made to move the rolling bridge. Overseeing it all was the man who designed it, Colonel David Laskov. Less than a month after celebrating his seventieth birthday, and with a son then fighting on the west bank of the canal, Laskov stood under the moon and oversaw the hitching of the rolling bridge to twelve tanks. As the convoy pulled away, the red taillights of the tanks barely visible through the dust, he raised his right arm and offered a smart salute. Then he lowered his hand and wept.[7]

The unit had received a three-hour crash course in how to drag a 450-ton bridge. The soldiers were inexperienced, exhausted, and forced to take breaks in their training to ward off Egyptian commandos.[8] The drivers quickly discovered that the trick to pushing the bridge was making sure that every tank moved in perfect unison. If even one went too fast or too slow, it would put pressure on that portion of the bridge and pull the sections apart.

They made it a mile down the road when they had to make a slight turn. Two lieutenants standing exposed in a turret heard a sound and instinctively jumped down off their ladders into the belly of the tank. When they looked up, they saw the rolling bridge sitting on top of the opening where they had been standing just moments before.[9] A quick inspection revealed that the cable snapped and the bridge somehow rolled up over the tank without being damaged. After easing it back down, the convoy continued its slow journey west toward the canal.

The bridge crawled for over eight hours, traveling just three miles.[10] At 2:30 A.M., in the early hours of October 16, as the battle raged farther west around the Tirtur-Lexicon intersection, they came to the most difficult terrain of the journey, a brief stretch where the bridge had to travel over sand dunes. Five additional tanks were added, creating five more opportunities for someone to drive too fast or too slow.

The bridge was inched successfully up the incline of a dune. But then on the way down, the tanks lost control, possibly because one of the exhausted drivers fell asleep. Someone shouted "Stop!" into the radio, and the tanks simultaneously slammed on the brakes. Tanks that weigh more than thirty tons cannot stop on a dime, particularly when they are traveling over soft sand. Everything lurched down the dune before coming to a stop. Following a quick inspection in the dark, the commanding officer was told that "it ripped apart." The commander, a gruff lieutenant colonel, barked, "Then replace the cable that ripped." The soldier replied, "It wasn't the cable that ripped. It was the bridge."[11]

That the Tirtur Road was blocked was now only half the problem. The rolling bridge had to be repaired with a battle raging nearby. The commanding colonel initially told Sharon the repairs would take days. He later called with good news. It would take only "at least twenty-four hours."[12]

Meanwhile, the pontoons headed south, much in the way the crocodiles had traveled, shoving everything in their path out of the way. A mobilized civilian commuter bus that only a week before was bringing people to work now sat on the road like a beached whale. The driver had been given strict instructions to protect the expensive vehicle from any harm and refused to drive it onto the sand. The commander of a pontoon-laden tank approached him and calmly explained that he did not mind if he left the bus exactly where it was. He merely hoped that the driver would exercise good judgment and jump off before he crushed it. The tank moved forward, the bus driver jumped out in the nick of time, and the transit bus was split in two across its length.[13]

Thirteen pontoons finally made it to the jump-off point at the head of the Akavish Road at 6:30 A.M. on the morning of October 16. The convoy arrived too late to benefit from the cover of darkness. A cloudless desert sky was now shining brilliantly over the white sand dunes. The tanks, the pontoons, and the combat bulldozers all fell into line and headed west, black dots crawling across a white horizon. In broad daylight, the smoke-belching procession was visible for miles to anyone with binoculars.

Barely a mile and a half in, Egyptians emerged from the dunes and opened fire with Saggers. After a week of firing these missiles with abandon, Egyptian commandos were perhaps the world's finest marksmen in that weapons class. From what must have been a distance of a mile or more, they hit three of the tanks and one of the bulldozers at the same moment. A group of senior Israeli officers that included General Adan stood on a hill and saw burning men jump out ("Not a very pleasant sight," Adan later wrote with characteristic understatement). The burning men included the commander of the armored column, who was badly wounded. The bulldozers carried no weapons of their own, so when one of them ignited in a fireball, the others steered off the road and took cover. The pontoons were stopped cold barely a mile from the jump-off point.[14]

Reports of disaster were coming hard upon each other. The rolling bridge was broken. The Tirtur Road was closed. The Akavish Road was now closed as well. Without both Tirtur *and* Akavish, it was impossible to lay a bridge—*any* bridge. There was no way to get bridging equipment to the canal traveling over the soft sand dunes.

The crocodiles, meanwhile, were still plying the waters of the canal, ferrying men and supplies in each direction right under the noses of the Egyptians. The Israelis traveled back and forth in broad daylight all through October 16 (providing more fodder for conspiracy theories). Still, the Israeli operation hung by a thread.

The crocodiles were soft vehicles, kept afloat by rubber inflatables, easily sunk by artillery or small-arms fire. Elazar and Bar-Lev knew that the Egyptians would eventually figure out what was afoot. When they did, the crocodile lifeline would be lost. Even if the Egyptians remained miraculously oblivious, there was still the problem of getting supplies to the crocodiles. With both roads closed, the only way to travel from east to west was over the dunes, and the IDF had no tracked vehicles that could carry supplies. A soldier stationed on the west bank of the canal later told an interviewer, "For all intents and purposes, we were cut off."[15]

*How could this have happened?* The night before, Colonel Mat's men made it through the Akavish Road without any trouble. Why was the road impassable now?

Bar-Lev had little doubt who was to blame. Sharon was supposed to send only a few tanks to protect the bridgehead and use the rest to protect the Akavish Road. Instead, Bar-Lev told a colonel, "The 'gentleman' began conducting raids, the Egyptians crawled south and now Akavish and Tirtur are closed."[16]

Sharon's supporters viewed this as scapegoating. There is no evidence of any "crawling south." The fire probably originated from north of the Tirtur Road. What's more, the Egyptians were far enough away that Sagger operators could spot targets only during the day. Supplies could still be sent under cover of night. Or, as Sharon put it, the Akavish Road was not closed. It was merely under "intermittent fire."[17] *

This, Sharon believed, was hardly a reason to slow down. The war would be won west of the canal, not east of it. Conquer territory, destroy surface-to-air missiles, and the Egyptian army would collapse as it did in 1967. The key, Sharon believed, was that the Egyptian High Command had failed to figure out what the IDF

---

* As proof that Akavish was open, Sharon told a postwar panel he sent Moshe Dayan in an APC down the road on October 17. One of the panel members said wryly that the fact he sent Dayan down the road in no way proved he thought it was safe (the room erupted in laughter).

was up to. When they did, they would send reinforcements to box the Israelis inside the bridgehead and saturate it with artillery fire. There was still time to get more tanks across, destroy more surface-to-air missiles, and fan out across the countryside. But only if they hurried.

Bar-Lev, Elazar, and Gonen would have none of it. An operation depending upon the crocodiles, they believed, was an operation floating on a leaky ship, figuratively and literally. And so, at eleven A.M. on the morning of October 16, Sharon received an order he described as "so outrageous I at first refused to believe it."[18] All crossing activity was to cease at once.

How on earth, Sharon wondered, could Elazar and Bar-Lev stop him now? *He was winning the war.* The heat of the moment brought mutual hatreds to a boil, hatreds that had simmered for decades. The argument eventually took on a life of its own and was dubbed the War of the Generals, with the two sides training their fire on each other long after the guns went silent on the battlefield.

Dayan, Elazar, and the rest of the General Staff believed that Sharon was surrounded. Sharon scoffed and said it was the other way around; it was the Egyptians that were surrounded. "We were in back of them," he said, "we were threatening them, not vice versa." Dayan and Elazar said that at least one bridge had to be laid across the canal by the morning of October 17 or Sharon would have to be called back. Sharon said the crocodiles were not only good enough, but better. They could be spread out over a wider area. The General Staff scoffed at that. The crocodiles would not last more than a few hours once the Egyptians commenced artillery fire. Bar-Lev demanded that Sharon open the Tirtur and Akavish roads. Sharon insisted he give that task to another division.[19]

Any semblance of discipline disintegrated. When asked to report what was happening, Sharon responded, "Don't worry, there's nothing to be afraid of." Eventually Elazar lost his temper and screamed, "Who asked you if I'm afraid?! There are no cowards here, just tell us what's going on!" Elazar and Bar-Lev demanded that Sharon come to them to discuss what to do. Sharon refused and insisted that they come to him to see the situation for themselves.[20]

As was somehow the case throughout his career, Sharon fought his superiors to a draw. On the one hand, no additional forces would cross the canal on October 16. There would be no creative interpretation of orders, either; Gonen was no longer taking any chances. He broke army protocol, bypassed the chain of command, and spoke directly to Sharon's brigade commanders, ordering them to stay put on the east bank of the canal until they got the order directly from him or Bar-Lev.[21] This served to further enrage Sharon, who found breaches in the military chain of command intolerable (at least when he was on the receiving end of them).

On the other hand, Sharon got his way in several key respects. First, he could keep the forces he had west of the canal. Dayan wanted to bring them back, as did Gonen, at least until a bridge was laid.[22] Second, Bar-Lev gave in and relieved Sharon of having to open the roads.

General Adan's division sat out the battle the night before in anticipation of crossing once Sharon opened the corridor and laid the bridges over the canal. Early on the morning of October 16, it was given the task of moving the pontoons to the canal. Bar-Lev gave the order to Adan, he later said, because he figured Sharon would never do it. Bar-Lev went so far as to write in his journal that Sharon lied to him—saying he could not get the pontoons to the jump-off point, even though he could—to free up more tanks to fight west of the canal. The record does not seem to support the idea that Sharon lied, but it overflows with statements like Bar-Lev's, laced with distrust and mutual contempt.[23]

* * *

Opening the two roads was to be the primary objective of October 16. Adan arrived on the scene, took one look, and quickly concluded that he would never dislodge the Egyptians in broad daylight. That just left the formality of losing as many men as orders required. A too-small force was formed in the dunes south of Akavish and feebly attacked north.[24]

The intense desert heat radiated from the asphalt road, leaving Egyptian commandos visible through the shimmering waves. Every tank attack was greeted with an unbearable volume of Sagger missiles, cascading down in sheets of flame. Adan's men made two assaults on the roads. Each advanced as far as it could, which was not very far, and then turned back. In all, the commander lost four tanks—the number he thought necessary to confirm the hopelessness of the situation—and broke off the attack for good. Adan agreed with the commander's decision to pull back, radioed Bar-Lev, and told him that there was no way for tanks to open the two roads. The only way to clear out Egyptian commandos was to send in paratroopers at night.[25]

For the Israelis, not all the news on October 16 was bad. The rolling bridge was repaired in less than eight hours. This miraculous turn of events was made possible by the fact that there were two other rolling bridges under construction when the war broke out. Someone had the good sense to cannibalize a section from an uncompleted bridge and send it into battle as a "spare." It was quickly swapped in place of the damaged portion and the rolling bridge resumed its journey to the canal.[26]

Sharon had called away the unit that moved the rolling bridge the night before, so yet another inexperienced tank company was brought in to replace it. The men in the second group of tanks received an even shorter crash course than those in the first, but they made good progress all the same. It turned out to be a lot easier to move the bridge during the day when tank drivers could see where they were going and were not falling asleep at the wheel. The convoy arrived at the jump-off point and parked the behemoth alongside the stalled pontoons. Everything was ready. The only thing left was to open the Tirtur and Akavish roads.[27]

As the sun set on the afternoon of October 16, it was clear the day would end as it began. The two roads were still closed. Bursts of fire kept breaking out in unexpected places. Time was running out for the men west of the canal.

Bar-Lev had one last card to play. He radioed Colonel Uzi Yairi (pronounced Yah-EEE-ree), commander of the 35th Parachute Infantry Brigade. He needed a battalion at once. His orders echoed those Colonel Reshef had received two days before: The Tirtur and Akavish roads were closed. And they had to be taken at all costs.[28]

# 18

## THE CHINESE FARM AND THE MEN WHO CONQUERED IT

Wars are not won by fighting battles. Wars are won by choosing battles.[1]

—George S. Patton Jr.

Tuesday, October 16, was a day of rejoicing and celebration in Egypt, the day the nation finally stepped out from the shadow of 1967. Crowds that had once chanted insults about Sadat spilled out into the streets of Cairo to cheer him. People hung from lampposts and craned their necks from sidewalks to catch a glimpse of Sadat's motorcade as it crossed the Nile from his residence. The motorcade passed beneath banners slung across the broad boulevards of Cairo, hailing THE HERO OF THE CROSSING.[2]

Appearing in public for the first time since the outbreak of war, Sadat stood triumphantly to deliver a speech to a special session of the People's Assembly. Speaking "in the name of God," he declared the previous week and a half "the most dangerous, magnificent and glorious of history." He declared that he had pledged before God that "the 1967 setback was an exception and not the rule." The pledge was fulfilled, for the Israelis were now "faced with a war of attrition we can bear much better than they." He concluded by saying that he had already taken steps to reopen the Suez Canal.[3]

The speech was well received in the Arab world. It was even better received by Israeli intelligence. Reopen the canal? It was self-evident Sadat had no idea what was going on. General Shazly said later that "confused" reports reached him of SAM units being attacked by tanks, some as far as ten miles west of the canal. But "nobody seemed to know where the tanks had come from."[4]

In trying to explain what went wrong, General Gamasy, the chief of operations, said that the 16th and 21st Divisions had been badly mauled on October 14–15 and were without their commander, General Saad Mamoun. Mamoun was bedridden for the remainder of the war with what some said was a heart attack and what Shazly described as a "breakdown." Gamasy wrote in his memoir that Mamoun's short-lived replacement—a brigadier general named Taysir al-Aqqad—made a good faith mistake as to the number of Israeli tanks that crossed the canal. Many have speculated that Egyptian soldiers returned to the practice of lying to their superiors.[5]

The Egyptians did not remain in the dark for long. Shortly after Sadat finished his speech, they were tipped off as to what was happening. And from the most unlikely source of all.

The night before, on October 15, Golda stayed up late waiting for news that the paratroopers had made it successfully across the canal. She did not return home until well after midnight. In her own words, she arrived at the Knesset the next day "very tired." She rose to deliver a forty-minute speech. Much of it, she said, "didn't make pleasant hearing." However, she was proud to report that, as she was speaking, "a task force was already operating on the west bank of the Canal."[6]

Elazar was horrified. He could not contradict his prime minister. So he had the army issue a statement acknowledging only that a "commando force" was operating west of the canal. Dayan asked

Elazar how this could have happened. Hadn't Golda submitted her speech to the military censor in advance for clearance? Elazar replied that she had, and they had removed much of what she planned to say. But somehow that sentence had slipped through. Following the debacle, Dayan instructed his generals to refuse to answer questions put by Golda's ministers, "even if they scream at you."[7]

The damage was done. And though the Egyptians remained in the dark a little longer—Heikal called this intelligence blunder Egypt's biggest mistake of the war—Elazar knew that the night of October 16–17 was likely to be the final chance to open the Tirtur and Akavish roads. After that, the Egyptians would move in reinforcements, shoot the crocodiles out of the water, and the window would close for good. Elazar told Tal he was heartsick that the pontoon bridge didn't get through the night before because of a "goddamn traffic jam."[8]

Elazar's mood only darkened as the day progressed. Jordanian engineers were spotted along the Jordan River inspecting the terrain for places where tanks could cross.[9] A third front might open at any time with practically nothing there to hold the line.

Then Elazar was told by General Ezer Weizman that Sharon was calling Menachem Begin, head of the opposition Likud Party, every day and passing along dirt about him and the General Staff. Worse still, Weizman said that he had heard from a low-level officer that Sharon asked to send *hundreds of tanks* over the canal but was rebuffed. Elazar took Dayan aside and asked for advice. Should he remove Sharon now or wait until after the war was over? On the one hand, he could not take much more of this. But on the other, he did not think this was the time to fire Sharon and spark a "War of the Jews."

Dayan said that the last thing the army needed at this delicate juncture was more turmoil, turmoil that would quickly enter the political arena as well. Both men knew that the Saturday before the war broke out, Sharon was on the banks of the canal filming an election campaign ad. Moreover, the plain fact was that despite everything—and everything was admittedly a lot—Dayan still admired Sharon as a commander. Of course, Dayan was all too familiar with the difficulties of dealing with him. But they had no choice but to suck it up. "In this regard," he said, "our country really is just pathetic."[10] *

* * *

The Sinai Peninsula was so barren that the view there was typically disturbed by nothing but the curvature of the earth. Ariel Sharon described its white sand dunes as the cleanest place on earth.[11] But there was a rare landmark abutting the north side of the Tirtur Road. It was known as the Chinese Farm.

The Chinese Farm was neither Chinese nor a farm. It was a Japanese agricultural research facility established in the 1960s to help combat world hunger. Israeli soldiers that came upon it in 1967 confused Japanese writing for Chinese and the name stuck. Like much of the Sinai, it was flat and sandy. But it was crisscrossed with irrigation ditches that gave perfect cover to infantry armed with shoulder-fired weapons. There was an especially large cluster of irrigation channels in an area measuring two square miles, around the Tirtur Road near kilometer marker 42. Bar-Lev told the paratroopers that Tirtur-42 had to be cleared. Otherwise the rolling bridge, and possibly the pontoon bridge, could not get through to the canal.[12]

The roads to the staging area, at the eastern end of the Akavish Road, were choked with vehicles as far as the eye could see. The only way for the paratroopers to get there was by helicopter. The helicopters tried to squeeze in flights to pick up wounded

---

* In 2001, the State of Israel passed a law requiring all military officers holding the rank of two-star general (*Aluf*) or higher to wait at least three years before running for public office. Under the National Security Act of 1947, the United States has a seven-year waiting period before a soldier leaving active duty may serve as secretary of defense, unless they receive a special waiver from Congress.

men, but it soon became apparent that if they continued, the paratroopers would never make it to the staging area while it was dark. Without seeking authorization, the helicopter commander made the difficult decision to abandon the wounded to their fate. He was careful to reveal the story only decades later, after the statute of limitations had lapsed and there was no longer any risk of criminal prosecution.[13]

The commander of the paratroopers, Colonel Uzi Yairi, was rushed into the staging area carrying a week-old reconnaissance photo that showed nothing in the Chinese Farm but a few Egyptian "tank hunters." He even told a group of medics that enemy soldiers had been in the field for days, were probably hungry, and that it would be easy to "shoo them off." What he did not know was that as he spoke, AMAN had updated pictures of the Chinese Farm showing thirty Egyptian tanks, dozens of armored vehicles, and *three thousand Egyptian soldiers* dug into the irrigation ditches and trenches. In the hectic chaos of getting the men into the field, these pictures never made it to Yairi or the men he commanded. A bitter Colonel Amnon Reshef complained after the war that this negligence reminded him of the verse in Genesis: "The blood of your brother cries out to you from the ground."[14]

Even without the photos, Yairi sensed that more time was needed to ready an assault. He called Bar-Lev. The paratroopers were late getting in, and there was no time to prepare a proper military plan. Couldn't the mission be postponed to the following night? The usually unflappable Bar-Lev grew emotional. "The fate of the Jewish nation rests upon your shoulders," he said. "You have to move tonight. If you don't open the road, then we will have to bring Sharon back and cancel the crossing." Both men knew what that meant—a grinding war of attrition along the canal that Israel could not possibly win. Egypt with its population of thirty-seven million could remain on a war footing for a long period of time. Israel with its population of 3.3 million could not. So long as Egypt's army was still fighting east of the canal, and Israel could not demobilize its reservists, Sadat could dictate his terms at the negotiating table. But just to reinforce the point, Bar-Lev added, "And then we've lost the war."[15]

Yairi organized four platoons from the elite 890th Parachute Infantry Battalion and told its commander, Lieutenant Colonel Yitzchak "Itzik" Mordecai, to spread his men out over a wide area to root out the "tank hunters." Mordecai said he could not proceed without an artillery officer. He was told one would arrive soon enough. He asked for air support and armor. He was told that "it was already worked out." In the meantime, he had to get into the field because there was no time.[16]

Mordecai and his men left the staging area at midnight, walking past silent vehicles that still clogged the roads. The paratroopers marched in an arc two miles long, each man standing thirty feet from the other. The men moved slowly, stumbling in the dark, sinking in the soft sand under the weight of their weapons. Two hours into the operation, at about two A.M., they received orders from General Adan to pick up the pace and focus on the Tirtur Road only. The men closed ranks and faced north, forming a line on the shallow dunes. There they were ordered by Mordecai to "dig in and prepare to take fire from every direction."[17]

Moments later, dozens of flares were fired into the sky from the Egyptian side. The flares lit up the heavens, turned night into day, and revealed the Israelis digging in the sand.[18] They might as well have been digging their own graves.

Hot metal poured down, in the words of one Israeli soldier, "like a heavy rain, a flood." The ammunition hit from every direction and from every type of weapon: mortars, Saggers, tanks, and what for Israelis would turn out to be the most fearsome weapon of all, Goryunov machine guns. Above the deafening sounds around him, a man radioed Mordecai and screamed, "We aren't facing tank hunters, we're facing a whole army!" The foxholes had not yet been dug, so the only cover was the bomb craters created by Egyptian artillery. No one had to crawl far to find one.[19]

As they attempted to fight back, the Israelis made another horrifying discovery. Egyptian soldiers were armed with that miracle of twentieth-century battlefield technology, the Kalashnikov rifle. Perhaps the most famous item ever produced by the Soviet Union—they sold over 100 million of them—the "Kalatch" had deadly range, massive firepower, and never jammed no matter the circumstances. The Israelis were armed with one of *their* country's most famous products, the Uzi submachine gun, but it was hopelessly ill-suited for the task at hand. The short-barreled weapon was designed for urban warfare and had limited range. One man raised his to a 45-degree angle, hoping it might reach the Egyptians. It didn't.[20]

He was one of the lucky ones. At least his weapon fired. For others, the only way to harm Egyptians was to throw bullets at them. Their Uzis jammed the minute they came in contact with the sand. One man literally begged his weapon to fire. When that did not work, he cursed it, then beat it like a stubborn mule. A platoon leader's Uzi jammed, so he grabbed his radioman's Uzi. It jammed also. He then looked over at a private but saw that he was busy taking his gun apart while bullets rained around him. The private coolly cleaned it. But he could not get it to fire.[21]

The objective of the mission was forgotten, overtaken by the need to evacuate the wounded. A brave soldier lifted an injured comrade onto his shoulders, but as he rose to make a run for it, the wounded man felt the bullets whizzing overhead and cried, "Put me down! We'll get killed up here!" Another wounded man had the strange experience of lying on his back in a bomb crater, light-headed from a morphine shot, and watching a sound and light show whistling above him. The Egyptians used green tracer bullets, the Israelis used reds, and the two danced in the sky back and forth like a psychedelic pendulum. The man had just enough presence of mind to notice that there were far more greens than reds. "I was completely stoned."[22]

As Mordecai's men were being slaughtered below, the air

force made an attempt under cover of darkness to supply Sharon's forces west of the canal using helicopters. In 1973, helicopters had been in full-scale production for only thirty years. Crashes were common. Those that stayed aloft flew with minimal armor. In Vietnam, the United States lost a staggering 5,607 helicopters out of a total 11,846 deployed, or almost half. The fragile machines were all the more vulnerable when they were laden with tons of supplies. On the night of October 16, the Egyptians spotted the Israeli group, fired on the lead helicopter, and the aerial convoy was compelled to turn back. If anyone harbored any doubts, this failure put them all to rest.[23]

Either the paratroopers opened the roads, or the war was lost.

\* \* \*

At 2:30 A.M. on the morning of October 17, General Adan sent a small group of half-tracks down the Akavish Road to see if it was open. The force, nicknamed Bomba, was comprised of reservists in World War II–era equipment. The unspoken expectation was that they would be wiped out. But there were only three more hours left before the sun came up, and Adan knew he had to do something.[24]

The nervous, middle-aged reservists took to the road heading west. The trip left each with the strange sensation of being deaf in one ear, for to the right was the earsplitting cacophony of bullets and bombs in the Chinese Farm just north of the Tirtur Road, while to the left all was quiet. It took them only forty-five minutes to drive the six miles to the intersection with the Lexicon Road. If it had taken any longer, it is unlikely the pontoons could have made it through before first light. At 3:15 A.M., the commander radioed back: *The Akavish Road is open.*

In his memoir, Adan remembered this as the moment in which the scales were evenly balanced between victory and defeat. The road might be open. Or maybe the Egyptians let them through, hoping to ambush bigger prey. If it was an ambush, and if the pontoons were hit, then the bridge would be lost, Sharon would be called back, and the General Staff would have to figure out how to fight an unwinnable war of attrition.[25]

Adan made his decision. He first positioned tanks north of Akavish to protect the road. Then, at 3:45 A.M., Adan ordered his assistant General Dov Tamari to move the pontoons to the Yard.[26] Tamari moved slowly, bulldozers at the head clearing the way. The pontoons made the sharp right turn onto the Lexicon Road, riding partly over sand that was packed down. Finally, at 6:50 A.M., with the sun now shining on the Yard, he handed off the pontoons to Ariel Sharon.

Tamari, always one to speak his mind, proudly proclaimed on the radio for the entire division to hear, "I have delivered the P's to Lakikon and handed them off to Fatso." "P" was the code letter for "pontoon." "Lakikon" was the code word for the Yard. "Fatso" was not in the codebook. But everyone knew to whom he was referring.[27] *

* * *

Back at the Chinese Farm, the ground seemed to swallow everyone that stumbled onto it. One soldier said that so many Saggers flew over him, he was not afraid of the missiles but of having his neck severed by the cables. The paratroopers' commander, Lieutenant Colonel Mordecai, could do little more than watch the carnage unfolding before him. However, he was able to take heart from what he saw behind him, for he was close enough to see and hear the pontoons heading for the canal. "We were the barrier that stopped all the Egyptian fire," he told a documentary filmmaker thirty years later. "The Israeli Army passed behind us that night and the following day without taking a bullet."[28]

---

* It turned out to be a bad career move. In 1981, Major-General Dov Tamari—a man marked to one day be appointed chief of staff—was invited to a meeting with newly appointed defense minister Ariel Sharon. At that meeting, one of the first Sharon held, Tamari was told that his military career was over.

The Egyptians, it seems, were so focused on killing every last Israeli soldier that walked into the ambush that they lost sight of what was happening just a few hundred yards farther south. An Israeli who escaped the slaughter remembered how stunned he was to see vehicles sitting peacefully on the Akavish Road just beyond the battle. There was even an army SHEKEM truck—the Hebrew acronym for "Snack Bar and Kiosk Service"—parked on the side selling coffee.[29]

But when the sun rose on the morning of October 17, the Israelis had only about half of what they needed. The pontoon bridge was through, but it was not yet assembled. It was anyone's guess if it could be snapped together in broad daylight within clear sight of Egyptian artillery spotters. Even if combat engineers managed that, the many parts would go back to being many parts—or worse, fragments—if the fragile bridge took fire.

All of Israel's war plans depended on the more durable rolling bridge. But the Tirtur Road was still closed, making it impossible for it to get through. The Akavish Road was open, but only at night. Vehicles traveling in sunlight would be visible to Egyptian Sagger operators in the Chinese Farm, just as they were the day before. In short, the Israeli operation west of the canal was still viable. But it was hanging by a thread.

\* \* \*

Meanwhile, on the west bank of the canal, early on the morning of October 17, Lieutenant Colonel Dan Ziv was taken aside by his superior, Colonel Danny Mat. Mat ordered Ziv to take a small force comprised of just two tanks and ten half-tracks, drive north along train tracks, and eliminate Egyptian artillery spotters. He was told he had to remain on the train tracks.[30]

Everything about the mission was strange. Why take a small force that could barely defend itself and send it deep into enemy territory? Why send it along such a prominent path where Egyptian soldiers were liable to see it?

Ziv took to the road without receiving answers to any of these questions. One of his tanks broke down, leaving the force with only one. They continued anyway, traveling a little over a mile without finding any artillery spotters. Each time Ziv radioed Mat that they had found nothing, and each time Mat told him to keep going. By now Ziv started to sense "something Sharon-ish" about the whole operation. But that raised yet another question. Ziv had known Sharon for twenty years, since serving under him in the 1950s. If Sharon wanted something, why didn't he tell him directly? Sharon hardly ever bothered with the chain of command.

An officer in the unit named Asa Kadmoni complained to Ziv. Why were they remaining on the train tracks where they were liable to get ambushed? Couldn't they travel along a less visible path? Ziv, still with complete confidence in Sharon, told him that these were their orders and they would follow them.[31]

The group continued four miles from the bridgehead until they came to the Egyptian town of Serapheum. No artillery spotter could possibly see the bridgehead from that far away. But then, inexplicably, Mat told them to attack it. They opened fire with everything they had, which was not much. And though they caught the startled Egyptians by surprise, they soon found themselves confronting two full battalions guarding a nearby logistics base. The force was exponentially larger than Ziv's.[32]

Ziv's lone remaining tank was quickly knocked out. The men in his half-track piled out and took refuge in a house, with Asa Kadmoni manning a machine gun.[33] Kadmoni had been wounded years before and had almost no feeling in his right hand. He'd had to fool an army panel to make it back into combat. But after emptying the machine gun, he joined the others in the house. Then he climbed onto the roof.

A ferocious battle ensued in Serapheum between hundreds of Egyptians—and Asa Kadmoni. He killed thirty Egyptian soldiers in a truck with a shoulder-fired missile. Then he destroyed another. Now out of missiles, and using nothing but a rifle and hand grenades, he manned the roof by himself, jumping from one place to another, killing anyone that came near. A radio message was intercepted of an Egyptian soldier reporting that there was a "crazy Jew" on the roof who was unkillable. A rescue party arrived over four hours later, with Kadmoni out of grenades and down to just seven bullets. Writing over thirty years later, an Israeli journalist wrote that Kadmoni was "perhaps the greatest hero of all Israel's wars."[34]

Of the eighty Israeli soldiers that went into battle in Serapheum, eleven were killed and forty wounded. The survivors, led by Kadmoni, bled fury from every wound in their bodies. How could they have been led into battle by such an incompetent commander? How could Lieutenant Colonel Ziv have ordered them into such a foolhardy attack?

Kadmoni was awarded the Order of Valor, the nation's highest military award, but he had no interest in medals. He became obsessed with but one thing: to publicize what had happened and make those responsible pay.[35]

* * *

Back at the Chinese Farm, it was clear that there was no longer any point in the paratroopers remaining along the dunes. The task of extracting them was handed off to the Bomba unit, the same reservists that had driven down the Akavish Road a few hours before and discovered that it was open.

The experience of the men of Bomba caused something of a spiritual awakening, even among the IDF's most ardent atheists. For the Bomba unit seemed to be protected by nothing less than the hand of God Almighty. Miraculously—for that is the only word that does the story justice—less than ten hours after taking no casualties on the Akavish Road, the men of Bomba drove straight into the Chinese Farm in broad daylight. Like the night before, the expectation was that they would be completely wiped out. But then a strange thing happened. They drew no fire at all.[36] It did not seem possible.

But it was. Because sometime late on the morning of October 17, the Egyptians withdrew from the Chinese Farm.

For Egypt, this was the greatest tactical blunder of the war, worse even than the ill-advised offensive on October 14. The tank attack was a painful setback, but it was only that, a setback. The formula leading to victory had not been altered. The loss of the Chinese Farm, on the other hand, opened Egypt's back door to the laying of bridges over the canal. From this there would be no recovery. In describing the battle, General Shazly later wrote that he was "ashamed" to recount his army's deployment.[37]

What Shazly did not know was that the IDF General Staff had already decided that if the bridge was not laid on October 17, the force west of the canal would be ordered back.[38] That withdrawal would have been more than a tactical defeat. The expectations created by Golda Meir's speech before the Knesset would have turned it into an enormous psychological blow as well. A grinding war of attrition would have ensued. Sadat's demands at the negotiating table would have multiplied. For Israel, the war would have been lost.

But why did the Egyptians withdraw? Why did thousands of well-armed troops pull out and flee north?

It was obvious to all who participated in the battle what the reason was *not*. It had little or nothing to do with the Israeli paratroopers who fought there. No one ever questioned their heroism. But in the words of one of Lieutenant Colonel Mordecai's men, "It doesn't matter what anyone thinks today—don't you believe a word of it. We didn't do anything." Another paratrooper said, "We didn't conquer the objective, and we didn't even inflict a lot of casualties." A medic probably said it best: "Our job was to be cannon fodder that doesn't run away. . . . We carried out the mission—to die in God's name (*al kiddush Hashem*)."[39]

But if the paratroopers did not force the Egyptians out, then who did?

The answer would emerge only years later. General Shazly wrote in his memoir:

> Fire from the west bank [of the canal] on to 21st Division's flank [on the east bank of the canal] forced it to pull back. In effect, the right or southern flank of the Second Army had been driven north to a line opposite Serapheum on the west bank—and the enemy's corridor correspondingly widened. Our first concern was to strengthen and encourage the 150th Parachute Brigade, which was now bearing the first brunt of Sharon's drive north. Every yard the enemy gained would widen the threat to the rears of 16th and 21st Divisions, forcing them to pull back north.[40]

It was not fire east of the canal that forced the Egyptians north. It was fire west of it. Ariel Sharon's near-suicidal, high-stakes gamble had paid off. Two days after the battle in Serapheum, Sharon saw Ziv while passing in his command APC. Sharon told the driver to stop abruptly, jumped out, and gave Ziv a big hug. He said, "I'm sorry, I didn't know there were so many Egyptians there." Ziv knew Sharon too well to believe a word of that. He smiled and winked at him. Sharon broke into a broad grin and exclaimed, "You bastard!"

The two men met privately the next day and Sharon told Ziv what he had already figured out on his own. On the morning of October 17, Sharon had been given a stern warning by Bar-Lev and Gonen. If he so much as attempted to act outside of his orders, he would be relieved of command. That was why Sharon could not speak to Ziv directly. That was why Ziv's force was so small and its mission defined as "searching for artillery spotters." And that was why they were ordered to travel along the train tracks. Sharon wanted the Egyptians to see them. He wanted them to think a huge offensive was under way.[41]

Like all successful generals, Ariel Sharon was a man who understood men. He knew the kind of man he needed to carry out a rogue operation. In 1973, Ziv was already a legend in the IDF. He had won an Order of Valor of his own for actions in the 1956 war, being one of just thirty-two men to win Israel's highest military honor up to that point. He was with the paratroopers when they liberated the Western Wall in 1967. He was the battalion commander who insisted they cross the canal with only half the planned force, promising that his unit would do the work of two. And in Serapheum, the rescue party found him completely unfazed. In fact, he wanted to continue north, convinced the Egyptians were at the point of collapse.[42]

Sharon's sixth sense for sizing up men extended not just to appointing those who would fight to the end. At every stop of his military career, then later in politics, he also had the uncommon gift for finding people who would protect him in the same manner. In all the years, no one close ever turned on him, even when they knew he was acting outside his authority.

Ziv's reputation suffered irreparable damage in the wake of the Serapheum battle. He became the only paratroop officer in Israeli history whose men demanded that he be replaced in the middle of a war. Though he held on to his command, an internal army investigation raised serious questions about his judgment. The investigator returned to Kadmoni to hear his testimony a second time. He believed he had to hear the story again. These were paratroopers. The officers were the best in the army. The level of Ziv's incompetence did not seem possible.[43]

Through it all, Ziv never breathed a word.

It was only in 2015, the year after Sharon died, that Ziv finally told the story to historian Uri Millstein. He was just shy of his eightieth birthday. To the obvious question of why he had remained quiet for so long, he responded: "I did my bit in the crossing and in Serapheum. The Israeli public knows it and God knows it. The rest isn't important."

In this, Ziv was wrong. God knew it. But the Israeli public was another story.

The paratroopers who fought in the Chinese Farm were hailed as conquerors, showered with more medals than any other unit in the Yom Kippur War, and by a large margin. They even outshined the unit that deserved the most credit—even more than Dan Ziv's—which was the 14th Armored Brigade commanded by Colonel Amnon Reshef. Reshef's tanks did most of the fighting and took most of the casualties. But years later, one of the unit's most celebrated heroes, a retired colonel named Rami Matan, visited Yad La-Shiryon, the Israeli Armored Corps Museum. There—in the very institution dedicated to honoring the IDF's tank warriors—he went to one of the computers and typed in the words *Chinese Farm*. His eyes darkened as the following appeared on the screen: "the Chinese Farm was conquered by the 890th Parachute Infantry Battalion under the command of Colonel Itzik Mordecai."[44]

It left many asking the obvious question of why. Why were the paratroopers given credit out of all proportion to their contribution to the battle?

All explanations point in one direction. The people in the know did not want Sharon to get any credit. Sharon himself could not take any credit because he was acting outside his authority. For all the years after the war, he boasted of being first to cross the canal. He never mentioned Serapheum. Except, that is, in private gatherings where he heaped praise on Dan Ziv.[45] By default, the only other unit that could be credited was Itzik Mordecai's paratroopers. To the public, the description made sense. The Tirtur and Akavish roads were closed before the paratroopers entered the Chinese Farm. They were open after.

The whole affair left a bad taste in the mouths of many

veterans.[46] Years later, a group demanded to see transcripts of the deliberations granting medals to the paratroopers. The army refused to release them. Legal action commenced. The matter made it all the way to the Israeli Supreme Court. On the courthouse steps the army gave in and agreed to release all the information in its possession. A short while later, all the records in the army's possession were delivered to the litigants.

The files were all empty.[47]

\* \* \*

On the afternoon of October 17, Itzik Mordecai assembled what was left of the 890th Parachute Infantry Battalion. There was a fearsome battle forming around the canal bridgehead, he said. He would not order anyone back into the fight, not after what they had been through in the Chinese Farm. Any man who wanted to leave could do so and no questions would be asked. But the entire war effort depended now on keeping the corridor open, and every able-bodied soldier was needed. Not a single man left.[48]

As the paratroopers were about to set off into the night, the unit's unofficial "combat rabbi"—the IDF had no such title, but he fought through the night and he was a rabbi—asked Mordecai to halt the operation. Like everyone, he had lost track of time. But he did a quick calculation and came to a realization. It was the Jewish holiday of Simkhat Torah. He ran back to the equipment truck, emerged with a Torah in hand, and began to dance. Two men joined him, and then two others. Before long, the shattered men of the 890th were holding hands, singing, and dancing in a circle. The celebration continued through the night.[49]

The paratroopers took to the road the following morning, October 18. They marched west toward the canal in a long line, passing the Chinese Farm on their right. Israeli dead were still being recovered from the battlefield. The unit given the thankless task was experienced in this sort of work, but surprised to find the bodies warm instead of cold, testament to how much of the sun's heat was captured by the sand. Egyptian dead littered the landscape as well, intertwined with the Israelis across the black moonscape left by three days of fighting.[50]

The stench of burning metal intensified as the paratroopers got closer to the canal. When they were a mile away, they came under air attack by Egyptian MiGs. Then, as they entered the Yard, they hustled into APCs. The APCs drove through intense shelling and crossed on the pontoon bridge that was at last floating on the canal. The bridge was pockmarked with small shrapnel holes. It had only one lane: all the traffic moved in the same direction. The tanks, the APCs, the trucks—every vehicle headed west into Africa.[51]

# 19

## THE RACE TO THE BRIDGEHEAD

One experience is often sufficient to establish a long-term fear . . .
even when there is no reason to expect it to happen again.[1]
—Daniel Kahneman, Nobel Prize–winning psychologist

Early on the morning of October 17, Dayan received a jubilant
call from Bar-Lev. The roads to the canal were open! Dayan later
wrote that he could feel Bar-Lev's joy over the telephone.[2] There
was one problem, however, a familiar one. Sharon had violated his
orders again. What was the infraction this time? Sharon had sent
more tanks over the canal.[3]

Sharon himself would later say that he "stole" ten tanks across.
Earlier that morning, he hoped that, with the pontoons in the
Yard, "we might finally be able to change some minds about getting our forces across fast." The pontoons did not change Dayan's
mind a bit. He angrily called Sharon, ordered him to drop everything and come to a meeting on the east bank of the canal.[4]

\* \* \*

It took the Egyptians longer than it should have to figure out
what the Israelis were up to. But by October 17 they understood
everything and attempted to make up for lost time. As Israeli

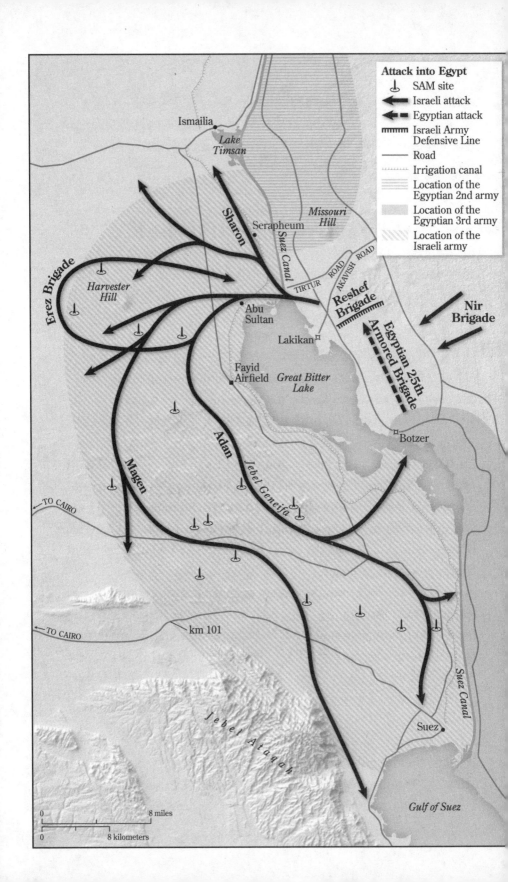

**Attack into Egypt**

⚓ SAM site
◄■■■ Israeli attack
◄┅┅ Egyptian attack
⊓⊓⊓⊓⊓ Israeli Army Defensive Line
——— Road
⋯⋯⋯ Irrigation canal
Location of the Egyptian 2nd army
Location of the Egyptian 3rd army
Location of the Israeli army

Ismailia

*Lake Timsan*

Serapheum

*Missouri Hill*

Sharon

Suez Canal

TIRTUR ROAD

AKAVISH ROAD

*Erez Brigade*

*Harvester Hill*

Abu Sultan

Lakikan

**Reshef Brigade**

Egyptian 25th Armored Brigade

Nir Brigade

Fayid Airfield

*Great Bitter Lake*

Botzer

Adan

Magen

Jebel Geneifa

TO CAIRO

TO CAIRO

km 101

Suez Canal

Jebel Ataqah

Suez

*Gulf of Suez*

0     8 miles

0     8 kilometers

combat engineers started assembling the bridge across the canal, an artillery barrage rained down upon them. Egyptian MiG fighter jets were next. Shells burst in every direction, tossing men like rag dolls and spraying them with hot metal splinters mixed with sand and canal water. The Yard measured only about five hundred yards by two hundred yards. In those tight confines—Israeli soldiers soon nicknamed it Yard of Death—the shells landed with devastating effect. The Israeli historian Ilan Kfir, who served in the battle as a combat medic, estimates that more than *one hundred thousand shells* were fired at the bridgehead area over the ensuing eight days.[5] *

Sitting in an armored vehicle was bad. Sitting in an unarmored vehicle like a truck or bus was worse. Standing exposed while directing traffic or assembling a bridge was worst of all. Ariel Sharon stood in the Yard directing tank drivers and combat engineers. Zev Amit, Sharon's best friend—formerly a paratrooper, currently a Mossad agent—accompanied him wearing army boots given to him by Sharon's wife.[6]

Early on the 17th, an Egyptian MiG swooped down and Amit screamed to Sharon to take cover. Sharon jumped into an APC and slammed the door shut. But the force of the blast pounded his head against a machine gun. The attack left the back of the vehicle in a bomb crater. Sharon momentarily blacked out, but opened his eyes just in time to hear someone scream, "The general is dead!" As it turned out, his face was covered in blood, but apart from a gash on his forehead he was fine. He swathed his head in a large white bandage and carried on.[7]

Ariel Sharon could not even get wounded without sparking controversy. To his admirers, he was a fearless warrior, the injury only adding to the legend. To his detractors, he was a shameless

* In 1974, following the signing of the Sinai Separation of Forces Agreement, later known as Sinai I, the Egyptians embarked on reopening the canal. With the help of the Americans, British, and French, they removed 686,000 land mines and 13,500 pieces of unexploded ordnance along the banks of the canal. They detonated an additional 7,500 pieces of unexploded ordnance in the waters of the canal itself.

faker, wrapping a minor cut with an oversize bandage to bolster his image.

Before he had a chance to finish wrapping the bandage, Sharon noticed that vehicles outside the Yard were being hit, not by artillery fire but by direct fire. He wiped the blood from his eyes, peered through binoculars, and saw what looked like a force of Egyptian tanks standing at the Lexicon Road shooting directly at them. "It was an absolutely critical moment," he remembered. He called Reshef, "screaming at the top of my lungs," to send Israeli tanks to the rescue. Reshef heard the usually restrained Sharon over the radio, raced to the junction himself, and destroyed a lone Egyptian tank.[8]

Enraged, Sharon radioed Gonen. He complained bitterly that Adan had left his flank exposed and that he was not allowed to use his own forces as he saw fit. Sharon was heated enough that Gonen pulled away from the microphone and muttered to an aide, "He's hysterical." Gonen was in no mood for Sharon, either, and said, "We'll talk about this after the war, just as we'll talk about other things." Sharon replied, "We'll talk about everything, and it won't be pleasant, that's for sure."

Shortly after hanging up, Sharon asked about Zev Amit and was told he had been "wounded and evacuated." He knew that no one was then being evacuated from the Yard and suspected what in fact was true. His best friend of over twenty years had been killed and no one had the heart to tell him.[9]

After all this, and with his head "pounding like a sledgehammer," Sharon left the Yard to attend the meeting with Dayan, Elazar, General Ze'evi, Bar-Lev, and Adan. Elazar had long complained that Sharon never seemed to travel anywhere without a posse of reporters in tow. Adan recognized at least one of the people in Sharon's entourage as a journalist. Someone asked Sharon why he was not wearing a helmet, and he replied, "Let the people in the rear wear helmets. I'll deal with them after the war." The men awaited Sharon with impatient fury, flanked by APCs and helicopters. Still sporting the large bandage, Sharon sat down in the sand.[10]

The encounter began with an awkward silence. It was Bar-Lev who finally broke it, saying to Sharon, "There's a lot of distance between what you promised and what you delivered." Sharon later said it took all his powers of self-control not to punch Bar-Lev in the face ("To this day I do not know how I kept myself from hitting him"). Sharon aide Jackie Even called the meeting the "greatest tragicomedy of the Yom Kippur War." But remarkably, once the ice was broken, and perhaps sensing what was at stake, the men overcame the mutual hostility and held a reasonably professional exchange of ideas. They even referred to one another collegially by their nicknames, "Dado," "Arik," "Bren."[11]

Sharon said the Egyptians were "beginning to collapse" and more tanks should be sent to Africa immediately using the crocodiles. As far as Sharon was concerned, the laying of the pontoon bridge was a foregone conclusion, Egyptian artillery notwithstanding. Bar-Lev scoffed at this: "I've been hearing about Egypt's 'collapse' for a week already." He and Elazar were also not as confident in the ability of the combat engineers to assemble thousands of pieces under fire. They remained adamant that no more tanks would cross the canal until the bridge was open for business.[12]

They left the most difficult question for last. Assuming the engineers succeeded in laying the pontoon bridge, who would spearhead the effort in Africa?

Sharon made a compelling argument. It was critical to get tanks across as quickly as possible so they could fan out and destroy SAM bases. There was no time to waste. An Egyptian defensive line was already forming.[13] If no tanks could cross until a bridge was laid, Sharon argued, let them at least cross the moment one became available. Adan's forces were then far to the south, preparing to head off an Egyptian attack on the bridgehead. It would be hours before they would be free to cross the canal. Better to let his tanks cross immediately.

Adan argued that the pontoon bridge was not yet ready anyway. It would take hours to assemble it, by which time he could complete the battle with the Egyptians and get across the canal. His forces were also in far better condition that Sharon's, because Sharon's had taken most of the casualties opening the corridor to the canal.[14]

Tensions were high, nerves were frayed. No one would budge. In exasperation, Bar-Lev proposed a compromise—*no one would cross first*. Instead, half of Adan's forces and half of Sharon's would cross at the same time.

From a military standpoint, this was an unorthodox proposal. How could an offensive involving hundreds of tanks and thousands of men operate without a clear hierarchy? Elazar understood this immediately. He lost his temper and cut off the debate. *Adan's tanks would cross first.* "Arik," he shouted, "finish the mission we gave you and then you can cross!"[15]

Elazar later said that the erstwhile compromise was the only bad decision Bar-Lev made in the war.[16] Left unspoken was that his decision to have Adan cross first was, if anything, even worse. In fact, it must take its place among the worst decisions of the war.

The meeting in the sand ended at 2:00 P.M. The combat engineers told them that the pontoon bridge would be ready "in the afternoon." As it turned out, it was ready at 4:00 P.M. That left Adan just two hours to defeat the Egyptians, return to the bridgehead, have his tanks rearm and refuel, and then cross into Africa. It was obvious that this timetable was impossible and that the bridge would sit idle until late into the evening. Sharon, by contrast, had over a hundred tanks armed, fueled, and ready to attack the Egyptian heartland.[17]

Somehow, it appears to have been lost on everyone that *Sharon had already crossed first*. A thousand paratroopers and more than thirty tanks under his command had been fighting west of the canal for over twenty-four hours. In every interview Sharon gave for the rest of his life, he boasted that he crossed the canal first. No one ever disputed him.[18] Why, then, did Elazar choose Adan over Sharon and waste at least eight crucial hours? The best answer might be found in an old saying in the Talmud: "Hatred distorts judgment."

Fortunately for the Israelis, the Egyptian leadership would match their dysfunction and overtake it. While the Israelis dithered, the Egyptians could have rushed forces to the bridgehead and attacked Sharon's tiny force west of the canal. Failing that, they could have moved over a hundred tanks and thousands of Sagger operators into the area and packed them in a line as tightly as the defensive line east of the canal. Once the Israelis broke out of the bridgehead and fanned out across the Egyptian heartland, that opportunity would be lost.

There was only one man in Egypt who seemed to understand this. It was Egypt's chief of staff, Sa'ad Shazly. What he did not yet understand was how sharply his superiors' thinking departed from basic principles of the soldier's art. He was about to learn.

Any competent commander will keep forces in reserve. It is impossible to be strong everywhere, and it is the reserves that plug the breach in the line if the enemy achieves a breakthrough. When Winston Churchill was told in 1940 that the collapsing French army had gone to battle against the Wehrmacht without leaving anything in reserve, he described it as "one of the greatest surprises I have had in my life."[19]

Keeping a fifth of one's forces in reserve is considered the minimum. A more cautious general, blessed with an overabundance of resources, might leave as much as a third. Shazly took no chances. As late as October 13, he had 780 tanks east of the canal and 680 tanks west of it, or almost half his army in reserve. The trouble began on the night of October 13 when Shazly was ordered by Sadat and General Ismail to send 330 tanks into Sinai for the October 14 offensive. That left him with only 350 tanks in reserve west of the canal.[20]

It was still a formidable force, at least on paper. But in comparison with the vast territory it had to defend, it was woefully inadequate. Many of the tanks could not be used because they were needed to defend Cairo, the Red Sea coast, and other high-value targets. Others could not be used because they were needed to defend something deemed even more important, which was the regime itself. Just two years removed from a coup attempt, Sadat held his Presidential Guard in reserve. Sadat went out of his way in his memoir to note that it "actually took part in the war, fought valiantly, and returned without losing a single tank." But Shazly wrote in *his* memoir that of his "strategic reserve" west of the canal, he could use only 130 tanks.[21]

Shazly's greatest problem was not even the lack of tanks, but the lack of infantry. A study by the Israelis after the war showed that 42 percent of their tanks were destroyed by Saggers and RPGs, while only 30 percent were destroyed by enemy tanks (the remaining 28 percent were destroyed by mines, artillery, and planes).[22] The foot soldiers and tanks were most effective when they were packed tightly together, each supporting the other. The Egyptian army fared badly in every encounter that pitted tanks against tanks only, or tanks against foot soldiers only.

As the curtain went up on this next phase of the war, Shazly knew that he had to act fast. Once the Israelis broke out of the bridgehead, it would be the war of movement that all his plans were designed to avoid. Fortunately, even after losing 250 tanks on October 14 and another 140 in the Chinese Farm, the Egyptians still had approximately 720 tanks east of the canal, plus thousands of available foot soldiers. The obvious next move was to bring a portion of that vanguard back across the canal to the western side to attack the Israelis inside the small bridgehead, or at least form a strong defensive line around it. It was all the more obvious because the Egyptian Third Army was under no pressure and two of its most important elements—the 4th Armored Division and the elite 25th Armored Brigade—had trained for exactly this mission.[23]

Shazly's military logic was unassailable. It was ignored by War Minister Ahmed Ismail. Ismail's thinking was dominated by a fear that bordered on a phobia: a withdrawal back across the canal, *any* withdrawal, might panic the Egyptian army and lead to its collapse.[24] Memories of the Six-Day War were still fresh in everyone's mind. Nasser's 1967 order to retreat led to the disintegration of discipline, morale, and everything else. It did not matter to General Ismail that this time Israeli jets did not control the skies, or that this time his army had proved itself. It did not even matter that Shazly did not ask to retreat but to attack in a different direction.

The bitter irony was that Ismail and Shazly were not that far apart. Both agreed that the elite 25th Armored Brigade, which to that point had seen little action, was the best unit to spearhead any attack. The choice was between having it travel north along the *western* shore of the Great Bitter Lake or north along the *eastern* shore of the Great Bitter Lake. The western shore was controlled by Egypt, both on the ground and in the air, courtesy of the SAMs. The tanks could thus travel safely until they reached Sharon's bridgehead. The eastern shore, on the other hand, was controlled on the ground and in the air by the Israelis. "Even when I explained to him," Shazly remembered, "Ismail seemed incapable of grasping the danger of asking an armored brigade, the 25th, to advance 25 miles with its left flank trapped against the water and its right flank open to enemy attack."[25] Forgetting everything else, the Israeli force in the bridgehead west of the canal was but a fraction of the force protecting the corridor east of the canal. In short, the choice was between traveling over safe terrain to attack a small force or traveling over dangerous terrain to attack a large one.

Sadat must have understood all of this—yet he sided with General Ismail. He had lived through the '67 debacle and was gripped with the same irrational fear. *No soldiers that crossed into Sinai would be allowed to withdraw back across the canal.* Shazly pleaded with Sadat to overrule General Ismail. Sadat exploded, "Why do you always propose withdrawing our troops from the east bank! If you persist in these proposals I will court-martial you!"

If Sadat had listened to Shazly instead of Ismail, it is very possible that Egypt would have won the war. With Sadat's stricture in place, the only thing Shazly had to attack the Israelis west of the canal was the 116th Infantry Brigade and the few tanks attached to it. The 116th was stopped by the Israelis right at the perimeter of the bridgehead along an irrigation channel. Colonel Chaim Erez, commander of the small Israeli force in the bridgehead, told his biographer that the Israelis only barely won the battle. He also noted that if Ariel Sharon had not "stolen" the additional ten tanks across the canal, there is "great doubt" that they would have held out at all. The bulk of Israel's army was still east of the canal. It was there that the Egyptians chose to attack.[26]

Shazly called the commander of the Egyptian Third Army, General Abdul Munim Wassel, and informed him that the 25th Armored Brigade would have to travel up the eastern shores of the Great Bitter Lake in broad daylight. A stunned Wassel pleaded to at least postpone the mission. If they waited until the late afternoon, they could travel with the setting sun on their left, blinding Israeli soldiers on their right. With a heavy heart, Shazly told him that even this was not possible.[27] Wassel accepted his fate and muttered the Muslim prayer of resignation: "Man has strength for nothing without the strength of God."[28]

\* \* \*

One of the most difficult feats in the military art is a coordinated assault, multiple forces attacking the same point at exactly the same time. The attack of the Egyptian 25th Armored Brigade on the Israeli bridgehead from south to north was but one prong of such an assault. Another prong was a north–south attack on the east bank of the canal by tanks of Egypt's 21st Division. As noted above, the third and final prong was a west-to-east attack by the 116th Infantry Brigade on the bridgehead. All three prongs were supposed to hit the bridgehead on both banks of the canal at the same time. But, General Shazly later wrote, "as usually happens in such cases, synchronization was lost. Each attacking force was left to fight its own battle." Amnon Reshef remembered it similarly but used more colorful language: "They fought like a bunch of schlemiels."[29]

Before any of this drama took place, on the morning of October 17 Israeli tanks in the 198th Armored Battalion under the command of Adan were sent to the Yard with orders to cross the canal on the crocodiles. Sharon and his officers, still fuming from the earlier meeting in the sand, interpreted this as a blatant maneuver by Elazar to upstage them and give Adan at least some claim to having crossed the canal first. The pontoon bridge was then still under assembly. And so with undisguised glee, Sharon explained to the battalion commander that only a few minutes before, Bar-Lev had prohibited any additional forces from crossing the canal until there was a bridge for them to travel over. Instead, Sharon sent the tanks north to the Shick Road to defend the northern line of the corridor and relieve the tired, battered men of the 184th Armored Battalion.[30]

It turned out to be an accidental masterstroke. The 184th had been decimated over the previous two days in the fight to open the corridor. The 198th had only fourteen tanks, but it was a fresh battalion, fully fueled and fully armed. It arrived just in time to defend against a frontal assault carried out by what was left of the Egyptian 21st Armored Division. The 21st was commanded by General Ibrahim el-Orabi, a competent officer who eventually rose to become chief of staff of the Egyptian army. But the 21st was down to just a hundred tanks, after having lost almost 150 over the previous two days. Orabi sent his 1st Armored Brigade with fifty-three battered tanks charging straight into the Israeli line along the Shick Road. It was not creative. There were no flanking maneuvers, no smoke screens, no diversions, just a headlong charge, once more unto the breach. With an advantage of fifty-three tanks to fourteen, the attack along a one-mile front had a decent chance of success. But the Egyptians were a spent force, attacking with no air or ground support, and doing so in broad daylight. The battle lasted only an hour. The Israeli commander claimed to have destroyed forty-five Egyptian tanks, though Egyptian sources put the figure closer to twenty. All agree the Israelis did not lose a single tank. All agree the Egyptians accomplished nothing.[31]

This drubbing, plus the failures of the Egyptian 116th Infantry Brigade west of the canal, would be largely forgotten by history. They were overtaken by a battle farther south that would later be studied by the military academies of the world.

* * *

On October 11, Israeli jets had destroyed a bridge near the city of Banha, twenty-five miles north of Cairo, not to disrupt transportation but to cut a communications cable that ran across its span. This forced the Egyptians to send more messages by wireless, which could then be intercepted by Israeli intelligence. One message intercepted by the Israelis was that the Egyptian 25th Armored Brigade, equipped with the most modern Soviet T-62 tanks, would be moving north along the eastern shores of the Great Bitter Lake.[32]

AMAN's warning gave the Israelis plenty of time to set up a two-sided ambush. Five tanks were positioned as a blocking force perpendicular to the Great Bitter Lake, six miles south of the Yard.[33] Farther south, two battalions spread out parallel to the Great Bitter Lake under the command of Colonel Nathan "Natke" Nir.

Nir, a Holocaust survivor, was one of the more noteworthy officers in the army. He had his legs shattered in the 1967 war while commanding a battalion in Sinai. Thirty-one operations in a Tel Aviv hospital accomplished nothing and left his doctors advising him to amputate both legs. Refusing to give up, he forged a doctor's signature on a medical report, sent it to Switzerland, and got himself accepted as a candidate for experimental titanium rods. The experiment succeeded. After enduring eight more operations he was able to walk again, albeit with a pronounced limp. IDF policy dictated that officers with physical limitations could not return to combat duty. But Adan let Nir command a reserve tank brigade, partly because he did not have the heart to refuse, and partly because he did not think a war would break out anyway. Jackie Even, Sharon's assistant, called Nir "one of the true heroes of the IDF."[34]

Sixty T-62 tanks, the finest in the Egyptian arsenal, began moving north accompanied by APCs, supply trucks, and field artillery. Military history has few examples of battles lost because forces arrived too early. Nevertheless, the group proceeded slowly, black dots inching across white dunes, a trail of dust and smoke billowing behind them. The procession moved at a snail's pace by design. Infantry armed with Saggers ran ahead on foot, established a defensive line, and then the tanks caught up. It was an unorthodox tactic that made the convoy look like the march along the Via Dolorosa pausing at the Stations of the Cross, rather than an armored counterattack. Adan remembered the six-mile procession as "shockingly slow, it stopped more than it moved."[35]

Nir positioned his tanks on the right flank of the Egyptians, employing a heavily drilled Israeli maneuver known as a "quick ambush." Nir's tanks were older-model Centurions. To have any hope of penetrating the heavy armor of the Egyptian T-62s, their guns had to be within 1,500 meters of the target, 500 meters closer than the firing range of the T-62s. But he had the element of surprise. The Egyptians inched forward, oblivious to what was taking shape on their right flank because Wassel thought the soft sand dunes overlooking the Great Bitter Lake were impassable to Israeli tanks.[36]

The Israelis sat quietly on the dunes with their engines off. Nir's assistant stood next to him, pleading with him to give the order to open fire and stop the Egyptians before they got too close to the bridgehead. Nir waited. He wanted as many tanks as possible to enter the ambush before he sprang the trap. He peered through his binoculars and calmly said, "A few more minutes."[37] At 2:45 P.M., with the sun high in the sky and the body of the Egyptian force at the top of the Lexicon Road near the blocking force, he finally gave the order.

Tank cannons thundered in unison across the dunes and the black dots in the distance instantly turned to orange fireballs. The Egyptians made a courageous effort to organize and charge Nir's position, but the Israeli tanks fired up their engines, closed in, and cut them to pieces. A few Egyptian tanks managed to slip away before the escape route sealed shut. But the vast majority of the brigade—the tanks, the trucks, the APCs, the Sagger teams, the very cream of the Egyptian army—all were incinerated in a box of fire. The slaughter continued until the sun set. The fires illuminated the night and left shadows of the wreckage flickering against the waters of the Great Bitter Lake. The Israelis lost three tanks.[38]

Barely an hour after the ambush began, at 4:00 P.M., Nir reported to Adan, "You can erase this brigade from the books. It's gone."[39] Adan hung up on Nir and breathlessly called Gonen. "The entire Egyptian 25th Armored Brigade has been wiped out! There isn't one of them left to piss against the wall." For the first time since the war began, the staff room of General Shmuel Gonen erupted in laughter.[40]

The Egyptian 25th Armored Brigade had not been erased from the books. It still had about a third of its strength, or thirty to forty tanks. But it ceased to exist as an effective fighting force. Earlier that day, Bar-Lev voiced the concern that the Egyptian 25th might tie down the bulk of Adan's division merely by traveling north and digging in. The 25th was now gone and the threat with it. The finish fight would take place west of the canal.[41]

The battlefield arithmetic had changed. Over the previous four days, the Egyptian army had lost *five hundred tanks*, or almost a third of its entire prewar strength. And there was still practically no Egyptian force opposite the bridgehead. The path to the Egyptian heartland was open. In past wars, these were the moments Israeli officers craved. The IDF prided itself as the ultimate instrument for finding weak spots and rushing to exploit them.

The pontoon bridge sat unused for almost eight hours.[42]

# 20

## BRIDGES

In war, events of importance are the result of trivial causes.

—Julius Caesar[1]

The arrival of Chaim Bar-Lev in Southern Command was welcomed by all who served there. Gonen's command operated in apoplectic disarray. Gonen routinely raged at his officers and at least once threw a bottle at one of them in his fury. The impression he left on those that visited his headquarters in the Dvaylah military base was not much better. Reshef writes that he found Gonen sitting on a seat that reminded him of a throne, sandwiched between a beautiful brunette manning a black phone to his right and a beautiful blonde manning a white phone to his left.[2]

Bar-Lev's appearance brought calm professionalism to a command that needed it. What it failed to bring was clarity. The German military theorist Carl von Clausewitz coined the term "fog of war" to describe the situational uncertainty one experienced in battle. Bar-Lev experienced an in-house variety in between battles as well. AMAN could give him a good understanding of the enemy's movements. No one, it seemed, could give him an understanding of Ariel Sharon's.

Moshe Dayan was also wondering what Sharon was up to. On

the afternoon of October 17, Dayan decided to drive to Sharon's command west of the canal to see for himself. With characteristic disregard for his own safety, he hitched a ride on one of the crocodiles ferrying equipment over the canal. Upon arriving at the bridgehead on the far bank, he ignored the shelling, refused to climb aboard an armored vehicle, and inspected the troops on foot. When his entourage passed a group of Egyptian prisoners, a captured major identified Dayan by his eye patch and asked for food. Dayan joked that it was Ramadan and so the Egyptians should be fasting. But then he turned serious and told an officer to see to it that the prisoners were treated properly.[3]

At 4:30 P.M. he headed back and was by then able to drive over the freshly laid pontoon bridge, one of the first to do so. This should have been a happy moment, a chance to savor the fruits of so much sacrifice, but Dayan could not fail to notice what was wrong with the picture: there was nothing traveling in the other direction.

Dayan drove straight to headquarters on the east bank of the canal and demanded to know why nothing was moving over the bridge. Elazar told him that he had ordered Adan to cross with seventy to eighty tanks that were near the bridgehead, but they were guarding the approaches to the corridor and could not move until Sharon's forces replaced them. Dayan lost patience. "Yes, replace them, no replace them," he retorted, "you've got to make a mad dash to the bridge."[4]

Sharon's assistant, Jackie Even, dedicates almost ten pages of his memoir to refuting the claim that Sharon was the cause of the delay. The real problem was that Adan's tanks had just completed the ambush of the Egyptian 25th Armored Brigade and had not refueled or rearmed. As Adan himself acknowledges in his own memoir, the supply trucks were late getting to the battlefield, blocked by the same traffic jam that had plagued the Israeli effort from the beginning.[5]

At 7:00 P.M. Gonen radioed Adan and pressed him to cross

the canal, ready or not. "If you don't cross then they'll tell Sharon to cross. Just cross now." Forty minutes later he radioed again and said, "Let them just cross with empty tanks and unorganized, just get to the other side." When Adan explained to him that this was foolish—it would be extremely difficult to refuel and reload on the far bank of the canal—Gonen said, "I can't talk to you now because we are on the radio. Just refuel as best as you can and get across."[6]

With each passing hour, Egyptian shelling of the Yard and the bridgehead intensified. Meanwhile, fresh Egyptian tanks were rushed to a defensive line near the bridgehead on the western side of the canal. At 9:30 P.M., Adan ordered his tanks to cease resupply and cross with whatever they had in their bellies. A little over an hour later, at 10:40 P.M., Adan radioed that he had crossed. What he did not report was that although he himself was in Africa, his tanks were all still in Asia. It seems clear he wanted to establish an earlier "crossing time" for the history books. In truth, the first tanks did not make it over the bridge until just before midnight.[7]

Descriptions of the crossing in the early morning hours of October 18 all contain the word *noise*. There was the noise of the tank engines, the noise of exploding artillery shells, and then to top it all off, the noise of fighter jets dogfighting above. Occasionally a truck loaded with fuel or ammunition was hit, setting off an earsplitting blast that wiped out everything in a hundred-yard radius.[8]

The pontoon bridge was a rickety floatation device made up of thousands of pieces assembled under fire. The combat engineers laid down the rules of the road. The tanks had to keep their distance from one another, and they had to travel at less than ten miles an hour. As fate would have it, the man given the task of issuing these orders was just a lowly second lieutenant. The third tank to cross was commanded by a senior officer in a hurry. The junior officer was ignored, three tanks raced across at the same time, and the bridge was torn in the middle. One of the tanks toppled off into the canal, drowning its crew of four.[9]

According to an old proverb, "for want of a nail a shoe was

lost, for want of a shoe a horse was lost," and so on, all the way up until a kingdom was lost. For the IDF, the tear in the bridge was potentially the nail. Everything stopped. The few operable crocodiles were pressed back into service. But they were limited in how much they could carry and were steadily being shot out of the water.[10]

What saved the day was a bridging tank—an armored vehicle with a heavy steel plate welded to the top in place of the turret— that was already in Africa, sent there in case it was needed to aid in crossing irrigation canals. Someone had the idea to tie the torn pieces of the pontoon bridge together with a cable and use a metal plate removed from a bridging tank to cover the tear. The exercise moved with admirable speed, and at 1:35 A.M. the pontoon bridge was back in service. The entire offensive was now held together by a cable and a metal plate, so this time strict discipline was enforced. Only one tank was permitted on the bridge at a time.[11]

The little metal plate was the symbolic straw that, once laid, broke the back of the Egyptian camel. As Israeli tanks crossed, Egyptian resistance started to break down. Egyptian soldiers were seen fleeing west across the canal. Israeli troops were under strict orders to hold their fire and let them flee. For Egyptian soldiers, that hardly meant it was safer in the rear than at the front. On October 21, the Israelis saw a group of withdrawing Egyptian soldiers deliberately mowed down by Egyptian machine-gun fire on the west bank of the canal.[12]

Egyptian artillery began to run low on ammunition as well. The shelling continued, but it weakened. Israeli efficiency increased as the drivers and their traffic cops got on the right side of the learning curve, optimizing travel over the delicate pontoon bridge. By the morning of October 18, Adan was on the west bank of the Suez Canal with 160 tanks at his disposal.[13]

The drama was far from over. A stray shell landed near the pontoon bridge and opened another gash in the middle. This time, a courageous Israeli soldier named Binyamin Mairnetz dove into the canal with a cable slung over his shoulder and lashed the two pieces of bridge back together.[14] *

The plain fact was that when Elazar said the crossing could not move forward without at least one bridge, this was not the bridge he had in mind. The 450-ton rolling bridge was going to have to do the job for which it was built. The need for it was so plain that for most of October 18 Sharon stopped pestering Bar-Lev to let him send more forces across the canal. With Adan's forces on the other side, even he knew that he had to stay put. The Israelis sent hundreds of vehicles through the supply route on the east bank of the canal, all but daring the Egyptians to try to cut it off. If such an attempt was made, Sharon's men were the only ones left to stop it.

Amnon Reshef was sent back to the Chinese Farm one last time on the morning of October 18 to make sure the Egyptians were gone. No resistance was encountered. The Tirtur Road at last secured, the rolling bridge was sent to the canal at 11:00 A.M. Israeli fighter jets patrolled above, no longer harassed by SAMs, to protect the procession below. Progress was slow. Shelling continued sporadically. The tanks broke off once to confront what was thought to be an attack of Egyptian commandos. Then, to top it all off, the group wandered into a hastily dug Egyptian minefield.[15]

The luckless bridge, for whom so many had already died, continued and came to a halt at the edge of the Lexicon Road at four in the afternoon. The group paused to catch its breath and make sure it was safe to proceed.[16] And the combat engineers knew that though they had fixed the bridge, braved artillery fire, and traversed the Chinese Farm, *now came the hard part.*

To travel the last two miles from the Lexicon Road to the canal, the convoy had to cross a narrow path between an Israeli-laid minefield on one side and swampland impassable to tanks on the other. Egyptian fire, they knew, would only intensify as they got

---

* In another of those strange decisions taken by the board that handed out commendations, his exploits earned him only the third highest award.

closer to the canal. Indeed, while the bridge was parked at the side of the road, six Egyptian MiG fighter jets slipped through the air defense and dove down out of the skies. Fortunately for the Israelis, the flying skills of the Egyptian pilots did not match their courage.* Somehow, miraculously, their shower of ordnance missed the two-hundred-yard-long bridge.[17]

But disaster struck all the same. The chief combat engineer of Southern Command, a lieutenant colonel named Aharon "Johnny" Teneh, took cover and was killed by Egyptian commandos hiding nearby (the commandos were quickly eliminated by a senior Israeli officer backed up by combat medics). At almost the same moment, the chief combat engineer for Sharon's 143rd Division, another lieutenant colonel named Baruch de Lion, was killed by shelling in the Yard. The Israelis had to thread a 450-ton bridge two more miles without the only two men who knew how to do it.[18]

General Even took command and led the bridge, in his words, "one grain of sand at a time."[19] The work continued into the night. The procession moved like a giant worm, slowly inching forward. At the head of the column stood a young combat engineer and a group of paratroopers guiding the effort by flashlight. At one in the morning in the early hours of October 19, the rolling bridge finally came to a stop along the water.

The tanks gave it a final shove into the canal. Small pyrotechnic devices exploded in unison to release the cables binding the bridge to the tanks. But even now the drama had one final act. The IDF's designers failed to account for the swift current of the canal. The bridge drifted with the waters and very nearly broke apart. A small boat working nearby on the pontoon bridge came to the rescue, caught the bridge, and helped anchor it to the other side. The floating behemoth finally spanned the Suez Canal.[20]

---

* Between October 16 and 18, the Israelis shot down thirty-six Egyptian planes and seven helicopters over the bridgehead. Against that, they lost only one plane, whose pilot safely ejected.

The payoff came when the "rolling" was complete. For once in place, the bridge was practically unsinkable. The "rollers" were metal cylinders filled with polyurethane. If the cylinders were hit by artillery shrapnel, the polyurethane would still float and prevent water from seeping in.[21] Only a direct hit could take out a section of the bridge, and that was all but impossible with artillery fire. The offensive west of the canal could finally proceed.

The logistical headache was not quite over. The rolling bridge could carry only vehicles on tracks, not those that traveled on rubber tires. Jeeps, supply trucks, ambulances, all had to cross on the pontoon bridge (the problem was solved after the war). Moreover, like the pontoon bridge, the rolling bridge had only one lane. The scale of what the IDF had to support on the west bank of the canal now required more than just one lane serving both directions. Combat engineers also pleaded with logistics officers to let them take the pontoon bridge out of service, even briefly, to repair the tears with something permanent, so that it would no longer rely on cables and metal plates.

There was only one potential solution. Far from the battlefield, a second pontoon bridge was under development. It had never been tested, but the greater concern was the bridge's location; it was over a hundred miles away. The only way to move it was with tanks. Not a single one could be taken off the line.

A white-haired officer named Senya Sirkin was part of a large cadre of reservists who were too old to be called up for duty but showed up on the battlefield anyway. Sirkin remembered that on his way in, he had seen repair yards filled with tanks that had been knocked out of battle. He gambled that just enough of them could drive even though they lacked their turrets. With a group of younger officers, he assembled a collection of headless tanks and together, the strange little force moved the experimental bridge into place on October 20. It was nicknamed the Tzneh Bridge.[22]

The Tzneh Bridge worked perfectly for the balance of the war. It allowed the pontoon bridge to be taken offline for permanent repairs. It also allowed the true heroes of the campaign—the croc-odiles and the men that piloted them—to come off the line.

By the time the rolling bridge was laid, only one crocodile was still operable. The rest had all been shot out of the water. Only a few hours before, a group of crocodiles was hit and the two tanks they carried slid off into the canal, drowning six of the nine men aboard. But in the brief thirty hours before Egyptian shell-ing began, they moved 120 vehicles across and did what no one before the war thought possible: rescued the State of Israel from certain defeat. The surrounding of the Egyptian Third Army, the early end of the war, the signing of the Camp David Accords five years later—all were made possible by discarded, secondhand ve-hicles bought for $5,000 a copy. Military history contains few ex-amples of such a good return on such a trivial investment.[23]

# 21

## AFRICA

The best electronic countermeasure against a surface-to-air
missile is a tank.

—Chaim Bar-Lev, speaking to Golda Meir[1]

Only in an army that contained an Ariel Sharon could generals
like David Elazar and Chaim Bar-Lev be accused of being overly
cautious. On the morning of October 19, the Israelis had about
650 tanks along the canal. Elazar and Bar-Lev sent 400 of them
into Africa.[2]

The plan was to have the 400 head south, destroy SAMs, and
cut off the Egyptian Third Army on the east bank of the canal
from its supply line west of it. It was an ambitious to-do list. To
accomplish everything, the task force had to conquer almost fifty
miles of territory in the Egyptian heartland. And every vehicle had
to pass through a corridor that from Egyptian lines north of the
Chinese Farm to the Akavish Road south of it measured only two
miles wide.[3] The narrow gauntlet was firmly in Israeli hands, but
every point of it was well within the range of Egyptian artillery.

Israel's zone of operations looked like an hourglass lying on
its side. If the Egyptians cut it off at the chokepoint in the middle, everything in Africa—the four hundred tanks, artillery, APCs,

trucks, and the thousands of men in the assault force—would be lost. On October 20, Ariel Sharon invited Colonel Tuvia Raviv, commander of the brigade defending the corridor, to a meeting with a "special guest." When Raviv arrived, he found Sharon still swaddled in the white bandage and a uniformed figure wearing an eye patch. "Tuvia," Moshe Dayan said, putting his hand on his shoulder, "I want you to know that the entire viability of the State of Israel rests on your brigade. If the Egyptians break through, we're finished."[4]

Elazar's high-wire act was not yet complete. He called General Yitzchak Hofi, commander of Northern Command, to congratulate him. Hofi's forces fighting in the "bulge" inside Syria had beaten back two Arab offensives, one on October 16 and the other on October 19. It was Napoleon who famously prayed that if he had to face an enemy, *please God let it be a coalition.* Israel's prayers were answered. Syrian, Iraqi, and Jordanian forces attacked one at a time; the Israelis defeated them one at a time. Elazar ignored the risk that Assad's coalition might launch a coordinated assault and ordered Hofi to pull a tank battalion off the line and send it to the canal. Hofi's protests fell on deaf ears. The redeployment left Northern Command with only 382 tanks.[5]

Back in Tel Aviv, Elazar's all-or-nothing approach electrified the General Staff with a fresh sense of optimism. The surprise of the war's opening days taught Elazar's generals that the only thing they had to fear was the lack of fear itself. Their fears melted away all the same. Photo reconnaissance revealed that east of the canal Egypt had more destroyed tanks than functioning ones. October 19 was also the first day of the war in which the IAF did not lose a single plane.[6]

This was probably the most encouraging news of all. The new tactic for destroying SAMs chipped away at Egypt's air defenses, even as tanks chewed them up on the ground. Elazar reported to Golda and her cabinet on the night of October 18 that out of a total of fifty-four SAM batteries, Egypt was down to its last twenty.* An Israeli pilot wrote in his memoirs that by October 20 he could fly over the bridgehead without worrying about Egyptian missiles.[7]

Egyptian fighter pilots flew into that breach and courageously attacked the bridgehead in waves. The Israeli air force blasted them out of the sky. Over the course of the war, the Israeli air force lost only 6 planes in air-to-air combat. They shot down 277, performing in 1973 much as they had in 1967, destroying Arab planes, only in the air instead of on the ground. On October 20, an Israeli pilot named Giora Even notched his seventeenth career kill, making him the world's most successful ace of the modern fighter-jet era.[8] [†]

The news from the field was just as encouraging. West of the canal, a hill code-named Harvester was where the Egyptians situated the bulk of the artillery that hammered the Israeli bridgehead. Given its shape and location, the hill appeared on Israeli maps like a bone lodged in a throat. The task of removing that bone was handed to Colonel Natke Nir, the hero of the October 17 ambush that destroyed the Egyptian 25th Armored Brigade. As Nir stood in the turret of his tank making plans, he took a direct hit that knocked him unconscious. Upon opening his eyes, lying in the belly of his tank, he discovered that he had taken a shrapnel wound to the neck. Nir calmly bandaged his wound, dusted himself off, and promptly led an east–west frontal assault straight up Harvester Hill. It was one of the most important Israeli victories of the war. Eighty Egyptian artillery pieces were taken out of action, and for a time the bridgehead was quiet. Israeli soldiers that crossed on October 19 were the lucky ones. One commander described his trip over the rolling bridge as "pastoral."[9]

The barriers into Egypt were finally pried loose. Once in open

---

* There are conflicting accounts of how many SAMs the Egyptians possessed. There is a consensus that about 70 percent were destroyed, two-thirds by the Israeli air force and one-third by ground forces.

† The record for an American is Charles B. DeBellevue, who recorded six kills in Vietnam.

country, the tanks sped through the desert, encountering light resistance. General Adan said that seeing the broad expanses before
him felt like a prize given to his tanks in recognition of all the
hard fighting it took to get there. Four Israeli brigades rolled west
in a broad counterclockwise thrust heading south. The path of the
tanks was dictated by the location of Egyptian surface-to-air missiles scattered along the way. The ultimate prize was a hill called
Jebel Geneifa, which dominated the horizon west of the Great
Bitter Lake and was the location of a cluster of SAM bases.[10]

The SAMs were easy to spot on hilltops, their distinctive radar
antennas poking up above large compounds. A good tank gunner
could take out the fragile radars at a distance of two and a half
miles. The Egyptians manning the SAM bases defended themselves in the only way they could, by lowering their sights and firing SAMs directly at the tanks. Israeli tank gunners later described
the missiles as giving off an enormous amount of heat and producing a sizable shock wave. But they were designed for targets in
the air and flew wildly in every direction.[11]

All in all, October 19 was a good day for the Israelis. They
advanced about fifteen miles south, parallel with the Great Bitter
Lake. The heights of Jebel Geneifa were just six miles away, close
enough to be visible without binoculars. Still, Elazar remained
unsettled. The all-important but unglamorous job of holding the
corridor on the east bank of the canal was given to Ariel Sharon,
the general least interested in unglamorous work. "I don't want
Arik doing any Tour de France," Elazar muttered. In laying out his
priorities, Elazar placed protecting the bridgehead at the top of
the list and then exclaimed, "I'm afraid of Asia, not Africa!"[12]

Sharon was, if anything, even more unsettled. The war was being won west of the canal and he was stuck protecting a corridor
east of it. On the morning of October 19, Sharon radioed Gonen
and pleaded for authorization to send more tanks across the canal. Gonen, who by now should have known better, gave an order
that left the door open a crack. He told Sharon he could cross "if

it becomes possible." Sharon predictably interpreted that to mean "yes" and immediately sent seventeen tanks and several hundred commandos across the canal.[13]

Gonen flew into another rage and demanded that Sharon be sacked. Elazar flew into a rage of his own. But instead of following through and relieving Sharon of command, Elazar made a concession, one that nearly cost him his life.

Sharon had long complained that those above him would see things his way if only they were there in the field. Sharon went out of his way to state that he was not questioning the courage of those who remained in the rear, but the implication was obvious. Thus goaded, Elazar rose to take the bait. He said that he would give the matter of Sharon's removal more thought and pass sentence later that day. But first he would fly west of the canal to where Sharon had moved his headquarters near the front line, to see what was happening for himself.[14]

Elazar's helicopter flew low over the bridgehead to avoid missiles and landed along the shores of the Great Bitter Lake near a place called Abu Sultan. Sharon emerged in a fiery mood and told Elazar that the surest way to push the Egyptians farther north on the east bank of the canal was to push them farther north on the west bank. Each time his men seized ground along the west bank of the canal, Sharon said, he made sure they planted a large Israeli flag so that the Egyptians on the east bank saw that they were being surrounded. Egyptian morale was wavering, panic was setting in. With enough manpower, Sharon insisted, he could push north of the city of Ismailia in a week to ten days and cut off the Egyptian Second Army.[15]

Elazar thought the plan senseless. Putting aside how overextended the IDF already was, moving north of Ismailia required crossing two large irrigation canals. Because the few bridges the IDF possessed were all in use on the Suez Canal, the only way forward was capturing Egyptian bridges—and those were almost certainly wired with explosives.[16]

Elazar told Sharon that the main effort would be south, not north, with the aim of surrounding the Egyptian Third Army. Whether they surrounded more Egyptians was less important than making sure they did not get surrounded themselves. He therefore ordered Sharon to extend the corridor on the *east bank* farther north and capture an important hill code-named Missouri. It would not be long before the Egyptians moved artillery onto Missouri Hill, and then the shelling of Israel's only supply line would commence again. Sharon was horrified. "I railed against it."[17] The two men spoke past each other for close to two hours, Sharon wanting to push north on the west bank, Elazar on the east. Nevertheless, Elazar left it at that. The unspoken compromise was that Sharon did not get his way on strategy, but Elazar did not sack him, either.

On the helicopter flight back, Elazar aide Avner Shalev looked down and noticed that the uniforms of the soldiers appeared brighter than those worn by Israelis. The pilot checked his instruments and realized that he had made a slight mistake in his navigation. *The men below were Egyptians.*

There was no time for a course correction. At that very moment, bullets filled the sky. The pop-pop sounds from below drowned out the chop-chop noise of the helicopter blade overhead. The pilot bobbed and weaved, angling the craft back and forth, but the chopper was hit anyway and even lost a hydraulic system. Nevertheless, the flight crew kept its cool; the Egyptians were apparently not armed with anything larger than assault rifles, and the helicopter somehow made a safe landing in an Israeli base in Sinai.[18] One can only imagine the damage that would have been caused if an Israeli chief of staff had been killed or, worse, fallen into captivity.*

---

* That evening, not far from where Elazar had flown, Colonel Nir was told that the only hope a wounded man had of survival was being evacuated to a hospital by helicopter. Nir insisted that a helicopter be sent immediately, even though the air force grounded all such missions, deeming the battle zone too dangerous. A helicopter was sent and shot down. All aboard were killed, except a copilot who fell into Egyptian captivity.

If Elazar learned anything on his trip, it was how daunting the challenges were. He confided in those around him that he thought it unlikely they could surround the Egyptian Third Army. When asked by Dayan later that evening, Bar-Lev said that he, too, thought the chances of surrounding the Egyptians were "fifty-fifty." All agreed that the effort south should not be diluted by diverting resources for another Sharon adventure to the north. And all agreed that the most important thing was guaranteeing the supply line east of the canal and conquering Missouri Hill.[19]

In any other army, the general tasked with protecting the corridor would have received his orders and attacked Missouri Hill. But in any other army, the man receiving those orders would not have been Ariel Sharon.

* * *

General Sa'ad Shazly, the Cassandra of the Egyptian army, watched helplessly as his situation crumpled. What was clear to Ariel Sharon instinctively was now clear to Shazly as well: the Egyptian plan was brilliant but brittle. It worked perfectly right up to the moment that it almost delivered victory. Then it did not work at all.

Shazly could draw solace from the fact that the faith he placed in his men was vindicated. Late on October 18, Sadat and General Ismail finally authorized him to move an armored brigade from the Egyptian Third Army back across the canal to the west side. As he had predicted, there had been no panic; the army east of the canal did not collapse. If the same had been done two days earlier, the 25th Armored Brigade would have still been in existence, and it would have been fighting at that moment to keep the Israelis bottled up in the bridgehead.[20]

Unfortunately, Shazly could also see that moving a single armored brigade now was too little too late. Before the brigade could get into position, the Israelis were already halfway down the Great Bitter Lake, tearing up SAM batteries as they went.

There was no longer any bridgehead to contain. The fight was out in the open across the wide expanses of the Egyptian heartland.

In Anwar Sadat's telling, Shazly returned to Cairo late on the night of October 19 "a nervous wreck." Writing in 1989—eight years after Sadat's assassination, when it was safe to speak freely— Field Marshal Muhammad el-Gamasy said that this was simply not true. Sadat also claimed that Shazly counseled withdrawing the entire army from the east bank of the canal. Gamasy writes that this was not true, either. Shazly recommended leaving the infantry on the east bank with their Saggers and RPGs, and moving four armored brigades—about two-thirds of the tanks—back across the canal for a final, decisive battle with the Israelis.[21]

Sadat assembled his war council just after midnight, in the early hours of October 20, and went around the table seeking advice from each general. The group, which included air force commander Hosni Mubarak, was unanimous that, as Gamasy put it, "it was essential to maintain the status quo east of the Canal, without the withdrawal of any significant number of troops." Before hearing any counterargument from Shazly, Sadat made his decision, a decision, he declared, "even more important than that of the fighting order of October 6." There would be no withdrawal from the east bank. "Not a soldier, not a rifle, nothing."[22]

It was almost certainly the right decision. Shazly was correct two days earlier when he advised moving forces west of the canal. That was when the SAMs were still in place, and the tanks could have been packed tightly with infantry to hem the Israelis inside the tiny bridgehead. The front now stretched in a sweeping arc across dozens of miles. A large tank battle in the open country, with few Saggers on the Egyptian side and the Israeli air force controlling the skies, would have been a replay of the '67 war. This was the fight Israel had craved from the first day.

Sadat had no intention of fighting Israel's war. Instead, he chose to fight in the forum where Egypt held all the advantages.

Right after Sadat's meeting with his generals, at two o'clock in the morning, Soviet diplomat Vladimir Vinogradov was awakened by "the ringing of the presidential telephone." He was asked to see Sadat urgently at Tahra Palace.

Together with an aide, Vinogradov rushed through the darkened streets of Cairo. Once inside the blacked-out palace, they were taken to a room with Sadat, Minister of War Supplies Abdullah Fattah, and General Ismail, who was smoking nervously in the corner. Sadat himself was, in Vinogradov's words, "not looking his best." His light-colored military tunic was creased, the collar was unbuttoned, and both Vinogradov and his aide "detected efforts to remain calm and confident."

As usual, the two sides spoke in English. After the usual diplomatic pleasantries, Sadat took a long drag on his pipe. He paused and then declared, "I can fight against Israel, but not against the United States." Sadat began in an even tone, but then grew emotional. "I am unable to fight against the flow of American tanks and aircraft . . . I would like you to urgently send this request to Moscow: could they achieve a ceasefire as soon as possible . . ."[23]

# 22

# EMBARGO

When the Americans speak of 'the Arabs,' they are talking about Saudi Arabia. They don't care if Syria or Iraq likes them.

—Abba Eban[1]

On April 18, 1973, Richard Nixon delivered the first-ever presidential address on energy to Congress. The policy statement noted that the American people constituted only 6 percent of the planet's population but used a third of its oil. The statement went on to describe far-reaching steps to increase domestic oil production, stating that "our energy demands have grown so rapidly that they now outstrip our available supplies."[2]

The historic address was barely noticed—as was the fact that by the summer, oil imports reached a record 6.2 million barrels a day—because April 1973 was also the month in which Nixon fired John Dean and accepted resignations from his attorney general as well as John Ehrlichman and H. R. Haldeman, two of his closest aides. In the middle of 1973, the American people were far more interested in the Watergate scandal than an economic trend.

Six months later, on October 17, 1973, the foreign ministers of four Arab countries came to Washington to meet with Nixon and Kissinger in the Oval Office. Among the Arabs, expectations were high. Kissinger had won the Nobel Peace Prize the day before and Saudi Foreign Minister Omar Saqqaf said, "The man who could solve the Vietnam War . . . can easily play a good role in settling and having peace in our area of the Middle East."[3]

Kissinger thought that Nixon handled the meeting "masterfully." But by this he meant that Nixon did an excellent job telling the Arabs things that they did not want to hear. The airlift to Israel, Nixon explained, was done to "maintain a balance" with the Soviets and was commenced only after Moscow sent "over three hundred planes." To the Arab request that Israel be forced back to the 1967 line, Nixon promised to "work within the framework of Resolution 242." The presentation ended awkwardly, with Nixon asserting that although Kissinger was Jewish, "he will not be moved by domestic pressures in this country." (Kuwait's foreign minister, el-Sabah, took it in stride and said, "We are all Semites together.") But everyone emerged to offer kind words to the press. Then Kissinger gave Saudi Foreign Minister Saqqaf a private audience with Nixon so that the president could personally thank him for the "very moderate and constructive role" that his country was playing.[4]

Late that afternoon, Nixon met with the WSAG—the special committee convened to manage the crisis—to thank everyone for their efforts. The worst seemed to be behind them. Kissinger said, "Mr. President, this has been the best run crisis since you have been in the White House. We have launched a massive airlift [to Israel] yet . . . you stand here getting Arab compliments in the Rose Garden."[5]

Just as the meeting adjourned, a news ticker jolted everyone's complacency. Arab oil ministers meeting in Kuwait announced that they would reduce production by 5 percent immediately, and an additional 5 percent each month, until Israel withdrew to the 1967 boundary. The day before, delegates from the Persian Gulf had announced that the "posted price" paid by oil companies to producing nations was being raised 70 percent, to over five dollars a barrel. This act brought pricing into line with the panicky spot market and left very little profit for oil companies. There was nothing the oil companies could do about it, because for the first time there was no spare capacity in the United States or elsewhere to fill any sudden loss of oil production. As Kissinger put it, "It became progressively evident that the producer cartel could set prices nearly arbitrarily . . . a new phase of postwar history began."[6]

The move stunned American officials. A cable from the US embassy in Kuwait City described a meeting with Kuwaiti Minister of Finance and Oil Abdul Rahman Ateeqi, who informed his American counterpart that the "cumulative effect of [the] initial reduction of five percent . . . was intended to result in a complete embargo on oil to the United States." A State Department official in Washington read the cable and scribbled a comment in the margin: "Really?"[7]

* * *

As the industrialized nations learned something new about oil markets, Anwar Sadat learned something old about war—namely, how quickly things can go from good to bad on a battlefield.[*] West of the canal, the Egyptians continued to give ground in what more and more looked like a flight from the inevitable. On October 21, an Israeli tank commander made it to the top of Jebel Geneifa and looked out on what he called a "breathtaking sight." Below him was farmland, gardens, and the Great Bitter Lake (though above him were artillery shells raining down in a steady whistle). The destruction of the SAMs on Jebel Geneifa seems to have been the tipping point. Moshe Dayan wrote that from that point forward, the IAF could do what it did best: give close ground support to

---

[*] As late as July 18, 1918, Imperial Germany refused to even consider negotiations to end World War I, so certain was the German High Command of victory. Just four days later an offensive failed, and they knew that the war was lost. A German general appeared in the Reichstag shortly thereafter and stubbornly predicted victory. He was met with gales of mocking laughter.

tanks pushing south. October 21 was another day in which the Israeli air force did not lose a single plane.[8]

The sudden turn of events did nothing to create harmony among Israel's generals. All through October 19–22, the debate raged at the highest levels as to whether Elazar should sack Sharon. The dispute this time was over Missouri Hill, the egg-shaped hill just north of the Chinese Farm. For days Sharon was ordered to conquer it, and for days he refused.[9]

Of all the disputes of what became known as the War of the Generals, this one was the bitterest. The men who ultimately paid the price were those sent into battle with too few resources to accomplish anything. Twenty-six tanks attacked Missouri Hill. Only four came back. We will never know if sending a larger force would have made a difference. But Sharon experienced a vindication of sorts. The hill was never taken and the corridor held firm just as he said it would.[10]

If the dispute hadn't burst forth onto the newspapers after the war, the battle would have remained a footnote. What commanded attention was the fight west of the canal where the endgame began to take shape. On October 22, the IAF launched the last mission against Egyptian SAMs. The new tactics were by now honed to perfection. The Israelis destroyed two more batteries without losing a plane. With that, Egypt's air defense system essentially ceased to exist. Not coincidentally, on October 22 the IAF flew 441 sorties over the canal, the most of any single day of the war. One pilot said it was so busy in the skies they needed a traffic cop. The Egyptian army was doomed.[11]

* * *

On October 19, Nixon asked Congress for what was termed a $2.2 billion aid package for Israel. Kissinger wrote in his memoir that this was a "routine, largely budgetary decision" taken to cover the costs of the airlift to Israel. A member of the WSAG team, William Quandt, describes the decision in less anodyne terms, saying that

Kissinger "argued for a very large aid bill for Israel." In Quandt's telling, Kissinger did this because he knew how grueling the up-coming diplomacy was likely to be, and he needed to obtain "max-imum credit with Israel." Of course, given his emotional ties to the Jewish state, the desire to lend a helping hand was probably a factor as well. Whatever the motive, Kissinger writes that no one warned of "an Arab reaction," and that "the worst was thought to be over."[12] The sentiment was understandable. It was the transfer of arms by airlift that was expected to cause friction, not the transfer of money.

As so often happens in the Middle East—a land of hot weather and high emotion—events quickly overtook what was expected. News of the aid package burst open a dam of pent-up rage in the Arab world, rage that easily surpassed the anger at the airlift. A palace official in Saudi Arabia told an American diplomat that "King Feisal was as furious as [I have] ever seen him." The cable to Washington describing the situation said the king was heard to call for a "Jihad."[13]

Brezhnev, at least, was calling for an immediate ceasefire. The Soviets did not attempt to conceal their desperation, concluding an October 19 invitation for talks in Moscow with an urgent plea: "It would be good if he [Kissinger] could come tomorrow, Oc-tober 20." Kissinger obliged them. In his words, delaying might cause the Soviets to respond by "raising the military ante" and anyway, Kissinger figured the long flight to Moscow would give the Israelis more time on the battlefield. He left in good spir-its, knowing that he held the stronger hand. He confidently told Schlesinger, Moorer, and William Colby, the director of the CIA, that "we can't humiliate the Soviet Union too much."[14]

While flying to the Kremlin, Kissinger was given news of a de-velopment that, in his words, "turned almost into an obsession for the next five months." Saudi Arabia declared a total embargo on oil exports to the United States. Coming on the heels of the Oc-tober 16 price hike and the October 17 cutback of 5 percent, the psychological effect on markets was electric. Panic buying ensued.

By mid-December, oil was selling for $17 a barrel—six times the pre-October 16 price.[15] *

Still playing for time, Kissinger landed and politely told his Soviet hosts that he never negotiated after long flights and would not be available until the following morning, October 21. When the sun rose the next day, he knew he could delay no longer, not even under the guise of seeking Nixon's consent. Nixon sent an ill-advised letter to Brezhnev informing him that "Dr. Kissinger speaks with my full authority." Kissinger later wrote that "history will not record that I resisted many grants of authority. This one I resented bitterly; it was a classic example of how 'full powers' can inhibit rather than enhance negotiating flexibility."[16]

During the Cold War, conflicts typically ended after years of negotiations. The Moscow talks lasted only four hours.[17] The Soviets capitulated on every substantive issue. The draft resolution to be submitted to the UN was a ceasefire-in-place. There was no reference to "withdrawal" as Sadat demanded only a week before. Nor did the resolution contain the other word that Jerusalem invariably fought: "Palestine." The agreement disregarded the Arab taboo against negotiating with Israel—one of the "Three No's"—stating that "negotiations shall start between the parties concerned under appropriate auspices." The toppling of yet another of the "Three No's"—no peace—was hinted at; the negotiations were "aimed to establish a just and durable peace in the Middle East." And there was no reference to the 1967 boundary, only "implementation of Security Council Resolution 242."

What the Soviets got in return was speed. The draft resolution would be presented to the UN Security Council immediately. Once it passed, shooting had to end "no later than 12 hours after the moment of the adoption of this decision."

---

* In his memoir, Kissinger states with admirable candor that it would have been wiser to delay the Israeli aid package until after the ceasefire was signed. That way, Washington could have explained it as an unavoidable part of the deal to end the war and rescue the Egyptian Third Army.

Under ordinary circumstances, Israel would have considered this an excellent deal. But these were not ordinary circumstances. As Kissinger knew from State Department reports, the quick ceasefire would prevent the Israelis from encircling the Egyptian Third Army. As Jerusalem saw it, only a few more hours separated victory from defeat. There were two east–west roads from Cairo used to supply the Third Army, and a third coming up from the south. The Israelis had captured the two east–west roads.[18] If the third eluded them, then the Third Army would soldier on and the Israelis would find themselves fighting a war of attrition from overextended lines deep in Egypt.

None of this concerned Kissinger. He had a potential crisis with the Soviets that he needed to avoid; he had an embargo imposed by the Arabs that he needed to lift. Israel was going to have to make do. In Washington, General Alexander Haig, Nixon's chief of staff, gave the proposed text of the resolution to Israeli ambassador Dinitz and told him that not a word could be changed. Golda attempted to contact Nixon directly to plead for more time, but he was unyielding. The Israelis had been promised that Kissinger would not present them with a fait accompli. Kissinger now did exactly that. He spoke first to the ambassadors of Britain, France, and Australia. Those were the nations he now deemed important, because those were the nations he needed to rush the resolution through the Security Council.[19]

Kissinger was in such a hurry that one aspect of the arrangement seems to have eluded him: the deal was terrible for the United States of America.

This was the moment when Washington had the most leverage over the Arabs. The destruction of the Egyptian Third Army was imminent. If ever there was a time to demand the end of the embargo and the 5 percent cutback in production, this was it. A rollback of the October 16 price hike was almost certainly impossible, given market conditions. But Kissinger could easily have contacted Feisal from Moscow and conditioned the rescue of the

Third Army on OPEC agreeing to a ceasefire for consumers. It is difficult to see how the king could have turned him down.

So why didn't Kissinger do this? One of his aides said in an interview for this account that he simply made a bad mistake. A retired senior American diplomat told this author the same thing. One of Kissinger's greatest admirers, former US ambassador Martin Indyk, wrote in his book *Master of the Game* that "Kissinger was too focused on his looming negotiations with Brezhnev to appreciate the significance of Feisal's decision."[20] Yet remarkably, even after the significance was apparent to every motorist on the planet, Kissinger only once raised the possibility of using the Third Army's predicament as leverage to end the embargo. It was in a conversation with Golda Meir.[21] *

\* \* \*

The Syrian force atop Mount Hermon was formidable on paper, numbering hundreds of well-trained commandos. But from a logistics standpoint it was hanging by a thread. There was no road leading to Mount Hermon from the Syrian side, so the primary means of supply was by helicopter. The Israelis dedicated artillery to keep watch over the mountain and opened fire each time they heard the chop-chop of rotor blades coming in for a landing. It left the Syrians with only one means of supply, and that was by donkey.[22]

Helicopters would be the centerpiece of Israel's October 21 operation to retake the mountain. Syrian artillery might have similarly prevented Israeli helicopters from landing, but an Israeli officer had learned how to overcome the problem while studying in America with the US Marine Corps. The operation thus began with bombardment from Israeli fighter jets. The mountain's altitude took them right into the sweet spot for Syrian SAMs, so the planes flew in from Lebanon pushing their jet engines to the limit,

---

* Henry Kissinger declined two requests to be interviewed for this account.

twisting and diving so violently that one pilot said he landed and "vomited out everything inside me, including my soul."[23]

The planes did not just drop bombs, but a smoke screen that gave cover to helicopters that flew up from a narrow wadi. The thin air required the blades to carry only half as many men as would have been possible under ordinary circumstances, so it took twenty-seven sorties to drop 626 men on the higher Syrian Hermon. The paratroopers set out at sunset and headed down the mountain toward the Israeli Hermon, fighting through the night. It was an elegant operation that by morning had the force in control of the higher portion of the mountain, stopping just short of the Israeli Hermon beneath them. Only two Israelis were killed, against thirty-nine Syrians killed and another seventeen captured.[24]

The larger battle took place farther south where a second Israeli force headed up the heights to retake the Israeli Hermon from below. The Syrians chose to make their stand around a position known as Hill 16; the battle raged for eight hours. Knowing that the ceasefire was imminent, the Israelis did not have time to devise anything complicated, so they conquered it with brute force. Over the entire battle they fired thirteen thousand artillery shells. Syrian records are filled with praise for their commandos, saying they fought until they ran out of ammunition. But in the end, Israeli troops from the crack Golani Brigade returned to the bunker where the conflict began and hung their nation's flag from an antenna. In one of the war's most memorable television moments, an Israeli soldier with a thick Sephardic accent said to the camera, "We knew that Mount Hermon was important. They told us it is the 'eyes of the State of Israel.'"[25] It has been known as the "eyes of the nation" ever since.

\* \* \*

Kissinger decided to stop in Israel on his way back from Moscow, landing in Lod airport in the early afternoon of October 22. Israeli

Foreign Minister Abba Eban met him on the tarmac and said that Golda was waiting to see him. Eban's tone sounded like a summons to see a stern school headmistress. Eban had seen Golda's anger that morning, and he did not envy Kissinger for what he was about to experience.[26]

To be sure, Golda had kind words for Kissinger for delivering the airlift. ("I know what you did. Without you, I don't know where we would have been.") But she had plenty to be angry about and was not shy about displaying it. There had been no consultation. How did she know there was no side deal between Washington and the Soviets? Kissinger said there was none. There was no provision on POWs. "How can I face the mothers and wives of these men?" Golda asked. Kissinger said, "I have the word of honor of Brezhnev. That is not worth much, but we can use it." When he saw that this did not make much of an impression, he relented and told Golda she did not have to negotiate until all POWs were freed.[27]

The greatest source of Golda's anger, of course, was the timing. The Israeli army was winning, and now it was being told it had to stop. Israel's ambassador to the UN, Yosef Takoah, bought the IDF some time. He delayed the Security Council meeting by six hours. Then, Soviet ambassador Yakov Malik—the verbal pugilist who is credited with introducing the Russian word *nyet* to the English-speaking world—got into a shouting match with the Chinese ambassador. Takoah bought a little more time by pouring fuel onto the fire and forcing a temporary adjournment. Then he goaded the Saudi representative into a debate about the origins of Zionism.[28] Nevertheless, by the time Kissinger sat down with Golda, the resolution had already passed, and the ceasefire was scheduled to take effect in just six hours.[*]

---

[*] UN Security Council Resolution 338 passed at 12:52 A.M., New York time, on October 22. Because the Suez Canal is six hours ahead of New York time, and because the resolution called for "all military activity" to terminate "no later than 12 hours" after adoption of the resolution, the ceasefire took effect along the canal on October 22 at 6:52 P.M. local time.

Golda did not let on as to just how close the Israelis were to surrounding the Third Army. She even implied that her army had some distance to go, telling Kissinger, "We would have been in a better position in a few days." Kissinger therefore thought he had some leeway to soften the blow.[29] The following exchange took place:

Kissinger: You won't get violent protests from Washington if something happens during the night, while I'm flying. Nothing can happen in Washington until noon tomorrow.
Golda: If they don't stop, we won't.
Kissinger: Even if they do . . .[30]

\* \* \*

Accepting a ceasefire before there are monitors to police it is a lot like accepting a law before there are judges to enforce it. That, Muhammad Heikal told Sadat, was why Egypt should continue to fight, at least until observers made it into the field. Sadat declined, knowing that anything that gave the Israelis a pretext to continue their drive south could spell disaster. When his national security adviser, Hafez Ismail, gently pressed Heikal's case, Sadat exploded. "What's got into you, Hafez? You're a military man, you ought to know better." The outburst brought Ismail to the verge of tears.[31]

There is perhaps no point on which the records of Israel and Egypt diverge so sharply as the question of what occurred immediately after the declaration of the October 22 ceasefire. Egypt's General Shazly is willing to concede only that "on the road south from Suez, a few shots were fired at them [the Israelis], usually on the initiative of some junior officer." Israeli accounts are just as adamant that their forces were attacked. One Israeli lieutenant colonel said, "We saw no sign of any ceasefire where we were; the enemy kept shooting like normal." A different field commander whose unit took casualties—they suffered two dead and seven wounded—wrote in his memoir that after they dug in for the night, the Egyptians "fired at us from every direction, missiles, anti-tank fire, mortars and light arms."[32]

Israeli records are themselves contradictory as to the army's intentions. In an emergency meeting of the government on October 22, Dayan told Golda and her ministers that if the Egyptians truly stopped shooting, then Israel would have no choice but to comply with the ceasefire. Indeed, the government's unanimous decision authorized the army to continue fighting, if and only if it was fired upon.[33]

Nevertheless, others in Southern Command had no intention of letting victory slip from their grasp. Starting on October 8, Gonen knew there was going to be an investigation after the war, so he placed a tape recorder in his headquarters. He had the recorder turned off on October 22 when he and the others presumably discussed breaching the ceasefire. When it was turned back on, Gonen could be heard explaining to General Dov "Dovick" Tamari, General Adan's assistant, that he should be prepared to go on the attack because Egyptian forces were going to attack him at 7:30 A.M. on October 23, some twelve hours after the ceasefire was in effect. Tamari wondered if Gonen had some fortuitous piece of intelligence and went back and forth with him several times, until Gonen finally said, "*I'm* telling you what's going to happen." With that, Tamari said, "Ooooh, *now* I understand." Southern Command erupted in laughter.[34]

In a confidential meeting with Golda, the details of which were not declassified until decades later, Bar-Lev strongly suggested that his forces would have driven farther south one way or the other under the guise of "linking up with forward positions." Fortunately, they were fired upon after the ceasefire went into effect, so they could rightly claim they advanced only under fire. And, Bar-Lev added dryly, "nobody can prove anything anyway."[35]

Sadat would have helped his cause if he had painted the letters "UN" on a small plane and used it to take photos of the battlefield on October 22. Additionally, he could have sent journalists to document where the parties were situated. As matters stood, no one could really say for sure where the lines were drawn when the ceasefire went into effect. Heikal's and Ismail's advice to keep fighting did not seem so foolish in hindsight. Regardless of whose version of the story is true, the ceasefire declaration seems to have made it easier for the Israelis to advance south. Shazly writes that IDF forces drove "unopposed past admin bases and rest camps full of wounded men." Israeli accounts paint a much more violent picture. But Bar-Lev told Golda in the confidential meeting that the Israelis advanced fully twelve miles after the ceasefire was declared. Shortly after the sun set on October 23, the Egyptian Third Army was completely surrounded.[36] *

The Soviets were irate. Using unusually strong language, the Kremlin charged that the IDF had "perfidiously attacked . . . Egyptian troops and peaceful populated localities." It then stated ominously, "The Soviet government warns the government of Israel of the gravest consequences that continuation of its aggressive actions against Egypt and Syria will entail."[37]

Messages by the Soviets to the Americans were far more dangerous. Throughout the Cold War, the fear was not a repeat of World War II, where one power brazenly invaded another. The fear was a World War I scenario in which complicated alliances turned a regional conflict into a global one. In gaming this out, military planners had long identified the Middle East as the modern successor to the Balkans.

The distrust between the parties reinforced the sense that perhaps the dark history of 1914 was repeating itself. Of all the secretaries of state he'd dealt with (there were nine of them), the one Gromyko always singled out was Kissinger. "Don't give him a finger," he said. "He will bite off your hand." Breaching protocol,

---

* When asked decades later why he had told the Israelis they could proceed after the ceasefire, Kissinger said, "It never occurred to me that it would make a huge strategic difference. . . . I didn't think they would capture the entire Third Army."

on the morning of October 23 Brezhnev sent a message not to Nixon, but to Kissinger. The message was read over the phone in imperfect English, suggesting it was dashed off in a hurry. It accused Jerusalem of "flagrant deceit" and demanded that the United States use all the tools at its disposal to "bring the Israelis to order." Brezhnev underlined to Kissinger "the urgency" of the matter and insisted upon an immediate answer.[38]

# 23

## DEFCON 3

Our dependence on the Americans is total. But they won't support us to the bitter end.

—Israeli General Yisroel Tal[1]

At 4:30 P.M. on the afternoon of October 23, Henry Kissinger assembled his staff for an emergency meeting. By now, two additional messages had come across from the Soviets via the "hotline," the emergency communications system established after the Cuban Missile Crisis. Apart from the Indo-Pakistani War of 1971, it was the first use of the apparatus since the 1967 Arab-Israeli War. Moscow had more time to draft the text, so the English was better than the first communication. But the messages were more menacing. "Why this treachery was allowed by Israel," the Soviets observed, "is more obvious to you." What was obvious to the Kremlin was that the ceasefire deal had to be implemented. "Too much is at stake," Moscow's message concluded, "not only as concerns the situation in the Middle East, but in our relations as well."[2]

Kissinger had plenty of anger himself, and he used the meeting with his staff to vent some of it in the open. He railed against the Europeans (they "behaved like jackals," doing everything to "egg on the Arabs"). He railed against the Israelis, claiming (inaccurately) that he never prevented a preemptive strike and (also inaccurately) that even if they had struck first, it would not have made any difference. He also said that "we could not make our policy hostage to the Israelis." Somehow, though facing an oil embargo and the prospect of World War III, Kissinger and his staff did not lose their sense of humor. Kissinger noted that UN Security Council Resolution 338 called for the immediate implementation of Resolution 242, but this was impossible since no one except for his aide Joe Sisco knew what it meant. To that, Sisco quipped, "And I'll never tell."[3]

What Kissinger described only a week before as the "best run crisis" of the Nixon administration he now described as a "serious predicament." If the Israelis destroyed the Third Army, the Soviets might intervene, plus Washington could write off any relationship it had with moderate Arab states. Israeli ambassador Simcha Dinitz told Kissinger that the IDF did not "initiate" any of the fighting. Kissinger noted in his memoir that Golda plainly had a creative definition of the word *initiate*. Nevertheless, he stood by Israel, resisting pressure inside the Pentagon to end the airlift and replying to Brezhnev that it was impossible to force Israel to withdraw to the October 22 line since "the positions actually occupied by both sides at that time are unclear."[4]

The war raged on, but, paradoxically, only in areas where the ceasefire was declared. In the north, Assad stubbornly refused to accept it, but the front nevertheless remained quiet. In the south, where the parties agreed to stop shooting, the fighting only intensified. Sadat sent an unprecedented personal message to Nixon— Egypt had broken off diplomatic relations with the United States immediately after the Six-Day War six years earlier—demanding that Washington intervene against Israel "even if that necessitates the use of force." Forty-five minutes later, at 4:00 P.M., the Security Council convened, at Egypt's request, for one of the most tumultuous sessions in its history. The proceedings were little more than a shouting match. But they still resulted in a unanimous, two-paragraph resolution, passed as UN Security Council Resolution 339. The first paragraph called on the parties to return to "the positions they occupied at the moment the ceasefire became effective." The second instructed the secretary-general to immediately dispatch UN observers to enforce the arrangement. [5]

The resolution came not a moment too soon for the Egyptian Third Army. The Israelis took thousands of prisoners on the morning of October 23. Intelligence officers told General Adan that the Egyptian military governor of Suez City was trying to find a way to communicate with him so he could arrange a formal surrender. The fuzzy information from the field convinced Gonen and Adan that it was possible to snatch the city before UN observers arrived. Though the city at the mouth of the canal had become a ghost town during the War of Attrition, it had a population of over a quarter million before 1967 and was a major logistics center. With or without the city, the Third Army was surrounded, so its value was limited. The mission was therefore approved with an unusual order, to take it "only if it isn't Stalingrad." Given the lack of any military intelligence, this was not a plan so much as a gamble.[6]

The gamble failed. Suez was not quite Stalingrad, but it was not open for the taking, either. The hastily assembled force took to the road on the morning of October 24 with little planning and drove right down the city's main thoroughfare. The Egyptians allowed it to traverse the entire east–west length of the city before springing an ambush. Fire poured from every window. The battle had a surreal moment when an old woman emerged from a building, enraged because the fighting had caused her prized rug to fall off the terrace of her apartment to the dusty ground below. Her curses and insults caused both sides to stop fighting. One soldier said it was as if they received an order to "cease fire!" But after she retrieved the rug and went back indoors, everyone went right back to shooting. The Israeli force miraculously extracted itself, but the battle did much to damage the reputation of General Adan. The Israelis inflicted few casualties and suffered eighty killed and over a hundred wounded.[7] *

* * *

News of Egypt's ceasefire reached President Assad as he was sitting with his generals planning a major offensive. The attack was designed to expel the Israelis from the "bulge" they had conquered inside Syria and was cause for alarm in Tel Aviv. The Syrians had by now been heavily resupplied by the Soviets. Against the IDF's 350 tanks, the Syrian coalition that included Iraq and Jordan boasted 751. And because the IAF had focused on Egypt, Syria's SAMs were still largely intact.[8]

Sadat was already planning his postwar narrative that he had to declare a ceasefire because he could not confront the Americans. To sell this, he knew he could not have a situation in which Egypt stood down but Syria soldiered on. For that reason, and perhaps out of concern that a continuation of the war anywhere might endanger his Third Army, he personally called Assad to request that he join the ceasefire. Assad was enraged that a ceasefire was declared right after he lost Mount Hermon, and right before his offensive to take it back. Most of all, the prickly Assad was angered that all of this was done without anyone consulting with him. But he knew that Syria could not face the Israelis alone, so late on October 23 he reluctantly agreed to a ceasefire. However, he left the door open to further hostilities by conditioning acceptance on *his* interpretation of Resolution 338—namely, "complete Israeli withdrawal from all Arab territory occupied since 1967" (without receiving a peace treaty), and "safeguarding the legitimate national rights of the Palestinians."[9]

In one of their communications, Sadat told Assad that the

---

* Adan later defended his decision, arguing that carefully prepared operations are obviously better than quickly improvised thrusts: "But he who never takes quick action does not properly exploit success on the battlefield and reduces its achievements."

Soviets were sending "personnel" to the region. The Arabic word for personnel—*quwat*—is also the word for "forces." Some have speculated that American intelligence intercepted this and interpreted it to mean the Soviets were about to send forces to the canal.* Such an interpretation would have been a mistake; Sadat meant observers. But there was no mistaking the letter that Dobrynin read to Kissinger over the phone at 10:00 P.M. on the evening of October 24. The message from Brezhnev to Nixon called on the two superpowers to send forces to the region to implement the two Security Council resolutions. But then the letter ended ominously: "I will say it straight that if you find it impossible to act jointly with us in this matter, we should be faced with the necessity to consider the question of taking appropriate steps unilaterally. We cannot allow arbitrariness on the part of Israel."[10]

The Soviets drafted the message cautiously, adding the caveats of "considering the question" to take "appropriate steps." But in the world of international diplomacy, where naked threats are often clothed in polite language, the word *unilaterally* drowned out everything else. Kissinger called it "one of the most serious challenges to an American President by a Soviet leader."[11]

What the Soviets did not fully appreciate was that they were turning up the heat on a Washington that was already boiling over. October 1973 was a busy time for the newsmen of the world. In addition to the war, the embargo, and the resignation of Vice President Agnew, it was also the month in which the Watergate scandal reached critical mass. When Kissinger landed in Moscow on October 20, he learned of the Saturday Night Massacre, in which Attorney General Elliot Richardson and his assistant resigned rather than fire Special Prosecutor Archibald Cox. The day before Moscow's warning was sent also happened to be the day

---

* Soviet diplomat Victor Israelyan's memoir suggests that there was even confusion in Moscow, recounting that Sadat requested "observers or troops."

that Nixon agreed to comply with a subpoena to turn the tapes over to Judge John J. Sirica.[12]

A Soviet ultimatum did little to raise Nixon's spirits. Kissinger writes that "Nixon was as agitated and emotional as I had ever heard him." Kissinger himself was not much better. After receiving the message, he called Dobrynin and said, "Don't you pressure us. I want to repeat again, don't pressure us!" Both Nixon and Kissinger were upset about the same thing, the sense that the Soviets were taking liberties because they thought the United States did not have a functioning president.[13]

The trouble was, the United States really *didn't* have a functioning president. Both Kissinger and Haig say in their memoirs that on the night the Soviet ultimatum arrived, Nixon was asleep and not to be awakened, exhausted from the ordeal of Watergate. There were credible rumors that in actuality he was drunk. To mask Nixon's condition, Haig insisted to Kissinger that a planned emergency meeting take place in the White House rather than the State Department.[14]

Admiral Moorer kept minutes of the meeting, which he included in a personal diary that was declassified in 2007. In it, he noted that "the Middle East is the worst place in the world for the U.S. to get engaged in a war with the Soviets" because it would not be a NATO war and because of the logistical challenge. Only one airfield in the Azores was available to the US Air Force between North America and the Middle East. He also noted that "if we do put Marines or troops in the Middle East it will amount to scrapping Détente and cutting off all relations with the Soviet Union." Nerves were frayed. Haig, a former national security adviser and two-star general, predicted that the Soviets would indeed send troops to the region.[15]

Despite this, the group agreed that Washington's response had to be "a tough one." In Moorer's words, the move was designed "to indicate to the Soviets that, while they may have thought they picked a moment of maximum U.S. weakness, we can still make responsible decisions concerning the use of force." Kissinger added that "when you decide to use force you must use plenty of it."[16]

* * *

At that very moment, Israel's government was meeting in Jerusalem. Golda and her ministers were the most mercurial cabinet in the history of the nation, constantly alternating between confidence and panic. The pendulum was then swinging high in the direction of confidence, superpower crisis notwithstanding. The Egyptian Third Army had attempted to break out of the siege. It was easily turned back. Earlier that day, Bar-Lev calmly explained to Golda that the Kremlin would never send forces to the region. The Soviets lacked aircraft carriers; it would take weeks to establish fighter wings or send in tanks. The most that Moscow could do was fly in four thousand to five thousand men per day, which meant it would take a minimum of five days for any sizable force to arrive. By then the ceasefire would have unraveled and the Third Army would be destroyed.[17]

The government never seriously considered pulling back to the October 22 line. Releasing the chokehold on the Third Army, Elazar said, "would bring us to the verge of catastrophe . . . we would be in a trap." Moshe Dayan spoke for many when he complained of the Americans, "They demand that we start wars when it is good for the Arabs, declare ceasefires when it is good for the Arabs, and withdraw when it is good for the Arabs. How are we going to end the conflict this way?"[18]

As the meeting drew to a close, the ministers took a break and Golda received a report from Ambassador Dinitz. She reconvened and said, "Contrary to all the rotten things we've been saying about the Americans, it looks like they're holding up quite well. Their answer to the Soviets is smart and strong. In fact, it couldn't be stronger."[19]

The Nixon administration announced that it was moving two aircraft carriers into the area to join a third that was already there; it

placed European forces and the 82nd Airborne on alert; it recalled
seventy-five B-52s from Guam. Lastly, Washington took a step guar-
anteed to create banner headlines around the globe: the US military
was placed on a Defcon 3 alert, a first step toward mobilizing for
war. This was not quite as dramatic as it seemed. The Sixth Fleet,
stationed in the Mediterranean, was already at that level of readiness. As for the remainder of the military, the Defcon 3 designation
was, in the words of an NSC staffer, "considerably short of a decision
to go on a war footing."[20] But it caught everyone's attention.

The Soviets were stunned. They indeed thought that Watergate
had given them room to flex their muscles. Only a few days before,
senior Soviet diplomat Victor Israelyan had assessed that Nixon
had no interest in a showdown. "He already has several irons in the
fire, and they are all red hot." Now Israelyan was left to lament "how
wrong was our forecast of the American reaction!"[21]

The situation was still dangerous. People do not always act
rationally when they are angry, and the Soviets were very angry.
Dobrynin wrote, "I was incensed rather than alarmed." Had it not
been the Israelis who violated the ceasefire by surrounding the
Third Army? Wasn't this a breach by Washington of the October 21
deal in Moscow?[22]

There was even greater cause for alarm, though it would not
become widely known for another forty-five years. As dysfunc-
tional as the American government was, the Kremlin was even
worse. Documents released in 2018 revealed that Brezhnev had
become addicted to sleeping pills, which when combined with
alcohol impaired his ability to think rationally. The irate Brezhnev
tossed out various ideas, such as sending a naval task force off Tel
Aviv and giving Sadat authorization to fire Scud missiles into Israeli cities. In the words of Sergey Radchenko, the American professor who unearthed and translated the documents, "Someone in
the Soviet leadership realized that the general secretary was going
off the rails." It was KGB head Yuri Andropov who worked quietly
to calm the situation and keep the USSR from blundering into a

third world war. The Defcon 3 alert also seems to have shocked Brezhnev back into a sober state of mind.[23]

The Soviet response that effectively ended the crisis came the following day, October 25, at 2:40 in the afternoon. Dobrynin read a letter to Kissinger from Brezhnev that retreated from the unilateral action threat, proposing nothing more than a joint observer group to implement the Security Council resolutions.[24]

This was cause for relief, if not celebration, in Washington, and Nixon chose to make the most of it. On October 26, the day the Defcon alert was rescinded, he held a press conference in which he said, "Many thought the President was shell shocked and couldn't act. Well, the president acted."

\* \* \*

At almost the same moment that Nixon faced reporters, Kissinger chaired a meeting with the leaders of Exxon, Mobil, and seven other large oil companies. Ken Jamieson, the chairman of Exxon, pointed out that World War II rationing had reduced domestic demand by only 6 percent. The embargo threatened to reduce supply by 18 percent. An economic catastrophe loomed on the horizon. Jamieson further noted that if something did not happen soon, King Feisal would be forced to act, and he might nationalize Saudi Aramco. When one of Kissinger's aides noted the success of American diplomacy getting Moscow to back down and asked, almost rhetorically, "Don't you think that he [Feisal] is more afraid of the Soviets than of the Israelis?" Jamieson replied that Feisal was afraid of neither. What really scared him were radical Arabs in his own kingdom.[25] \*

Golda had held firm against the Soviets. But she knew she would have a far more difficult time with the Americans. The Israelis expressed an unconditional commitment to live up to both Security Council resolutions and return to the October 22 ceasefire

---

\* Feisal was assassinated by his nephew in 1975.

line, but alas, no one knew where that line was. Kissinger's heart was plainly in Israel's corner. He knew exactly where the October 22 line ran. On November 2, Israeli general Aharon Yariv surprisingly acknowledged to him that Israel had conquered only two of the three roads supplying the Third Army when Security Council Resolution 338 went into effect. In an October 23 conversation with Dinitz, Kissinger said it was time to "put that Jewish mind to work so that when the pressure starts you can withdraw a few hundred yards," but still leave the Third Army encircled.[26]

Nevertheless, Kissinger had his limits. "You will not be permitted to capture [the Third] Army," he told Dinitz on October 26. Dinitz protested that never in the history of war had an invading army been released by the nation invaded. Kissinger shot back that it likewise never happened that a small nation was permitted to spark a world war by winning.[27]

In a conversation on October 29 with Egypt's new foreign minister Ismail Fahmi, Kissinger said, "We have told them [the Israelis] we will not tolerate the destruction of the Third Army." Fahmi pushed Kissinger to force the Israelis back to the October 22 line, but Kissinger sidestepped the question, saying it would be better to focus on broader peace talks rather than where the ceasefire line ran. Fahmi then tipped his hand as to how desperate the Third Army's plight was, agreeing not to send in any military equipment and asking only that the Israelis be compelled to allow food and water. The meeting concluded with him repeating the importance of getting a convoy through. This might have been another moment for Kissinger to demand that the embargo be lifted. The most he could bring himself to say was, "There must not be any threats from other countries, your friends, while we are trying to do something."[28]

* * *

The news that they would have to allow food and water to reach the Third Army brought the IDF rank and file to what one Israeli general called a "borderline mutiny."* That the enemy was being let off the hook was bad enough. What really set off ordinary soldiers was the fact that their leaders agreed to this without first securing the return of their POWs. The arrangement was just as unpopular among senior officers. Ariel Sharon advocated inducing the Egyptians to fire first and then using it as a pretext to finish them off. The idea was rejected. But the Israelis sent Egyptian POWs back to the Third Army carrying the message, backed up by radio broadcasts, that any soldier who wanted to could drop his weapon and go home. None took up the offer.[29]

On November 1, Golda traveled to Washington to meet Kissinger in what would be one of the most acrimonious meetings ever between an Israeli prime minister and an American secretary of state. Kissinger resented an October 27 letter he'd received from Golda, which stated, among other things, that "there is only one thing that nobody can prevent us from doing and that is to proclaim the truth of the situation: that Israel is being punished not for its deeds, but because of its size and because it is on its own." He told her, in unusually blunt language, that "you rely too much on Jewish Senators." She shot back, "Who should we rely on?"[30]

Golda tried to sell Kissinger on the idea of a mutual withdrawal: Israel would pull back from the west bank of the canal and Egypt from the east. Kissinger said that Cairo would never accept it and that she might as well advocate the overthrow of Sadat. Kissinger said the Egyptians were still pushing hard for a return to the October 22 line, and that only he, Kissinger, had prevented Nixon from supporting them. He added, "It won't take much to get the U.S. Government to support a return to the '67 borders [with Israel not receiving a peace treaty]." To Golda's protests he said, "There is no sense in debating the issue of justice here. You're only three million. It is not the first time in the history of the Jews that unjust things have happened."[31]

---

* The first truck into the Third Army contained food, water, and something perhaps more important: cigarettes.

The talks dragged on for days with Kissinger shuttling between the State Department, where he met with Fahmi, and Blair
House, where he met with Golda. The Egyptians were adamant
that Israel had to pull back to the October 22 ceasefire line. "She
cannot bargain on the return to the October 22 positions," Fahmi
insisted. "The Security Council has decided the matter." Golda
stiffened her back and refused. Israeli soldiers would stay put.
They would allow supply of the Egyptian army, but only if POWs
were exchanged. Israel would negotiate only a full separation
agreement, and only while the Third Army was surrounded.[32]

Late on November 3, Kissinger finally lost patience with her.
"You will have a helluva time," he said, "explaining to the American people how we can have an oil shortage over the issue of
your right to hold territory you took after the ceasefire." He also
pointed out how important it was to get a deal done now, so they
could all get through the winter. "Oil pressure in April is different
from oil pressure in November," he said.[33]

Golda wouldn't budge. If the IDF pulled back and the Third
Army was allowed resupply, the fighting would break out again.
The only hope of ending the war was keeping all forces in place.
Then she repeated her position yet again: the Third Army could
continue to receive food and water, but only if POWs were exchanged. They went back and forth for over two hours. In frustra-
tion, Kissinger told Golda that if fighting broke out again, Israel
could not count on American resupply. He also offered the opinion that there was "next to no chance" that the Egyptians would
accept her proposal.[34] Golda demanded that he march over to
the State Department and present it to Fahmi anyway. Kissinger
reluctantly obliged her.

Several hours later, Kissinger notified Golda and her team that
there had been a breakthrough. The Egyptians gave in.

Kissinger flew to Cairo on November 7 for a first-ever meeting
with Sadat to finalize the arrangement. Discussions would commence to settle the issue of returning to the October 22 ceasefire

line, but only "in the framework of agreement on the disengagement and separation of forces." In the meantime, food, water, and medicine would continue to reach the Third Army, and POWs would be exchanged. Cairo also announced that it was renewing diplomatic ties with the United States.[35]

Golda had pulled off the impossible. She defied the United Nations. Then, a lioness in orthopedic shoes, she stared down the Soviets, steamrolled the Egyptians, and outlasted the Americans. On the battlefield of international diplomacy, outnumbered by men in fine tailored suits, she fought each and every one to the point of exhaustion. For in the end, what dictated the outcome in Washington was the same thing that dictated the outcome on all the smoking battlefields of the Yom Kippur War.

Golda Meir held out one minute longer.

# 24

## A FUNERAL IN JERUSALEM

Military justice is to justice what military music is to music.

—Georges Clemenceau[1]

On December 1, 1973, David Ben-Gurion died in hospital of a stroke at the age of eighty-seven. Ben-Gurion's body lay in state at the Knesset before being taken by helicopter to the remote desert kibbutz of Sde Boker for burial next to his wife, Paula. At the funeral, two black crows flew overhead and were seen swooping down on Ben-Gurion's tombstone. It was taken as a bad omen.[2]

Israeli reality has a way of exceeding expectations, whether for good or for bad. When the nation's losses were tallied up the month before, they came in remarkably low, at least by the blood-soaked standards of the twentieth century. In the eighteen days of October now known as the Yom Kippur War, the State of Israel suffered 2,222 killed and 7,251 wounded.* Commentators invariably hastened to add that, taken as a percentage of the population, it was the equivalent of the United States losing over 200,000

---

* Egypt and Syria never released casualty figures. The Agranat Commission estimated that Egypt sustained 11,000 dead and 25,000 wounded. Assad told both Kissinger and his biographer that Syria suffered 6,000 dead. It is estimated that an additional 870 Palestinians died fighting in the Syrian army.

men. But that was a reflection on how tiny Israel was, not how many casualties it took. Modern warfare is just as lethal for small countries as it is for large ones. And 2,222 was fewer dead than the United States suffered at Pearl Harbor in the opening hours of American involvement in World War II.[3]

In economic terms, the war was estimated to have cost the Jewish state approximately $7 billion, or about one year of gross domestic product. But the Israeli taxpayer paid for only about half of that. The United States offered a generous $2.2 billion package—about half the emergency aid Washington gave around the world that year—and Jewish donors abroad covered another $1.3 billion to $1.4 billion. The war broke out almost thirty years to the day after the Nazis levied a tribute from the Jewish community of Rome, forcing it to pay fifty kilos of gold. In a nice touch, the Jews of Rome raised a hundred kilos of gold for Israel (worth about $10 million). Egyptian editor Muhammad Heikal complained that the Jewish donors gave Israel in one year what all the Arab governments of world had not given Egypt in five.[4]

Israeli equipment losses were quickly restored as well. The IAF lost ninety-eight fighter jets (plus two small planes and two helicopters). Of the fighter jets, thirty-two were F-4 Phantoms. By November, Washington had already sent thirty-six to replace them. Israel lost eight hundred tanks. But Elazar told the government that half could be repaired, and the United States supplied three hundred more. And then there was the haul of captured equipment. Israel went to war with 147 Soviet tanks captured in 1967 that had been outfitted with Israeli cannons. This time Israel captured between three and four hundred Soviet tanks, a quarter in perfect working order with ammunition inside. A new "Soviet Brigade" was already in the works.[5]

To be sure, it had been a close shave. But it ended in less than three weeks with the Egyptian Third Army surrounded and Damascus practically within artillery range. Countless nations have fought countless wars over the millennia; any one of them would have deemed the Yom Kippur War a victory for the ages. Yet somehow, the Israeli public viewed it as if through a funhouse mirror. Victory assumed the shape of defeat.

The '67 war raised eyebrows, but it also raised expectations. The failure to achieve another easy victory, the loss of the sense of invincibility, these things were bound to take a toll. But that offers only a partial explanation. "We Jews are perfectionists," a former member of Knesset said with a smile.[6] His words harked back to an ancient tradition. Long before Socrates and the method of critical thinking he pioneered, the children of Israel were excoriated by prophets who spewed fire and brimstone. In the Bible, Jewish transgression is a barrel without a bottom. Of course, there is a positive side to all the self-criticism. When you accept criticism, you also improve.

The Israelis made a vice of a virtue. On November 18, 1973, in response to a public outcry, the government appointed a commission of inquiry to be headed by Shimon Agranat, president of the Israeli Supreme Court.[7] It seemed a deft political move. Golda could sense that Israel was on a collision course with itself. Appointing the Commission placated critics and kicked the can until after December elections.

But in doing this, Golda forgot her Bible. The Jews were not just the nation of angry prophets like Isaiah and Jeremiah. They were also the people that regularly sacrificed a scapegoat.[8]

* * *

The funhouse mirror extended into Egypt as well, where the government (and the media it controlled) did everything to ensure that defeat assumed the shape of victory. Years later, Sadat and his wife each wrote in their memoirs that it was the Israeli army that was surrounded, not the Egyptian. Field Marshal Gamasy wrote the same thing in his memoir. As late as November 1973, Gamasy seems to have truly believed that Egypt had won the war. Then Henry Kissinger arrived in Cairo.[9]

Months of grueling negotiations ensued. All through this time, the Egyptian Third Army was hanging by a thread, kept alive with food, water, and other non-military supplies that the Israelis allowed through. The Egyptians were horrified to see the Israelis lay an enormous additional bridge over the canal and fortify their positions west of it, seemingly setting the stage to remain there permanently. The Egyptians responded by skirmishing, killing fifteen Israeli soldiers in the months after the ceasefire. But when things got out of hand, the Israelis prevented supplies from reaching the Third Army, and the Egyptians stood down. Sadat saw his dream of reclaiming Sinai slip away and took ill. In November he was urinating blood.[10]

In mid-January, Sadat gave in on all three sticking points: the Israelis could remain in Sinai west of the passes, the Egyptians would be permitted only a token force east of the canal and, most important, Egyptian SAMs had to be withdrawn west, beyond the range of any future Sinai battlefield. Were Egypt to attack Israel again, its forces would be naked to attack from the air and stand little chance against the Israeli air force. In short, Egypt received the canal. But it no longer possessed the option of going to war.

In sum and substance, this was identical to Moshe Dayan's interim agreement proposal that Cairo had rejected in 1972. Muhammad Heikal wrote, "From a military viewpoint, the disengagement agreement left Egypt in a worse position than it had been before October 6, in that resumption of the war of attrition was impossible." After hearing the terms, General Gamasy rose from his chair, walked over to a window, and attempted to hide his tears. Golda and her ministers did not sign on easily, either. But when they did, Kissinger joked that he had performed a miracle. He had gotten the Israelis to agree to their own proposal.[11]

The Israelis wisely permitted the SAM and troop restrictions to be codified outside the disengagement agreement in a separate letter signed by all the parties.[12] It allowed Sadat to conceal that aspect of the deal from his public and at least realize one of his war goals. Egypt had reclaimed its national honor.

To outsiders, it really seemed as if Egypt had won the war. After all, isn't it the winning party that expands its territory? Only a few students of the region knew that Egypt had merely received what Dayan had offered it years before. And only a few understood that Jerusalem had achieved *its* primary war goal: Egypt's days of waging war against Israel were over. The troop reductions and the removal of the SAMs left Cairo with but two choices: make peace with losing more than 90 percent of the Sinai Peninsula—or make peace with Israel.

Upon hearing that Egypt agreed to a separate deal, Syria's President Assad was outraged. "Do you understand the meaning of what you are doing?" he shouted into the phone at Sadat. Assad pleaded with Feisal to maintain the oil embargo. In a November 21, 1973, press conference, Kissinger hinted that the United States might resort to force to break it. Saudi Arabia threatened to blow up the oil fields if it did. But in the end cooler heads prevailed. The oil states needed the money and were eager to cash in on the sudden surge in pricing. On March 18, 1974, the embargo was lifted.[13]

Assad was left with little leverage. He handed over a list with the names of Israeli POWs in Syrian captivity. In return, Kissinger got the shah of Iran to mass troops on the border with Iraq, compelling Saddam Hussein to return his forces from Syria. A major threat to the Assad regime was thus removed. With almost no remaining leverage, Assad launched a ferocious war of attrition against Israel. In April 1974 alone, Syria fired forty-one thousand shells into the Israeli "bulge," or almost one per minute twenty-four hours a day. In all, 442 Israelis died in the 1974 war of attrition, while Syrian losses are unknown. But in the end, Assad was compelled to accept a deal similar to Egypt's. Syria received a tiny sliver of land that included the empty border town of Kuneitra in return for withdrawing SAMs far enough away to render any future military adventure impossible. The Israelis achieved their primary military goal. The Golan border remained the quietest in the Middle East for decades. As for Syria, it received barely enough ground to bury its dead.[14]

* * *

On Sunday, February 3, 1974, a newspaper reporter emerged from the prime minister's office and saw a soldier standing on a hill opposite the gate holding a handwritten sign that read DAYAN RESIGN!. The soldier was Captain Moti Ashkenazi, commander of the Budapest *maoz*, the only *maoz* to hold out against the Egyptian onslaught.[15]

The reporter ran a story about a reserve captain holding a handwritten sign, and the next day a wounded soldier joined Ashkenazi straight from his hospital bed. Word of mouth attracted more reservists to come, some immediately upon returning from the front. When a television crew came for the first time on February 6, Ashkenazi fulfilled a promise to jittery policemen and asked that soldiers who arrived directly from active duty should please not come with their guns. Then he dipped into his meager savings and took out a tiny, two-inch ad in a newspaper, advertising a protest on February 17. By now he knew that such protests required a permit, so he went down to the government office to fill out the forms. One of the questions was how many people he estimated would come. He thought for a minute and, wanting to play it safe, he projected a thousand. With permit in hand, he went back to the gate and saw something that took his breath away. There were a thousand people there already.[16]

* * *

The Agranat Commission was empaneled by the government on November 18, 1973. The first order of business for Justice Agranat was to appoint the other members of the Commission. He first selected Moshe Landau, a respected Supreme Court justice who had achieved fame by presiding over the trial of Adolf Eichmann. Agranat also made a safe choice in State Comptroller Yitzchak Nebentzal, a relatively minor figure chosen because of his sterling reputation for integrity.[17] That left two final choices, both of which were reserved for men with a military background.

Decades later, just before she died, Golda's stenographer said that she witnessed Dayan telling Golda that he would support a commission of inquiry only if former Chief of Staff Chaim Laskov was included on the panel. Laskov was appointed, as was former Chief of Staff Yigael Yadin, who was also known to be close to Dayan. Then there was the question of what the Commission was empowered to investigate. The government gave it authority to explore only two things: the intelligence failure leading up to the surprise attack, and the army's defense in the early days of the war.[18] It was a curious mandate, not unlike judging the performance of the US Navy in World War II on the basis of the Pearl Harbor attack alone.

The Commission sat for over a year. It heard testimony from ninety witnesses and had investigators gather testimony from another 188. In all, its findings ran to over two thousand pages, divided up among two interim reports issued in 1974 and a final one released in 1975.[19]

From the start there was a glaring irregularity. Justice Agranat told each and every army officer, "I advise you not to get a lawyer. If you do, it will make our job more difficult." Elazar asked the Commission members if he needed a lawyer, and they told him, "You have five defense lawyers here on the panel." This gross breach of judicial ethics caused most of the generals to naively appear without the aid of counsel. The one figure that understood where everything was headed was Moshe Dayan. He ignored the Commission's request and assembled a crack legal team that was led by a future Israeli Supreme Court justice.[20]

There were rumors of other irregularities. It was said that transcripts of Commission proceedings were secretly sent by hand to Dayan, allowing him to tailor his testimony.[21] Others said they saw documents being shredded. Witnesses colluded, particularly about not disclosing King Hussein's September 1973 warning to Golda. And the Commission refused to hear testimony from General Bar-Lev. Bar-Lev was one of the central architects of Israel's defense plan before the war. But he was known to be close to Elazar.[22]

The first interim report of the Agranat Commission was released on April 2, 1974. It ran to only thirty-three pages, or barely 1 percent of the final report's length. But the first interim report is the one that people remember. The other two reports were not declassified until decades later. And strangely, though the bulk of the investigation had not yet occurred, the first interim report is the one that contains the Commission's conclusions.

The core findings were not controversial, and for those in the know, even a little obvious. The Commission found that the intelligence failure was caused by three things: (1) a "stubborn" adherence to "the Concept," described by the Commission as the assumption that Egypt would not go to war until it acquired long-range fighter jets; (2) Zeira promising the army that he could give adequate warning of the enemy's intentions, even though he could not; and (3) a failure by AMAN to read unmistakable signs of war. In the classified second interim report, the Commission acknowledged that every intelligence agency had to rely on "concepts" or it could not function. Thus, the "lesson" to follow these assumptions only as a "starting point," but not "stubbornly," smacks of hindsight. However, the Commission's other lesson has merit. AMAN's chief failure—apart from hubris—was its reliance on "golden intelligence" from top sources, such as Marwan, the Egyptian officer, or the Extraordinary Measures. The Commission cited a study of the Pearl Harbor attack and concluded that assessments are more accurate when they rely upon numerous indications gathered from the field, rather than on a single source, no matter how good that source might be.[23]

It was the findings related to personal responsibility that caused an earthquake.

The Commission absolved Golda. It found that much of the key intelligence was kept from her, and that she did all the things expected of a prime minister in the days leading up to the war. Though she bore overall responsibility as prime minister, this was hardly grounds to call for her resignation, particularly when the Israeli public gave her a resounding vote of confidence at the polls just two months after the war ended.[24] *

Moshe Dayan got off as well. The Commission found that although he held overall responsibility for military matters, he did not have a private intelligence agency to contradict what AMAN was telling him. The Commission further concluded that it was reasonable for him to rely on AMAN given its record of success, and that he had no obligation to go into the field to form his own judgment.

Predictably, the Commission found that General Zeira had failed in carrying out his duties. Strangely, the report makes only a passing reference to the Extraordinary Measures—AMAN's listening devices thought to be the ultimate "insurance policy"— and the fact that Zeira lied to his superiors, saying he deployed them when he didn't.† Colonel Yakov Khasdai, one of the lead investigators for the Commission, was still alive in 2022 to be interviewed for this account. He said that many documents related to the Extraordinary Measures did not reach the Commission, so they had only a basic understanding of them. Moreover, they did not believe that the surprise would have been prevented even if they had been deployed or if Zeira had told the truth.[25] Instead, the report criticized him for canceling out contrary views, as well

---

* In elections held on December 31, 1973, Golda's Labor Alignment Party received fifty-one seats in the Knesset. It was the second highest total in Israeli history.

† The Israelis have released very little information regarding the Extraordinary Measures. But published reports indicate that they delivered little useful intelligence during the war. It is possible that the Egyptians discovered the Extraordinary Measures prior to October and used them to feed the Israelis false information.

as for his "overconfidence and his appointing himself the last word on all intelligence assessments." The Commission recommended that Zeira and three of his assistants be removed from their positions in AMAN. It was a swift end for the man who was widely viewed as the leading candidate to replace Elazar as the next chief of staff. [26]

Gonen was a casualty as well, but the finding cost him only a minor post. Dayan sacked him the day after the war ended and gave him a command that had previously been held by a colonel. The interim report was merely the last nail in the coffin.[27]

Had the Agranat Commission stopped there, its report might not have been considered controversial. Its factual findings were spot-on accurate and survived the test of time. Even after Gonen's secret tape recordings came to light thirty years later, none of the new material contradicted anything in the report.[28] As for the conclusions of personal responsibility, at least those described above, all were sensible and grounded in fact.

But the Agranat Commission arrived at one additional conclusion. It related to Chief of Staff David Elazar.

* * *

Late on the night of April 2, Elazar called for a special meeting of the General Staff. Those invited were asked to listen to the 10:00 P.M. news report on the radio prior to coming. In the words of one general, what they heard struck "like lightning on a sunny day." The Agranat Commission had concluded that General David Elazar had failed to carry out his duties as chief of staff of the army and recommended that he be replaced.

When the meeting of the General Staff was convened a half hour later, Elazar entered and read a letter he had drafted defending his actions. Upon finishing, he took no questions and exited. His assistant then appeared and informed everyone that the meeting was over. No one moved. No one spoke. They were stunned. Yes, Elazar had made mistakes; all generals do. But he made all the key decisions that won the war. He took a calculated risk that Jordan would not attack and sent his only spare division north. He deterred Jordan from entering the war by bombing Damascus and carried the fight into Syria. In the south, he did not withdraw to the passes as Dayan recommended; he ordered the crossing of the canal in a high-stakes gamble that delivered victory. It was a remarkable performance, one that the generals sitting around the table had witnessed in that very room. "How did the Commission not see this?" one asked.[29]

The Agranat Commission's findings echoed what it said about Dayan, only in reverse: Elazar should *not* have relied on AMAN's assessments despite its track record of success; Elazar *should* have gone out into the field to assess the situation for himself. The Commission ignored the fact that Zeira kept vital intelligence from Elazar and lied to him about the deployment of the Extraordinary Measures.[30]

Golda was horrified. After reading the report she went to see an old friend, Ephraim Katzir, who held the ceremonial position of president. She told him that she recognized the writing style and it belonged to Laskov and Yadin, not Agranat. She added that Dayan's fingerprints were all over the report.[31]

Plainly, the Commission had judged Dayan and Elazar by different standards. As a member of the General Staff pointed out, the two men literally sat next to each other when Zeira and AMAN gave their assessments. Yet the Agranat Commission found that Elazar had an obligation to go out into the field, whereas Dayan did not. The finding was all the more bizarre because under Israeli law, the person with ultimate authority to call up reservists was the defense minister, not the chief of staff. To top everything off, on the morning of October 6, it was Elazar that wanted the larger mobilization, not Dayan. Laskov told his biographer that the Commission's only goal in calling for Elazar's resignation was to send a strong message that the IDF's unpreparedness was unacceptable. Viewed in isolation, this is a harsh but arguably defensible conclusion. But viewed in the context of how Dayan was treated, it is a verdict that can only shock the conscience.[32] *

If Dayan engineered the whole thing, then it was the mistake of a lifetime. Had Elazar gotten off, there is a reasonable chance that Golda and Dayan would have escaped as well. When Elazar went down, the Israeli public did not conclude that the Agranat Commission was too harsh with him. Rather, it viewed this as evidence that it was not harsh enough on Golda and Dayan.

By now, Moti Ashkenazi's vigil at the gate had swelled to twenty-five thousand protesters. In May 1967, a public outcry had swept Dayan into office as defense minister; now another one compelled his resignation. At the government meeting held on April 9, 1974, with Dayan present, the ministers openly debated whether they should wait to appoint Elazar's replacement, seeing as there might soon be a new defense minister who would want to appoint his own man. On June 3, Moshe Dayan resigned.[33]

Golda herself remained popular among the ministers, but her health faltered. Her cancer had returned before the war in June 1973; she suffered a painful bout of shingles in January 1974. Moreover, something seems to have broken inside her during the war. Despite her charisma and command of the English language, she made practically no public appearances, even those typically done by wartime politicians, such as visiting the wounded in the hospital. She visited the wounded; she just did it without the press being present. She also played no role in an area where she had shined in the past: raising money from Jewish donors abroad. She barely appeared in public during the December election campaign, either. West German chancellor Willy Brandt saw her at an

---

* On some level, the Commission members seem to have understood the injustice that was perpetrated. Justice Agranat's biographer writes that he became defensive when the subject came up. Justice Moshe Landau was unfailingly polite to Adolf Eichmann during the latter's trial. But he started screaming at me when I reached him on the phone in the early 2000s and asked if I could pose questions about the Agranat Commission.

international conference after the war and said she looked to be suffering from clinical depression.[34]

On April 10, 1974, Golda Meir resigned as prime minister. By the time all the dust settled, a complete changing of the guard took place. For the first time in Israeli history, the prime minister, defense minister, foreign minister, and finance minister were all replaced at once.[35] Egyptian media reported this with glee.

Golda's final years were difficult. Her old friend President Katzir said that she came to his house once, lit a cigarette with a trembling hand, and said, "I don't want to live." She confided that she suffered a recurring nightmare. In it, every corner of her home had a telephone that rang and rang. She was afraid to lift a single receiver . . . and then she would wake up covered in sweat, to a quiet, dark house.[36]

Golda Meir died on December 8, 1978, at the age of eighty. Resisting pressure from the Arab world, Moscow, and, most of all, Washington is part of the job description for any Israeli prime minister. Upon leaving office, Moshe Dayan—a hard man not given to handing out praise—said emotionally that no Israeli prime minister had resisted that pressure with greater fortitude than Golda Meir.[37] Those words are as true today as they were when he uttered them in 1974. It remains the finest flower on her grave.

* * *

Shmuel Gonen never had any doubt as to who engineered his downfall. By the fall of 1973, his hatred for Dayan burned with the heat of a thousand suns. A rumor made the rounds that he planned to kill Dayan and then commit suicide.[38] Before the war, Gonen struck terror in all around him. After the war, people felt free to wise off at him. Gonen left the country hoping to strike it rich in Africa. Israelis who saw the 1979 movie *Apocalypse Now* thought that the mad Colonel Kurtz character was modeled after him.

In reality, he became a soldier of misfortune, living in the jungle, penniless and alone. An Israeli reporter caught up with him in 1987 and described him as having "an enormous belly pressing against his shirt, not a belly made of beer, but of depression and hopelessness." The reporter landed a scoop when Gonen confirmed that he really did seriously consider killing Dayan.[39]

Paradoxically, the one person who tried to make it right was Gonen's old nemesis, Ariel Sharon. Sharon was a beast of a man to command but later showed moments of humanity. As a senior official in Likud, Sharon offered to make Gonen a candidate for mayor of Beersheva, one of Israel's largest cities.[40] Gonen would have none of it.

Shmuel "Gorodish" Gonen died of a heart attack on September 30, 1991, at the age of sixty-one. One of Israel's leading columnists, Amnon Abramovitch, wrote that "he was a victim of nothing but himself . . . he wanted to remove the stain of the Agranat Commission, but if he hadn't been such an idiot, he would've known how to do it without travelling all the way to Africa." Yitzchak Rabin remembered Gonen differently. Yes, he had made his share of mistakes in the early days of the Yom Kippur War. But there were other days, too. Three wars, in fact, where he had been an authentic hero. "Why are we like this," Rabin asked, "bouncing from one extreme to the other, raising people to the stars then pounding them into the dust? And how do we cure ourselves of this disease?"[41]

* * *

The experience of the Israeli air force demonstrated the foolishness of the approach adopted by the Agranat Commission. If the early mistakes of the war had become known, IAF commander Benny Peled would have been compelled to resign, too. But the senior officers of the air force banded together, kept quiet, and let the wave pass over them. The air force went practically unmentioned in the three Agranat Commission reports. It allowed Peled to go back to what he did best—planning, engineering, technology—and devise a plan to overcome the SAMs. The plan remains classified, though

Soviet sources suggest that a new weapon developed in Israel—
pilotless drones—took over the role of the "femme fatale" planes.
In the 1982 First Lebanon War, the IAF wiped out all the Soviet
SAMs without losing an aircraft. Peled was remembered fondly
upon his death in 2002.[42]

Chaim Bar-Lev similarly emerged unscathed in all three of
the Agranat Commission's reports. But just as Moti Ashkenazi's
protest movement seemed to wane, Asa Kadmoni—the hero of
Serapheum—arrived, bringing all his energy with him. Where
Ashkenazi focused on Dayan, Kadmoni directed all his fury at
Bar-Lev.[43] In the twentieth century, the surest way for a military
man to lose his reputation was to have his good name attached
to the word *line*, whether in the case of André Maginot or, as it
turned out, Chaim Bar-Lev.

The Bar-Lev Line became the tomb of the well-known soldier, blamed for much of what went wrong in the early days of
the war. Bar-Lev pointed out that the *maozim* that made up the
line were only a small part of a broader plan that involved tanks
and artillery, and it was unfair to criticize that plan, because it
was not followed. Bar-Lev analogized it to an elaborate lock built
for a bank vault that ultimately fails because someone forgets to
close the door. Lost in the controversy was the fact that his plan
worked in the northern Golan Heights, where it *was* followed.
Moreover, not a single Israeli soldier died inside a *maoz* during
the intense shelling of the war of attrition.[44] Bar-Lev was attacked
in 1974 even as Israeli soldiers were dying by the hundreds from
Syrian shelling in the bulge because there were no *maozim* there
to protect them. No one saw the irony in any of this.

Chaim Bar-Lev died of amyotrophic lateral sclerosis on May 7,
1994, at the age of sixty-nine (in Israel, Lou Gehrig's disease
is known as "Chaim Bar-Lev's disease"). The first person in the
line of mourners to shake the hand of Bar-Lev's widow was his
old nemesis, Ariel Sharon, who again showed the decent side of
his complicated personality. The gesture was well received by

the Bar-Lev family. His son even interpreted it as an "apology of sorts."[45]

The gesture was all the more impressive because if Bar-Lev had had his way in 1969, Sharon's military career would have ended then, and it is unlikely that anyone would have heard from him again. The Yom Kippur War made Ariel Sharon. He had an impressive record before 1973, but so did dozens of other generals. Now he emerged a first among equals, the hero of the crossing. One of Israel's most distinguished historians, Uri Millstein, called Sharon "the undisputed hero of the Yom Kippur War." His fame grew so wide that he was credited by the Egyptians for things he did not do.[46]

In one of the secret portions of its report, the Agranat Commission criticized an unnamed general for having "court journalists" that traveled with him. That is as close as the Commission came to criticizing Sharon. In January 1974, he made ill-advised comments to a reporter to the effect that there are times when an officer should not follow orders. While appearing before the Commission, he knew better. He claimed to have been misquoted and said, "I believe that you must strictly follow all orders."[47]

It did not take long before an emboldened Sharon demonstrated his true feelings about ignoring orders. His political career—which was an even wilder roller-coaster ride than his military one—began by leading Israel into a failed war in Lebanon in 1982. Menachem Begin, the prime minister under whom Sharon ostensibly served, said sheepishly, "I am kept informed either before or after action has been taken."[48] But that roller coaster also included a successful five-year term as prime minister from 2001 to 2006, during which Sharon defeated the Palestinian al-Aqsa intifada and disengaged from Gaza.

In the end, after Sharon was disabled by a stroke in 2006, most of his countrymen looked back on his tumultuous tenure and thought the State of Israel had come out ahead in the bargain. The warmest statements came from the men that served under him. Looking back on the war forty years later, Amnon Reshef said, "With all the mistakes and irregularities that Sharon committed over the course of the Yom Kippur War, there is no doubt that without his daring, elite leadership, the crossing of the Canal would never have succeeded. The Nation of Israel owes him an enormous debt."

* * *

"Chief of Staff David Elazar was one of the truly noble men I have met," Henry Kissinger wrote in his memoir. "[He] knew he would become—unjustly—the sacrificial victim for Israel's frustrations in the October war and yet bore his fate in silence and dignity." Elazar told his friend Yitzchak Rabin that he would have put up a legal defense if he had had an inkling of what was going to happen. More than a few top lawyers volunteered to represent him for free. But Elazar was busy rebuilding the army and had no time for the Agranat Commission, which he was certain would exonerate him anyway. In 1979, the Knesset passed a law requiring all future commissions of inquiry to warn those under investigation if their reputations are in jeopardy.[49]

The reform came too late for David Elazar. His wife said that after he resigned, he would drive around alone at night, stewing in his own rage. Outwardly, he carried on with quiet dignity. But it happened a few times in intimate circles that he broke down and cried. In 1976, he decided to tell his story. He met once with an author named Hanoch Bartov. But then he died suddenly of a heart attack at the age of fifty.[50] Elazar was given a hero's funeral in Jerusalem.

With the help of Elazar's assistant, Bartov went ahead with the project and produced perhaps the greatest biography yet written in the Hebrew language. In a nation of three million, it sold fifty thousand copies in the first month.[51] It would be the first of many books that would pass a far different verdict from the one rendered by the Agranat Commission.

His widow said in an interview forty years later that she believed his heart attack was related to the resignation. But she was
quick to add that one can never really know.[52] What can be said
with certainty is that David Elazar had a glittering military record
across a lifetime of sacrifice and service to his nation. That nation
repaid him with slander and ingratitude.

* * *

AMAN chief Eli Zeira largely disappeared after the war. The Labor Party knew how to take care of its own and offered him a
plum position in Israel's largest bank. But he had had enough of
the Labor Party establishment and turned down the offer, saying
he wanted to work independently as a consultant.[53] On the twentieth anniversary of the war, he released a memoir that did little
to repair his reputation. His central argument was that he took
the lion's share of the blame even though Israel's entire leadership
was fooled. It was a vague way of arguing something he had been
saying in classified circles for years: Ashraf Marwan was a double
agent.

His suspicion began when General Sa'ad Shazly released his
memoir in 1980. Following its release, Shazly was sentenced to
death and had to flee the country, suggesting its contents were
accurate.* Shazly said—as did Gamasy in his memoir—that Egypt
had no intention of attacking in either December 1972 or in April
1973. Sadat writes in his memoir that "I had no intention of starting a war in May, but as part of my strategic deception plan I . . .
took various civil defense measures which led the Israelis to believe that war was imminent." Why, then, did Marwan warn of
an attack in both December and May? Moreover, Marwan said
in an interview for a biography of Saudi Sheikh Yamani that he
was present at the August 1973 meeting between Sadat and King

---

* Shazly returned to Egypt after Sadat's death. In 2012, he was given the Order of the Nile,
Egypt's highest award, for his role in the October war. General Gamasy served as Egypt's
minister of defense until 1978.

Feisal.[54] At that meeting, Sadat told Feisal that war would come very soon. Why did Marwan tell the Israelis in August that no war was planned, and then wait until the last minute to sound the warning?

Others, particularly former head of the Mossad Zvi Zamir, were equally adamant that Marwan was a legitimate spy for Israel. The Egyptian officer also thought that Egypt would attack in December and May, so plainly there was some basis for Marwan to arrive at that conclusion.* Why had Marwan waited so long to sound the alarm in October? Perhaps it was because it was only then that he found out the actual date. Or perhaps it could be best explained by something attributed to Israeli spymaster Rafi Eitan. You must always remember, he would say, that there are no double agents; there are only triple agents. There is the nation they serve, the nation they betray, and then there is that third and highest loyalty, which is to themselves. What he meant was that Marwan was a traitor, but he still had some measure of loyalty to Egypt as well, and thus wanted to give the Israelis only the minimum needed to keep the money flowing. Zamir made another more important point: if Marwan had been a double agent, he would not have warned the Israelis at all.

On December 21, 2002, the Egyptian newspaper *al-Ahram* reported that Ashraf Marwan was an Israeli spy. It based the story on an interview with a London-based Israeli historian named Ahron Bregman. The news landed like a clap of thunder. Marwan was then a wealthy businessman living in London, enjoying life at the pinnacle of Arab society. At various times, he was close to both Mu'ammar al-Qaddafi and to Muhammad Fayed, the billionaire London-based businessman whose son Dodi was romantically involved with Lady Diana, until the two were killed in a Paris car crash. Marwan's daughter was married to the son of Amr Moussa,

---

* There is no suspicion that the Egyptian officer was a double agent. His existence was disclosed by the Israelis only in late 2020. They added that he was never discovered by Egyptian counterintelligence and had died of natural causes years earlier.

Egypt's former foreign minister and then secretary-general of the Arab League.[55]

Zamir accused Zeira of leaking Marwan's name to Bregman. An arbitration headed by a former Israeli Supreme Court justice found that this was true. Zeira never disclosed his motive for revealing the name of one of Israel's greatest spies. Whatever the reason, criminal complaints were filed against him. But after sitting on the case for years, on July 8, 2012, the state prosecutor chose to drop the matter because of Zeira's age—he was then eighty-four—and because of "the significance of putting an Israeli Major General on trial." This is another of those legal decisions that shocks the conscience.

On June 27, 2007, Ashraf Marwan was found dead on the sidewalk beneath the fifth-story balcony of his London apartment. Scotland Yard could not rule out murder, accident, or suicide. Marwan's family was certain it was not suicide. Most Israeli intelligence analysts believe he was murdered by the Egyptians. Nevertheless, he was given a hero's funeral in Cairo. President Hosni Mubarak issued a statement that Marwan had performed great service to his country.[56] Whether the statement was heartfelt or issued to avoid embarrassment is impossible to say. The only thing that is certain is that Ashraf Marwan died a hero. The question is, for which country?

* * *

On a cool morning in January 1977, Anwar Sadat was giving an interview to a Lebanese journalist when the journalist suddenly noticed something strange taking place behind him. Sadat turned around and saw a column of smoke rising in the distance, as well as a throng of protesters heading toward his house. Sadat fled in the company of his guards and learned that similar protests had broken out all over Egypt. The trigger for the crisis was the cancellation of subsidies that kept basic food staples affordable to Egypt's poor. Sadat broke a promise and called out the army against the Egyptian people. By the time the unrest was put down, 171 Egyptians were dead.[57]

Sadat tried to solve his economic woes by snatching some of Libya's oil wells. The effort failed. Now at the end of his rope, he shocked the world and traveled to Jerusalem to talk peace.* His counterpart was Israeli prime minister Menachem Begin, an enigma, wrapped in a mystery, wrapped in an ill-fitting suit. To some a terrorist, to some a freedom fighter, to all a strange political contradiction: a fierce right-wing radical on foreign policy and an equally fierce liberal on domestic policy.[58]

It got off to a rocky start. Sadat gave a speech in the Knesset in which he said he would settle for nothing less than "complete withdrawal from [the 1967] territories including Arab Jerusalem." He added that "you have found the moral and legal justification to set up a national home on a land that did not all belong to you." Begin rose to deliver not so much a speech as a rebuttal. "No, Sir, we did not take a foreign country. We came back to our homeland."[59]

Negotiations limped for almost a year. The hardest sticking point was the old issue of "linkage"—Sadat refused to sign a separate peace treaty, or any treaty, that did not include a Palestinian state. By the time the parties signed a framework agreement at Camp David on September 17, 1978, Sadat gave in. Israel achieved full peace with normalization, it retained control of the other territories (promising only autonomy to the Palestinians), and it withdrew from Sinai only. It was the offer that Levi Eshkol had made to Nasser back in the summer of 1967. It was the offer that Golda had made to Sadat in early 1973.[60]

The deal was popular in Israel. It passed by a lopsided majority in the Knesset. And it burnished Begin's reputation, posi-

---

* The level of distrust was so great that the Israelis stationed hundreds of commandos around the plane in case terrorists came out shooting. Egyptian president Hosni Mubarak laughed when he heard about it later. "What did you think, Sadat would come running out with a machine gun and spray everyone??"

tioning him in the front rank of prime ministers in poll after poll among the Israeli public (despite mismanagement of the economy and the failed war in Lebanon). Those same polls invariably placed Golda at the very bottom. Golda had won the victory that allowed Begin to achieve the peace. But no one seemed capable of connecting the dots between the two.

This is no accident. There were many in Israel who chose to glean the "lesson" from the Yom Kippur War that Israel had to trade land for peace. The history, as they told and retold it, was that Golda chose war over withdrawal, so Israel got war and then withdrawal. The fundamental tenets of this mythology are that Sadat wanted peace all along, the Yom Kippur War would have been prevented had Golda accepted a land-for-peace offer in 1971, and that only after losing the Yom Kippur War did Israel come to its senses and agree to give back Sinai. Nothing, it seemed, could explode this myth, not even an interview that Sadat's widow, Jihan, gave to an Israeli newspaper in 1987 in which she said, "I don't agree with those that say that Sadat tried to reach true peace before 1973. I believe he wanted only a ceasefire agreement, and nothing more."[61]

The peace deal was wildly unpopular in Egypt. A nation told that it had won the 1973 war was in no mood to abandon Nasser's pan-Arab struggle. After the treaty was signed, Israeli diplomats took office space in Cairo in the same building as Muhammad Heikal. He made a point of turning his back on the Israelis and facing the wall every time they rode together in the elevator. Jihan Sadat writes that there were days her husband went to work and she did not know if he would return. One of the few days she did not fear for his life was October 6, 1981, the day Egypt celebrated the crossing of the canal.[62] But it was at that day's parade that an Islamic radical named Khalid Islambuli ran up to the reviewing stand and gunned down Anwar Sadat. He was sixty-two.

In the words of Muhammad Heikal, Sadat was "the first Egyptian Pharaoh to be killed by his own people." His funeral was well attended by foreign leaders, less so by the Egyptian public.

Celebrations broke out across the Arab world. The street in Tehran where the Egyptian embassy was located was renamed after Islambuli, the assassin.[63]

A particularly large celebration took place in Damascus. Unlike his Egyptian counterpart, Assad never trumpeted any grand Syrian victory. He had no intention of making peace, and probably figured he would be better off striking a pose of defiance and hunger for revenge. When faced with the same choices as Sadat—make peace with losing land or make peace with Israel—Assad chose to soldier on. Syria thus never retrieved the Golan Heights. It is now a near certainty that it never will.

Sadat's replacement, Hosni Mubarak, was a cautious man who always made sure to keep relations with Israel as cool as possible. The term "cold peace" was coined. Relations have remained in that state to this day.[64] * A second peace treaty signed with Jordan in 1994 resulted in a similarly chilly relationship.

But recent years have seen a shift. On September 15, 2020, Israel signed the Abraham Accords with the United Arab Emirates and Bahrain. These small Arab nations have chosen a different kind of relationship with Israel. Less than two years later, annual trade between Israel and the UAE reached almost $1 billion, or more than double the amount between Israel and Egypt.[65] There is reason for optimism.

None of these treaties would have occurred had there not been peace between Egypt and Israel. And that peace treaty would never have occurred if Israel had not won the Yom Kippur War.

* * *

After Sadat's assassination, Moshe Dayan was invited to appear on Israeli television to praise the memory of the man that was first

---

* In an unguarded moment, while addressing students at Cairo University, Mubarak was heard to say: "Against us stood the most intelligent people on earth—a people that controls the international press, the world economy and world finances. . . . We have proven that making peace with Israel does not entail Jewish domination and that there is no obligation to develop relations with Israel beyond those we desire."

to sign a peace treaty with Israel. Dayan was appointed by Begin to serve as his foreign minister and had gotten to know Sadat over the course of the negotiations. By now Dayan's health had begun to fail. At Camp David, he walked right into a tree.

The television interview was Dayan's last public appearance. Shortly thereafter, a politician visited him at home and asked why all the lights were off. Dayan felt his way into the room and said that he had no reason to turn them on. He had gone blind. Sensing his visitor's discomfort, he hastened to add, "My suffering won't last much longer."[66] Two weeks later he died. He was sixty-six.

His final years had not been easy. Once while giving a speech at a memorial for the war dead on Mount Herzl, someone shouted at him: "Murderer!" A senior Labor politician was asked by a reporter what he thought Dayan would do after the war. He replied that he hoped Dayan spent the rest of his days as a groundskeeper in a military cemetery. It did not get much better after he died. Following a typically scathing newspaper piece in 2003, his son Udi could take it no longer and wrote a letter to the editor: "Keep it up everybody, keep firing bullet holes into my father's body buried in Nahalal, there's ammo for everyone."[67]

Dayan's aide and protégé, Shimon Peres, remained true to him. He said, "Dayan had a rare quality: he knew how to fight and win when necessary, and he knew to negotiate when possible."[68] Peres could have added that Dayan was also the tactical and spiritual founder of the Israeli army, the Jewish state's most valuable possession. Yet like Elazar, his career and legacy somehow ended in slander and ingratitude.

One can only hope that a reassessment will come someday, one that offers a more balanced view of Dayan and a more accurate view of Golda Meir. If that day comes, Golda will assume her rightful place in the front rank of Israeli prime ministers, joining Ben-Gurion and Eshkol as one of Israel's great wartime leaders.

Golda ended her own memoir with a prediction that one day there would be peace, so long as Israel remained strong.[69] And though she did not live quite long enough to see the first treaty signed—the ceremony between Sadat, Begin, and President Carter occurred three months after her death—she, as much as anyone, created an Israel that was strong enough to earn the prize. Her memoir must therefore stand as yet another example of history being written by the winners.

# ACKNOWLEDGMENTS

"So how do you get a book published?" I have asked that question to many people over the years. And now that my name finally appears as an author, I think I know the answer.

The first thing is to find an editor like Peter Ginna. Peter not only played a vital role in helping me craft this work, he offered invaluable advice in navigating the publishing world. Another great mentor was my agent, Mel Berger. Perhaps the greatest mentor of them all was my editor at St. Martin's, Elisabeth Dyssegaard, to whom I will always owe a debt for her trust, her input, and her patience in guiding this project over the finish line. Any mistakes are mine and mine alone.

There would not have been a book to guide had it not been for the many researchers that assisted me over more than twenty years. Thanks to Adva Chen and to Eyal Tzur for helping me uncover obscure sources in Israel, particularly those that have been declassified in recent years. Other great resources were Israel's Yad La-Shiryon, as well as Avi Zohar of the Israel War Institute. Perhaps the best thing Zohar did was to introduce me to Pesach Malovany, a walking encyclopedia who acted as a sounding board and offered key insight into the war with Syria. Malovany, a retired senior intelligence officer, has made much of the record accessible by translating Arabic source material in his spare time.

Of all the extraordinary people I met while researching this project, there was perhaps none quite as remarkable as Maozia Segal. Segal was one of the Yom Kippur War's most seriously wounded soldiers. He went on to raise a family, have a successful career, and write one of the best histories of the war, all despite being a triple amputee. Segal was kind enough to allow me to join IDF veterans on a January 2006 trip to the Chinese Farm battlefield. On that trip, a retired lieutenant colonel named Gil David was especially kind with his time and helped me understand the Israeli army of the 1970s. To all of them, this thanks is extended.

For Soviet source material, I was fortunate to have the help of the author and historian Lyuba Vinogradova. (Lyuba was introduced to me by Antony Beevor, who is not just one of our most distinguished World War II historians but also a real mensch.) Another researcher, who I will refer to only as Oleksii, tracked down and interviewed retired Soviet soldiers living in Ukraine. Oleksii did great work but quit before the project ended to enlist in the Ukrainian army and join the fight against Putin's invasion.

Syria is something of a Middle Eastern hermit kingdom. Good information is extremely hard to find. But one source is the files of the East German Stasi, which had a large presence in Syria in the 1970s. To review this material in Berlin, I had the help of Julie Moskovits. In another sign of the times, Julie had to quit before the project ended because she suffered a serious bout of COVID. I also want to thank my old pals Steve Schwell and Steve Alter for their friendship and support.

In this, as with everything else, my wife, Esther, was a source of encouragement and loving support. She, and my kids, often had to get by while Daddy was holed up in the basement. I only hope that the final result was worth their sacrifice.

# NOTES

**Chapter 1: A Parade in Jerusalem**

1. *Jerusalem Post*, May 5, 1968, p. 3.
2. *New York Times*, May 3, 1968, p. 1; *Jerusalem Post*, May 3, 1968, p. 1.
3. Schiff & Dor, *Yisroel 50* [Israel 50] (Galei Alfa Tikshoret, Jerusalem) (1997); *Jerusalem Post*, May 10, 1968.
4. Meshal, *V'Eleh Shnot, 50 L'Medinat Yisroel* [These Are the Years, Israel at 50] (Miskal Publishing, Tel Aviv) (1997), p. 147; *Jerusalem Post*, May 3, 1968, p. 1.
5. Ben-Gurion, *Israel: A Personal History* (Funk & Wagnalls, Inc., New York) (1971), p. 815.
6. *Jerusalem Post*, May 3, 1968, p. 1.
7. *Jerusalem Post*, May 3, 1968, p. 7.
8. *Ma'ariv, Mosaf Shabbat*, November 19, 2004, p. 18; Israel Channel 10 Television, June 5, 2017; Cohen, *Hatabu Ha'Acharon* [The Last Taboo] (Kinneret, Zmora-Bitan, Dvir Publishing House, Or Yehuda) (2005), p. 47.
9. Shalom, writing in Zohar & Malovany (Editors), *Milkhemet Sheshet Hayamim* [The Six Day War] (Israel War Research Institute, Kfar Chabad) (2018), p. 349.
10. Hod, writing in Mickelson & Meltzer (Editors), *Milkhemet Sheshet Yamim* [The Six Day War] (Effi Meltzer Publishing, Tel Aviv, 1996), p. 91; Weizman, *Lekha Shamayim Lekha Aretz* [To You Heaven, To You Earth] (Ma'ariv Books, Tel Aviv) (1975), p. 269.
11. Sadat, *In Search of Identity* (Harper & Row Publishers, New York) (1977), p. 176; *Bamahane*, June 12, 1967, p. 36; Amit, writing in Mickelson & Meltzer (Editors), *Milkhemet Sheshet Yamim*, p. 82.
12. Raphael, *Destination Peace* (Stein & Day, New York) (1981), p. 162.
13. Zohar & Malovany (Editors), *Milkhemet*, p. 379; Kfir & Dor, *Revah L'Shmona* [At a Quarter to Eight] (Yediot Ahronot, Sifrei Chemed, Rishon Lezion) (2019), p. 161.
14. Zohar, writing in Zohar & Malovany (Editors), *Milkhemet*, p. 404; Levkovitz, writing in Mickelson & Meltzer (Editors), *Milkhemet*, p. 267.
15. Segev, *1967* (Keter Book, Jerusalem) (2005), p. 454.
16. *Jerusalem Post*, May 5, 1968, p. 1.
17. Ben-Gurion, pgs. 821–822.

**Chapter 2: "That Which Was Taken by Force Will Be Returned by Force"**

1. Nutting, *Nasser* (E.P. Dutton & Co., New York) (1972), p. 41.
2. Farid, *Nasser: The Final Years* (Ithaca Press, Reading) (1994), p. 1.
3. *Ha'aretz Magazine*, Mosaf Ha'aretz, March 11, 2005, p. 26; Zohar, *Lokhamei Kav Hamayim V'Ha'esh* [War of Attrition, 1967–1970] (Israel War Institute, Tel Aviv) (2012), pgs. 143–145.
4. Kfir & Dor, *Masah Chaim* [Chaim Erez—A Journey of Life] (Kinneret, Zmora-Bitan, Dvir Publishing House, Or Yehuda) (2017), p. 176; Koryavin, *Na Blizhnem Vostoke* [In the Middle East] (Izvestiya, Moscow) (1982), p. 303; Zohar, p. 146.
5. *New York Times*, February 21, 1968; *New York Times*, January 23, 1968.
6. Egorin, *Egipet Nashego Vremeni* [Egypt of Our Time] (Moscow, 1998); Dayan, *Avnei Derekh* [Milestones] (Edanim Publishers & Dvir Publishing House, Jerusalem & Tel Aviv) (1976), p. 512; *Voenno-Istoricheesky Zhurnal*, No. 4, 1994, pgs. 36–43.
7. Farid, pgs. 36 & 124; interview with Mikhin Viktor Leonovich, July 9, 2004; Saenko, *The Role of Political Officers* (Institut Vostokovedeniya RAN, Moscow) (1988), p. 181.
8. Rabin, *Pinkas*, Volume 1 (Ma'ariv Books, Tel Aviv) (1979), pgs. 233, 236–243.
9. Zohar, p. 76; Avner, *The Prime Ministers, An Intimate Narrative of Israeli Leadership* (The Toby Press, Jerusalem) (2010), p. 167.
10. Korn, *Stalemate: The War of Attrition and Great Power Diplomacy in the Middle East, 1967–1970* (Westview Press, Boulder) (1992), pgs. 66–67.
11. Korn, p. 15; Sadat, *In Search of Identity* (Harper & Row Publishers, New York) (1977), p. 167.
12. Greenberg, writing in Golan & Shai (Editors), *Milkhama Hayom* [War Today] (Ma'arakhot, Israel) (2003), p. 72; Zohar, p. 134.
13. Kollek, *For Jerusalem* (Random House, New York) (1978), pgs. 201–203; Terrence Smith, then a correspondent for the *New York Times* on the *Newshour*, June 2, 1967; www.youtube.com/watch?v=OSuD-1hmMqo.
14. Argaman, *Zeh Hayah Sodi B'Yoter* [It was Top Secret] (Bamahane, Israel) (2007), p. 254.
15. Israel Government Transcript ("IGT"), June 18, 1967, p. 17, www.archives.gov.il /en/; Avneiri, *Optimi II* [Optimistic II] (Miskal-Yediot Ahronot & Chemed Books, Tel Aviv) (2016), p. 204.
16. Segev, *1967* (Keter Book, Jerusalem) (2005), p. 587; Sapir, *Hayesh Hagadol, Biographia Shel Pinchas Sapir* [The Big Have: A Biography of Pinchas Sapir] (Miskal-Yediot Ahronot & Chemed Books, Israel) (2011), p. 486; *Mamone*, June 16, 2017, p. 3; Halevi, "A Brief Economic History of Modern Israel," EH.net, https://eh.net /encyclopedia/a-brief-economic-history-of-modern-israel/; Herzog, *Who Stands Accused, Israel Answers Its Critics* (Random House, New York) (1978), p. 71.
17. *Ma'ariv, Mosaf Shabbat*, May 6, 1967; Tevet, *Khasufim B'Tzareakh* [Exposed in the Turret] (Schocken Books, Jerusalem & Tel Aviv) (1968), p. 278.
18. *Ma'ariv, Sofshavua*, October 16, 2011, p. 33; *Yediot Ahronot, 7 Yamim*, December 16, 2016, p. 20.
19. *Yediot Ahronot, 7 Yamim*, November 23, 1998.
20. Bar-On, *Moshe Dayan, Korot Khayav 1915–1981* [Moshe Dayan, His Life and Times 1915–1981] (Am Oved Publishers, Tel Aviv) (2014), p. 53; Yisraeli, *Megilat Chaim* [Chaim Yisraeli, A Life Story] (Miskal-Yediot Ahronot Books & Chemed Books, Israel) (2005), p. 254; Dayan, p. 56.
21. Bar-On, pgs. 74, 76 & 91.

22. Dayan, p. 109; Milstein, *B'Dam V'Esh Yehudah* [By Blood and Fire Judah] (Epstein-Modan Publishing, Israel) (1975), p. 196.
23. Avneiri, pgs. 462–463 and author's notes.
24. Dayan, p. 98; "Good Morning with Avri Gilad and Tali Metz," Israel Channel 13 TV, March 7, 2019.
25. Olmert, *B'Guf Rishon* [In Person] (Miskal—Yediot Ahronot & Chemed Books, Rishon LeZion) (2018), p. 380.
26. Bar-On, p. 177; *Yediot Ahronot, Hamosaf LeShabbat*, April 1, 2005, p. 15; Jackont, *Meir Amit Ha'Ish VeHaMossad* [Meir Amit—The Man and the Mossad] (Miskal—Yediot Ahronot & Chemed Books, Tel Aviv) (2012), p. 60; Sharon, *Warrior, The Autobiography of Ariel Sharon* (Simon & Schuster, New York) (1989), p. 126; Yisraeli, p. 308; Kollek, p. 243; Bar-On, p. 270; Eitan, *Raful, Sipur Shel Khayal* [Raful, A Soldier's Story] (Ma'ariv Books, Tel Aviv) (1985), pgs. 137–138.
27. Robinson (Editor), *Under Fire: Israel's 20 Year Fight for Survival* (W.W. Norton & Company, New York) (1968), p. 335; Avneiri, p. 388; Shamgar, *Meir Shamgar: Tam V'Loh Nishlam* [Meir Shamgar: An Autobiography] (Miskal—Yediot Ahronot & Chemed Books, Tel Aviv) (2015), p. 85.
28. Nutting, pgs. 430 & 431.
29. Farid, p. 54; Riad, *The Struggle for Peace in the Middle East* (Quartet Books, London) (1981), p. 52.
30. Riad, pgs. 51, 53 & 57; *New York Times*, February 28, 1958; Recorded conversation between Ambassador Vinogradov and President Nasser, November 14, 1967, F087 Op.30 P.89 D.9 L.33–42; Korn, pgs. 84–85; Farid, p. 52.
31. Farid, p. 59.

## Chapter 3: The Wars Between the Wars

1. Neumark, *Mishtar H'Neo-Baath B'Suriya, 1966–1970, Politika U'Mediniut* [The Neo-Baath Regime in Syria, 1966–1970: Politics and Policy] (Doctoral Thesis, submitted to History Department of Bar-Ilan University) (2002), pgs. 146–147.
2. Interview with Mikhin Viktor Leonovich, July 9, 2004.
3. Neumark, p. 206; *Yediot Ahronot*, Sheva Yamim, May 31, 2002, p. 8.
4. Korn, *Stalemate: The War of Attrition and Great Power Diplomacy in the Middle East, 1967–1970* (Westview Press, Boulder) (1992), p. 93; Zohar, *Lokhamei Kav Hamayim V'Ha'esh* [War of Attrition, 1967–1970] (Israel War Institute, Tel Aviv) (2012), pgs. 80, 99; Nadel, *HaMay'iz Minatzeakh* [Who Dares Wins] (Modan Publishing House, Ben Shemen) (2015), p. 55; Millstein & Doron, *Sayeret Shaked* [Shaked Patrol] (Yediot Ahronot, Sifrei Chemed Publishers, Tel Aviv) (1994), pgs. 164–166.
5. Zohar, p. 149; Vinogradov, *Grif Sekreto Snyat* [Declassified] (Institut Vostokovedeniya RAN, Moscow) (1997), p. 11.
6. Eitan, *Raful, Sipur Shel Khayal* [Raful, A Soldier's Story] (Ma'ariv Book, Tel Aviv) (1985), pgs. 103–104.
7. Haber, *Hayom Tifrotz Milkhama* [Today, War Will Break Out] (Edanim, Israel) (1987), pgs. 324–325, 347 & 349.
8. Zamir, *B'aynayim Pakukhot* [With Open Eyes] (Kinneret, Zmora-Bitan, Dvir Publishing House, Or Yehuda) (2011), p. 61; Gluska, *Eshkol Ten Pekuda!* [Eshkol, Give the Order!] (Modan Publishing, Tel Aviv) (2016), p. 43.
9. Medzini, *Golda Biographia Politit* [Golda, a Political Biography] (Miskal-Yediot Ahronot & Chemed Books, Tel Aviv) (2008), p. 27.
10. Kollek, *For Jerusalem* (Random House, New York) (1978), p. 149.

11. *Yediot Ahronot, 7 Yamim,* December 5, 2008, p. 19; Medzini, pgs. 87 & 199; Meir, *My Life* (G.P. Putnam's Sons, New York) (1975), p. 235.
12. *Ha'aretz,* October 10, 2003, p. 43.
13. *Ma'ariv, Mosaf Shabbat,* December 5, 2003, p. 2.
14. *Yediot Ahronot, 7 Yamim,* December 5, 2008, p. 21; Medzini, p. 436; *Yediot Ahronot, Mosaf Sukot,* October 12, 1984, p. 7; Eban, *Personal Witness: Israel Through My Eyes* (G.P. Putnam's Sons, New York) (1992), p. 476.
15. *Yediot Ahronot, Mosaf Sukot,* October 12, 1984, p. 7.
16. Korn, p. 108; Zohar, p. 158; Nadel, p. 64.
17. Zohar, p. 167.
18. Zohar, p. 188.
19. Zohar, p. 382.
20. Zohar, p. 368.
21. Zohar, pgs. 202 & 376.
22. Zohar, p. 203.
23. Zohar pgs. 354 & 367.
24. Nadel, pgs. 121–123; Shazly, *The Crossing of Suez: The October War (1973)* (Third World Centre for Research & Publishing, London) (1980), p. 16.
25. Kfir & Dor, *Revah L'Shmona* [At a Quarter to Eight] (Yediot Ahronot, Sifrei Chemed, Rishon Lezion) (2019), p. 172; Gordon, *30 Sha'ot B'October* [30 Hours in October] (Ma'ariv Book Guild, Tel Aviv) (2008), p. 63.
26. Gordon, p. 90; Korn, p. 168.
27. Gordon, p. 72; Dayan, *Avnei Derekh* [Milestones] (Edanim Publishers & Dvir Publishing House, Jerusalem and Tel Aviv) (1976), p. 517; Gamasy, *The October War* (The American University in Cairo Press, Cairo) (1993), p. 111; Schiff, *Re'idat Adamah B'October* [Earthquake in October] (Zmora, Bitan Modan Publishers, Tel Aviv) (1975), p. 197; Zohar, p. 239; Sadat, *A Woman of Egypt* (Simon & Schuster, New York) (1987), p. 242; Zohar, p. 277; Gordon, p. 72.
28. Shazly, *Crossing,* p. 16; Sadat, p. 242.
29. Vinogradov, *Grif Sekretno Snyat* [Declassified] (Institut Vostokovedeniya RAN, Moscow) (1997), p. 11; Heikal, *The Road to Ramadan* (Ballantine Books, New York) (1975), p. 81.
30. Heikal, pgs. 82 & 83; Nutting, *Nasser* (E.P. Dutton & Co., New York) (1972), p. 446.
31. *Yediot Ahronot, 7 Yamim,* March 22, 2019, p. 26; Herzog, *The Arab-Israeli Wars* (Random House, New York) (1982), p. 234; Eban, p. 483.
32. Rabin, *Pinkas,* Volume 1 (Ma'ariv Books, Tel Aviv) (1979), p. 287; Gordon, p. 74; Sharon, *Warrior, The Autobiography of Ariel Sharon* (Simon & Schuster, New York) (1989), p. 234; *Yediot Ahronot, 7 Yamim,* March 22, 2019, p. 28.
33. Kissinger, *White House Years* (Little, Brown & Co., New York) (1979), pgs. 224–225.
34. Kissinger, pgs. 559 & 564.
35. Schiff, p. 109; Kissinger, pgs. 564–565; Quandt, *Decade of Decisions* (University of California Press, Berkeley) (1977), p. 97.
36. Kfir & Dor, *Yanush* [Yanush] (Kinneret, Zmora-Bitan, Dvir Publishing House, Hevel Modi'in) (2017), p. 91; Gordon, p. 104; Kissinger, p. 569; Zohar, pgs. 270–271; Gordon, p. 66.
37. Egorin, *Egipet Nashego Vremeni* [Egypt of Our Time] (Moscow, 1998), pgs. 188, 191 & 195.
38. Spector, *Ram U'Barur* [Loud and Clear] (Yediot Ahronot, Sifrei Chemed) (2008), p. 196; Kfir & Dor, *Revah,* p. 190.
39. Zohar, p. 288; *Yediot Ahronot, 7 Yamim,* October 11, 2019, p. 22.

40. *Ma'ariv Sofshavua*, August 12, 2005, pgs. 11–14; *Yediot Ahronot, 7 Yamim*, March 22, 2019, p. 26; Spector, p. 191; Heikal, p. 164.

41. Interview with Vinogradov, *Grif Sekretno Snyat* [Declassified] (Institut Vostoko-vedeniya RAN, Moscow) (1997), p. 12; Interview with Goryachkin, Zhaivoronok, *Grif Sekretno Snyat* [Declassified] (Moscow, Lespromekonomika, Vinogradov ed.1997), p. 180.

42. Kissinger, p. 566.

43. Editorial Note, Foreign Relations of the United States, 1969–1976, Volume XII, Soviet Union, January 1969–October 1970, https://history.state.gov /historicaldocuments/frus1969–76v12/d170; Kissinger, p. 576; Rabin, *Pinkas I*, p. 292; Eban, p. 478; Quandt, p. 101.

44. Kissinger, p. 582; Medzini, p. 466.

45. Gamasy, p. 121; Zohar, p. 180.

46. Sharon, *Warrior*, p. 235.

47. Zeira, *Milkhemet Yom HaKippurim, Mitoos Mul Metziut* [The Yom Kippur War: Fact versus Fiction] (Yediot Ahronot, Tel Aviv) (1993), pgs. 35–39; Kissinger, p. 591; Zohar, p. 109.

48. Gamasy, p. 115; Zohar, p. 182; Sadat, p. 181.

49. Sadat, pgs. 203 & 248; Farid, *Nasser: The Final Years* (Ithaca Press, Reading) (1994), pgs. 212–213; Riad, *The Struggle for Peace in the Middle East* (Quartet Books, London) (1981), p. 167.

50. Gamal Abdel Nasser Quotes, BrainyQuote, www.brainyquote.com/authors/gamal -abdel-nasser-quotes.

## Chapter 4: Yesmanship: Peace and Its Process

1. Kissinger, *Years of Upheaval* (Little, Brown & Co., Boston) (1982), pgs. 843–844.

2. Telegram from First Deputy Minister of Foreign Affairs of the USSR to ambassa-dors of the USSR in Bulgaria, Hungary, DDR, Poland, Czechoslovakia, Vietnam, Mongolia, China, and Cuba, F.059 Op.56 P.116 D.522 L.8–16; Riad, *The Struggle for Peace in the Middle East* (Quartet Books, London) (1981), p. 183.

3. Telegram from the First Deputy Minister of Foreign Affairs of the USSR to ambassadors of the USSR in Bulgaria, Hungary, DDR, Poland, Czechoslovakia, Vietnam, Mongolia, China and Cuba. F.059 Op.56 P.116 D.522 L.8–16; Heikal, *The Sphinx and the Commissar* (Harper & Row Publishers, New York) (1978), p. 190; V.A. Kirpichenko, *Razvedka: Litsa I Lichnosti* [Intelligence Service: Persona and Personalities], (Moscow) (1998), p. 103.

4. K.N. Brutents, *Tridtsat Let na Staroi Ploshchadi* [Thirty Years in the Staraya Square] (Moscow) (1998), p. 368.

5. Medzini, *Golda Biographia Politit* [Golda, a Political Biography] (Chemed Books) (2008), p. 344; Eban, *Personal Witness: Israel Through My Eyes* (G.P. Putnam's Sons, New York) (1992), pgs. 439–440; Raphael, *Destination Peace* (Stein & Day, New York) (1981), p. 186.

6. Eban, p. 439; Korn, *Stalemate: The War of Attrition and Great Power Diplomacy in the Middle East, 1967–1970* (Westview Press, Boulder) (1992), p. 33; Riad, p. 62.

7. Kissinger, *White House Years* (Little, Brown & Co., New York) (1979), p. 341.

8. *New York Times*, June 2, 2002, p. 43.

9. Heikal, *Autumn of Fury* (Corgi Books, Transworld Publishers, London) (1983), pgs. 17 & 33; Sadat, *A Woman of Egypt*, (Simon & Schuster, New York) (1987), p. 95.

10. Heikal, *Autumn of Fury*, p. 36; Sadat, *Revolt on the Nile*, (The John Day Company,

New York) (1957), p. 109; Nutting, *Nasser* (E.P. Dutton & Co., New York) (1972), p. 36; *New York Times*, July 18, 1971.

11. Sadat, *A Woman*, p. 148.

12. Farid, *Nasser: The Final Years* (Ithaca Press, Reading) (1994), p. 85.

13. Farid, p. 153; Sadat, *In Search of Identity* (Harper & Row Publishers, New York) (1977), pgs. 199 & 200; Heikal, *Autumn of Fury*, pgs. 42 & 43; Nutting, p. 430; Heikal, *Secret Channels* (HarperCollins Publishers, London) (1996), p. 161.

14. Shazly, *The Crossing of Suez* (Third World Centre for Research and Publishing, London) (1980), p. 64; Eban, p. 499; Rabin, *Pinkas II* (Ma'ariv Books, Tel Aviv) (1979), p. 325; Sadat, *In Search*, p. 215; Avneiri, *Optimi II* [Optimistic II] (Miskal-Yediot Ahronot & Chemed Books, Tel Aviv) (2016), p. 379; *New York Times*, March 21, 1976; Golan, *The Secret Conversations of Henry Kissinger* (Quadrangle/The New York Times Book Co.) (1976), p. 145.

15. Farid, pgs. 92, 95 & 129; Riad, pgs. 90–91; Office of the Historian, Foreign Relations 1964–1968, Volume XX, Arab-Israeli Dispute 1967–1968, https://2001-2009.state.gov/r/pa/ho/frus/johnsonlb/xx/2673.htm.

16. Gazit, *Ta'halikh HaShalom 1969–1970* [Peace Process] (Yad Tabenkin, Israel) (1984), p. 12.

17. U.N. Security Council Report S/10070, par. 8 (March 5, 1971).

18. Gazit, p. 76. King Hussein followed the same practice. See Heikal, *The Road to Ramadan* (Ballantine Books, New York) (1975), p. 51.

19. U.N. Security Council Report S/10070, par. 9 (March 5, 1971).

20. Gazit, p. 86; Medzini, p. 500; Heikal, *The Road to Ramadan*, p. 120.

21. Eban, p. 501.

22. Gazit, p. 88; U.N. Security Council Report S/10070, par. 12 (March 5, 1971).

23. Dayan, *Avnei Derekh* [Milestones] (Edanim Publishers & Dvir Publishing House, Jerusalem & Tel Aviv) (1976), pgs. 526–527; Eban, p. 499; Heikal, *Secret Channels*, p. 162.

24. Sadat, *In Search*, p. 219; Sadat, *A Woman*, p. 254; Terence Smith, "Sadat Spells Out Position on Withdrawal by Israelis," *New York Times*, February 15, 1971, www.nytimes.com/1971/02/15/archives/sadat-spells-out-position-on-withdrawal -by-israelis.html; Excerpts from a Speech by President Sadat Further Defining the Peace Initiative, https://sadat.umd.edu/sites/sadat.umd.edu/files/Excerpts%20 from%20a%20Speech%20by%20President%20Sadat%20Further%20Defin- ing%20the%20Peace%20Initiative.pdf.

25. Sadat, *In Search*, p. 219; Excerpts from a Speech by President Sadat Further Defining the Peace Initiative, https://sadat.umd.edu/sites/sadat.umd.edu/files /Excerpts%20from%20a%20Speech%20by%20President%20Sadat%20Fur- ther%20Defining%20the%20Peace%20Initiative.pdf; Gamasy, *The October War* (The American University in Cairo Press, Cairo), p. 171.

26. Medzini, p. 507.

27. Kissinger, *Years of Upheaval*, pgs. 210 & 212.

28. Transcript of Secret Talks between Egyptian National Security Adviser Hafez Ismail and US National Security Adviser Henry Kissinger, February 25–26, 1973, https://israeled.org/resources/documents/transcript-secret-talks-Egyptian -national-security-hafez-ismail-us-national-security-adviser-henry-kissinger/; Kissinger, *Years of Upheaval*, p. 216.

29. Kissinger, *Years of Upheaval*, p. 216.

30. Rabin, *Pinkas II*, p. 387.

31. Rabin, *Pinkas II*, p. 393.

32. Gazit, p. 137; Riad, p. 237.
33. Kissinger, *White House Years*, pgs. 351 & 567; Gamasy, p. 176; Office of the Historian, Foreign Relations of the United States, 1969–1976, Volume XXV, Arab-Israeli Crisis and War, 1973, https://history.state.gov/historicaldocuments /frus1969–76v25/d47; Kissinger, *Years of Upheaval*, p. 222.
34. Interview with Arnaud de Borchgrave, June 2, 2002; Kipnes, *HaDerekh L'Milkhama 1973* [The Path to War 1973] (Kinneret, Zmora-Bitan, Dvir Publishing House, Or Yehuda) (2012), p. 86; "The Battle Is Now Inevitable," *Newsweek*, April 9, 1973, pgs. 44–46; Raphael, p. 280.
35. Sadat, *In Search*, p. 242.

**Chapter 5: To Prepare for the War That Must Come**
1. Twain, *The Innocents Abroad* (The Readers Digest Edition) (1990—first published in 1869), pgs. 391 & 395.
2. Millstein & Doron, *Sayeret Shaked* [Shaked Patrol] (Yediot Ahronot, Sifrei Chemed Publishers, Tel Aviv) (1994), p. 176.
3. Bar-Yosef, *HaTzopheh Shenirdam* [The Watchman That Fell Asleep] (Zmora-Bitan Publishers, Ganei Aviv-Lod) (2001), p. 76.
4. Adan, *Al Shtay Gadot Suez* [On Both Banks of the Suez] (Edanim & Yediot Ahronot, Jerusalem) (1979), p. 46; Herzog, *The War of Atonement* (Little, Brown & Co., Boston) (1975), p. 6.
5. Adan, p. 47; Dayan, *Avnei Derekh* [Milestones] (Edanim Publishers & Dvir Publishing House, Jerusalem and Tel Aviv) (1976), p. 515.
6. Sakal, *Hasadir Yivlome?* [The Regulars Will Hold?] (Ma'ariv Book Guild, Tel Aviv) (2011), pgs. 28 & 110.
7. Greenberg, writing in Golan & Shai (Editors), *Milkhama Hayom* [War Today] (Ma'arakhot, Israel) (2003), p. 61; Millstein, *B'Dam V'Esh Yehudah* [In Blood and Fire Judea] (Levin-Epstein Publishers, Tel Aviv) (1975), p. 285; Arbel & Ne'eman, *Shigayon LeLoh Kippur* [Unforgiveable Self-Delusion] (Miskal-Yediot Ahronot & Chemed Books) (2005), p. 150; Adan, p. 53; Hefetz & Bloom, *HaRoeh* [The Shepherd] (Miskal-Yediot Ahronot & Chemed Books) (2005) pgs. 195–200; Gai, *Bar-Lev Biographia* [Bar-Lev, a Biography] (Am Oved Safrit Poalim) (1998), p. 186.
8. Reshef, *Lo Nekhdal! Khativah 14 B'Milkhemet Yom HaKippurim* [We Will Never Cease! The 14th Brigade in the Yom Kippur War] (Dvir Publishing House, Tel Aviv) (2013), p. 47.
9. Agranat Commission, Final Report, Volume 1 (Jerusalem, 1975), p. 70; Agranat Commission, Interim Report, Second Report (1974), p. 151; Bar-Yosef, pgs. 190–191.
10. Reshef, p. 46.
11. Gai, p. 209.
12. Millstein, *B'Dam*, p. 216.
13. Arbel & Ne'eman, p. 272
14. Arbel & Ne'eman, *Hakhraot Gevuleot*, [Borderline Choices] (Miskal – Yediot Ahronot & Chemed Books, Tel Aviv) (2011), p. 103.
15. Amidror writing in Yephezkaili (Editor), *Milkhemet Yom HaKippurim Uleka-Kheha* [The Yom Kippur War and Its Lessons] (Israeli Ministry of Defense, Israel) (2005), p. 22; Gordon, *30 Sha'ot B'October* [30 Hours in October] (Ma'ariv Book Guild, Tel Aviv) (2008), p. 49; Golan & Shai (Editors), p. 66.
16. Wolfe, *The Purple Decades* (Penguin Books, New York) (1984), p. 242.
17. Zhaivoronok, *Looking Back*, pgs. 47, 48 & 53, in Vinogradov (Editor), *Grif Sekretno Snyat* (Lespromekonomika, Moscow) (1997).

18. Gordon, p. 154; interview with Colonel Yitzchak David on YouTube, February 28, 2021; interview with Colonel Menachem Paz on YouTube.

19. Wikipedia, "List of US Aircraft Losses to Missiles during the Vietnam War," https://en.wikipedia.org/wiki/List_of_US_aircraft_losses_to_missiles_during_the _Vietnam_War

20. Hirst & Beeson, *Sadat* (Faber & Faber, Ltd., London) (1982), p. 18; Heikal, *The Road to Ramadan*, p. 128; Sadat, *In Search of Identity* (Harper & Row Publishers, New York) (1977), pgs. 223–224 & 226; Sadat, *A Woman of Egypt* (Simon & Schuster, New York) (1987), pgs. 267–268; Heikal, *Autumn of Fury* (Corgi Books, Transworld Publishers, London) (1983), pgs. 48–49; Heikal, *Secret Channels* (HarperCollins Publishers, London) (1996), pgs. 165 & 172; Hirst & Beeson, pgs. 107–108.

21. *Newsweek*, June 19, 1967, p. 35.

22. Shazly, *The Crossing of Suez* (Third World Centre for Research and Publishing, London) (1980), p. 69.

23. Shazly, p. 18.

24. Sadat, *In Search*, p. 244.

25. Herzog, p. 27; Gilbert, *The First World War, A Complete History* (Henry Holt & Company, New York) (1994), p. 221.

26. Sadat, *In Search*, p. 244; Shalev, *Kishalone V'Hatzlakha B'Hatra'ah* [Failure and Success in Alert] (Ma'arachot, Tel Aviv) (2006) p. 63.

27. Shalev, p. 80.

28. Tal, writing in *Milkhemet*, p. 39.

29. Shalev, p. 80.

30. Shazly, pgs. 25–26.

31. Seale, *Asad: The Struggle for the Middle East* (University of California Press, Berkeley) (1988), p. 197; Shazly, p. 31.

32. Bartov, *Dado I* [Daddo] (Dvir Publishing House, Or Yehuda) (2002), pgs. 41–42.

33. Bartov, p. 40; Gai, p. 29.

34. Bartov, p. 64.

35. Bovin, *Zapiski Nenastoyashchego posla* [Notes of a Mock Ambassador] (Moscow) (2001), p. 182; Shalev, pgs. 167–168.

36. Hirst & Beeson, p. 127; Gamasy, *The October War* (The American University in Cairo Press, Cairo) (1989), p. 140; Heikal, *Autumn of Fury*, p. 56.

37. Shazly, p. 125; Heikal, *The Road*, p. 184.

38. Gamasy, pgs. 150 & 152; Shazly, pgs. 27, 83 & 126–129.

## Chapter 6: The Angel and the Noise

1. Kahneman, *Thinking Fast and Slow* (paperback edition) (Farrar, Straus & Giroux, New York) (2011), p. 277.

2. Zeira, *Milkhemet Yom HaKippurim, Mitoos Mul Metziut* [The Yom Kippur War: Fact versus Fiction] (Yediot Ahronot, Tel Aviv) (1993), p. 86; Heikal, *The Road to Ramadan* (Ballantine Books, New York) (1975), p. 7; *Pirkei Avos* [Ethics of Fathers], Chapter 5, Mishna 7; Bar-Yosef, *HaTzopheh Shenirdam* [The Watchman That Fell Asleep] (Zmora-Bitan Publishers, Ganei Aviv-Lod) (2001), p. 152.

3. *Yediot Ahronot, Hamosaf LeChag*, October 5, 2003, p. 26; Adan, *Al Shtay Gadot Suez* [On Both Banks of the Suez] (Edanim & Yediot Ahronot, Jerusalem) (1979), p. 63.

4. *Ma'ariv, Sofshavua*, April 18, 1997, p. 13.

5. Agranat Commission, Interim Report, Second Report (1974), p. 62.

6. Agranat Commission, Interim Report (Second Report), p. 389; Bar-Yosef, pgs. 115 & 117.

7. *Yediot Ahronot, 7 Yamim*, June 6, 2005, p. 26; Zamir, *B'aynayim Pakukhot* [With Open Eyes] (Kinneret, Zmora-Bitan, Dvir Publishing House, Or Yehuda) (2011), p. 130.

8. *Yediot Ahronot, 7 Yamim*, June 6, 2005, p. 26; Jeff Asher, "Spying Doesn't Pay— Unless You're Really Good At It," https://fivethirtyeight.com/features/spying -doesnt-pay-unless-youre-really-good-at-it/.

9. Bar-Joseph, *The Angel: The Egyptian Spy Who Saved Israel* (HarperCollins Publishers, New York) (2016), pgs. 7 & 14–15.

10. Zamir, p. 135; "World: Egypt: Sadat in the Saddle," *Time*, May 31, 1971; Mendes, writing in Bronstein (Editor), *Nitzakhon B'Svirut Nemookha* [The October 1973's Unlikely Victory] (Effi Melzter Inc., Israel) (2017), p. 30; Bar-Joseph, pgs. 91 & 96.

11. Zamir, pgs. 135–136 & 141.

12. Bar-Joseph, pgs. 25 & 29; Zamir, p. 141; Kirpichenko, *Razvedka: Litsa I Lichnosti* [Intelligence Service: Persona and Personalities], (Moscow) (1998), p. 108.

13. Zamir, p. 138; *Yediot Ahronot, 7 Yamim*, June 6, 2005, p. 26; Heikal, *Autumn of Fury* (Corgi Books, Transworld Publishers, London) (1983), p. 43; Kirpichenko, p. 121; Bar-Joseph, p. 50.

14. Zamir, p. 129; Bar-Joseph, p. 51.

15. Agranat Commission, Interim Report (1974), p. 19.

16. Agranat Commission, Interim Report (Second Report) (1974) (declassified January 1, 1995), p. 61.

17. Agranat Commission, Final Report (1975) (declassified January 1, 1995), p. 1212; Zeira, p. 68.

18. Shalev, *Kishalone V'Hatzlakha B'Hatra'ah* [Failure and Success in Alert] (Ma'arachot, Tel Aviv) (2006), p. 173; Zeira, p. 87.

19. Agranat Commission, Interim Report (Second Report) (1974), p. 50; Zeira, pgs. 86–88.

20. Agranat Commission, Interim Report (Secret Portion) (1974), p. 64.

21. Ze'evi, *HaHona'ah HaMitzrit* (The Egyptian Deception) (Schocken Books, Jerusalem & Tel Aviv) (1980), p. 30; Shazly, *The Crossing of Suez* (Third World Centre for Research and Publishing, London) (1980), p. 55.

22. *Yediot Ahronot, 7 Yamim*, September 25, 2020, p. 12; Zeira, p. 119; Bar-Joseph, pgs. 159–160.

23. Zamir, p. 121; Bar-Joseph, p. 167; Colonel Langotsky (ret.), *Milkhemet Yom Hakipurrim Hamikhdal Hamodi'ini, Ee Hafalat Hemtza'im Hameyukhadim* [Yom Kippur War, the Intelligence Failure, Failure to Employ the Extraordinary Measures], Presentation, October 2013, p. 6. The author is indebted to Colonel Langotsky for sharing the presentation.

24. Langotsky, p. 22; *Galili Testimony Before Agranat Commission*, February 13, 1974, pgs. 32–33, cited in Zohar (Editor), *40 Shana Akharay* [40 Years After] (Israel War Institute, Israel) (2014), p. 124.

25. Langotsky, p. 17; *Zeira Testimony Before Agranat Commission*, pgs. 686 & 1032, cited in Langotsky, p. 20.

26. *Ha'aretz Magazine*, March 3, 2006, p. 18; Bronstein (Editor), *Nitzakhon B'Svirut Nemookha* [The October 1973's Unlikely Victory] (Effi Melzter Inc., Israel) (2017), p. 140.

27. Langotsky, p. 13; Bronstein, p. 151, endnote 114.

28. Ehud Barak, Interview on Yoel Ben Porat on YouTube, June, 2021.
29. Braun, *Moshe Dayan B'Milkhemet Yom HaKippurim* [Moshe Dayan in the Yom Kippur War] (Edanim Publishers, Ltd., Yediot Ahronot) (1992), p. 33; Arbel & Ne'eman, p. 183.
30. Zeira, pgs. 87–88 & 92.
31. Golan & Shai (Editors), *Milkhama Hayom* [War Today] (Ma'arakhot, Israel) (2003), p. 304, fn. 10; Asher, *HaSurim Al Hagderot* [The Syrians Are on the Fences] (Ma'arachot, Tel Aviv) (2008), p. 23; Braun, p. 33; Gordon, *30 Sha'ot B'October* [30 Hours in October] (Ma'ariv Book Guild, Tel Aviv) (2008), p. 164; Arbel & Ne'eman, p. 166.
32. Bar-Yosef, pgs. 235–236; Gordon, p. 187; Zeira, p. 134.
33. *Ha'aretz*, October 4, 2002, p. B3.
34. *Ha'aretz*, October 4, 2002, p. B3; Asher, p. 45.
35. Shazly, *The Crossing of Suez*, p. 136; Seale, *Asad: The Struggle for the Middle East* (University of California Press, Berkeley) (1988), p. 194.
36. Shazly, *The Crossing of Suez*, p. 136; Seale, *Asad*, p. 194; Friedman, *From Beirut to Jerusalem* (Farrar Straus Giroux, New York) (1989), p. 104; Sadat, *In Search*, p. 242.
37. Sadat, *In Search*, p. 245; Zamir, p. 112.
38. Sadat, *In Search*, p. 245.
39. *Yediot Ahronot, HaMosaf LeChag*, October 10, 2003, p. 10; Shazly, p. 32.
40. Shalev, p. 109; *Ha'aretz, Gilyon Rosh Hashana*, September 26, 2003, p. B4.
41. Interview of Dudu Halevi in *Ma'ariv*, October 23, 1998, cited in Shalev, p. 109; Shalev, pgs. 110–112; Arbel & Ne'eman, pgs. 190–191; *Ma'ariv, Mosaf Rosh Hashana*, September 26, 2003, pgs. 3–6; Bar-Yosef, pgs. 243 & 245; *Yediot Ahronot, 7 Yamim*, October 5, 2001, p. 14; Bartov, *Dado I* [Daddo] (Dvir Publishing House, Or Yehuda) (2002), p. 309.
42. Shazly, *The Arab Military Option* (American Mideast Research, San Francisco) (1986), pgs. 37, 39, 210–211; Golan & Shai, (Editors) *Milkhama Hayom*, p. 293; *Milkhemet Yom Hakippuring UliKakhehah*, p. 99; Dayan, *Avnei Derekh* [Milestones] (Edanim Publishers & Dvir Publishing House, Jerusalem and Tel Aviv) (1976), p. 593; Gordon, p. 163.
43. Sakal, *Hasadir Yivlome?* [The Regulars Will Hold?] (Ma'ariv Book Guild, Tel Aviv) (2011), p. 104; Shalev, p. 193.
44. Shalev, p. 187; Agranat Commission, Interim Report (Second Report), p. 414; Bar-Yosef, p. 158.
45. Langotsky, p. 13; *Yediot Ahronot, 7 Yamim*, September 25, 2020, pgs. 12–13.
46. *Yediot Ahronot, 7 Yamim*, September 25, 2020, p. 14.
47. Agranat Commission, Secret Report, April 1, 1974, p. 50.
48. Langotsky, p. 16; Langotsky Interview on YouTube, www.youtube.com/watch?v=3H8l87zwvLE; *Ma'ariv Sofshavua*, July 13, 2018, p. 29.
49. *Ha'aretz Magazine*, March 3, 2006, p. 18; Yossi Langutsky, Israel Channel 1 Television, January 6, 2014.
50. Langotsky, pgs. 13–15 & 23; Bronstein, p. 141; Agranat Commission, Interim Report, p. 34; Bartov, p. 322; Bar-Yosef, p. 270; Arbel & Ne'eman, p. 289, fn. 2; *Yediot Ahronot, Hamosaf LeShabbat*, October 24, 2003, p. 16.
51. *Ma'ariv, Mosaf Shabbat*, March 18, 2005, pgs. 12–13; Bartov, p. 331; Israelyan, *Inside the Kremlin During the Yom Kippur War* (Penn State University Press, University Park) (1995), p. 3.
52. Zeira, p. 144; Bergman & Meltzer, *Milkhemet Yom Kippur Zman Emet* [The Yom

Kippur War—Moment of Truth] (Miskal-Yediot Ahronot Books & Chemed Books) (2003), p. 33; Langotsky Interview on YouTube, www.youtube.com/watch ?v=3H8l87zwvLE; Bronstein, p. 141.

53. Agranat Commission, Additional Materials to Interim Report, April 1, 1974, p. 21; Braun, pgs. 57–59; Agranat Commission, Interim Report, p. 34; Bartov, *Dado I*, p. 322; Bar-Yosef, p. 270; Arbel & Ne'eman, p. 289, fn. 2; *Yediot Ahronot, Hamosaf LeShabbat*, October 24, 2003, p. 16; Langotsky, p. 23.

54. Agranat Commission, Additional Materials to Interim Report, April 1, 1974, pgs. 22 & 24; Langotsky, p. 16.

55. Dayan, p. 732; Bartov, p. 327.

56. *Yediot Ahronot, Hamosaf LeShabbat*, October 10, 2021, p. 22; *Yediot Ahronot Mosaf HaChag*, April 3, 2015, p. 18; Shalev, p. 194; Bar-Joseph, p. 209; Barkai, *B'Shem Shamayim* [For Heaven's Sake] (Kinneret, Zmora-Bitan, Dvir Publishing House, Or Yehuda) (2013), p. 97.

57. Zamir, pgs. 146–147; *Ma'ariv, Sofshavua*, December 28, 2007, p. 10.

58. Arbel & Ne'eman, p. 234; Bar-Joseph, p. 211.

59. Zamir, p. 150.

**Chapter 7: Judgment Day**

1. Ashkenazi, *HaErev B'shesh Tifrotz Milkhama* [Today at Six War Will Break Out] (Hakibbutz Hameukhad, Tel Aviv) (2003), p. 55.

2. Bartov, *Dado, 48 Shana V'ode 20 Yamim II* [Dado, 48 Years and Another 20 Days, Volume II] (Dvir Publishing House, Or Yehudah) (2002), p. 343; *Yediot Ahronot, Mosaf HaChag*, October 10, 2003, p. 10.

3. Bergman & Meltzer, *Milkhemet Yom Kippur Zman Emet* [The Yom Kippur War—Moment of Truth] (Miskal-Yediot Ahronot Books & Chemed Books) (2003), p. 42.

4. Zamir, *B'aynayim Pakukhot* [With Open Eyes] (Kinneret, Zmora-Bitan, Dvir Publishing House, Or Yehuda) (2011), p. 150.

5. Bartov, *Dado II*, p. 367; Agranat Commission, Interim Report (Second Report), p. 137; Gordon, *30 Sha'ot B'October* [30 Hours in October] (Ma'ariv Book Guild, Tel Aviv) (2008), p. 244.

6. Dayan, *Avnei Derekh* [Milestones] (Edanim Publishers & Dvir Publishing House, Jerusalem and Tel Aviv) (1976), p. 575; Bartov, *Dado II*, p. 370.

7. Kipnes, *HaDerekh L'Milkhama 1973* [The Path to War 1973] (Kinneret, Zmora-Bitan, Dvir Publishing House, Or Yehuda) (2012), p. 126; Dayan, p. 575; Braun, *Moshe Dayan B'Milkhemet Yom HaKippurim* [Moshe Dayan in the Yom Kippur War] (Edanim Publishers, Ltd., Yediot Ahronot) (1992), p. 68; Langotsky, *Milkhemet Yom Hakipurrim Hamikhdal Hamodi'ini, Ee Hafalat Hemtza'im Hameyukhadim* [Yom Kippur War, the Intelligence Failure, Failure to Employ the Extraordinary Measures], Presentation, October 2013, p. 16.

8. Agranat Commission, Partial Report, p. 47; Bar-Yosef, *HaTzopheh Shenirdam* [The Watchman That Fell Asleep] (Zmora-Bitan Publishers, Ganei Aviv-Lod) (2001), p. 346.

9. Agranat Commission, Interim Report (Second Report), pgs. 42–43; Zeira, *Milkhemet Yom HaKippurim, Mitoos Mul Metziut* [The Yom Kippur War: Fact versus Fiction] (Yediot Ahronot, Tel Aviv) (1993), p. 212; Kipnes, p. 238.

10. Dayan, p. 480; Agranat Commission, Interim Report (Second Report), pgs. 36–38; Bar-Yosef, p. 346.

11. Haver, *Hayom Tifrotz Milkhama* [Today War Will Break Out] (Edanim Publishers & Yediot Ahronot) (1987), pgs. 24–25.
12. Yisraeli, *Megilat Chaim* [Chaim Yisraeli, A Life Story] (Miskal-Yediot Ahronot Books & Chemed Books, Tel Aviv) (2005), pgs. 247–248; Zamir, p. 109.
13. Agranat Commission, Interim Report (Second Report), p. 43.
14. Agranat Commission, Interim Report, p. 50; Haver, p. 28.
15. Agranat Commission, Interim Report (Second Report), p. 43; Sakal, *Hasadir Yivlome?* [The Regulars Will Hold?] (Ma'ariv Book Guild, Tel Aviv) (2011), p. 118.
16. Agranat Commission, Interim Report (Second Report), p. 31.
17. Gordon, p. 142; Braun, p. 28.
18. Rabin, *Pinkas II* (Ma'ariv Books, Tel Aviv) (1979), p. 380; Kipnes, p. 61.
19. Henry A. Kissinger, https://nsarchive2.gwu.edu/NSAEBB/NSAEBB98/octwar -10.pdf (declassified November 3, 2000); Agranat Commission, Interim Report (Second Report), p. 42.
20. Langotsky, p. 16; Bar-Yosef, p. 286; Eilam, *Eidut Min Habor* [Testimony from the Bunker] (Miskal—Yediot Ahronot & Chemed Books, Israel) (2013), p. 39.
21. Kfir & Dor, *Masah Chaim* [Chaim Erez—A Journey of Life] (Kinneret, Zmora-Bitan, Dvir Publishing House, Hevel Modi'in) (2017), pgs. 191–192; Regev, *Khatzi HeDerekh L'Kaheer* [Half Way to Cairo] (Tavliti Publishers, Bnei Brak) (2012), p. 40.
22. Agranat Commission, Full Report (1975), pgs. 22 & 38; Regev, *Khatzi HeDerekh*, p. 36; *Yediot Ahronot, Yom Kippur*, September 27, 2020, p. 4; Sharon, *Warrior, The Autobiography of Ariel Sharon* (Simon & Schuster, New York) (1989), p. 292.
23. Yisraeli, p. 337.
24. Sharon, *Warrior*, pgs. 272–273; Bloom & Hefez, *HaRoeh* [The Shepherd] (Miskal—Yediot Achornot Books & Chemed Books, Tel Aviv) (2005), p. 222.
25. Tevet, *Khasufim*, pgs. 58, 147–148; *Yediot Ahronot, Hamosaf LeShabbat*, October 4, 1991, p. 3.
26. Tevet, p. 148
27. Reshef, *Lo Nekhdal! Khativah 14 B'Milkhemet Yom HaKippurim* [We Will Never Cease! The 14th Brigade in the Yom Kippur War] (Dvir Publishing House, Jerusalem and Tel Aviv) (2013), p. 54; Kfir & Dor, *Yanush* [Yanush] (Kinneret, Zmora-Bitan, Dvir Publishing House, Hevel Modi'in) (2017), pgs. 60–61; *Ma'ariv, Sofshavua*, p. 20.
28. Agranat Commission, Interim Report (Second Report), p. 44; *Yediot Ahronot, Hamosaf LeShabbat*, October 11, 1992, p. 5.
29. *BaMachane*, October 3, 2003, p. 9; Bar-Yosef, p. 360.
30. Ashkenazi, pgs. 17, 34–35 & 41; *Yediot Ahronot, 7 Yamim*, October 6, 2000, p. 37.
31. Ashkenazi, pgs. 48 & 51.
32. *Yediot Ahronot, HaMosaf LeShabbat*, September 10, 2021, p. 22; Ashkenazi, p. 54.
33. Ashkenazi, pgs. 60 & 61.
34. Zohar, *40 Shana Akharei* [40 Years After] (Israel War Institute, Tel Aviv) (2013), p. 401; *Ha'aretz*, August 8, 2003, p. 1; *Ma'ariv, Mosaf Shabbat*, August 15, 2003, p. 8; Arad & Laskov, *Hilukh Khozer* [A Walk Back] (Israel Defense Ministry) (2003), p. 71; Kfir, *Akhai Giboray HaTi'alah* [My Brothers, the Heroes of the Canal] (Miskal—Yediot Ahronot & Chemed Books, Tel Aviv) (2003), p. 40.
35. Barkai, *Al Blimah* [On the Edge] (Ma'ariv Book Guild, Tel Aviv) (2009), p. 101;

Asher, *HaSurim Al Hagderot* [The Syrians Are on the Fences] (Ma'arachot, Tel Aviv) (2008), p. 89.

36. *Yediot Ahronot, Hamosaf LeChag*, October 5, 2003, p. 4; Barkai, p. 153.

37. Heikal, *The Road to Ramadan* (Ballantine Books, New York) (1975), p. 5; Hirst & Beeson, *Sadat* (Faber & Faber, Ltd., London) (1982), p. 26; *Yediot Ahronot*, October 10, 2003, p. 11; Zeira, p. 116.

38. Heikal, *Autumn of Fury*, p. 60; Shazly, *The Crossing of Suez* (Third World Centre for Research and Publishing, London) (1980), pgs. 40 & 152.

39. Shazly, pgs. 38 & 42.

40. Shazly, pgs. 153 & 157; *Milkhamot Yisroel* (Mercaz HaHazbarah, Jerusalem) (1984), p. 9; Golan & Shai (Editors), *Milkhama Hayom* [War Today] (Ma'arakhot, Israel) (2003), p. 253, fn. 15; *Ma'ariv, Hamosaf LeShabbat*, October 25, 1974, p. 11.

41. Sakal, p. 114.

42. *Milkhemet Yom HaKippurim UleKakheha*, p. 181; Shazly, p. 157; Heikal, *Autumn of Fury*, p. 59.

43. Reshef, p. 71; Dayan, p. 583.

44. Weizman, *Lekha*, pgs. 327–328. A long list of senior Israeli officers who agreed with Weizman can be found in Bar-Yosef, *Milkhama Mishelo* [A War of Its Own] (Kinneret, Zmora, Dvir Publishing House, Israel) (2021), p. 379, fn 10.

45. *HaTzofeh, Hashavua*, October 3, 2003, p. 9; Braun, p. 81; Agranat Commission, Interim Report (Second Report), pgs. 332–333.

46. Bronstein (Editor), *Nitzakhon B'Svirut Nemookha* [The October 1973's Unlikely Victory] (Effi Melzter Inc., Israel) (2017), p. 157.

47. Gordon, pgs. 241 & 264.

48. Gordon, p. 149.

49. Interview with Colonel Yitzchak David (ret.), YouTube, March 9, 2021.

50. Gordon, pgs. 264–265; *Ma'ariv Mosaf Shabbat*, October 3, 2008, p. 12; Barkai, *B'Shem Shamayim* [For Heaven's Sake] (Kinneret, Zmora-Bitan, Dvir Publishing House, Or Yehuda) (2013), p. 141; *Ha'aretz*, October 3, 2008, p. B7.

51. Gordon, p. 285; Barkai, p. 151.

52. Barkai, p. 152; Gordon, p. 285.

53. Gordon, p. 262.

54. Halutz, *B'Govah Aynayim* [Straightforward] (Yediot Ahronot, Chemed Books, Tel Aviv) (2010), p. 81; interview with Colonel Yitzchak David (ret.), YouTube, March 9, 2021.

55. Interview with Colonel Yitzchak David (ret.), YouTube, March 9, 2021; Gordon, p. 487.

56. Barkai, p. 158; Gordon, pgs. 274–275, 279 & 487; Barkai, p. 187; Wallach, *Atlas Carta L'Toldot Medinat Yisroel Asor Shlishi* [Carta's Atlas of Israel The Third Decade 1971–1981] (Carta, Jerusalem) (1983), p. 115.

57. Agranat Commission, Interim Report (Second Report), p. 285.

58. Gordon, p. 286.

**Chapter 8: "The Third Temple Is at Risk"**

1. Givati, *Ha'Ma'aracha B'Khermon* [The Hermon Mountain Operation] (Modan Publishing House Ltd., Ben Shemen) (2015), pgs. 25–27 & 38; Mickelson & Meltzer (Editors), *Milkhemet*, p. 256; Kfir & Dor, *Revah L'Shmona* [At a Quarter to Eight] (Yediot Ahronot, Sifrei Chemed, Rishon Lezion) (2019), pgs. 161–162.

2. Givati, pgs. 39, 50–51, 53, 56, 57.

3. Givati, pgs. 82 & 98.
4. Givati, pgs. 111–114.
5. Givati, pgs. 115, 121–123 & 172.
6. Givati, pgs. 168–169.
7. BArch, MfS, AIM Nr. 10825/91 4; interview with Oleksei Ivashin, February 8, 2022.
8. Agranat Commission, Final Report (1975), p. 965; Malovany, *Milkhemet Hashikhrur Shel October 1973, HaKhazit Hasurit* [The War of Liberation of October 1973 on the Syrian Front] (Israel War Institute, Israel) (2021), p. 140; Barkai, *Al Blimah* [On the Edge] (Ma'ariv Book Guild, Tel Aviv) (2009), pgs. 29–30 & 216; The Editors of Encyclopaedia Britannica, Golan Heights, www.britannica.com /place/Golan-Heights.
9. Malovany, p. 174.
10. Malovany, p. 142; *Bamachane*, October 3, 2003, p. 26; Nir, *Natke HaKatzin HaPatzua SheKhazar L'sdeh HaKrav* [Natke, The Wounded Officer that Returned to the Battlefield] (Miskal-Yediot Ahronot Books & Chemed Books, Tel Aviv) (2010), pgs. 123–124; Zohar, *40 Shana Akharei* [40 Years After] (Israel War Institute, Tel Aviv) (2013), p. 401; Malovany, pgs. 186–187.
11. Agranat Commission, Interim Report (Second report), pgs. 169 & 303; see also Agranat Commission, Final Report (1975), p. 133.
12. Agranat Commission, Interim Report (Second report), pgs. 186, 197 & 200.
13. Malovany, pgs. 142–143.
14. Agranat Commission, Interim Report (Second report), pgs. 237 & 288; Agranat Commission, Final Report (1975), p. 967; Bartov, *Dado, 48 Shana V'ode 20 Yamim II* [Dado, 48 Years and Another 20 Days, Volume II] (Dvir Publishing House, Or Yehuda) (2002), p. 390.
15. Agranat Commission, Final Report (1975) (Second report, Declassified in 2012), p. 912; Agranat Commission, Interim Report (Second report), p. 109.
16. Agranat Commission, Final Report (1975), pgs. 916, 944, & 948; Barkai, pgs. 137 & 146.
17. Agranat Commission, Interim Report (Second report), p. 318; Agranat Commission, Final Report (1975) (Second report, Declassified in 2012), pgs. 1216–1217.
18. Agranat Commission, Interim Report (Second report), pgs. 320 & 321.
19. Agranat Commission, Interim Report (Second report), p. 285 (there is a typo in the report that resulted in there being two page 285s and no page 286. The citation is taken from the first page 285).
20. Agranat Commission, Interim Report (Second report), p. 226.
21. Ashkenazi, *HaErev B'shesh Tifrotz Milkhama* [Today at Six War Will Break Out] (Hakibbutz Hameukhad, Tel Aviv) (2003), p. 81.
22. Sakal, *Hasadir Yivlome?* [The Regulars Will Hold?] (Ma'ariv Book Guild, Tel Aviv) (2011), pgs. 344–356; Mickelson & Meltzer (Editors), *Milkhemet*, p. 107; Bar-Yosef, pgs. 121 & 395–396.
23. Bar-Tov, *Dado II*, p. 376.
24. Sakal, pgs. 159, 162–163; Even & Maoz, *B'Nikudat Hacoved, Matzbiut B'Khazit HaTealah B'Milkhemet Yom HaKippurim* [At the Decisive Point, Generalship in the Yom Kippur War in the Canal Front] (Ma'arachot) (2012), pgs. 26–27; Golan & Shai (Editors), *Milkhama Hayom*, p. 226.
25. Bartov, p. 397; Braun, *Moshe Dayan B'Milkhemet Yom HaKippurim* [Moshe

Dayan in the Yom Kippur War] (Edanim Publishers, Ltd., Yediot Ahronot) (1992), p. 87; Even & Maoz, p. 27.

26. Sakal, pgs. 46 & 148–149; Bartov, p. 376.
27. Hirst & Beeson, *Sadat* (Faber & Faber, Ltd., London) (1982), p. 26.
28. Thornton, *Asymmetric Warfare: Threat and Response in the 21st Century* (U.S. Naval War College, Newport) (2007), p. 82.
29. Greengold, *Koach Tzvika* [Force Tzvika] (Modan Publishing House, Moshav Ben-Shemen) (2008), p. 51.
30. Catton, *The Civil War* (American Heritage Press, New York) (1971), pgs. 160–161; Sakal, p. 110; Agranat Commission, Final Report (1975), p. 1443; Kfir, *Akhai Giboray HaTi'alah* [My Brothers, the Heroes of the Canal] (Miskal—Yediot Ahronot & Chemed Books, Tel Aviv) (2003), p. 27.
31. Sakal, pgs. 169 & 171; Golan & Shai (Editors), p. 214; Reshef, *Lo Nekhdal! Khativah 14 B'Milkhemet Yom HaKippurim* [We Will Never Cease! The 14th Brigade in the Yom Kippur War] (Dvir Publishing House, Jerusalem and Tel Aviv) (2013), p. 126.
32. Braun, p. 94.
33. Bartov, p. 418.
34. Barkai, p. 192.
35. Barkai, pgs. 254–255; Malovany, p. 145; Givati, p. 170; Agranat Commission, Final Report (1975), pgs. 1010 & 1062.
36. Malovany, p. 147; Agranat Commission, Final Report (1975), p. 962; Barkai, p. 204.
37. Agranat Commission, Final Report (1975), p. 963; Barkai, pgs. 193, 218, 255, 274.
38. Clausewitz, *On War* (U.S. Army War College, Carlisle) (1832), Book 8, Chapter 4.
39. Arad & Laskov, *Hilukh Khozer* [A Walk Back] (Israel Defense Ministry) (2003), p. 154; Barkai, p. 270.
40. Greengold, pgs. 59–60; Barkai, p. 271.
41. Barkai, p. 289; Greengold, p. 83; Agranat Commission, Final Report (1975), p. 998.
42. Barkai, p. 233; Malovany, p. 423.
43. Barkai, pgs. 257 & 287; *Ma'ariv, Mosaf Shabbat*, October 22, 2004, pgs. 20–21; *Halokhem*, October 2004, p. 20.
44. Greengold, pgs. 84, 88 & 91.
45. Barkai, p. 295; Sharon, *Shafuy B'Damesek* [Sane in Damascus] (Orly Levy, Israel) (2005), p. 22; *Ma'ariv, Mosaf Yom Hakippurim*, October 12, 2005, p. 14.
46. Sharon, pgs. 22–26; Greengold, pgs. 104–106; Barkai, pgs. 302–303; *Ma'ariv, Mosaf Shabbat*, October 22, 2004, p. 21.
47. Bartov, p. 405; Agranat Commission, Final Report (1975), p. 1018; Braun, p. 92; Bar-Yosef, *Milkhama*, p. 129.
48. Agranat Commission, Final Report (1975), p. 982; Asher, *HaSurim Al Hagderot* [The Syrians Are on the Fences] (Ma'arachot, Tel Aviv) (2008), p. 97; Kfir & Dor, *Yanush* [Yanush] (Kinneret, Zmora-Bitan, Dvir Publishing House, Hevel Modi'in) (2017), pgs. 127–128; Barkai, pgs. 228, 258 & 321.
49. Braun, p. 92; *Yediot Ahronot, 7 Yamim*, October 6, 1989, pgs. 9 & 11; *Ma'ariv, Sofshavua*, July 28, 2006, p. 17.
50. Kfir & Dor, p. 122; Agranat Commission, Final Report (1975), p. 911.
51. Bar-Yosef, *HaTzopheh Shenirdam* [The Watchman That Fell Asleep] (Zmora-Bitan Publishers, Ganei Aviv-Lod) (2001), p. 389; Braun, p. 92; Bartov, p. 407; *Ma'ariv Sofshavua*, September 17, 2010, p. 16.

52. Dayan, *Avnei Derekh* [Milestones] (Edanim Publishers & Dvir Publishing House, Jerusalem and Tel Aviv) (1976), p. 598; Shushar, *Sikhot im Rehavam Ze'evi, Ghandi* [Conversations with Rehavam Ze'evi, Ghandi] (Yediot Ahronot, Chemed Books, Tel Aviv) (2001), p. 169.

**Chapter 9: Syrians at the Gate**
1. Joachim von Puttkamer, Dissidence—Doubt—Creativity, www.eurozine.com /dissidence-doubt-creativity/.
2. Bar-Yosef, *Milkhama Mishelo* [A War of Its Own] (Kinneret, Zmora, Dvir Publishing House, Israel) (2021), pgs. 67–69.
3. Bar-Yosef, *Milkhama*, p. 124.
4. Gordon, *30 Sha'ot B'October* [30 Hours in October] (Ma'ariv Book Guild, Tel Aviv) (2008), p. 154; Halutz, *B'Govah Aynayim* [Straightforward] (Miskal—Yediot Ahronot, Chemed Books, Tel Aviv) (2010), p. 90; Bar-Yosef, *Milkhama*, pgs. 125–126; Spector, *Ram U'Barur* [Loud and Clear] (Miskal—Yediot Ahronot, Chemed Books, Tel Aviv) (2008), p. 231.
5. Agranat Commission, Interim Report (Second report), (1974), p. 219; Halutz, pgs. 88–89; Spector, p. 244; Bar-Yosef, *Milkhama*, p. 128.
6. Agranat Commission, Final Report (1975), pgs. 1021 & 1024; Braun, *Moshe Dayan B'Milkhemet Yom HaKippurim* [Moshe Dayan in the Yom Kippur War] (Edanim Publishers, Ltd., Yediot Ahronot) (1992), p. 93.
7. Herzog, *The War of Atonement* (Little, Brown & Co., Boston) (1975), p. 104; Bronstein (Editor), *Nitzakhon B'Svirut Nemookha* [The October 1973's Unlikely Victory] (Effi Melzter Inc., Israel) (2017), p. 182; interview with a former Syrian officer (identity with the author), December 29, 2020.
8. Agranat Commission, Final Report (1975), pgs. 240 & 1075; Bartov, *Dado, 48 Shana V'ode 20 Yamim II* [Dado, 48 Years and Another 20 Days, Volume II] (Dvir Publishing House, Or Yehuda) (2002), p. 408.
9. Gordon, pgs. 319 & 324; Bar-Yosef, *Milkhama*, p. 403, fn. 68; *Ma'ariv, Sofshavua*, September 17, 2010, p. 14; Agranat Commission, Final Report (1975), p. 1074.
10. Gordon, p. 326.
11. Halutz, p. 89; Spector, p. 245; Gordon, p. 348; Barkai, *B'Shem Shamayim* [For Heaven's Sake] (Kinneret, Zmora-Bitan, Dvir Publishing House, Or Yehuda) (2013), p. 225; Bar-Yosef, *Milkhama*, p. 140.
12. Gordon, p. 350; Bar-Yosef, *Milkhama*, p. 109.
13. Spector, p. 244; Tlass, *Mirat Hayati* [Reflections of My Life] (Damascus) (2004), Volume 3, pgs. 846–847, cited in Bar-Yosef, *Milkhama*, p. 149; Gordon, pgs. 335 & 329.
14. Gordon, p. 335; Barkai, p. 217; Bar-Yosef, *Milkhama*, p. 144. Gordon gives a slightly different version, saying that Elazar suggested carrying out Dougman 5, though he left the ultimate decision to Peled. Gordon, p. 324.
15. *Ma'ariv, Sofshavua*, September 17, 2010, p. 16.
16. *Yediot Ahronot, 7 Yamim*, June 14, 1985, p. 9; Agranat Commission, Final Report (1975), p. 1081; *Ma'ariv Mosaf Shabbat*, October 8, 2010, p. 15; Bartov, p. 409; Barkai, p. 332.
17. Agranat Commission, Final Report, Volume 1 (Jerusalem, 1975), p. 101; Halevi, *K'Neged Kol HaSikuyim, Aluf Mussa Peled* [Against All Odds, General Mussa Peled] (Modan Publishing House, Moshav Ben-Shemen) (2019), p. 212.
18. Halevi, p. 214.
19. Agranat Commission, Final Report (1975), p. 133; Herzog, p. 115; Bar-Yosef,

*HaTzopheh Shenirdam* [The Watchman That Fell Asleep] (Zmora-Bitan Publishers, Ganei Aviv-Lod) (2001), p. 418; Agranat Commission, Final Report (1975), pgs. 1146, 1162 & 1196; Barkai, p. 338; Asher, *HaSurim Al Hagderot* [The Syrians Are on the Fences] (Ma'arachot, Tel Aviv) (2008), p. 122.

20. Agranat Commission, Final Report (1975), p. 1139; Kahalani, *Oze 77* [Oze 77] (Schocken Publishing House Ltd., Tel Aviv) (1975), pgs. 78–83.

21. Agranat Commission, Final Report (1975), pgs. 1001–1002, Malovany, *Milkhemet Hashikhrur Shel October 1973, HaKhazit Hasurit* [The War of Liberation of October 1973 on the Syrian Front] (Israel War Institute, Israel) (2021), p. 163.

22. Barkai, pgs. 349 & 373; Gordon, p. 328; Zohar, *40 Shanah Akharay* [40 Years After] (Israel War Institute, Tel Aviv) (2014), p. 527; Sakal, *Hasadir Yivlome?* [The Regulars Will Hold?] (Ma'ariv Book Guild, Tel Aviv) (2011), p. 375; Bartov, p. 410; Bar-Yosef, *Milkhama*, pgs. 154–156; Herzog, p. 101.

23. Halevi, p. 215; Agranat Commission, Final Report (1975), p. 1138.

24. Eitan, *Raful, Sipur Shel Khayal* [Raful, A Soldier's Story] (Ma'ariv Book, Tel Aviv) (1985), pgs. 20 & 98.

25. Barkai, p. 355; Eitan, p. 130.

26. Orr, *Eleh Ha'achim Shelee* [These Are My Brothers] (Miskal-Yediot Ahronot and Chemed Books, Tel Aviv) (2003), pgs. 25 & 81.

27. Greengold, *Koach Tzvika* [Force Tzvika] (Modan Publishing House, Moshav Ben-Shemen) (2008), pgs. 109 & 116; Barkai, pgs. 382–383.

28. Agranat Commission, Final Report (1975), pgs. 1089, 1093 & 1097.

29. Agranat Commission, Final Report (1975), p. 1101.

30. Orr, pgs. 84–85; Agranat Commission, Final Report (1975), p. 1101.

31. Barkai, p. 390; Tlass, p. 732, quoted in Malovany, p. 166.

32. Barkai, pgs. 394–395.

33. Orr, pgs. 22 & 89–103; Malovany, p. 163; Barkai, p. 408.

34. Asher, p. 130; Nir, *Natke HaKatzin HaPatzua SheKhazar L'sdeh HaKrav* [Natke, The Wounded Officer that Returned to the Battlefield] (Miskal-Yediot Ahronot Books & Chemed Books, Tel Aviv) (2010), p. 36; Barkai, p. 277.

35. Orr, p. 95; Greengold, pgs. 126–129; Agranat Commission, Final Report (1975), p. 1155.

36. Dayan, *Avnei Derekh* [Milestones] (Edanim Publishers & Dvir Publishing House, Jerusalem and Tel Aviv) (1976), p. 632; Israelyan, *Inside the Kremlin During the Yom Kippur War* (Pennsylvania State University Press, University Park) (1995), p. 46.

37. Malovany, p. 171.

38. Arad & Laskov, *Hilukh Khozer* [A Walk Back] (Israel Defense Ministry) (2003), pgs. 28 & 154.

39. Braun, p. 95; Agranat Commission, Final Report (1975), pgs. 229, 242, 278 & 341–342.

40. *Yediot Ahronot, 7 Yamim*, October 4, 2013, p. 11; *Ha'aretz Magazine*, October 29, 2010, p. 10.

41. *Yediot Ahronot, 7 Yamim*, October 4, 2013, p. 12.

42. *Ha'aretz*, July 27, 2007, p. B2.

**Chapter 10: *Mikhdal:* The Counterattack**

1. Joint Committee on the Investigation of the Pearl Harbor Attack Congress of the United States, Investigation of the Pearl Harbor Attack, www.ibiblio.org/pha /congress/Vol40.pdf, p. 282.

2. Shushar, *Sikhot im Rehavam Ze'evi, Ghandi* [Conversations with Rehavam Ze'evi, Ghandi] (Yediot Ahronot, Chemed Books, Tel Aviv) (2001), p. 169; Gonen, speaking on *Fifteen Years Since the Yom Kippur War*, Israeli Channel 1 Television, October 1988, quoted in Zohar, *40 Shanah Akharay* [40 Years After] (Israel War Institute, Tel Aviv) (2014), p. 425; Agranat Commission, Final Report (1975), pgs. 246 & 249; Bartov, *Dado, 48 Shana V'ode 20 Yamim II* [Dado, 48 Years and Another 20 Days, Volume II] (Dvir Publishing House, Or Yehuda) (2002), p. 423.

3. Agranat Commission, Final Report (1975), pgs. 221, 246, 250, 259; Bartov, p. 424; *Ma'ariv, Sofshavua*, December 28, 2007, p. 31; *Yediot Ahronot, 7 Laylot*, October 30, 2020, p. 4; *Yediot Ahronot, 7 Yamim*, February 8, 2008, p. 34; *Yediot Ahronot, 7 Yamim*, July 11, 2003, p. 42; Yisraeli, *Megilat Chaim* [Chaim Yisraeli, A Life Story] (Miskal-Yediot Ahronot Books & Chemed Books, Tel Aviv) (2005), p. 270; Bar-On, *Moshe Dayan, Korot Khayav 1915–1981* [Moshe Dayan, His Life and Times 1915–1981] (Am Oved Publishers, Tel Aviv) (2018), p. 281; Zohar, p. 432, fn. 100.

4. Agranat Commission, Final Report (1975), pgs. 185 & 188; Zohar, p. 430.

5. Zohar, p. 430, fn 91.

6. Spector, *Ram U'Barur* [Loud and Clear] (Yediot Ahronot, Sifrei Chemed) (2008), pgs. 247–249; Bronstein (Editor), *Nitzakhon B'Svirut Nemookha* [The October 1973's Unlikely Victory] (Effi Melzter Inc., Israel) (2017), p. 455.

7. Bar-Yosef, *Milkhama Mishelo* [A War of Its Own] (Kinneret, Zmora, Dvir Publishing House, Israel) (2021), p. 153; Gordon, *30 Sha'ot B'October* [30 Hours in October] (Ma'ariv Book Guild, Tel Aviv) (2008), p. 368.

8. Bartov, p. 426.

9. Agranat Commission, Interim Report (Second report), p. 108.

10. Agranat Commission, Final Report (1975), p. 256; Zohar, p. 420, fn 59.

11. Bar-Yosef, pgs. 162–163.

12. Agranat Commission, Final Report (1975), pgs. 24, 71, 74–75, 136, 155, 203, 206; Agranat Commission, Interim Report (Second report), p. 3.

13. Zamir, *B'aynayim Pakukhot* [With Open Eyes] (Kinneret, Zmora-Bitan, Dvir Publishing House, Jerusalem and Tel Aviv) (2011), p. 157; Zohar, p. 414.

14. Even & Maoz, *B'Nikudat Hacoved, Matzbiut B'Khazit HaTealah B'Milkhemet Yom HaKippurim* [At the Decisive Point, Generalship in the Yom Kippur War in the Canal Front] (Ma'arachot) (2012), p. 32; Sakal, *Hasadir, Yivlome?* [The Regulars Will Hold?] (Ma'ariv Book Guild, Tel Aviv) (2011), pgs. 207–208.

15. Agranat Commission, Final Report (1975), pgs. 246–251; Meir, *My Life* (G.P. Putnam's Sons, New York) (1975), p. 428.

16. Agranat Commission, Final Report (1975), pgs. 246–247; Bartov, pgs. 424–426.

17. Meir, p. 429. Braun says that the offer to resign occurred not on October 7, but on October 12. Braun, *Moshe Dayan B'Milkhemet Yom HaKippurim* [Moshe Dayan in the Yom Kippur War] (Edanim Publishers, Ltd., Yediot Ahronot) (1992), p. 167.

18. Golan & Shai (Editors), *Milkhama Hayom* [War Today] (Ma'arakhot, Israel) (2003), p. 206.

19. Agranat Commission, Final Report (1975), pgs. 274–275; Sakal, p. 110.

20. Agranat Commission, Final Report (1975), p. 277.

21. Bartov, p. 429; Bronstein, p. 197; Sharon, *Warrior, The Autobiography of Ariel Sharon* (Simon & Schuster, New York) (1989), p. 298; Agranat Commission, Final Report (1975), pgs. 265–266.

22. Agranat Commission, Final Report (1975), pgs. 283 & 321.
23. Agranat Commission, Final Report (1975), pgs. 329 & 519; Sakal, p. 210.
24. Agranat Commission, Final Report (1975), pgs. 520, 1220 & 1224; Even & Maoz, p. 60.
25. Sharon, p. 301; Agranat Commission, Final Report (1975), pgs. 346 & 553.
26. Agranat Commission, Final Report (1975), p. 303; Shamshi, *Sa'arah B'October* [Storm in October] (Ma'arachot, Israel) (1986), p. 22.
27. Agranat Commission, Final Report (1975), pgs. 347–349; Bronstein, pgs. 455 & 476–477.
28. Agranat Commission, Final Report (1975), pgs. 387–388.
29. Agranat Commission, Final Report (1975), p. 508.
30. Sakal, *Ki Milkhamta Ko Arukha* [A War That Is So Long] (Sakal, Israel) (2018), pgs. 325–326; Even & Maoz, p. 54; *Ma'ariv Mosaf Shabbat*, October 8, 2010, p. 14; Agranat Commission, Final Report (1975), pgs. 390, 397 & 495; Braun, p. 114; Bartov, pgs. 452–453; Dayan, *Avnei Derekh* [Milestones] (Edanim Publishers & Dvir Publishing House, Jerusalem and Tel Aviv) (1976), p. 602.
31. Sharon, p. 302; Agranat Commission, Final Report (1975), p. 770; Even & Maoz, p. 58.
32. Agranat Commission, Final Report (1975), pgs. 769–771; Wallach, *Atlas Carta L'Toldot Medinat Yisroel Asor Shlishi* [Carta's Atlas of Israel The Third Decade 1971–1981] (Carta, Jerusalem) (1983), p. 94.
33. Agranat Commission, Final Report (1975), p. 786.
34. Even & Maoz, p. 44; Sharon, p. 302; Agranat Commission, Final Report (1975), p. 777; Megiddo, *Hamutal UMakhshir Lo B'Yadaynu* [Hamutal and Makhshir Are Not in Our Hands] (Kinneret, Zmora, Dvir Publishing House, Israel) (2019), p. 51; Even & Maoz, pgs. 44–45.
35. Megiddo, p. 83; Agranat Commission, Final Report (1975), p. 791; Sharon, p. 302; Even & Maoz, p. 58; Agranat Commission, Final Report (1975), p. 775; Bronstein, p. 258.
36. Israel Center for the Yom Kippur War, https://kippur-center.gal-ed.co.il/Web/He/Medal/247.aspx?id=741.
37. Agranat Commission, Final Report (1975), pgs. 536 & 1344; Zaken, *Suez Ayno Stalingrad* [Suez Isn't Stalingrad] (Ma'arachot, Jerusalem) (2021), p. 48.
38. Shamshi, p. 24; Sakal, p. 236; Agranat Commission, Final Report (1975), pgs. 479, 526 & 529; *Yediot Ahronot, Hamosaf LeShabbat*, October 15, 1978, p. 6; Nir, *Natke, HaKatzin HaPatzua SheKhazar L'sdeh HaKrav* [Natke, The Wounded Officer That Returned to the Battlefield] (Miskal-Yediot Ahronot Books & Chemed Books, Tel Aviv) (2010), p. 137.
39. Agranat Commission, Final Report (1975), pgs. 770 & 778–785; *Hatzofeh Ha-shavua*, October 3, 2003, p. 5.
40. Sharon, p. 302; Megiddo, p. 42, citing Egyptian sources; Agranat Commission, Final Report (1975), p. 686; Adan, *Al Shtay Gadot Suez* [On Both Banks of the Suez] (Edanim & Yediot Ahronot, Jerusalem) (1979), p. 108.
41. Agranat Commission, Final Report (1975), p. 496; Even & Maoz, pgs. 50 & 58; Megiddo, pgs. 22, 27, 37, 42.
42. Megiddo, pgs. 42 & 54 (endnote 19), 77 & 118–119; Agranat Commission, Final Report (1975), pgs. 713 & 821–822.
43. *Yediot Ahronot, 7 Yamim*, January 13, 2006, p. 17.
44. Even & Maoz, p. 53.
45. Bar-Yosef, p. 153; *Yediot Ahronot*, August 2, 2002, p. 6.

**Chapter 11: Valleys of Tears**

1. *Ma'ariv Hamosaf LeShabbat*, October 11, 1992, p. 4; *Yediot Ahronot, Hamosaf Le-Shabbat*, October 8, 2010, p. 7; Bartov, *Dado, 48 Shana V'ode 20 Yamim II* [Dado, 48 Years and Another 20 Days, Volume II] (Dvir Publishing House, Or Yehuda) (2002), p. 477.

2. Dayan, *Avnei Derekh* [Milestones] (Edanim Publishers & Publishing House, Jerusalem and Tel Aviv) (1976), p. 609; Bartov, p. 752; but see, Medzini, *Golda Biographia Politit* [Golda, a Political Biography] (Chemed Books) (2008), pgs. 552 & 561; *Bamahane*, October 3, 2003, p. 10; *Yediot Ahronot, 7 Yamim*, December 5, 2008, p. 21.

3. Bar-On, *Moshe Dayan, Korot Khayav 1915–1981* [Moshe Dayan, His Life and Times 1915–1981] (Am Oved Publishers, Tel Aviv) (2018), p. 286.

4. Hersh, The Samson Option (Random House, New York) (1991), p. 237; *Yediot Ahronot, Hamosaf LeShabbat*, October 8, 2010, p. 7; Cohen, *HaTabu HaAkharon* [The Last Taboo] (Kinneret, Zmora-Bitan, Dvir Publishing House, Jerusalem and Tel Aviv) (2005), p. 52; *Yediot Ahronot, 7 Yamim*, October 4, 2013, p. 13; Bergman & Meltzer, *Milkhemet Yom Kippur Zman Emet* [The Yom Kippur War— Moment of Truth] (Miskal-Yediot Ahronot Books & Chemed Books, Tel Aviv) (2003), p. 138; Israel Government Transcript (IGT), October 9, 1973, p. 12.

5. Dayan, p. 609; Agranat Commission, Final Report (1975), p. 473; Bar-Yosef, *Milkhama Mishelo* [A War of Its Own] (Kinneret, Zmora, Dvir Publishing House, Israel) (2021) pgs. 192–193; Malovany, *Milkhemet Hashikhrur Shel October 1973, HaKhazit Hasurit* [The War of Liberation of October 1973 on the Syrian Front] (Israel War Institute, Israel) (2021), p. 429.

6. Bar-Yosef, p. 193; Agranat Commission, Final Report (1975), p. 473.

7. Bartov, p. 478; Bergman & Meltzer, p. 136.

8. Israelyan, *Inside the Kremlin During the Yom Kippur War* (Pennsylvania State University Press, University Park, Pennsylvania) (1995), p. 14.

9. Israelyan, p. 43; Dayan, p. 632; interview with Oleksei Ivashin, Kiev, January 2022.

10. Israelyan, pgs. 31, 32 & 39.

11. Sadat, *In Search*, p. 254; Dobrynin, *Sugubo Doveritelno. Posol V Vashingtone Pre Shesti Prezidentakh SSHA (1962–1986)* [Absolutely Confidential. Ambassador in Washington During the Rule of Six Presidents of the U.S.A. (1962–1986)] (Moscow) (1997), p. 269; Israelyan, pgs. 40 & 47; Heikal, *The Road to Ramadan* (Ballantine Books, New York) (1975), p. 5; Hirst & Beeson, *Sadat* (Faber & Faber, Ltd., London) (1982), p. 217.

12. Malovany, p. 175.

13. Malovany, p. 175.

14. Sahar, *Ad K'Tzeh Hayekholet* [To the Utmost Ability] (Modan Publishing House, Moshav Ben-Shemen) (2013), p. 116.

15. Bolger, *Why We Lost: A General's Inside Account of the Iraq & Afghanistan Wars* (Houghton Mifflin Harcourt, New York) (2014), p. 126; Barkai, *Al Blimah* [On the Edge] (Ma'ariv Book Guild, Tel Aviv) (2009), pgs. 540–542; author's notes; Greengold, *Koach Tzvika* [Force Tzvika] (Modan Publishing House, Moshav Ben-Shemen) (2008), p. 115.

16. Halevy, *K'Neged Kol HaSeekuyim* [Against All Odds] (Modan Publishing House, Ben Shemen) (2019), pgs. 233 & 235–236; Arad & Laskov, *Hilukh Khozer* [A Walk Back] (Israel Defense Ministry) (2003), p. 168.

17. Peled, *Ish Tzavah* [Soldier] (Ma'ariv Book Guild, Tel Aviv) (1993), p. 179.

18. Peled, p. 165.
19. Peled, p. 168.
20. Arad & Laskov, pgs. 142–143; *Yediot Ahronot, 7 Yamim*, October 3, 2003, pgs. 24–26 & 51.
21. Peled, p. 173; Malovany, p. 198.
22. Peled, p. 174; Halevy, p. 225.
23. Malovany, p. 191; Kfir & Dor, *Yanush* [Yanush] (Kinneret, Zmora-Bitan, Dvir Publishing House, Jerusalem and Tel Aviv) (Hevel Modi'in) (2017), p. 154; Orr, *Eleh Ha'achim Shelee* [These Are My Brothers] (Miskal-Yediot Ahronot and Chemed Books, Tel Aviv) (2003), p. 143; Wallach, *Atlas Carta L'Toldot Medinat Yisroel Asor Shlishi* [Carta's Atlas of Israel The Third Decade 1971–1981] (Carta, Jerusalem) (1983), p. 59.
24. Orr, p. 148; Malovany, pgs. 186–189, relying on Syrian records. Bar-Yosef has slightly different figures, relying on Israeli records. Bar-Yosef, p. 197.
25. Orr, pgs. 143 & 145.
26. Orr, pgs. 144 & 146; Peled, p. 174.
27. Peled, pgs. 172–174.
28. Arnon Lavoshin, YouTube, December 25, 2018.
29. Spector, *Ram U'Barur* [Loud and Clear] (Yediot Ahronot, Sifrei Chemed, Israel) (2008), pgs. 253 & 254.
30. Arnon Lavoshin, YouTube, December 25, 2018; Arad & Laskov, p. 215.
31. Arad & Laskov, pgs. 216 & 219–220; Arnon Lavoshin, YouTube, December 25, 2018; Bar-Yosef, p. 195.
32. Arad & Laskov, pgs. 207 & 220; Arnon Lavoshin, YouTube, December 25, 2018.
33. Bar-Yosef, p. 195.
34. Arnon Lavoshin, YouTube, December 25, 2018.
35. Spector, pgs. 255 & 259.
36. Spector, p. 260.
37. Peled, p. 174; Halevy, *K'Neged*, p. 241; Bar-Yosef, p. 197.
38. Sahar, *Ad K'Tzeh*, p. 118; Kfir & Dor, p. 155.
39. Barkai, p. 542; Sahar, p. 117; Malovany, p. 184.
40. Kfir & Dor, pgs. 10 & 65.
41. Sahar, pgs. 117, 118 & 120.
42. Sahar, p. 118; Kfir & Dor, p. 157; Bronstein (Editor), *Nitzakhon B'Svirut Nemookha* [The October 1973's Unlikely Victory] (Effi Melzter Inc., Israel) (2017), p. 398; General Aryeh Mizrahi, *HaYekholet L'Kroe Haytev et HaKrav* [The Ability to Properly Read the Battle], kippur-center.org.
43. General Aryeh Mizrahi, *HaYekholet*; Sahar, p. 125.
44. Kfir & Dor, p. 158; Kahalani, *Oze 77* [Oze 77] (Schocken Publishing House Ltd., Tel Aviv) (1975), p. 115; *Yediot Ahronot, Hamosaf LeShabbat*, September 27, 2020, p. 27.
45. Kahalani, pgs. 116–117.
46. Kfir & Dor, p. 162; Eitan, *Raful, Sipur Shel Khayal* [Raful, A Soldier's Story] (Ma'ariv Book Guild, Tel Aviv) (1985), p. 134.
47. Eitan, pgs. 134–135; Sahar, 128–129.
48. Eitan, p. 135; Hofi in *Milkhemet*, pgs. 94–95.
49. *Ma'ariv*, September 24, 1993, p. 16; Malovany, p. 194.
50. Malovany, p. 427.
51. Seale, *Asad: The Struggle for the Middle East* (University of California Press, Berkeley)

(1988), p. 209; Kfir & Dor, p. 153; Malovany, p. 190; *New York Times*, October 28, 1973, p. 27.

52. Malovany, p. 190.

## Chapter 12: Command and Control

1. Shazly, *The Crossing of Suez* (Third World Centre for Research and Publishing, London) (1980), p. 162.

2. Bartov, *Dado, 48 Shana V'ode 20 Yamim II* [Dado, 48 Years and Another 20 Days, Volume II] (Dvir Publishing House, Or Yehuda) (2002), p. 376; Dayan, *Avnei Derekh* [Milestones] (Edanim Publishers & Dvir Publishing House, Or Yehuda) (1976), p. 582.

3. *Ma'ariv, Mosaf Shabbat*, August 15, 2003, p. 11; Israel Channel 10 Television, September 7, 2018; Dayan, pgs. 586–587; Kfir, *Akhai Giboray HaTi'alah* [My Brothers, the Heroes of the Canal] (Miskal—Yediot Ahronot & Chemed Books, Tel Aviv) (2003), pgs. 29–32.

4. *Ma'ariv, Mosaf Shabbat*, August 15, 2003, p. 11.

5. Even & Maoz, *B'Nikudat Hacoved, Matzbiut B'Khazit HaTealah B'Milkhemet Yom HaKippurim* [At the Decisive Point, Generalship in the Yom Kippur War in the Canal Front] (Ma'arachot) (2012), p. 65; Kfir, p. 102.

6. Sharon, *Warrior, The Autobiography of Ariel Sharon* (Simon & Schuster, New York) (1989), p. 307; Even & Maoz, p. 65.

7. Megiddo, *Hamutal UMakhshir Lo B'Yadaynu* [Hamutal and Makhshir Are Not in Our Hands] (Kinneret, Zmora, Dvir Publishing House, Israel) (2019), p. 310.

8. Bartov, pgs. 473 & 478; Even & Maoz, p. 65.

9. Even & Maoz, pgs. 65–66.

10. Megiddo, p. 170; Agranat Commission, Final Report (1975), p. 845.

11. Megiddo, p. 135.

12. Agranat Commission, Final Report (1975), p. 839.

13. Bronstein (Editor), *Nitzakhon B'Svirut Nemookha* [The October 1973's Unlikely Victory] (Effi Melzter Inc., Israel) (2017), p. 259; Even & Maoz, p. 66; Megiddo, pgs. 137 & 166.

14. Megiddo, pgs. 166 & 225.

15. *Ma'ariv, Mosaf Shabbat*, August 15, 2003, p. 11; Bergman & Meltzer, *Milkhemet Yom Kippur Zman Emet* [The Yom Kippur War—Moment of Truth] (Miskal–Yediot Ahronot Books & Chemed Books, Tel Aviv) (2003), pgs. 420–421.

16. Bergman & Meltzer, p. 420; Reshef, *Lo Nekhdal! Khativah 14 B'Milkhemet Yom HaKippurim* [We Will Never Cease! The 14th Brigade in the Yom Kippur War] (Dvir Publishing House, Jerusalem and Tel Aviv) (2013), p. 147; Agranat Commission, Final Report (1975), p. 869.

17. Reshef, p. 145; *Ma'ariv, Mosaf Shabbat*, August 15, 2003, p. 11; Kfir & Dor, *Masah Chaim* [Chaim Erez—A Journey of Life] (Kinneret, Zmora-Bitan, Dvir Publishing House, Jerusalem and Tel Aviv) (2017), p. 208.

18. Megiddo, pgs. 161, 162 & 185; Agranat Commission, Final Report (1975), p. 849.

19. Agranat Commission, Final Report (1975), p. 849; Megiddo, p. 169.

20. Kfir & Dor, *B'Neteevay HaAish* [In Paths of Fire] (Miskal—Yediot Ahronot & Chemed Books, Israel) (2018), pgs. 19, 23–24 & 42; Megiddo, pgs. 188 & 226.

21. Kfir & Dor, *B'Neteevay*, pgs. 43 & 53; Kfir & Dor, *Masah*, p. 205; Megiddo, p. 208; Kfir, pgs. 97 & 98.

22. Agranat Commission, Final Report (1975), pgs. 845, 849–852 & 867; Kfir & Dor, *B'Neteevay*, p. 58; Megiddo, pgs. 220 & 247; Even & Maoz, p. 72.

23. Agranat Commission, Final Report (1975), pgs. 845; Even & Maoz, p. 72; Bergman & Meltzer, p. 141; Megiddo, p. 191.
24. Even & Maoz, p. 72; Agranat Commission, Final Report (1975), p. 845; *Yediot Ahronot*, *7 Yamim*, January 13, 2006, p. 17; Bergman & Meltzer, p. 145.
25. Bergman & Meltzer, p. 147.
26. Bergman & Meltzer, p. 149.
27. Reshef, p. 152; Wallach, *Atlas Carta L'Toldot Medinat Yisroel Asor Shlishi* [Carta's Atlas of Israel The Third Decade 1971–1981] (Carta, Jerusalem) (1983), p. 100; Bar-Yosef, *Milkhama Mishelo* [A War of Its Own] (Kinneret, Zmora, Dvir Publishing House, Israel) (2021), p. 198.
28. Reshef, p. 153.
29. Bartov, p. 485.
30. Megiddo, p. 256.
31. Bartov, p. 489; Braun, *Moshe Dayan B'Milkhemet Yom HaKippurim* [Moshe Dayan in the Yom Kippur War] (Edanim Publishers, Ltd., Yediot Ahronot) (1992), pgs. 139 & 142–143; Bartov, pgs. 495–496.
32. Gai, *Bar-Lev Biographia* [Bar-Lev, a Biography] (Am Oved Safrit Poalim) (1998), p. 254; Braun, pgs. 139 & 142; Dayan, *Avnei Derekh* [Milestones] (Edanim Publishers & Dvir Publishing House, Jerusalem and Tel Aviv) (1976), p. 278; Bar-On, *Moshe Dayan, Korot Khayav 1915–1981* [Moshe Dayan, His Life and Times 1915–1981] (Am Oved Publishers, Tel Aviv) (2018), p. 165; Bartov, p. 492; Braun, p. 142.
33. Sharon, p. 305.
34. Megiddo, pgs. 248 & 257–258; Even & Maoz, p. 78.

## Chapter 13: Frenemies

1. Zaken, *Suez Ayno Stalingrad* [Suez Isn't Stalingrad] (Ma'arachot, Jerusalem) (2021), p. 66.
2. Schiff, *Re'idat Adamah B'October* [Earthquake in October] (Zmora, Bitan Modan Publishers, Tel Aviv) (1975), p. 119.
3. Polikanov, *Perevodchik Voiny* [Interpreter of War] (Moscow) (2014), published in part on www.artofwar.ru; Malovany, *"Milkhemet HaShikhrur" Shel October 1973 B'Khazit HaSurit* [The "War of Liberation" of October 1973] (Israel War Institute, Israel) (2021), p. 201.
4. Seale, *Asad: The Struggle for the Middle East* (University of California Press, Berkeley) (1988), p. 208.
5. Halutz, *B'Govah Aynayim* [Straightforward] (Miskal—Yediot Ahronot, Chemed Books, Tel Aviv) (2010), p. 100; Bar-Yosef, *Milkhama Mishelo* [A War of Its Own] (Kinneret, Zmora, Dvir Publishing House, Israel) (2021), p. 196; Heikal, *The Road to Ramadan* (Ballantine Books, New York) (1975), p. 5; Hirst & Beeson *Sadat* (Faber & Faber, Ltd., London) (1982), p. 220; Seale, p. 210.
6. Golan & Shai (Editors), *Milkhama Hayom* [War Today] (Ma'arakhot, Israel) (2003), pgs. 127, 129–131 & 141; Malovany, pgs. 249–251; Seale, p. 215.
7. State Department Situation Report 22, October 12, 1973, NPMP, NSCF, Box 1174, 1973 Middle East War—1 October 1973 File No. 7; Kissinger, *Years of Upheaval* (Little, Brown & Co., Boston) (1982), p. 506.
8. Golan & Shai (Editors), p. 129; Lunt, *Hussein of Jordan* (William Morrow & Company, New York) (1989), p. 168; Seale, p. 215.
9. Heikal, *The Sphinx and the Commissar* (Harper & Row Publishers, New York) (1978), p. 259; Zohar, *40 Shanah Akharay* [40 Years After] (Israel War Institute, Tel Aviv) (2014), p. 67.

10. Indyk, *Master of the Game: Henry Kissinger and the Art of Middle East Diplomacy* (Alfred A. Knopf, New York) (2021), pgs. 116 & 118; Findley, *They Dare to Speak Out: People and Institutions Confront Israel's Lobby* (Lawrence Hill, Chicago) (1989), p. 87.

11. Memorandum from William Quandt to Brent Scowcroft, "Arab-Israeli Tensions," October 6, 1973, NPMP, NSCF, Box 1173, 1973 War (Middle East) 6 Oct. 1973 File No. 1; Memorandum from William Quandt and Donald Stukel, NSC Staff, "WSAG Meeting—Middle East, Saturday October 6, 1973, 3:00 P.M.," NPMP, NSC Institutional Files Box H-94, WSAG Meeting, Middle East 6 Oct. 1973, 7:30 P.M., Folder 1.

12. Memcon between Kissinger and Ambassador Huang Zhen, PRC Liaison Office, October 6, 1973, 9:10–9:30 P.M., RG 59, Records of the Policy Planning Staff, Director's Files (Winston Lord), 1969–1977, Box 328, China Exchanges, July 10—October 31, 1973, pgs. 1–2.

13. Memcon between Kissinger and Ambassador Huang Zhen, PRC Liaison Office, October 6, 1973, 9:10–9:30 P.M., RG 59, Records of the Policy Planning Staff, Director's Files (Winston Lord), 1969–1977, Box 328, China Exchanges, July 10—October 31, 1973, pgs. 1–2.

14. Memcon between Dinitz and Kissinger, October 9, 1973, 8:20–8:40 A.M., RG59, Records of Henry Kissinger, Box 25, Cat C, Arab-Israeli War.

15. Memcon between Dinitz and Kissinger, October 9, 1973, 8:20–8: 40 a.m., RG59, Records of Henry Kissinger, Box 25, Cat C Arab-Israeli War.

16. A number of these sources can be found in Zohar, *40 Shanah Akharay*, p. 86, fn. 35; Kissinger, *Years of Upheaval*, p. 493; interview with Ambassador Martin Indyk, April 5, 2022.

17. Zaken, p. 48.

18. Amos Yadlin writing in *Milkhemet Yom Hakipurrim Ul'kakheha*, p. 10.

19. Bartov, *Dado, 48 Shana V'ode 20 Yamim II* [Dado, 48 Years and Another 20 Days, Volume II] (Dvir Publishing House, Or Yehuda) (2002), pgs. 511–512.

20. Dayan, *Avnei Derekh* [Milestones] (Edanim Publishers & Dvir Publishing House, Jerusalem and Tel Aviv) (1976), p. 633; Bartov, p. 511; Braun, *Moshe Dayan B'Milkhemet Yom HaKippurim* [Moshe Dayan in the Yom Kippur War] (Edanim Publishers, Ltd., Yediot Ahronot) (1992), pgs. 151–152.

21. Voronstov, Minister-Counselor, Soviet Embassy, to Scowcroft, October 10, 1973, 11:15 A.M., NPMP, HAKO, Dobrynin/Kissinger Vol. 19, July 1, 1973–October 11, 1973; Bartov, p. 517; Braun, p. 155.

22. Halutz, *B'Govah Aynayim* [Straightforward] (Yediot Ahronot, Chemed Books, Tel Aviv) (2010), p. 103; Bar-Yosef, p. 232; Amos Yadlin writing in *Milkhemet Yom Hakipurrim Ul'kakheha*, p. 82; Interview with Syrian professor who wishes to remain anonymous, December 29, 2020.

23. Bar-Yosef, pgs. 210 & 214–215.

24. Interview with Oleksei Ivashin, February 2022; Bar-Yosef, pgs. 201–203 & 205; Bartov, p. 481.

25. Sahar, *Ad K'Tzeh Hayekholet* [To the Utmost Ability] (Modan Publishing House, Moshav Ben-Shemen) (2013), p. 165; Malovany, p. 201; Seale, pgs. 211 & 214; Tlass, *Mirat Hayati* [Reflections of My Life] (Damascus) (2004), Volume 3, pgs. 895–903, cited in Malovany, p. 212.

26. Sahar, p. 181.

27. Sahar, p. 173; Indyk, p. 135.

28. Kahalani, *Oze 77* [Oze 77] (Schocken Publishing House Ltd., Tel Aviv) (1975),

pgs. 156–158 & 164–166; Sahar, p. 267; Eitan, *Raful, Sipur Shel Khayal* [Raful, A Soldier's Story] (Ma'ariv Book, Tel Aviv) (1985), p. 139.

29. Zohar, p. 239; Sahar, pgs. 178–179; Orr, *Eleh Ha'achim Shelee* [These Are My Brothers] (Miskal-Yediot Ahronot and Chemed Books, Tel Aviv) (2003), p. 197.
30. Golan & Shai (Editors), pgs. 136–137.
31. Orr, p. 197.
32. Orr, p. 200; Sahar, p. 230; Braun, p. 163.

## Chapter 14: Never Call Surrender

1. Bartov, *Dado, 48 Shana V'ode 20 Yamim II* [Dado, 48 Years and Another 20 Days, Volume II] (Dvir Publishing House, Or Yehuda) (2002), p. 376; Ashkenazi, *HaErev B'shesh Tifrotz Milkhama* [Today at Six War Will Break Out] (Hakibbutz Hameukhad, Tel Aviv) (2003), pgs. 37 & 115–116; Arad & Laskov, *Hilukh Khozer* [A Walk Back] (Israel Defense Ministry) (2003), p. 62.
2. *Yediot Ahronot, Hamosaf LeShabbat*, September 3, 2010, p. 16; *Yediot Ahronot, Magazine Yom Kippur*, October 1, 2006, p. 10.
3. *Yediot Ahronot, Magazine Yom Kippur*, October 1, 2006, p. 11; *Jerusalem Post*, March 26, 2010.
4. *Ha'aretz Magazine*, March 12, 2004, p. 15
5. *Yediot Ahronot, Hamosaf LeShabbat*, September 3, 2010, p. 16; *Yediot Ahronot, Magazine Yom Kippur*, October 1, 2006, p. 12.
6. Schiff & Haver, *Lexicon L'Bitakhon Yisroel* [Lexicon of Israeli Defense] (Zmora, Bitan, Modan Publishers, Jerusalem) (2nd Edition, 1976), p. 307; *Yediot Ahronot, Hamosaf LeShabbat*, September 3, 2010, p. 17; Zalmi, He Took Torah into War, http://zalmi.blogspot.com/2018/09/he-took-torah-into-war.html.
7. Segal, *Eduyot M'Govah HaKhol* [Testimony from Across the Dunes] (Modan Publishers, Ben-Shemen) (2007), p. 58.
8. *Report of an Amnesty International Mission to Israel and the Syrian Arab Republic to Investigate Allegations of Ill Treatment and Torture, October 10–24, 1974* (Amnesty International Publications, London) (1975), pgs. 26–27; *Yediot Ahronot, Mosaf Yom Kippur*, September 13, 2013, p. 21.
9. *Report of an Amnesty International Mission to Israel and the Syrian Arab Republic to Investigate Allegations of Ill Treatment and Torture, October 10–24, 1974* (Amnesty International Publications, London) (1975), pgs. 2 & 8; author's notes.
10. Sharon, *Shafuy B'Damesek* [Sane in Damascus] (Orly Levi, Israel) (2005), pgs. 39, 46, 55, 58, 62, 79, 81, 82, 135; *Yediot Ahronot, Hamosaf LeShabbat*, October 3, 2003, p. 15; *Yediot Ahronot, 7 Yamim*, November 27, 2020, p. 18; Bergman & Meltzer, *Milkhemet Yom Kippur Zman Emet* [The Yom Kippur War—Moment of Truth] (Miskal-Yediot Ahronot Books & Chemed Books, Tel Aviv) (2003), p. 451; Barkai, *B'Shem Shamayim* (For Heaven's Sake) (Kinneret, Zmora-Bitan, Dvir Publishing House, Or Yehuda) (2013), p. 97; *Ma'ariv, Sofshavua*, p. 25.
11. *Yediot Ahronot, Mosaf Erev Yom Kippur*, October 10, 1997; Israel Channel 2 Television, September 3, 2016; Bergman & Meltzer, p. 361; Sharon, p. 106.
12. Israel Channel 10 Television, September 7, 2018.
13. *Ma'ariv, Mosaf Shabbat*, December 24, 2004, p. 16; *Yediot Ahronot, Hamosaf LeShabbat*, October 3, 2003, p. 16; Arad & Laskov, p. 53.
14. Israel Channel 2 Television, September 3, 2016.
15. *Yediot Ahronot, Magazine Yom Kippur*, October 1, 2006, p. 12.
16. *Yediot Ahronot, Magazine Yom Kippur*, October 1, 2006, p. 12.

## Chapter 15: Armageddon on a Road Called Talisman

1. Memcon between Muhammad Hafez Ismail and Henry Kissinger, May 20, 1973, 10:15 A.M., RG 59, Records of Henry Kissinger, Box 25, Cat C Arab-Israeli War, p. 18.
2. Zohar, *40 Shanah Akharay* [40 Years After] (Israel War Institute, Tel Aviv) (2014), p. 321.
3. Luntz, writing in *Milkhemet Sheshet Yamim* [The Six Day War] (Effi Meltzer Publishing, Tel Aviv, 1996), p. 86; Golan & Shai (Editors), *Milkhama Hayom* [War Today] (Israel Defense Ministry, Israel) (2003), pgs. 389–391; Luntz, writing in *Milkhemet*, p. 85.
4. Golan & Shai (Editors), *Milkhama Hayom*, p. 392.
5. Golan & Shai (Editors), *Milkhama Hayom*, p. 392; *Yediot Ahronot, 7 Yamim*, June 13, 1975, pgs. 16–17; Arad & Laskov, *Hilukh Khozer* [A Walk Back] (Israel Defense Ministry) (2003), pgs. 250–253.
6. Arad & Laskov, pgs. 18–19 & 158.
7. Gordon, *30 Sha'ot B'October* [30 Hours in October] (Ma'ariv Book Guild, Tel Aviv) (2003), pgs. 404–405.
8. Gordon, p. 338; Spector, *Ram U'Barur* [Loud and Clear] (Yediot Ahronot, Sifrei Chemed) (2008), p. 235.
9. Spector, p. 236.
10. Gordon, p. 418.
11. Memcon between Dinitz and Kissinger, October 9, 1973, 6:10–6:35 P.M., RG 59, SN 70–73, Pol Isr-US, pgs. 1–3; Indyk, *Master of the Game: Henry Kissinger and the Art of Middle East Diplomacy* (Alfred A. Knopf, New York) (2021), p. 128.
12. William Quandt to Kissinger, "Middle Eastern Issues," October 9, 1973, NPMP, NSCF, Box 664, Middle East War Memos & Misc. October 6–17, 1973.
13. Memcon between Deputy Secretary of State Kenneth Rush and Petroleum Company Executives, "The Middle East Conflict and U.S. Oil Interests," October 10, 1973, RG 59, SN 70–73, POL 27 Arab-Isr.
14. Yuli Vorontsov, Minister-Counselor, Soviet Embassy, to Scowcroft, October 10, 1973, delivered 11:15 A.M., NPMP, HAKO, Dobrynin/Kissinger Volume 19 (July 1, 1973–October 11, 1973); Kissinger, *Crisis* (Simon & Schuster, New York) (2003), pgs. 161, 165 & 206.
15. Kissinger, *Years of Upheaval* (Little, Brown & Co., Boston) (1982), p. 497; Kissinger, *Crisis*, pgs. 153 & 180; Government Protocol, October 12, 1973 (Diary of Eli Mizrahi), p. 19.
16. Zohar, pgs. 285–286; Kissinger, *Crisis*, p. 193.
17. State Department Routing Message, October 12, 1973, RG 59, SN 70–73, POL 15–1 US/Nixon; Kissinger, *Crisis*, pgs. 196 & 197.
18. Bartov, *Dado, 48 Shana V'ode 20 Yamim II* [Dado, 48 Years and Another 20 Days, Volume II] (Dvir Publishing House, Or Yehuda) (2002), pgs. 533–534.
19. Bartov, p. 536; Zohar, pgs. 281 & 282; Israel Government Protocol, October 12, 1973, p. 1; Gordon, p. 411.
20. Bar-Yosef, *Milkhama Mishelo* [A War of Its Own] (Kinneret, Zmora, Dvir Publishing House, Israel (2021), p. 220; Gordon, pgs. 216 & 410; Tal, *Prakim L'Milkhemet Yom Hakippurim* [Episodes of the Yom Kippur War] (Miskal Publishing, Israel) (2019), pgs. 566 & 854; Peled, Interview on YouTube, November 2000; Zohar, p. 282; Israel Government Protocol, October 12, 1973, p. 1; Gai, *Bar-Lev Biographia* [Bar-Lev, a Biography] (Am Oved Safrit Poalim) (1998), p. 258; Israel Government Protocol, October 12, 1973 (Diary of Eli Mizrahi), p. 1.

21. Kissinger, *Crisis*, pgs. 194 & 207; Eban, *Personal Witness: Israel Through My Eyes* (G.P. Putnam's Sons, New York) (1992), p. 534.

22. Eban, p. 533.

23. Israel Government Protocol, October 12, 1973 (Diary of Eli Mizrahi), p. 19; Kissinger, *Years of Upheaval*, p. 510; Dobrynin, *Sugubo Doveritelno. Posol V Vashingtone Pre Shesti Prezidentakh SSHA (1962–1986)* [Absolutely Confidential. Ambassador in Washington During the Rule of Six Presidents of the U.S.A. (1962–1986)] (Moscow) (1997), p. 269; Heikal, *The Road to Ramadan* (Ballantine Books, New York) (1975), p. 5; Hirst & Beeson, *Sadat* (Faber & Faber, Ltd., London) (1982), p. 229.

24. Heikal, p. 229; Israelyan, *Inside the Kremlin During the Yom Kippur War* (Pennsylvania State University Press, University Park) (1995), p. 81; Sadat, *In Search of Identity* (Harper & Row Publishers, New York) (1977), pgs. 256–258.

25. Dobrynin, p. 270; Kissinger, *Years of Upheaval*, pgs. 517–518.

26. Quandt, *Decade of Decisions* (University of California Press, Berkeley) (1977), pgs. 182–183; Kissinger, *Years of Upheaval*, p. 517.

27. Israel Government Protocol, October 12, 1973, p. 4.

28. Gamasy, *The October War* (The American University in Cairo Press, Cairo) (1989), pgs. 270 & 272; for another senior Egyptian who thought the plan was to go to the Passes, see Riad, *The Struggle for Peace in the Middle East* (Quartet Books, London) (1981), p. 245; Heikal, p. 225.

29. Shazly, *The Crossing of Suez* (Third World Centre for Research and Publishing, London) (1980), pgs. 164–165.

30. Israel Government Protocol, October 12, 1973, pgs. 12 & 17.

31. See, e.g., *International Symposium on the 1973 October War*, First Volume (October 27–31, 1975), p. 284.

32. Seale, *Asad: The Struggle for the Middle East* (University of California Press, Berkeley) (1988), p. 210; Badri, Magdoub, Zohdy, *The Ramadan War, 1973* (Dupuy Associates, Inc., Dunn Loring, Virginia) (1978), pgs. 97–98; Heikal, p. 227.

33. Memcon between Kissinger and Acting Egyptian Foreign Minister Ismail Fahmi, October 29, 1973, RG, SN 70–73, POL 27 Arab-Isr, p. 9.

34. U.S. Interests Section in Egypt, Cable 3942 to State Department, "Current Egyptian Military Situation," October 10, 1973, NPMP, NSCF, Box 638, Arab Republic of Egypt IX (Jan–Oct '73).

35. Israel Government Protocol, October 12, 1973, pgs. 2–3.

36. Israel Government Protocol, October 12, 1973, pgs. 10, 11, 13, 19; *Yediot Ahronot, 7 Yamim*, September 25, 2020, p. 14.

37. *Yediot Ahronot, 7 Yamim*, September 25, 2020, p. 14.

38. Zamir, pgs. 158–159; *Yediot Ahronot, 7 Yamim*, September 25, 2020, p. 14.

39. *Yediot Ahronot, 7 Yamim*, September 25, 2020, p. 14; Israel Government Protocol, October 12, 1973, p. 17.

40. Israel Government Protocol, October 12, 1973, p. 18.

41. Megiddo, *Hamutal UMakhshir Lo B'Yadaynu* [Hamutal and Makhshir Are Not in Our Hands] (Kinneret, Zmora, Dvir Publishing House, Israel) (2019), pgs. 259–262.

42. Polikanov, *Interpreter of War*, www.artofwar.ru.

43. Arad & Laskov, pgs. 64–67.

44. Bar-Yosef, p. 269; Wallach, *Atlas Carta L'Toldot Medinat Yisroel Asor Shlishi* [Carta's Atlas of Israel The Third Decade 1971–1981] (Carta, Jerusalem) (1983), p. 102; *Ma'ariv Sofshavua*, September 12, 2013.

45. Shazly, p. 167; Gamasy, p. 277; Wallach, *Atlas*, p. 101.
46. Meir, *My Life* (G.P. Putnam's Sons, New York) (1975), p. 431.

### Chapter 16: "We Will Cross with What We Have"

1. Bergman & Meltzer, *Milkhemet Yom Kippur Zman Emet* [The Yom Kippur War—Moment of Truth] (Miskal-Yediot Ahronot Books & Chemed Books, Tel Aviv) (2003), p. 229.
2. Reshef, *Lo Nekhdal! Khativah 14 B'Milkhemet Yom HaKippurim* [We Will Never Cease! The 14th Brigade in the Yom Kippur War] (Dvir Publishing House, Jerusalem and Tel Aviv) (2013), pgs. 180–181; Wallach, *Atlas Carta L'Toldot Medinat Yisroel Asor Shlishi* [Carta's Atlas of Israel The Third Decade 1971–1981] (Carta, Jerusalem) (1983), p. 102.
3. Braun, *Moshe Dayan B'Milkhemet Yom HaKippurim* [Moshe Dayan in the Yom Kippur War] (Edanim Publishers, Ltd., Yediot Ahronot) (1992), pgs. 177 & 182.
4. Herzog, *The War of Atonement* (Little, Brown & Co., Boston) (1975), pgs. 198–199.
5. Reshef, p. 133; Bronstein, *Nitzakhon B'Svirut Nemookha* [The October 1973's Unlikely Victory] (Effi Meltzer Ltd., Israel) (2019), p. 241; *Yediot Ahronot, Calcalah Chag*, October 1, 2006, pgs. 14–15; *Hatzofeh Hashavua*, October 3, 2003, p. 5.
6. Herzog, *The Arab-Israeli Wars* (Random House, New York) (1982), p. 124; *Yediot Ahronot, Mosaf*, October 21, 1983, p. 11; *Yediot Ahronot, Yom Kippur*, October 2, 1987, p. 20.
7. Even & Maoz, *B'Nikudat Hacoved, Matzbiut B'Khazit HaTealah B'Milkhemet Yom HaKippurim* [At the Decisive Point, Generalship in the Yom Kippur War in the Canal Front] (Ma'arachot) (2012), p. 134.
8. Reshef, p. 182.
9. *Ha'aretz Magazine*, November 15, 2002, p. 20.
10. Reshef, p. 224.
11. Bar-Yosef, *Milkhama Mishelo* [A War of Its Own] (Kinneret, Zmora, Dvir Publishing House, Israel) (2021), pgs. 220 & 280–281; Reshef, p. 224.
12. Even & Maoz, p. 135; Sharon, *Shafuy B'Damesek* [Sane in Damascus] (Orly Levi, Israel) (2005), p. 313; *Yediot Ahronot, Hamosaf LeShabbat*, September 29, 2006, p. 9.
13. Bronstein, p. 37; Adan, *Al Shtay Gadot HaTi'ah'lah* [On Both Banks of the Canal] (Edanim, Jerusalem) (1979), p. 243; Gai, *Bar-Lev Biographia* [Bar-Lev, a Biography] (Am Oved Publishers, Tel Aviv) (1998), pgs. 262–263; Bartov, *Dado, 48 Shana V'ode 20 Yamim II* [Dado, 48 Years and Another 20 Days, Volume II] (Dvir Publishing House, Or Yehuda) (2002), pgs. 591–592, Even & Maoz, p. 135.
14. Reshef, pgs. 246–248; Bronstein, p. 309.
15. *Yediot Ahronot, 7 Yamim*, January 13, 2006, p. 18; Even & Maoz, p. 145.
16. Bronstein, p. 379.
17. Reshef, pgs. 183 & 192.
18. Reshef, p. 197; *Ma'ariv, Yom Kippur, 30 Shana*, October 5, 2003, p. 13; Kfir, *Akhai Giboray HaTi'alah* [My Brothers, the Heroes of the Canal] (Miskal—Yediot Ahronot & Chemed Books, Tel Aviv) (2003), p. 205; Even & Maoz, p. 145.
19. Harel, *Avirei HaLev* [The Stouthearted] (Keren Khativat Tzankhanim) (1974), pgs. 28–29; Sharon, *Warrior* (Simon & Schuster, New York) (1989), pgs. 314–315.
20. Bronstein, pgs. 509–535; YouTube, *Milkhemet Yom HaKippurim*, UKrav HaKhava Hasinit, Uri Millstein, November 29, 2016 (minute 55:00).
21. Sharon, *Warrior*, p. 315; Even & Maoz, p. 145; Bergman & Meltzer, *Milkhemet Yom Kippur Zman Emet*, p. 229; Harel, p. 32.
22. Reshef, p. 184, 197 & 202; Even & Maoz, p. 151.

23. Wallach, *Atlas*, p. 105; Reshef, p. 198; Sharon, *Warrior*, p. 315.

24. Sharon, *Warrior*, p. 315; Reshef, p. 200.

25. Arad & Laskov, *Hilukh Khozer* [A Walk Back] (Israel Defense Ministry) (2003), p. 74; Even & Maoz, p. 152.

26. Arad & Laskov, p. 76; Reshef, p. 205; Bronstein, pgs. 306 & 340–341.

27. Reshef, p. 200.

28. Arad & Laskov, p. 77; *Jerusalem Post Magazine*, September 13, 2002, p. 6; Sharon, *Warrior*, p. 315.

29. Bronstein, p. 312.

30. Bronstein, p. 313; Reshef, p. 213.

31. Littwitz, *Z-817831, B'Khazit HaDarom B'Milkhemet Yom Hakippurim* [Z-817831, On the Southern Front During the Yom Kippur War] (Effi Meltzer, Ltd., Israel) (2011), p. 18; Reshef, p. 214.

32. Littwitz, pgs. 80 & 85.

33. Reshef, pgs. 218–219; Bronstein, p. 287.

34. *Yediot Ahronot, 7 Yamim*, October 3, 2003, p. 16; Reshef, p. 220.

35. Bronstein, pgs. 314–315; *Yediot Ahronot, 7 Yamim*, October 3, 2003, pgs. 16 & 17; *Ma'ariv, Sofshavua*, April 23, 2004, p. 14.

36. Bergman & Meltzer, p. 231; Sharon, *Warrior*, p. 313.

37. Givati, *Ha'Ma'aracha B'Khermon* [The Hermon Mountain Operation] (Modan Publishing House Ltd., Ben Shemen) (2015), p. 201.

38. Even & Maoz, pgs. 121 & 159; Arad & Laskov, p. 112.

39. Even & Maoz, p. 122.

40. Even & Maoz, pgs. 122–123 & 125; Kfir & Dor, *Masah Chaim Aluf Chaim Erez* [Chaim Erez: A Journey of Life] (Kinneret, Zmora-Bitan, Dvir Publishing House, Jerusalem and Tel Aviv) (2017), p. 219; Bronstein, p. 310.

41. Bergman & Meltzer, p. 239; Arad & Laskov, p. 85.

42. Arad & Laskov, pgs. 87 & 88.

43. Arad & Laskov, pgs. 88–89.

44. Bronstein, p. 310; *Ma'ariv, Yom Kippur, 30 Shana*, October 5, 2003, p. 13.

45. Bergman & Meltzer, pgs. 233 & 241.

46. Even & Maoz, p. 149.

### Chapter 17: The War of the Generals

1. Arad & Laskov, *Hilukh Khozer* [A Walk Back] (Israel Defense Ministry) (2003), p. 88; *Ma'ariv, Mosaf Yom Kippur*, October 5, 2003, p. 16.

2. Sharon, *Warrior* (Simon & Schuster, New York) (1989), p. 317; Arad & Laskov, pgs. 108, 110, 111, 114–115.

3. Kfir, *HaKhavah HaSinit* [The Chinese Farm] (Ma'ariv Book Guild) (2012), p. 190; Sharon, p. 317; Even & Maoz, *B'Nikudat Hacoved, Matzbiut B'Khazit HaTealah B'Milkhemet Yom HaKippurim* [At the Decisive Point, Generalship in the Yom Kippur War in the Canal Front] (Ma'arachot) (2012), p. 172; Kfir & Dor, *Masah Chaim Aluf Chaim Erez* [Chaim Erez: A Journey of Life] (Kinneret, Zmora-Bitan, Dvir Publishing House, Jerusalem and Tel Aviv) (2017), p. 234; Bergman & Meltzer, *Milkhemet Yom Kippur Zman Emet* [The Yom Kippur War—Moment of Truth] (Miskal–Yediot Ahronot Books & Chemed Books , Tel Aviv) (2003), p. 234; *Yediot Ahronot, Hamosaf LeShabbat*, September 29, 2006, p. 9.

4. Sharon, p. 316; Dayan, *Avnei Derekh* [Milestones] (Edanim Publishers & Dvir Publishing House, Or Yehuda) (1976), p. 652; Kfir, *HaKhavah*, pgs. 82 & 162; Arad & Laskov, p. 79.

5. *Ma'ariv, Sofshavua,* April 23, 2004, p. 15.
6. Reshef, *Lo Nekhdal! Khativah 14 B'Milkhemet Yom HaKippurim* [We Will Never Cease! The 14th Brigade in the Yom Kippur War] (Dvir Publishing House, Jerusalem and Tel Aviv) (2013), p. 210.
7. Givati, *Ha'Ma'aracha B'Khermon* [The Hermon Mountain Operation] (Modan Publishing House Ltd., Ben Shemen) (2015), p. 17; Kfir, *Akhai Giboray Ha-Ti'alah* [My Brothers, the Heroes of the Canal] (Miskal—Yediot Ahronot & Chemed Books, Tel Aviv) (2003), p. 272.
8. Segal, *Eduyot MiGovah HaKhol* [Voices Across the Dunes] (Lemoden Hotza L'Ohr) (2007), p. 71.
9. Segal, p. 72.
10. Segal, p. 72; Even & Maoz, p. 146.
11. Segal, p. 72.
12. Kfir & Dor, p. 226.
13. Segal, p. 73.
14. Adan, *Al Shtay Gadot HaTi'ah'lah* [On Both Banks of the Canal] (Edanim, Jerusalem) (1979), p. 201; Even & Maoz, pgs. 160–161 & 169–170.
15. Bronstein, *Nitzakhon B'Svirut Nemookha* [The October 1973's Unlikely Victory] (Effi Meltzer Ltd., Israel) (2019), p. 481; Arad & Laskov, pgs. 91–92.
16. Segal, p. 76.
17. Bronstein, p. 319; Sharon, p. 318; *Yediot Ahronot, 7 Yamim,* August 29, 2003, p. 19.
18. Sharon, p. 317; Bergman & Meltzer, p. 241; Gai, *Bar-Lev Biographia* [Bar-Lev, a Biography) (Am Oved Safrit Poalim) (1998), p. 265.
19. Bar-Tov, *Dado, 48 Shana V'ode 20 Yamim II* [Dado, 48 Years and Another 20 Days, Volume II] (Dvir Publishing House, Or Yehuda) (2002), p. 609; Sharon, p. 321; Bar-Tov, p. 609; *Yediot Ahronot, 7 Yamim,* August 29, 2003, p. 19.
20. Kfir, *HaKhavah,* p. 192; Sharon, p. 319.
21. Adan, p. 204.
22. *Yediot Ahronot, Mosaf Yom Kippur,* September 13, 2013, p. 11.
23. Adan, p. 200; *Yediot Ahronot, Mosaf Yom Kippur,* September 13, 2013, p. 11; See, e.g., Even & Maoz, p. 176.
24. Even & Maoz, p. 183.
25. Nir, *Natke HaKatzin HaPatzua SheKhazar L'sdeh HaKrav* [Natke, The Wounded Officer That Returned to the Battlefield] (Miskal-Yediot Ahronot Books & Chemed Books, Tel Aviv) (2010), pgs. 177–178; Adan, p. 203; Bergman & Meltzer, p. 243.
26. Givati, p. 14.
27. Even & Maoz, p. 175.
28. Segal, pgs. 76–77.

## Chapter 18: The Chinese Farm and the Men Who Conquered It

1. George S. Patton Quotes, www.azquotes.com/author/11404-George_S_Patton?p=2.
2. Hirst & Beeson, *Sadat* (Faber & Faber, Ltd., London) (1982), p. 17.
3. Excerpts of a Speech Calling for an Arab-Israeli Peace Conference, https://sadat.umd.edu/sites/sadat.umd.edu/files/Excerpts%20of%20a%20Speech%20Calling%20for%20an%20Arab-Israeli%20Peace%20Conference.pdf.
4. Bergman & Meltzer, *Milkhemet Yom Kippur Zman Emet* [The Yom Kippur War—Moment of Truth] (Miskal-Yediot Ahronot Books & Chemed Books, Tel Aviv)

(2003), p. 243; Shazly, *The Crossing of Suez* (Third World Centre for Research and Publishing, London) (1980), p. 171.

5. Shazly, p. 168; Gamasy, *The October War* (The American University in Cairo Press, Cairo) (1989), pgs. 285 & 287.

6. Meir, *My Life* (G.P. Putnam's Sons, New York) (1975), pgs. 432–433.

7. Braun, *Moshe Dayan B'Milkhemet Yom HaKippurim* [Moshe Dayan in the Yom Kippur War] (Edanim Publishers, Ltd., Yediot Ahronot) (1992), pgs. 191–192.

8. Bergman & Meltzer, p. 244; Heikal, *The Road to Ramadan* (Ballantine Books, New York) (1975), p. 236; Bartov, *Dado, 48 Shana V'ode 20 Yamim II* [Dado, 48 Years and Another 20 Days, Volume II] (Dvir Publishing House, Or Yehudah) (2002), p. 600.

9. Dayan, *Avnei Derekh* [Milestones] (Edanim Publishers & Dvir Publishing House, Jerusalem and Tel Aviv) (1976), p. 646.

10. Sharon, *Warrior* (Simon & Schuster, New York) (1989), pgs. 295–296; Bartov, p. 612; Braun, p. 193.

11. Sharon, p. 314.

12. Bronstein, *Nitzakhon B'Svirut Nemookha* [The October 1973's Unlikely Victory] (Effi Meltzer Ltd., Israel) (2019), pgs. 314–315 & 354.

13. Segal, *Eduyot M'Govah HaKhol* [Testimony from Across the Dunes] (Modan Publishers, Ben Shemen) (2007), pgs. 85–86.

14. *Yediot Ahronot, 7 Yamim*, October 3, 2003, p. 18; Segal, p. 223; Reshef, *Lo Nekhdal! Khativah 14 B'Milkhemet Yom HaKippurim* [We Will Never Cease! The 14th Brigade in the Yom Kippur War] (Dvir Publishing, Jerusalem and Tel Aviv) (2013), p. 271.

15. *Yediot Ahronot, 7 Yamim*, October 3, 2003, p. 18.

16. Segal, p. 89.

17. Segal, pgs. 91, 94–95 & 97; Wallach, *Atlas Carta L'Toldot Medinat Yisroel Asor Shlishi* [Carta's Atlas of Israel, The Third Decade 1971–1981] (Carta, Jerusalem) (1983), p. 107.

18. Kfir, *Akhai Giboray HaTi'alah* [My Brothers, the Heroes of the Canal] (Miskal— Yediot Ahronot & Chemed Books, Tel Aviv) (2003), p. 204.

19. Segal, pgs. 111, 112 & 127.

20. Segal, p. 131.

21. Segal, pgs. 114, 129 & 138–139.

22. Segal, pgs. 128, 137 & 282.

23. Gary Roush, Vietnam Helicopter Pilots Association, Helicopter Losses During the Vietnam War, www.vhpa.org/heliloss.pdf; Dayan, p. 646.

24. Adan, *Al Shtay Gadot HaTi'ah'lah* [On Both Banks of the Canal] (Edanim, Jerusalem) (1979), p. 212; Segal, p. 174.

25. Adan, p. 213.

26. Segal, p. 177.

27. Bergman & Meltzer, p. 245.

28. *Ma'ariv, Sofshavua*, April 23, 2004, p. 14; Segal, p. 266.

29. Segal, p. 266.

30. Bronstein, p. 379.

31. Bronstein, p. 380.

32. Bronstein, pgs. 381–382.

33. Bronstein, p. 381.

34. Kfir, *Akhai*, p. 277; Center for the Yom Kippur War: https://kippur-center.gal-ed.co .il/Web/He/Medal/247.aspx?id=37; *Ma'ariv, Sofshavua*, September 29, 2006, p. 14.

35. *Ma'ariv, Sofshavua,* September 29, 2006, p. 18.
36. Kfir, *HaKhavah,* p. 239; *Ma'ariv, Mosaf Yom HaKippurim,* September 24, 2004, p. 6.
37. Shazly, p. 174.
38. Bartov, p. 609; Braun, p. 194.
39. Segal, pgs. 243, 245–246 & 251.
40. Shazly, pgs. 177–178.
41. Bronstein, p. 383.
42. Bronstein, pgs. 380–382.
43. Bronstein, p. 382; *Ma'ariv, Sofshavua,* September 29, 2006, p. 18.
44. Bronstein, p. 559; Kfir, *HaKhavah,* p. 270.
45. Bronstein, p. 383.
46. See, e.g., *Ma'ariv, Sofshavua,* April 23, 2004, p. 14.
47. Bronstein, p. 558.
48. Segal, p. 236.
49. Segal, pgs. 286–287.
50. Segal, pgs. 206 & 238.
51. Segal, pgs. 241, 242 & 287.

## Chapter 19: The Race to the Bridgehead

1. Kahneman, *Thinking Fast and Slow* (paperback edition) (Farrar, Straus & Giroux, New York) (2011), p. 237.
2. Dayan, *Avnei Derekh* [Milestones] (Edanim Publishers & Dvir Publishing House, Jerusalem and Tel Aviv) (1976), p. 646.
3. Adan, *Al Shtay Gadot HaTi'ah'lah* [On Both Banks of the Canal] (Edanim, Jerusalem) (1979), p. 215.
4. Bergman & Meltzer, *Milkhemet Yom Kippur Zman Emet* [The Yom Kippur War—Moment of Truth] (Miskal-Yediot Ahronot Books & Chemed Books, Tel Aviv) (2003), p. 263; Sharon, *Warrior* (Simon & Schuster, New York) (1989), p. 322; Dayan, p. 648.
5. Even & Maoz, *B'Nikudat Hacoved, Matzbiut B'Khazit HaTealah B'Milkhemet Yom HaKippurim* [At the Decisive Point, Generalship in the Yom Kippur War in the Canal Front] (Ma'arachot, Ben-Shemen) (2012), p. 205; Kfir, *HaKhava HaSinit* [The Chinese Farm] (Ma'ariv Book Guild) (2012), p. 233; U.S. Navy, *All Hands Magazine,* February, 1976, pgs. 4–6.
6. Sharon, p. 292.
7. Bloom & Chefetz, *HaRoeh* [The Shepherd] (Miskal—Yediot Ahornot Books & Chemed Books, Tel Aviv) (2005), p. 276.
8. Reshef, *Lo Nekhdal! Khativah 14 B'Milkhemet Yom HaKippurim* [We Will Never Cease! The 14th Brigade in the Yom Kippur War] (Dvir Publishing House, Jerusalem and Tel Aviv) (2013), p. 337.
9. Bergman & Meltzer, p. 264.
10. Braun, *Moshe Dayan B'Milkhemet Yom HaKippurim* [Moshe Dayan in the Yom Kippur War] (Edanim Publishers, Ltd., Yediot Ahronot) (1992), p. 185; Adan, p. 218; Gai, *Bar-Lev Biographia* [Bar-Lev, a Biography] (Am Oved Safrit Poalim) (1998), p. 266.
11. Sharon, p. 326; Even & Maoz, p. 210.
12. Bronstein, *Nitzakhon B'Svirut Nemookha* [The October 1973's Unlikely Victory] (Effi Meltzer Ltd., Israel) (2019), p. 323; Gai, p. 267; Even & Maoz, p. 211.
13. Dayan, p. 649.
14. Even & Maoz, p. 214.

15. Adan, p. 218; Bartov, *Dado, 48 Shana V'ode 20 Yamim II* [Dado, 48 Years and Another 20 Days, Volume II) (Dvir, Or Yehudah) (2002), p. 617.

16. Bartov, p. 617.

17. Bartov, p. 617; Dayan, pgs. 648 & 649; Even & Maoz, pgs. 216–217.

18. See, e.g., YouTube: *Eser Shanim l'Milkhemet Yom Hakippurim: Rayon im Ariel Sharon.*

19. Churchill, *Memoirs of the Second World War* (abridged edition) (Houghton Mifflin Company, Boston) (1959), p. 252.

20. Shazly, *The Crossing of Suez* (Third World Centre for Research and Publishing, London) (1980), pgs. 164–167.

21. Shazly, pgs. 164 & 171; Sadat, *In Search of Identity* (Harper & Row Publishers, New York) (1977), p. 262.

22. Reshef, p. 377.

23. Shazly, p. 171.

24. Shazly, p. 172.

25. Shazly, p. 171.

26. Arad & Laskov, *Hilukh Khozer* [A Walk Back] (Arad Family, Israel) (2003), p. 121; Kfir & Dor, *Masah Chaim Aluf Chaim Erez* [Chaim Erez: A Journey of Life] (Kinneret, Zmora-Bitan, Dvir Publishing House, Jerusalem and Tel Aviv) (2017), pgs. 239–240; Kfir & Dor, p. 238.

27. Shazly, p. 173.

28. Shazly, p. 173.

29. Shazly, p. 174; Reshef, p. 277.

30. Even & Maoz, p. 191.

31. Even & Maoz, p. 203; Reshef, p. 279.

32. Bar-Yosef, *Milkhama Mishelo* [A War of Its Own] (Kinneret, Zmora, Dvir Publishing House, Israel) (2021), p. 240; Even & Maoz, p. 201.

33. Reshef, p. 261.

34. Nir, *Natke HaKatzin HaPatzua SheKhazar L'sdeh HaKrav* [Natke, The Wounded Officer That Returned to the Battlefield] (Miskal-Yediot Ahronot Books & Chemed Books, Tel Aviv) (2010), pgs. 13, 109, 112, 113, 115; Adan, p. 143; Even & Maoz, p. 183.

35. Adan, p. 215; Even & Maoz, pgs. 206–207; Wallach, *Atlas Carta L'Toldot Medinat Yisroel Asor Shlishi* [Carta's Atlas of Israel The Third Decade 1971–1981] (Carta, Jerusalem) (1983), p. 108.

36. Wallach, p. 108; Bergman & Meltzer p. 265; Nir, pgs. 180 & 181.

37. Nir, p. 182.

38. Nir, p. 182; Shamshi, p. 55; Wallach, p. 108.

39. Adan, pgs. 220–221; Bergman & Meltzer, p. 265.

40. Bergman & Meltzer, p. 266.

41. Even & Maoz, pgs. 207 & 212; Wallach, p. 108.

42. Even & Maoz, p. 219.

## Chapter 20: Bridges

1. Good Reads, Gaius Julius Caesar Quotes, www.goodreads.com/author/quotes /16535395.Gaius_Julius_Caesar.

2. *Ma'ariv, Hamosaf LeShabbat*, October 4, 1991, p. 3; Reshef, *Lo Nekhdal! Khativah 14 B'Milkhemet Yom HaKippurim* [We Will Never Cease! The 14th Brigade in the Yom Kippur War] (Dvir Publishing House, Jerusalem and Tel Aviv) (2013), p. 329.

3. Reshef, p. 284; Dayan, *Avnei Derekh* [Milestones] (Edanim Publishers & Dvir Publishing House, Tel Aviv) (1976), p. 650; Braun, *Moshe Dayan B'Milkhemet Yom HaKippurim* [Moshe Dayan in the Yom Kippur War] (Edanim Publishers, Ltd., Yediot Ahronot) (1992), p. 197.
4. Braun, p. 198; Adan, *Al Shtay Gadot HaTi'ah'lah* [On Both Banks of the Canal] (Edanim, Jerusalem) (1979), p. 223.
5. Even & Maoz, *B'Nikudat Hacoved, Matzbiut B'Khazit HaTealah B'Milkhemet Yom HaKippurim* [At the Decisive Point, Generalship in the Yom Kippur War in the Canal Front] (Ma'arachot, Ben-Shemen) (2012), pgs. 225–226; Adan, p. 223; Even & Maoz, pgs. 226–227.
6. Even & Maoz, pgs. 229–230.
7. Adan, p. 224; Even & Maoz, pgs. 231 & 232; Dayan, p. 650; Sharon, *Warrior* (Simon & Schuster, New York) (1989), p. 330.
8. Adan, p. 226; Bergman & Meltzer, *Milkhemet Yom Kippur Zman Emet* [The Yom Kippur War—Moment of Truth] (Miskal-Yediot Ahronot Books & Chemed Books, Tel Aviv) (2003), p. 278; Harel, *Avirei HaLev* [The Stouthearted] (Keren Khativat Tzankhanim, Israel) (1974), p. 43; Bergman & Meltzer, p. 276.
9. Bronstein, *Nitzakhon B'Svirut Nemookha* [The October 1973's Unlikely Victory] (Effi Meltzer Ltd., Israel) (2019), p. 329; Bergman & Meltzer, p. 273; Kfir & Dor, *Masah Chaim Aluf Chaim Erez* [Chaim Erez: A Journey of Life] (Kinneret, Zmora-Bitan, Dvir Publishing House, Jerusalem and Tel Aviv) (2017), p. 242.
10. Even & Maoz, p. 232.
11. *Ma'ariv, Mosaf Yom Kippur*, October 5, 2003, p. 16; Adan, p. 226.
12. Bronstein, p. 332; Herzog, *The Arab-Israeli Wars* (Random House, New York) (1982), p. 241.
13. Even & Maoz, pgs. 234–235; Bergman & Meltzer, p. 271.
14. Kfir, *Akhai Giboray HaTi'alah* [My Brothers, the Heroes of the Canal] (Miskal—Yediot Ahronot & Chemed Books, Tel Aviv) (2003), p. 274.
15. Reshef, p. 289; Segal, *Eduyot M'Govah HaKhol* [Testimony from Across the Dunes] (Modan Publishers, Ben-Shemen) (2007), p. 238; Even & Maoz, pgs. 236–237; Givati, *Mavkee'ay Khomot* [The Wall Buster] (Miskal—Yediot Ahronot & Chemed Books, Tel Aviv) (2019), p. 211.
16. Givati, p. 211.
17. Even & Maoz, pgs. 237 & 238; Barkai, *B'Shem Shamayim* [For Heaven's Sake] (Kinneret, Zmora-Bitan, Dvir Publishing House, Or Yehuda) (2013), p. 438; Dayan, p. 654.
18. Even & Maoz, p. 238; Givati, p. 211.
19. Even & Maoz, p. 238.
20. Givati, p. 212; Bronstein, p. 332.
21. Givati, p. 204.
22. Bergman & Meltzer, p. 279; Even & Maoz, p. 239.
23. Even & Maoz, p. 291; Adan, p. 237; Shamshi, *Sa'arah B'October* [Storm in October] (Ma'arachot, Ben-Shemen) (2011), pgs. 63–65; Bronstein, p. 482.

**Chapter 21: Africa**
1. Israel Government Transcript, Mizrahi Diary, October 23, 1973, p. 12.
2. Braun, *Moshe Dayan B'Milkhemet Yom HaKippurim* [Moshe Dayan in the Yom Kippur War] (Edanim Publishers, Ltd., Yediot Ahronot) (1992), p. 201; see Nir, *Natke HaKatzin HaPatzua SheKhazar L'sdeh HaKrav* [Natke, The Wounded Of-

ficer That Returned to the Battlefield] (Miskal-Yediot Ahronot Books & Chemed Books, Tel Aviv) (2010), p. 174 for slightly different figures.

3. Reshef, *Lo Nekhdal! Khativah 14 B'Milkhemet Yom HaKippurim* [We Will Never Cease! The 14th Brigade in the Yom Kippur War] (Dvir Publishing House, Jerusalem and Tel Aviv) (2013), p. 291.

4. Kfir & Dor, *B'Neteevay HaAish* [In Paths of Fire] (Miskal—Yediot Ahronot & Chemed Books, Israel) (2018), p. 164.

5. Golan & Shai (Editors), *Milkhama Hayom* [War Today] (Israel Defense Ministry, Israel) (2003), pgs. 145–146; Bartov, *Dado, 48 Shana V'ode 20 Yamim II* [Dado, 48 Years and Another 20 Days, Volume II] (Dvir Publishing House, Or Yehuda) (2002), p. 648; Eilam, *Eidut Min Habor* [Testimony from the Bunker] (Miskal— Yediot Ahronot & Chemed Books, Israel) (2013), p. 121.

6. Eilam, p. 112; Bar-Yosef, *Milkhama Mishelo* [A War of Its Own] (Kinneret, Zmora, Dvir Publishing House, Israel) (2021), p. 310.

7. Israel Government Transcript, October 18, 1973, p. 4; Bartov, p. 634; Yonay, *No Margin for Error* (Pantheon Books, New York) (1993), pgs. 353–354; *Milkhemet Yom HaKippuring UleKakheha* [The Yom Kippur War and its Lessons] (Israeli Ministry of Defense, Israel) (2005), p. 80; Halutz, *B'Govah Aynayim* [Straightforward] (Miskal—Yediot Ahronot, Chemed Books, Tel Aviv) (2010), p. 124.

8. Gordon, *30 Sha'ot B'October* [30 Hours in October] (Ma'ariv Book Guild, Tel Aviv) (2008), p. 491; Wallach, *Atlas Carta, L'Toldot Medinat Yisroel Asor Shlishi* [Carta's Atlas of Israel The Third Decade 1971–1981] (Carta, Jerusalem) 91983), p. 91; Bar-Yosef, *Milkhama*, p. 318; Bennett, "7 of the Greatest Flying Aces throughout History," *Popular Mechanics*, Nov. 29, 2015, www.popularmechanics .com/flight/g2323/greatest-flying-aces/.

9. Nir, pgs. 198–199; Adan, *Al Shtay Gadot HaTi'ah'lah* [On Both Banks of the Canal] (Edanim, Jerusalem) (1979), p. 249; Litwitz, *Z-817831: B'Khazit HaDarom B'Milkhemet Yom HaKippurim* [Z-817831: In the Southern Front during the Yom Kippur War] (Effi Meltzer, Ltd., Israel) (2011), p. 166.

10. Zaken, *Suez Ayno Stalingrad* [Suez Isn't Stalingrad] (Ma'arachot, Jerusalem) (2021), p. 113; Adan, p. 248; Wallach, p. 110.

11. Zaken, p. 116; Adan, p. 232; Nir, pgs. 196 & 200.

12. Wallach, p. 110; Bartov, p. 638.

13. Even & Maoz, *B'Nikudat Hacoved, Matzbiut B'Khazit HaTealah B'Milkhemet Yom HaKippurim* [At the Decisive Point, Generalship in the Yom Kippur War in the Canal Front] (Ma'arachot) (2012), p. 249.

14. Bartov, p. 641; Bergman & Meltzer, *Milkhemet Yom Kippur Zman Emet* [The Yom Kippur War—Moment of Truth] (Miskal Yediot Ahronot Books & Chemed Books) p. 291.

15. Bartov, p. 641; Sharon, *Warrior, The Autobiography of Ariel Sharon* (Simon & Schuster, New York) (1989), p. 329; Bergman & Meltzer, *Milkhemet Yom Kippur Zman Emet* [The Yom Kippur War—Moment of Truth] (Miskal Yediot Ahronot Books & Chemed Books) (2003), p. 291.

16. Bronstein (Editor), *Nitzakhon B'Svirut Nemookha* [The October 1973's Unlikely Victory] (Effi Melzter Inc., Israel) (2017), p. 333.

17. Bartov, p. 642; Sharon, p. 329.

18. Bartov, p. 642; Nir, p. 201.

19. Bartov, pgs. 641 & 643; Dayan, *Avnei Derekh* [Milestones] (Edanim Publishers & Dvir Publishing House, Or Yehuda) (1976), p. 644.

20. Shazly, *The Crossing of Suez: The October War (1973)* (Third World Centre for Research & Publishing, London) (1980), p. 176.

21. Sadat, *In Search of Identity* (Harper & Row Publishers, New York) (1977), p. 262; Gamasy, pgs. 290 & 292; Shazly, p. 179.
22. Gamasy, p. 291; Sadat, p. 263.
23. Vinogradov, *Grif Sekretno Snyat* [Declassified] (Institut Vostokovedeniya RAN, Moscow) (1997), pgs. 247–248.

## Chapter 22: Embargo

1. Israel Government Transcript, October 21, 1973 (11:00 A.M.) p. 36.
2. Richard Nixon, "Special Message to the Congress on Energy Policy," April 19, 1973, American Presidency Project, www.presidency.ucsb.edu/documents/special -message-the-congress-energy-policy; Yergin, *The Prize: The Epic Quest for Oil, Money & Power* (Simon & Schuster, New York) (1991), p. 590.
3. Kissinger, *Crisis* (Simon & Schuster, New York) (2003), p. 281.
4. Kissinger, *Years of Upheaval* (Little, Brown & Co., Boston) (1982), p. 535; Memcon between Nixon and Arab Foreign Ministers, Wednesday, October 17, 1973, 11:10 A.M., NPMP, NSCF, Box 664, Middles East War Memos & Misc. October 6– 17, 1973, pgs. 5–6 & 9–10; Kissinger, *Crisis*, p. 276; Quandt, *Decade of Decisions* (University of California Press, Berkeley) (1977), p. 190.
5. Memcon, "SAG Principles: Middle East War," October 17, 1973, 4:00 P.M., NPMP, NSC Institutional Files, Box H—92, WSAG Meeting Middle East, Folder 6.
6. Kissinger, *Years of Upheaval*, pgs. 536–537; Yergin, p. 606.
7. U.S. Embassy Kuwait Cable 3801, Cable to State Department, "Atiqi Comment on OAPEC [*sic*] Meeting," October 18, 1973, NPMP, NSCF, Box 1175, 1973 Middle East War, October 18, 1973, File No. 13, p. 2.
8. Gilbert, *The First World War, A Complete History* (Henry Holt & Company, New York) (1994), pgs. 444 & 455; Zaken, *Suez Ayno Stalingrad* [Suez Isn't Stalingrad] (Ma'arachot, Jerusalem) (2021), p. 120; Dayan, *Avnei Derekh* [Milestones] (Edanim Publishers & Dvir Publishing House, Or Yehuda) (1976), p. 656; Eilam, *Eidut Min Habor* [Testimony from the Bunker] (Miskal—Yediot Ahronot & Chemed Books, Israel) (2013), p. 120.
9. Eilam, p. 122; Bar-Tov, *Dado, 48 Shana V'ode 20 Yamim II* [Dado, 48 Years and Another 20 Days, Volume II] (Dvir Publishing House, Or Yehuda) (2002), p. 658.
10. Sharon, *Warrior, The Autobiography of Ariel Sharon* (Simon & Schuster, New York) (1989), p. 330; Kfir & Dor, *B'Neteevay HaAish* [In Paths of Fire] (Miskal— Yediot Ahronot & Chemed Books, Israel) (2018), p. 189.
11. Spector, *Ram U'Barur* [Loud and Clear] (Yediot Ahronot, Sifrei Chemed) (2008), p. 263; Bar-Yosef, *Milkhama Mishelo* [A War of Its Own] (Kinneret, Zmora, Dvir—Publishing House Ltd., Israel) (2021), pgs. 332–333.
12. Kissinger, *Years of Upheaval*, p. 873; Quandt, p. 188.
13. Embassy in Saudi Arabia Cable 4663 to State Department, October 23, 1973, NPMP, NSCF, Box 1175, 1973 Middle East War, October 23, 1973—File No. 18, p. 2.
14. Brezhnev to Nixon, October 19, 1973, delivered to Kissinger 11:45 A.M., NPMP, HAKO, Box 69, Dobrynin/Kissinger Volume 20 (October 12-November 27, 1973); Kissinger, *Years of Upheaval*, p. 544; Memcon between Kissinger, Schlesinger, Colby, and Moorer, October 19, 1973, 7:17–7:28 P.M., NPMP, NSCF, Box 1027, Memoranda of Conversations, April-November 1973, HAK & President.
15. Kissinger, *Years of Upheaval*, p. 873; Yergin, p. 615.
16. Kissinger, *Years of Upheaval*, pgs. 545 & 548; Nixon to Brezhnev, October

20, 1973, NPMP, HAKO, Box 69, Dobrynin/Kissinger, Volume 20 (October 12-November 27, 1973).

17. Quandt, p. 192.

18. State Department Cable 208776 to all Diplomatic and Consular Posts, "Middle East Situation," October 21, 1973, NPMP, NSCF, Box 1175, 973 Middle East War, October 20, 1973, File No. 15, p. 2; Israel Government Transcript, October 22, 1973 (10:00 P.M.) p. 3.

19. Eban, *Personal Witness: Israel Through My Eyes* (G.P. Putnam's Sons, New York) (1992), p. 536; Quandt, pgs. 192–193; Braun, *Moshe Dayan B'Milkhemet Yom HaKippurim* [Moshe Dayan in the Yom Kippur War] (Edanim Publishers, Ltd., Yediot Ahronot) (1992), p. 228; Israel Government Transcript, October 21, 1973, p. 31; Memcon between Kissinger and Western Ambassadors, October 21, 1973, 6:30–6:45 P.M., RG59, SN 70–73, POL 7 US/Kissinger.

20. Indyk, *Master of the Game: Henry Kissinger and the Art of Middle East Diplomacy* (Alfred A. Knopf, New York) (2021), p. 161.

21. Memcon between Kissinger, Meir and Party, November 2, 1972, 10:00 P.M.—12:45 P.M., RG 59, SN 70–73, POL Israel-U.S., p. 4.

22. Givati, *Ha'Ma'arakha B'Hermon* [The Hermon Mountain Operation] (Modan Publishing House, Ltd., Ben-Shemen) (2015), p. 245.

23. Givati, pgs. 247 & 277.

24. Givati, pgs. 285, 288 & 300.

25. Givati, pgs. 278 & 399; Malovany, *Milkhemet Hashikhrur Shel October 1973, HaKhazit Hasurit* [The War of Liberation of October 1973 on the Syrian Front] (Israel War Institute, Israel) (2021), p. 221; YouTube, Interview with Benny Messess (Hebrew), The Battle of the Hermon, posted August 20, 2017.

26. Kissinger, *Years of Upheaval*, p. 560; Eban, p. 537.

27. Memcon between Meir and Kissinger, October 22, 1973, 1:35–2:15 P.M., RG 59, SN 70–73, POL 7 US/Kissinger, pgs. 2–4.

28. Israelyan, *Inside the Kremlin During the Yom Kippur War* (Pennsylvania State University Press, University Park) (1995), pgs. 49 & 142; Golan, *The Secret Conversations of Henry Kissinger* (Quadrangle/The New York Times Book Co., New York) (1976), pgs. 79–82.

29. Memcon between Meir and Kissinger, p. 4; Kissinger, *Years of Upheaval*, pgs. 561 & 569.

30. Memcon between Meir and Kissinger, p. 6.

31. Heikal, *Secret Channels: The Inside Story of Arab-Israeli Peace Negotiations* (Harper Collins Publishers, London) (1996), p. 204.

32. Shazly, *The Crossing of Suez* (Third World Centre for Research and Publishing, London) (1980), p. 181; Zaken, p. 137; Eilam, p. 125; Adan, p. 282; Shamshi, *Se'arah B'October* [Storm in October] (Ma'arachot, Israel) (2011), pgs. 94 & 103.

33. Israel Government Transcript, October 22, 1973, pgs. 14 & 18.

34. Bergman & Meltzer, *Milkhemet Yom Kippur Zman Emet* [The Yom Kippur War—Moment of Truth] (Miskal-Yediot Ahronot Books & Chemed Books, Tel Aviv) (2003), pgs. 118–119; Bergman & Meltzer, p. 318.

35. Israel Government Transcript, Mizrahi Diary, October 25, 1973, p. 16.

36. Shazly, p. 181; Israel Government Transcript, Mizrahi Diary, October 25, 1973, p. 16; Adan, p. 289; Indyk, p. 174.

37. Israelyan, p. 160, quoting *Izvestia*, October 24, 1973.

38. Israelyan, p. 124; Message from Brezhnev to Kissinger as read by Minister

Vorontsov to the Secretary on the telephone on October 23, 1973 at 10:40 A.M., NPMP, HAKO, Box 69, Dobrynin/Kissinger Vol. 20 (October 12–November 27, 1973).

## Chapter 23: Defcon 3

1. Eilam, *Eidut Min Habor* [Testimony from the Bunker] (Miskal—Yediot Ahronot & Chemed Books, Israel) (2013), p. 171.
2. *The New York Times Magazine*, September 18, 1988, p. 60; Hotline Messages from Brezhnev to Nixon, October 23, 1973, NPMP, HAKO, Box 69, Dobrynin/ Kissinger Volume 20 (October 12–November 27, 1973).
3. Transcripts of Secretary of State Henry A. Kissinger Staff Meetings, 1973–1977, Box 1, pgs. 2, 4, 6, 7, 14–15.
4. Kissinger, *Years of Upheaval* (Little, Brown & Co., Boston) (1982), pgs. 570–571; Kissinger, *Crisis* (Simon & Schuster, New York) (2003), pgs. 316–317; Kissinger to Brezhnev, October 23, 1973, 5:15 P.M., NPMP, HAKO, Box 69, Dobrynin/ Kissinger Vol. 20 (October 12-November 27, 1973).
5. Eilam, p. 126; Kissinger, *Years of Upheaval*, pgs. 573–574; Israelyan, *Inside the Kremlin During the Yom Kippur War* (Pennsylvania State University Press, University Park) (1995), pgs. 158–159.
6. Bergman & Meltzer, *Milkhemet Yom Kippur Zman Emet* [The Yom Kippur War— Moment of Truth] (Miskal-Yediot Ahronot Books & Chemed Books, Tel Aviv) (2003), p. 329; Adan, *Al Shtay Gadot HaTi'ah'lah* [On Both Banks of the Canal] (Edanim, Jerusalem) (1979), pgs. 302–303; Zaken, *Suez Ayno Stalingrad* [Suez Isn't Stalingrad] (Ma'arachot, Jerusalem) (2021), p. 154.
7. Zaken, pgs. 151, 168, 188, 221, 238, 294; Adan, p. 305.
8. Malovany, *Milkhemet Hashikhrur Shel October 1973, HaKhazit Hasurit* [The War of Liberation of October 1973 on the Syrian Front] (Israel War Institute, Israel) (2021), p. 351; Israel Government Transcript, Mizrahi Diary, October 23, 1973, p. 3; Eilam, p. 127.
9. Seale, *Asad: The Struggle for the Middle East* (University of California Press, Berkeley) (1988), pgs. 221–224; State Department Cable 210444 to all Diplomatic and Consular Posts, "Middle East Situation," October 25, 1973, NPMP, NSCF, Box 1175, 1973 Middle East War, File No. 20, p. 2.
10. Heikal, *The Road to Ramadan* (Ballantine Books, New York) (1975), pgs. 259–260; Israelyan, p. 166; Message from Brezhnev to Nixon, October 24, 1973, received at State Department, 10:00 P.M., NPMP, HAKO, Box 69, Dobrynin/ Kissinger Volume 20 (October 12–November 27, 1973).
11. Israelyan, p. 169; Kissinger, *Crisis*, p. 342.
12. Kissinger, *Years of Upheaval*, p. 552; *New York Times*, October 24, 1973, p. 1.
13. Kissinger, *Years of Upheaval*, p. 581; Kissinger, *Crisis*, p. 345; Diary of Admiral Thomas Moorer, paragraphs 7 & 9–11. https://history.state.gov /historicaldocuments/frus1969–76v25/d269.
14. Kissinger, *Crisis*, pgs. 343 & 347; Haig, *Inner Circles: How America Changed the World, A Memoir* (Warner Books, New York) (1992), pgs. 415–416; Weiner, *One Man Against the World* (Henry Holt & Co., New York) (2015), pgs. 290 & 292.
15. Diary of Admiral Moorer, paragraphs 6, 12 & 14.
16. Diary of Admiral Moorer, paragraph 16.
17. Shazly, *The Crossing of the Suez* (Third World Centre for Research and Publishing, London) (1980), p. 183; Israel Government Transcript, Mizrahi Diary, October 25,

1973, p. 5; Israel Government Transcript, Mizrahi Diary, October 25, 1973,
pgs. 15–16.

18. Israel Government Transcript, October 25, 1973, p. 12; Israel Government Transcript, October 25, 1973, p. 7.

19. Israel Government Transcript, October 25, 1973, pgs. 31–32.

20. Diary of Admiral Moorer, paragraph 17; Quandt, *Decade of Decisions* (University of California Press, Berkeley) (1977), p. 197.

21. Israelyan, p. 173.

22. Dobrynin, *Sugobo Doveritelno. Posol V Vashingtone Pri Shesti Prezidentakh SShA (1962–1986)* [Absolutely Confidential. Ambassador in Washington During the Rule of Six Presidents of the U.S.A. (1962–1986)] (Moscow) (1997), p. 275.

23. *New York Times*, October 9, 2018, www.nytimes.com/2018/10/09/opinion /stumbling-toward-armageddon.html.

24. Kissinger, *Crisis*, pgs. 360–361.

25. Memcon, Meeting with Oil Company Executives, October 26, 1973, 5:30 P.M., RG 59, SN 70–73, PET 6, pgs. 8–10.

26. Kissinger, *Crisis*, pgs. 311 & 322; Memcon between Kissinger, Meir and Party, November 2, 1973, 10:00 P.M.–12:45 A.M., RG 59, SN 70–73, POL Israel-U.S., p. 6.

27. Kissinger, *Crisis*, pgs. 375 & 379.

28. Memcon between Kissinger and Acting Egyptian Foreign Minister Ismail Fahmi, October 29, 1973, RG 59, SN 70–73, POL 27, Arab-Isr, pgs. 6, 12 & 15.

29. Eilam, p. 141; Memcon between Nixon, Kissinger and Meir. November 1, 1973, 12:10 P.M., RG 59, Records of Henry Kissinger, 1973–1977. Box 2. NODIS Action Memos 1973–1976, p. 10; Eilam, p. 168; Israel Government Transcript, Mizrahi Diary, October 25, 1973, p. 10; Israel Government Transcript, Mizrahi Diary, October 25, 1973, p. 5.

30. Kissinger, *Years of Upheaval*, p. 610; Memcon between Kissinger, Meir, Dinitz and General Yariv, November 1, 1973, 8:10 A.M.-10:25 A.M., RG 59, Records of Henry Kissinger, 1973–1977, Box 2. NODIS Action Memos 1973–1976, p. 10.

31. Memcon between Kissinger, Meir, Dinitz and General Yariv, November 1, 1973, 8:10 A.M.–10:25 A.M., RG 59, Records of Henry Kissinger, 1973–1977, Box 2, NODIS Action Memos 1973–1976, pgs. 9, 12, 14.

32. Memcon between Fahmi and Kissinger, November 1, 1973, 5:30 P.M., RG 59, Records of Henry Kissinger, Box 24, Cat C, Material November–December 1973, p. 2.

33. Memcon between Kissinger, Meir and Party, November 3, 1973, 10:45 P.M.–1:10 A.M., RG 59, Records of Henry Kissinger, 1973–1977, Box 3, pgs. 8 & 11.

34. Memcon between Kissinger, Meir and Party, November 3, 1973, 10:45 P.M.–1:10 A.M., RG 59, Records of Henry Kissinger, 1973–1977, Box 3, pgs. 18 & 21.

35. Scowcroft to President, "Meeting with Sadat," November 7, 1973, NPMP, HAKO, Box 132, Egypt—Volume VIII, November 1–December 31, 1973.

## Chapter 24: A Funeral in Jerusalem

1. Georges Clemenceau Quotes, goodreads.com, www.goodreads.com/author /quotes/8261670.Georges_Clemenceau#:~:text=%E2%80%9CWar%20is%20 a%20series%20of,that%20results%20in%20a%20victory.%E2%80%9D&- text=%E2%80%9CWar%20is%20too%20serious%20a,to%20entrust%20 to%20military%20men.%E2%80%9D&text=%E2%80%9CThe%20right%20 to%20insult%20members%20of%20the%20government%20is%20inviola- ble.%E2%80%9D&text=%E2%80%9CAll%20that%20I%20know%20I%20 learned%20after%20I%20was%20thirty.%E2%80%9D.

2. *Yediot Ahronot, Hamosaf LeShabbat,* August 2, 2002, p. 4.

3. Agranat Commission, Final Report (1975), p. 1; Malovany, *Milkhemet Hashikhrur Shel October 1973, HaKhazit Hasurit* [The War of Liberation of October 1973 on the Syrian Front] (Israel War Institute, Israel) (2021), p. 243; Kissinger, *Years of Upheaval* (Little, Brown & Co., Boston) (1982), p. 957; "Overview of the Pearl Harbor Attack, 7 December 1941," Naval History and Heritage Command, https: //web.archive.org/web/20210602043203/; www.history.navy.mil/content/history /nhhc/research/library/online-reading-room/title-list-alphabetically/p/the-pearl -harbor-attack-7-december-1941.html.

4. Sachar, *A History of Israel from the Rise of Zionism to Our Time* (Knopf, New York) (2001), p. 78; Israel Government Transcript, October 21, 1973, pgs. 7, 17 & 35; Israel Government Transcript, October 25, 1973, p. 37.

5. Israel Government Transcript, October 22, 1973, p. 8; Israel Government Transcript, October 24, 1973, p. 5; Israel Government Transcript, October 22, 1973, p. 7.

6. Interview with Yakov "Ketzele" Katz, July 3, 2022.

7. Agranat Commission, Interim Report (1974), p. 1.

8. Leviticus, 16:21–22.

9. Sadat, *In Search of Identity* (Harper & Row Publishers, New York) (1977), p. 270; Sadat, *A Woman of Egypt* (Simon & Schuster, New York) (1987), p. 297; Gamasy, *The October War* (The American University in Cairo Press, Cairo) (1993), pgs. 300 & 302.

10. Dayan, *Avnei Derekh* [Milestones] (Edanim Publishers & Dvir Publishing House, Jerusalem & Tel Aviv) (1976), pgs. 704–705; Sadat, *A Woman,* p. 296.

11. Heikal, *Secret Channels* (HarperCollins Publishers, London) (1996), pgs. 232 & 234; Gamasy, pgs. 336–338; Kissinger, *Years of Upheaval,* pgs. 828, 831 & 835.

12. Heikal, *Secret Channels,* p. 233.

13. Seale, *Asad: The Struggle for the Middle East* (University of California Press, Berkeley) (1988), p. 237; Kissinger, *Years of Upheaval,* pgs. 880 & 932.

14. Indyk, *Master of the Game: Henry Kissinger and the Art of Middle East Diplomacy* (Alfred A. Knopf, New York) (2021), pgs. 347–348; Malovany, p. 429; Agranat Commission, Final Report (1975), p. 2.

15. Ashkenazi, *HaErev B'shesh Tifrotz Milkhama* [Today at Six War Will Break Out] (Hakibbutz Hameukhad, Tel Aviv) (2003), pgs. 152–153.

16. Ashkenazi, pgs. 154, 157–158.

17. Lahav, *Yisroel B'Mishpat, Shimon Agranat V'Hamayah HaTzionut* [Judgment in Israel: Shimon Agranat and the Zionist Century] (Am Oved Publishers, Tel Aviv) (1999), pgs. 314–315.

18. *Yediot Ahronot, 7 Yamim,* May 8, 2009, p. 19; Agranat Commission, Interim Report (1974), p. 1.

19. Agranat Commission, Final Report (1975), p. 1.

20. *Yediot Ahronot, 7 Yamim,* May 6, 2016, p. 17; Zeira, *Milkhemet Yom HaKippurim, Mitoos Mul Metziut* [The Yom Kippur War: Fact versus Fiction] (Yediot Ahronot, Tel Aviv) (1993), pgs. 190–191; Bergman & Meltzer, p. 465; Bergman & Meltzer, p. 455.

21. *Yediot Ahronot, 7 Yamim,* May 8, 2009, p. 19.

22. *Ha'aretz Magazine* (English Edition), May 22, 2009, p. 10; Zeira, p. 199.

23. Agranat Commission, Interim Report (1974), p. 8. Agranat Commission, Interim Report (Second Part) (1974), p. 81; Agranat Commission, Interim Report (Second Part) (1974), p. 100; Agranat Commission, Interim Report (1974), pgs. 18–19.

24. Agranat Commission, Interim Report (1974), pgs. 31–32; Agranat Commission,

Interim Report (Second Part) (1974), pgs. 50 & 54; Interview with Yakov Khas-dai, May 30, 2022; Agranat Commission, Interim Report (1974), p. 27.

25. Interview with Yakov Khasdai, May 30, 2022.

26. Agranat Commission, Interim Report (1974), p. 19; Agranat Commission, Interim Report (1974), p. 20.

27. Bergman & Meltzer, *Milkhemet Yom Kippur Zman Emet* [The Yom Kippur War—Moment of Truth] (Miskal-Yediot Ahronot Books & Chemed Books, Tel Aviv) (2003), p. 484; *HaTzofeh Hashavua*, October 3, 2003, p. 9; Agranat Commission, Interim Report (1974), pgs. 26–27.

28. *Ha'aretz*, August 8, 2003, p. 1.

29. Eilam, *Eidut Min Habor* [Testimony from the Bunker] (Miskal—Yediot Ahronot & Chemed Books, Israel) (2013), pgs. 233–235.

30. Agranat Commission, Interim Report (1974), pgs. 23–25.

31. *Yediot Ahronot, 7 Yamim*, November 7, 2003, p. 20.

32. Eilam, p. 235; Bartov, *Dado, 48 Shana V'ode 20 Yamim II* [Dado, 48 Years and Another 20 Days, Volume II] (Dvir Publishing House, Or Yehudah) (2002), p. 730; Naor, *Laskov* (Keter Publishing House, Jerusalem) (1988), p. 337; Lahav, *Yisroel B'Mishpat* [Judgment in Jerusalem: Chief Justice Simon Agranat and the Zionist Century] (Am Oved Publishers, Ltd., Tel Aviv) (2002), p. 309.

33. Israel Government Transcript, April 9, 1974, p. 89.

34. Zohar, *40 Shana Akharei* [40 Years After] (Israel War Institute, Tel Aviv) (2013), pgs. 180–182; Medzini, *Golda Biographia Politit* [Golda, a Political Biography] (Chemed Books) (2008), pgs. 581 & 588.

35. Meir, *My Life* (G.P. Putnam's Sons, New York) (1975), p. 458; Medzini, p. 615.

36. *Yediot Ahronot, 7 Yamim*, December 5, 2008, p. 21.

37. *Yediot Ahronot*, June 7, 1974, p. 5.

38. *Ma'ariv, Sofshavua*, p. 35.

39. *Yediot Ahronot*, October 7, 1983, p. 7; *Ma'ariv Shabbat*, October 4, 1991, p. 1.

40. *Hotzofeh HaShavua*, October 3, 2003, p. 8.

41. *Ma'ariv Shabbat*, October 4, 1991, p. 2; Bergman & Meltzer, p. 486.

42. Bar-Yosef, *Milkhama Mishelo* [A War of Its Own] (Kinneret, Zmora, Dvir Publishing House Ltd., Israel) (2021), pgs. 358 & 435, fn. 31.

43. Ashkenazi, pgs. 165–166.

44. Givati, *Mavkee'ay Khomot* [The Wall Buster] (Miskal—Yediot Ahronot & Chemed Books, Tel Aviv) (2019), p. 164.

45. *Yediot Ahronot, Mosaf Yom Kippur*, September 13, 2013, p. 9.

46. Millstein, October 4, 2003, "Ariel Sharon, Hero of the Yom Kippur War," http://nfc.msn.co.il/archive/002-D-3651–00.html?tag=20–09–18; Heikal, *The Road to Ramadan* (Ballantine Books, New York) (1975), p. 256.

47. Agranat Commission, Second Interim Report (1974), p. 181; *Ma'ariv*, January 25, 1974; Agranat Commission, Final Report (1975), p. 62.

48. Eban, *Personal Witness: Israel Through My Eyes* (G.P. Putnam's Sons, New York) (1992), p. 610.

49. Kissinger, *Years of Upheaval*, p. 963. Bartov, p. 727; *Yediot Ahronot, 7 Yamim*, May 6, 2016, p. 17; *Yediot Ahronot, Hamosaf LeShabbat*, September 25, 2009, p. 13.

50. Interview with Talma Elazar on "5 with Rafi Reshef," Israel Channel 10 Television, October 6, 2013; *Ha'aretz Magazine*, September 13, 2002, p. 9; *Yediot Ahronot, Hamosaf LeShabbat*, September 25, 2009, p. 13.

51. Bartov, p. 16.

52. Interview with Talma Elazar on "*5 with Rafi Reshef*," Israel Channel 10 Television, October 6, 2013.
53. Zeira, p. 236.
54. "Morsi Grants Sadat & El-Shazli Highest Medal for October War 'Victory,'" ahramonline, Oct. 4, 2012, https://english.ahram.org.eg/NewsContent/1/64/54754/Egypt/Politics-/Morsi-grants-Sadat—ElShazli-highest-medal-for-Oct.aspx; Gamasy, p. 398; *Ha'aretz Magazine*, June 9, 2006, p. 16; Sadat, *In Search*, p. 241; *Ha'Aretz, Gilyon Rosh Hashana*, September 26, 2003, p. B4.
55. Bar-Yosef, *The Angel: The Egyptian Spy Who Saved Israel* (HarperCollins Publishers, New York) (2016), p. 289; *Yediot Ahronot, 7 Yamim*, June 6, 2005, p. 26.
56. Bar-Yosef, *The Angel*, pgs. 300–303; *Yediot Ahronot, 7 Yamim*, September 7, 2007, pgs. 12 & 15.
57. Heikal, *Secret Channels*, p. 245.
58. Heikal, *Secret Channels*, p. 247; *Yediot Ahronot, Homasaf LeShabbat*, October 31, 2008, p. 8.
59. "President Sadat's Speech to the Knesset," https://sadat.umd.edu/sites/sadat.umd.edu/files/President%20Sadat%E2%80%99s%20Speech%20to%20the%20Knesset.compressed.pdf, pgs. 10 & 12; "Prime Minister Begin's Speech to the Knesset," https://sadat.umd.edu/sites/sadat.umd.edu/files/Prime%20Minister%20Begin%E2%80%99s%20Speech%20to%20the%20Knesset.pdf, p. 6.
60. Gazit, *Tahalikh HaShalom 1969–1970* [Peace Process] (Yad Tabenkin, Israel) (1984), p. 86.
61. *Yediot Ahronot*, November 6, 1987, quoted in Medzini, p. 669.
62. Sadat, *A Woman*, p. 13.
63. Heikal, *Autumn of Fury* (Corgi Books, Transworld Publishers, London) (1983), pgs. 13–14; Sadat, *A Woman*, p. 450; *Ma'ariv, Mosaf Shabbat*, January 9, 2004, p. 15.
64. *Commentary*, April 2002, p. 26, citing Dowek, *Israeli-Egyptian Relations, 1980–2000* (Routledge, London) (2001).
65. Turak, "Israel Signs Historic Trade Deal with UAE, Its Biggest with Any Arab Country," CNBC, May 31, 2022, www.cnbc.com/2022/05/31/israel-signs-trade-deal-with-uae-its-biggest-with-any-arab-country.html.
66. Bar-On, *Moshe Dayan, Korot Khayav 1915–1981* [Moshe Dayan, His Life and Times 1915–1981] (Am Oved Publishers, Tel Aviv) (2018), p. 357.
67. Braun, p. 359; *Yediot Ahronot, Yom Kippur*, September 13, 2013, p. 2; *Yediot Ahronot, 7 Yamim*, August 29, 2003, p. 10.
68. Braun, p. 359.
69. Meir, p. 460.

# INDEX

Adan, Avraham "Bren," 136–38, 140, 228–29, 262–63
  Akavish Road opening by, 238–39
  bridges and, 265–67
  crocodile amphibious boats crossing by, 259
  first for Suez Canal bridge crossing of, 253–54
Africa, Yom Kippur War and, 205, 253, 272–80
Agranat, Shimon, 310
Agranat Commission, 68, 75, 84, 101, 310
  on AMAN Concept, 67
  Bar-Lev release from testimony to, 314
  on Ben-Gal refusal to follow Hofi orders, 111
  on Dayan and Meir, 83, 316
  on Elazar, 317–19
  on Elazar and Bar-Lev Line, 136
  exploration items of, 314
  on Gonen, 102, 138–41, 317
  Hofi praise for shortened mobilization time by, 120
  irregularities of, 314–15
  members of, 313–14
  personal responsibility findings of, 316
  on Sharon October 9 order defiance, 164–65, 168
Akavish Road, 139–40, 208, 211, 217–19, 223–27, 229–30
  Adan and opening of, 238–39
Allon, Yigal, 23, 127

AMAN Concept, 65–68, 70, 71, 75, 78
AMAN Concept r, 70
AMAN military intelligence. *See also* Zeira, Eli
  Egypt war plans obtained by, 101–2, 131–32, 202–3
  on Iraqi forces arrival to Syria, 181–82
  Marwan espionage for, 63, 78, 102
  prior to Yom Kippur War, 61–78
  on Scud missiles in Egypt information, 69–70
  Yariv as head of, 61
Amit, Zev, 251, 252
antitank guided missiles (ATGMs) (Sagger)
  casualties from, 134–35
  of Soviets, 105, 106, 167, 191, 214, 216, 226, 229
Arab League summit. *See* Khartoum Conference
Arabs, Jews comparison to, 13
Ardenest, Shlomo, 185, 189
Ashkenazi, Motti
  Dayan resignation request from, 313, 319
  on *maozim* disrepair, 88
el-Assad, Hafez, 20, 57, 125, 172, 312
  on ceasefire, 298
  disappointment with Egypt by, 173
  on Golan Heights war plan, 99–100
  request for Hussein, S., forces by, 148–49, 173–74, 179

el-Assad, Hafez (*continued*)
  Sadat, A., agreement on October 6
    war start with, 72
  on Soviet ceasefire arrangement, 147
  Valley of Tears and, 147–49
ATGMs. *See* antitank guided missiles

Banha bridge destruction, 260
Bar-Lev, Chaim, 3, 33, 149, 205, 226,
    264, 272, 314
  on Chinese Farm mission, 235
  death of, 322–23
  Elazar complacency and, 77
  Meir confidential ceasefire meeting
    with, 292–93
  name change from Brotzlewsky of, 58
  service above Gonen and Sharon by,
    170
  Sharon opposition from, 50
  on Suez Canal crossing end, 227
  on Suez Canal fort building, 49
Bar-Lev Line, 102, 133, 134–36, 322
Begin, Menachem, 50, 233, 323, 328–29,
    331
Ben-Gal Avigdor "Yanush," 158–61,
    180–81
  Agranat Commission on refusal to
    follow Hofi orders by, 111
Ben-Gurion, David, 7–8, 23
  death of, 308
  as Israeli army chief of staff, 16
Ben-Shoham, Yitzchak, 110, 125
Bomba men, at Chinese Farm, 242–43
de Borchgrave, Arnaud, 46
Brezhnev, Leonid, 35
  ceasefire and, 285–86, 288, 290–94,
    296, 299
  instability of, 302
bridgehead, race to, 249–50, 259, 262–63
  Egypt attack of Suez Canal east and,
    258, 266
  Ismail Ali on, 257–58
  Israel ambush set up during, 260–61
  Sharon at, 251–53
  Shazly on, 255–56
bridges, across Suez Canal, 210, 253–54
  Adan and, 265–67
  Banha bridge destruction, 260
  crocodile amphibious boats for Suez
    Canal crossing as, 218–19, 221–22,
    224–25, 259

Laskov rolling, 202, 216–19, 223–25,
    229, 234, 240, 268–71
  Peled, B., order to bomb Egypt,
    130–31
  pontoon, 217–18, 266
  single assembled, 217, 223, 229,
    268–70
  Tzneh Bridge, 270–71
Brotzlewsky, Chaim, 57–58
Budapest *maozim*, 79, 88, 184, 313

Canal Zone. *See* Suez Canal; War of
    Attrition
Carmeli, Ben-Zion "Bentzi," 139–40
casualties, of Yom Kippur War, 134–35,
    309
ceasefire, War of Attrition, 34, 43–44, 49
ceasefire, Yom Kippur War
  el-Assad on, 147, 298
  Bar-Lev confidential meeting with
    Meir on, 292–93
  Brezhnev and, 285–86, 288, 290–94,
    296, 299
  challenges to, 298–302
  Gonen plan to breach, 292
  Israel POW release condition of, 290,
    305–6
  Meir anger over, 287, 288
  Meir confidential meeting with Bar-
    Lev on, 292–93
  October 22 ceasefire line and, 292–93,
    296, 301, 303–6
  oil negotiation for, 194
  Sadat, A., on, 197–98, 201, 280, 298,
    306–7, 311
  Soviet Union on, 147, 195, 285–86,
    288, 290–94, 296, 299
  UN Security Council and, 196, 286,
    290, 296–97
Chinese Farm, 206, 231–34, 248
  Bar-Lev on mission of, 235
  Egyptian withdrawal from, 243–44
  men of Bomba at, 242–43
  Mordecai team at, 236–38, 239,
    247
  Reshef on, 246, 253, 268
  Sharon on, 244, 284
  Yairi on Egyptians in, 235
command and control, in Yom Kippur
    War, 162–71
Concept. *See* AMAN Concept

crocodile amphibious boats, for Suez
Canal crossing, 218–19, 221–22,
224–25, 259, 271

Damascus bombing, by Israel, 146–47,
154–56, 172
Dayan, Moshe, 3, 15–18, 23, 249,
283–84, 331
Agranat Commission on, 83, 316
Ashkenazi request for resignation of,
313, 319
Gonen hatred of, 320
Hofi and Elazar October 7 report to,
115
imminent attack skepticism by, 81
on interim peace proposal, 42–44
on Meir, 145
nuclear power display support of, 127
resignation of, 134, 319
Sharon meeting with, 265
on Syria civilian infrastructure
bombing, 146–47
on Third Temple risk, 112, 119–20
on withdrawal to passes, 129–30, 133
Defcon 3, Yom Kippur War and,
298–303
Diary of the Sinai Campaign (Dayan), 17
Dinitz, Simcha, 176, 177, 193, 195, 287
diplomacy, after War of Attrition, 35–39,
45–46
ceasefire and, 34, 43–44, 49
Jarring Egypt/Israel negotiation
attempt for, 40–44
Nixon Israel arms sales cease and, 30
Rogers Plan and, 32–33
UN Security Council ceasefire and, 49
Dobrynin, Anatoly, 32–33

Eban, Abba, 16, 25, 36, 290
economic costs, of Yom Kippur War, 309
Egypt, 11, 18–19. See also Sadat, Anwar
AMAN obtaining of war plans of,
101–2, 131–32, 202–3
el-Assad disappointment with, 173
Chinese Farm withdrawal by, 243–44
Dayan guidance for occupation of,
13–14
Eilat Israeli ship sinking by, 9–10, 190
Israel attack into, 249, 250, 251–63
Kissinger arrival in, 310–11
Sinai invasion war exercises of, 67

Six-Day War losses for, 67
Suez Canal east attack from,
258, 266
Talisman Road tank battle of, 203–4
War of Attrition costly failure to,
33–34
Egyptian army officer, as AMAN
Concept source, 67–68, 75
Egypt/Israel negotiation attempt, by
Jarring
Dayan on interim peace proposal for,
42–44
Meir agreement to Sinai withdrawal
in, 41–42
Sadat, A., and, 40–42
Eilat Israeli ship, Egypt sinking of, 9–10,
190
Eitan, Rafael, 18, 122–23
Elazar, David, 58, 103, 104, 118,
196–97, 273
Agranat Commission on, 317–19
Bar-Lev complacency and, 77
on Bar-Lev Line solidification,
134–36
on Bar-Lev service above Gonen, 170
Dayan October 7 report from, 115
Kissinger on, 324
Meir briefing by, 126
on nuclear power use, 146
October 6 early morning meeting with
Gonen and Hofi of, 101
Peled, B., call for Golan defense and
SAMs destruction from, 116
preemptive strike order by, 83
on Suez Canal crossing end, 227
Zamir warning phone call to, 79, 81
Zeira imminent attack concealment
to, 75
equipment losses, of Yom Kippur War,
309
Erez, Chaim, 164, 222, 258
Eshkol, Levi Yitzchak, 3, 11–12
death of, 22
description of, 22–23
Meir replacement for, 23–26
Mumble Speech of, 9, 15, 23
on Sharon, 85
Extraordinary Measures
Galili on, 68
lack of deployment of, 75–77
Zeira on, 69, 75–76

F-4 fighter jets, U.S., 11–12
  Kissinger sale opposition for, 126
  Sakal on slingshot bomb method of,
    103–4
Fawzi, Mohamed, as Egypt Defense
    Minister, 21
Feisal, of Saudi Arabia (king), 18, 285,
    303, 325–26
Forman, Giora, 92–93, 117
fort. See maozim
Freier, Shalhevet, 127
Fulbright, J. William, 198

Gabriel missile, of Israel navy, 190–91
Galili, Yisroel, 127
  on Extraordinary Measures, 68
Golan Heights. See also Nafekh military
    base
  el-Assad war plan of, 99–100
  Hofi defense of northern, 100
  Hofi on retreat from, 111–12
  IAF cluster bombing of Syrians in, 157
  Israel defensive line on, 50–51
  Peled, M., sent to, 118–20
  Syria attack on Nafekh military base
    in, 107–9, 113–27, 152–54
  Syria breakthrough at, 107–8
  Syria shelling of, 89, 93
Golda's Balcony (play), 25
Goldberg, Arthur, 37
Gonen, Shmuel, 264
  Agranat Commission on, 102, 138–41,
    317
  AMAN information on Egypt war
    plan and, 101–2
  Bar-Lev service above, 170
  Dayan hatred by, 320
  death of, 321
  Elazar October 6 meeting with Hofi
    and, 101
  maozim withdrawal decisions from,
    104–6
  Mikhdal counterattack failure and
    command by, 136–38
  plan to breach ceasefire by, 292
  repugnancy of, 86–87
  Sharon defiance of, 163–69, 274
  Sharon replacement by, 86
  Sharon response to order of, 137–39
  in Six-Day War, 86
Greengold, Tzvika, 109–10, 123, 125

Haig, Alexander
  on ceasefire, 287, 300
Hamadia Hill defense, 168
Hamtana (Waiting), 4
Hamutal Ridge, 178
  loss of, 141–42
  Sharon operation to regain, 163–66
  withdrawal from, 167
Heikal, Muhammad, 61
Hod, Mordecai, 27
Hofi, Yitzchak "Haka," 273
  Agranat Commission praise for
    shortening mobilization time by,
    120
  Dayan October 7 report from, 115
  Elazar October 6 meeting with Gonen
    and, 101
  on Golan Heights retreat, 111–12
  northern Golan Heights defense by,
    100
Honecker, Erich, 21
Humphrey, Hubert, 29
Hussein, Saddam, Syria assistance from,
    148–49, 173–74, 179
Hussein of Jordan (king), 4
  el-Assad assistance request of, 148
  Meir meeting with, 73–74
  Syria support by, 174

IAF. See Israel Air Force
Ibrahimi Mosque, division of, 13
IDF. See Israel Defense Forces
initial attack, in Yom Kippur War, 79–80,
    80, 82–84, 95. See also preparation,
    for Yom Kippur War
  Egypt minor achievement in, 94
  Elazar strategy in, 103
  Elazar warning phone call from Zamir
    about, 79, 81
  IAF pandemonium for, 93–94
  Israel mobilization pandemonium in,
    85
  Peled, B., on Syrian airfields in, 92–93
  Syria and Golan Heights shelling in,
    89, 93
  Syria suicide missions in, 100
interim peace proposal, of Dayan, 42–44
international support, for Egypt, Syria,
    Israel, 172–83
  Hussein, S., for Syria, 148–49, 173–74,
    179

King Hussein of Jordan Syria support, 174
Kissinger and Israel, 174–77, 193–95, 199, 204
Soviet Union for Syria, 70–71, 174, 195
Iraq diplomat, on signs of war, 77
Iraqi forces, for Syria
AMAN on, 181–82
Hussein, S., and, 148–49, 173–74, 179
removal of, 312
Ismail, Muhammad Hafiz, 44–45
Ismail Ali, Ahmed, 199
on bridgehead, 257–58
Operation High Minarets and, 60
Israel
air force tactical mission of, 4–5
bridgehead ambush from, 260–61
ceasefire condition of POW release by, 290, 305–6
LBJ lifting of arms embargo for, 11–12
night-fighting equipment and, 109–10
Nixon lack of support for, 29–30
October 5 emergency meeting in, 76–77
prevention of Nasser using Suez Canal by, 9
Sadat, A., contempt by, 59
Six-Day War profit for, 14
Suez Canal crossing by, 205, 207–20
Suez Canal shelling by, 10
Syria invasion by, 178–80
Valley of Tears and, 145–47
War of Attrition deep-penetration bombings by, 28, 29, 34, 66
Yariv on mobilization of, 62
Zeira on mobilization of, 62
Israel Air Force (IAF)
Arab invasion contingency plan by, 92
D-Day low-altitude routes of, 5
defense and protection of, 52
Elazar plan for use of, 102
initial attack pandemonium for, 93–94
loss for, 6, 197
Operation Dougman 5 as biggest disaster of, 118
SAM destruction by, 53, 131, 273–74, 283, 284
SAMs defense by, 52–53, 102
Six-Day War single tactical mission of, 4–7

Syria infrastructure bombing, 179–80
tactical mission of, 4
Israel Defense Forces (IDF), 14
complacency of, 77
quality of, 8
in War of Attrition, 30–31
Israel Hermon level, of Mount Hermon, 97–98, 289
Israel navy
failure of, 190
Gabriel missile and, 190–91
Israeli army
Ben-Gurion as chief of staff of, 16
Dayan establishment of, 17

Jarring, Gunnar, 37
Egypt and Israel negotiation attempt by, 40–41
Jerusalem
under Jewish sovereignty, 6
lifting of barriers in, 12
Jews
Arabs comparison to, 13
Western Wall prayers at, 14
Johnson, Lyndon B. "LBJ," 11–12
Jordan border, Israel lack of defense of, 119
al-Jundi, Abdel Karim, 20

Kadmoni, Asa, 241–42, 322
Kahalani, Avigdor, 120, 160–61
Kahneman, Daniel, 61, 249
Kalashnikov rifle, Egyptians use of, 227
Khamdun, Walid, 122
Khartoum Conference, 18–19, 35–37
Kissinger, Henry, 12, 35, 37, 190, 310–11
Brezhnev ceasefire message to, 294
Dinitz meeting with, 176
F-4 fighter jets sale opposition from, 126
Ismail, M., meeting with, 44–45
Israel support from, 174–77, 193–95, 199, 204
meeting with Nixon and Arab foreign ministers, 281–82
Meir meeting with, 305
on nuclear power use, 177
on preemptive strike opposition, 84, 92
on Sadat, A., 40
sovereignty for security proposal of, 45
War of Attrition and, 32

Kosygin, Alexei, 35
Kundera, Milan, 113

Laner, Dan, 50, 116
Laskov, David, 202, 216–19, 223–25,
    229, 234, 268–70
Levinberg, Amos, 187–89
linkage concept of Nasser, 40, 41, 43,
    44, 328

Malkin, Tzvi, 65
maozim (fort), on Suez Canal, 49,
    184–85
  Ashkenazi on disrepair of, 88
  attack map, 80
  Budapest, 79, 88, 184, 313
  Egypt movement through gaps in, 90
  Gonen withdrawal decisions for,
    104–6
  Mifreket, 87–89
  Purkan rescue, 163, 165–66
  Sharon on, 50, 90
  War of Attrition rescue exercise and,
    104–5
Marwan, Ashraf, 54, 74, 325
  AMAN and Mossad espionage from,
    63, 78, 102
  AMAN Concept information from,
    65–66, 78
  Malkin on, 65
  marriage to daughter of Nasser by,
    63, 64
  on Operation 41, 66
  as Sadat, A., right-hand-man, 63
  Zamir and, 78, 79, 326–27
Mat, Danny, 210–12, 240–41
Meir, Golda, 44, 82, 320
  Agranat Commission on, 83, 316
  Bar-Lev confidential ceasefire meeting
    with, 292–93
  ceasefire agreement anger of, 287, 288
  Dayan briefing with, 126–27
  Dayan on, 145
  Elazar briefing to, 126
  as Eshkol replacement, 23–26
  Hussein of Jordan meeting with,
    73–75
  Kissinger meeting with, 305
  mistaken Suez Canal speech of,
    232–33, 243
  Nixon meeting with, 45

Sinai withdrawal agreement by,
    41–42
  Zeira imminent attack concealment
    to, 75
Mezakh maozim request to surrender,
    184–85
Mifreket maozim, 87–89
MiG-23 and MiG-25 fighter jets, from
    Soviet Union, 59, 66
Mikhdal counterattack failure, 128, 143,
    146
  Dayan on withdrawal to passes and,
    129–30, 133
  Gonen commanding of, 136–38
  Hamutal Ridge loss and, 141–42
Moorer, Thomas, 175, 300–301
Mordecai, Yitzchak "Itzik," at Chinese
    Farm, 236–38, 239, 247
Mossad
  Marwan espionage for, 63, 78, 102
  Zamir on imminent war complacency
    of, 77
Mount Hermon, 107, 147, 154–55,
    178, 187, 288–89. See also Israel
    Hermon; Syria Hermon
Mubarak, Hosni, 279, 330
Mumble Speech, of Eshkol, 9, 15, 23

Nafekh military base
  Eitan defense of, 122–23
  Greengold and, 109–10
  Hofi call to Elazar on, 111
  Syria Golan Heights and attack on,
    107–9, 113–27, 152–54
Nasser, Gamal Abdel, 4, 8, 9, 39
  Khartoum Conference and, 18–19
  linkage concept of, 40, 41, 43, 44,
    328
  Marwan marriage to daughter of,
    63, 64
  Sadat, A., and, 38, 39
  sudden death of, 34, 40
  Three No's of, 19, 36–37
  Yemen war withdrawal by, 19
National Security Council, Sadat, A.,
    meeting with, 72
Nir, Nathan "Natke," 260–62, 274
Nixon, Richard Milhouse, 12
  Israel lack of support by, 29–30
  Kissinger and Arab foreign ministers
    meeting with, 281–82

Meir meeting for weapons with, 45
  request for Israel aid package by,
    284–85
  Sadat, A., personal message to, 296
  Watergate and, 195, 281, 299, 300,
    302
nuclear power
  Dayan support of display of, 127
  Elazar on use of, 146
  Kissinger and Dinitz on, 177

October 9 failed offensive, 162–71
October 22 ceasefire line, 292–93, 296,
    301, 303–6
oil
  Khartoum Conference on sale of, 19
  negotiation for ceasefire, 194
  Nixon on domestic production of, 281
oil embargo, Yom Kippur War and,
    281–94, 303, 312
Operation 41, of Shazly, 56, 59, 66
Operation Dougman 5, to destroy SAMs,
    116–18, 121, 142, 193
Operation Dovecote, 49–51, 91
Operation High Minarets, 56–57, 60
Operation Tagar mission, of Peled, B.,
    114, 115, 117, 131, 193
Orr, Ori, 123–24, 153–54, 182
outcome, of Yom Kippur War, 308,
    310–32
  casualties in, 134–35, 309
  economic costs of, 309
  equipment losses of, 309

parade, Jerusalem, 4–8
  attendance at, 1–2
  Bar-Lev, Dayan, Eshkol at, 3
Peled, Binyamin "Benny," 83, 321–22
  Elazar call for Golan defense and
    SAMs destruction to, 116
  Operation Tagar mission of, 114, 115,
    117, 131, 193
  order to bomb Egypt bridges for,
    130–31
  on Syrian airfields attack, 92–93
Peled, Moshe "Mussa," 118–20
Peled, Yossi, 150–52, 157
Podgorny, Nikolai, 35, 46
pontoon bridges, 217–18, 266
POW release, Israel ceasefire condition
  of, 290, 305–6

preemptive strike, in Six-Day War, 83,
    84, 92
preparation, for Yom Kippur War, 47–60
  by Egypt, 53–60
  Elazar, Zeira, senior officer meeting
    for, 81
  by Israel, 47–53
  Israel on SAMs location and
    destruction and, 53
  maozim building along Suez Canal in,
    49–50
  Operation Dovecote and, 49–51
  signs of war, 74–77
  Sinai Peninsula geography and, 47–48
  Suez Canal and, 48–49
  Zeira dismissal of imminent threat for,
    74–78
Purkan maozim rescue, 163, 165–66

Rabin, Yitzchak, 4, 11, 23, 45, 84, 324
Reshef, Amnon, 205, 207, 209, 211,
    214–16, 230
  on Chinese Farm, 246, 253, 268
  on Sharon, 324
Riad, Abdul Munim, 11, 26, 34, 40
Rogers, William P., 32–33
Rogers Plan. See Stop Shooting and Start
    Talking plan
RPG-7, of Soviets used in Yom Kippur
    War, 105, 106, 133, 134–35

Sadat, Anwar, 5, 39, 327–30
  el-Assad agreement on October 6 war
    start, 72
  assassination of, 279, 329
  background of, 38
  on ceasefire, 197–98, 201, 280, 298,
    306–7, 311
  coup attempt against, 54
  east bank withdrawal refusal by, 279
  as Egypt president, 34, 38, 40
  Israel contempt for, 59
  Jarring Egypt/Israel negotiation
    attempt and, 40–42
  Marwan as right-hand man to, 63
  as Nasser replacement, 38
  on Nasser Three No's, 40–41
  National Security Council
    September 30 meeting and, 72
  Soviet Union contempt for, 59
  on War of Attrition, 34, 231–32

Sadat, Jihan, 28
Sagger. *See* antitank guided missiles
Sakal, Emmanuel, 103–4
SAM antiaircraft missiles, 31, 192
  Egypt agreed removal of, 312
  IAF defense for, 52–53, 102
  IAF destruction of, 53, 131, 273–74,
    283, 284
  Operation Dougman 5 for destruction
    of, 116–18, 121, 142, 193
  Operation Tagar target of, 114, 115
  Syria delivery of, 70, 71
*Sane in Damascus* (Sharon), 187, 188
Scud missiles, from Soviet Union, 66,
  69–70
Sharaf, Sami, 40
Sharon, Ariel, 4, 33, 187, 188, 205, 226,
  275, 321
  Bar-Lev opposition to, 50
  Bar-Lev service above, 171
  Begin calls from, 233
  bridge crossing and, 268
  at bridgehead, 251–53
  on Chinese Farm, 244, 284
  Dayan on, 223–24
  defiance of orders by, 163–69, 227–28,
    244–46, 249, 253, 274, 276, 294,
    323
  difficult tasks assigned to, 207–8
  Eshkol on, 85
  on first of bridge crossing, 253–54
  Gonen replacement of, 86
  lying habit of, 85, 170–71, 228
  on *maozim*, 50, 90
  Reshef on, 324
  response to Gonen order by, 137–39
  at Suez Canal, 130
Shazly, Sa'ad, 28, 162, 183, 199, 325
  on bridgehead, 255–56
  on move of Egyptian army across
    canal to west side, 278–79
  Operation 41 of, 56, 59, 66
  Operation High Minarets and, 60
  Sinai Peninsula war plan by, 54–57
  war plan lies to Assad, 57
  signs of war, 74–77
Sinai Peninsula, 4, 17
  Egypt invasion war exercises in, 67
  geography of, 47–48
  Meir withdrawal agreement in, 41–42
  Shazly war plan at, 54–57

single assembled bridges, 217, 223, 229,
  268–70
Six-Day War (1967), 3
  Dayan praise after, 18
  Egypt losses in, 9, 18, 56
  Gonen in, 86
  IAF single tactical mission in, 4–7
  Israel profit from, 6, 14
  preemptive strike in, 83, 84, 92
  sovereignty for security proposal, of
    Kissinger, 45
Soviet Union, 11. *See also* SAM
  antiaircraft missiles
  ATGMs supplied by, 105, 106, 134–35,
    167, 191, 214, 216, 226, 229
  on ceasefire, 147, 195, 285–86, 288,
    290–94, 296, 299
  Dayan contact with, 29
  Egypt MiG-23 and MiG-25 fighter jets
    from, 59, 66
  Nasser request for War of Attrition
    support by, 28–29
  RPG-7 supply from, 105, 106, 133,
    134–35
  Sadat, A., contempt by, 59
  SAM antiaircraft missiles for Egypt, 31
  Scud missiles provision to Egypt by,
    66, 69–70
Stop Shooting and Start Talking plan
  (Rogers Plan), for War of Attrition
  end, 32–33
Suez Canal, 22. *See also* bridgehead, race
  to; bridges; *maozim*
  Dayan interim peace proposal and,
    42–44
  Elazar and Bar-Lev order to end
    crossing, 227
  Israel crossing of, 205, 207–20
  Israel strategy to stop Egypt at, 49–50
  Meir mistaken speech on, 232–33,
    243
  Nasser prevention of Israeli use of, 9
  Sharon given task of crossing, 208
  Shazly and Sadat, J., on, 28
  War of Attrition Israel bombing of,
    32–33
  west bank of, 221–22, 278–79
Suez Canal, east bank
  destruction of, 222–23
  Egypt attack on, 258, 266
  Sadat, A., withdrawal refusal in, 279

surrender, in Yom Kippur War
  captives severe treatment in, 186, 187
  Levinberg betrayal of Israel and,
    187–89
  Mezakh *maozim* request for, 184–85
Syria, 71. *See also* el-Assad, Hafez
  breakthrough at Golan Heights, 107–8
  Dayan on civilian infrastructure
    bombing in, 146–47
  on Golan Heights and Israel Nafekh
    military base, 107–9, 113–27,
    152–54
  Golan Heights shelling by, 89, 93
  Israel bombing of infrastructure in,
    179–80
  Israel Damascus bombing by, 146–47,
    154–56, 172
  Israel invasion of, 178–80
  Peled, B., on airfields attack, 92
  SAM missiles Soviet delivery to, 70, 71
  Soviet airlift to, 195
  Valley of Tears attack and, 158–61
Syria Hermon level, of Mount Hermon,
  97–98, 288

Takoah, Yosef, 290
Tal, Yisroel, 14, 102, 121, 146, 154, 203,
  295
Talisman Road, 141, 190–202
  tank battle at, 203–4
Tamari, Dov, 239, 292
Tarif, Hassan, 153
Third Temple, Dayan on risk for, 112,
  119–20
Three No's, of Nasser, 19, 275
  Sadat, A., on, 40–41
Tirtur Road, 208–9, 213–19, 223–27,
  229–30, 233–34, 240, 246
Tlass, Mustafa, 71–72, 117–18, 124, 180
Tzneh Bridge, 270–71

UN Security Council, 1
  War of Attrition ceasefire and, 49
  Yom Kippur War ceasefire and, 196,
    286, 290, 296–97
Unger, Amos, 167, 168
United States (U.S.), 11–12, 32–33,
  103–4, 126, 175, 282. *See also*
  Kissinger, Henry; Nixon, Richard
  Milhouse
  Haig of, 287, 300

Humphrey of, 29
  on nuclear power, 177
  Watergate in, 195, 281, 299,
    300, 302

Valley of Tears, *144*
  el-Assad and, 147–49
  Israel and, 145–47
  Syria attack of, 158–61

Waiting. *See Hamtana*
War of Attrition (July 1967 - August
    1970), 25–27, 310
  Dayan contact with Soviet Union
    for, 29
  Egypt costly failure of, 33–34
  IAF loss of aircraft in, 31
  Israel bombing of Canal Zone in,
    32–33
  Israel deep-penetration bombings in,
    28, 29, 34, 66
  *maozim* rescue exercise in, 104–5
  Meir Sinai withdrawal agreement in,
    41–42
  Nasser request for Soviet support in,
    28–29
  Sadat, A., on, 34, 231–32
  Shazly and Sadat, J., on Egypt Canal
    Zone cities destruction in, 28
  Soviet and U.S. Rogers Plan for end of,
    32–33
  Soviet SAM antiaircraft missiles for
    Egypt, 31
War of Generals, between Sharon, Elazar,
    and Bar-Lev, 221–30
Washington Special Action Group
    (WSAG), meeting with, 175, 282
Weizman, Ezer, 5, 207, 233
  on Operation Dovecote
    implementation failure, 91
Western Wall prayers, of Jews, 14
WSAG. *See* Washington Special Action
    Group

Yaguri, Asaf, 140–41
Yairi, Uzi, 230, 235
Yamani, Zaki, 194
Yariv, Aharon, 61–62
Yom Kippur War (October 6 - October
    25, 1973). *See specific subject
    topics for*

Zamir, Zvi, 202
    Elazar warning phone call from, 79, 81
    imminent war complacency by, 77
    Marwan and, 78, 79, 326–27
    as Mossad Chief, 77
Zeira, Eli, 325–26, 327
    Agranat Commission on, 316–17
    AMAN Concept and, 66–68

    on Extraordinary Measures, 69, 75–76
    imminent attack concealment to
        Elazar and Meir by, 75
    imminent threat dismissal of, 74–78
    on Israeli mobilization, 62
    replacement of Yariv to AMAN, 62
    on signs of war, 74–75
Ziv, Dan, 210–11, 240–41, 244–146